GREAT LOCOMOT
OF THE LNER
O.S. Nock

PSL

Patrick Stephens
Wellingborough, Northamptonshire

First published in 1988

British Library Cataloguing in Publication Data

Nock, O.S.
    Great locomotives of the LNER.
    1. London and North Eastern Railway—
History 2. Locomotives—England
—History
I. Title
625.2'6'0942   TJ603.4.G72L66

    ISBN 0-85059-856-7

Note
At the time the LNER ceased to exist in January 1948, and became part of British Railways, the art of railway photography in colour had barely started. The colour pictures in this book were all taken after this change and show LNER locomotives either in their working days in post-nationalization colours or restored to their former glory on some of the country's many preserved railways.

Patrick Stephens Limited is part of the Thorsons Publishing Group, Wellingborough, Northamptonshire, NN8 2RQ, England

Printed and bound in Great Britain by Butler & Tanner Ltd, Frome and London

10 9 8 7 6 5 4 3 2 1

Contents

Preface

In any account of 'Great Locomotives of the LNER', one personality stands out above all others, that of Sir Nigel Gresley. He strides across the scene like a Colossus. Many times during the eighteen years since the formation of the London and North Eastern Railway Company in 1923, the top management must have been glad that they appointed him at once to the office of Chief Mechanical Engineer. In later years it became known that he was not the first choice of the Chairman, William Whitelaw, or the Deputy Chairman, Lord Faringdon. The former CME of the Great Central, J.G. Robinson, was by many years the senior of the pre-grouping engineers, having been appointed Locomotive Engineer as long ago as 1900; although he was in his 67th year, there was then no fixed age at which senior officers retired and being in excellent health it was hoped that he would continue for a few more years. But 'the Great J.G.', as his men on the GCR called him, thought otherwise, and it was largely on his recommendation that Gresley was appointed.

While Great Central men, both former directors and senior officers, continued to exert much influence in the affairs of the amalgamated company, Gresley quickly established himself as 'commander in chief' of the CME's department, and, indeed, within six or seven years of his appointment he had attained a position of such stature in the profession as to already outshine some of the most eminent mechanical engineering personalities of pre-grouping days. The extent to which this was so among certain very leading railwaymen of the hour is shown by an incident which was kept very private at the time for very obvious reasons and which only leaked out to a minimal extent later. It was at the time when Sir Josiah Stamp, President of the Executive on the LMS, was seeking an outstanding engineer to replace Sir Henry Fowler as Chief Mechanical Engineer, and had come to the conclusion that an outsider was essential. His Vice-President (Works and Ancillary Undertakings), Sir Harold Hartley, who was also Director of Scientific Research and who had behind him a very brilliant university career at Oxford before joining the LMS, was at first inclined to seek someone of high academical attainments, 'another blue-eyed boy from Balliol' as one of my railway friends sarcastically put it! But Gresley's production of the high-pressure water-tube boilered No 10000, and the learned paper that followed, convinced Sir Harold that the LNER had in its CME a man who was seemingly able to think far ahead of the ordinary realms of railway motive power. But the approach to Gresley, however it was made, was unacceptable, and for the good of the LNER he stood firmly at Kings Cross.

Nevertheless, in 1931, when No 10000 was making its experimental running, the railway position in the country generally was far from propitious. The LNER in particular was suffering so severe a decline in traffic, both passenger and freight, that the Board was compelled to impose a uniform reduction in salaries and basic wage rates throughout the Company. With capital expenditure on new locomotives and rolling stock cut to the barest minimum, it was fortunate that the constituent companies had locomotives that were soundly built, had been well maintained and were capable of being used on all but the fastest and heaviest express passenger duties for many years to come. The retention of these older classes, 4-4-0s and 'Atlantics', on major express duties added much to the interest and charm of the LNER scene in the grouping years, not forgetting the byways and branches that were still worked by still older types. Furthermore, throughout all this period it was evident that Gresley himself, for all his modern developments, had a very real love of old stalwarts, and devoted the utmost enthusiasm to refurbishing the Stirling 8 ft 'Single' No 1 for her main-line running in 1938.

The London and North Eastern Railway was a prime mover in the project of setting up the Railway Museum at York. The pageantry surrounding the celebration of the centenary of the opening of the Stockton and Darlington Railway in 1925 gave the opportunity to restore to their original condition and colouring certain historic locomotives that were then on the active list in the North Eastern Area. These famous engines, the Fletcher '901' Class, the S & D long-boilered goods and the 'Tennant', came to form the nucleus around which was built the splendid collection of locomotives of former LNER types now included in the ranks of those exhibited in the National Railway Museum. But for the onset of war in 1939, and the untimely death of Sir Nigel Gresley, one believes that the collection would have been larger still, certainly including the remaining North British 'Atlantic' *Midlothian*, which had been set aside for preservation and was withdrawn from service at St Margarets shed, Edinburgh, in November 1939.

Even so, in any study of great and historical British locomotives the London and North Eastern and its constituents has been more fortunate than the others in having more representative types preserved, either as static or working exhibits. Also, having regard to the pre-eminent position of the former

North Eastern Railway as a freight and mineral carrier, it is a source of much gratification that examples of such notable work-horses as the 'P3' 0-6-0 and the 'T2' and 'T3' 0-8-0s have been preserved in working order. Had the industrial scene on the eastern side of Great Britain been more favourable in the late 1920s and early 1930s, one can be fairly sure that Gresley would have developed his freight engine programme which had been initiated in such striking fashion with the introduction, in Railway Centenary Year, of the two 'P1' 'Mikado' freight engines Nos 2393 and 2394, and the very impressive 6-cylinder 'Garratt'. In the event, however, no new Gresley 'O2' Class heavy freight locomotives were built between 1924 and 1932, and then multiplication up to 1934 was only to the extent of 16 more engines. For power in this category on an all-line basis, the LNER had to rely on the ex-GCR 'O4' Class, which from its pre-grouping strength of 130 was increased by subsequent purchases from Government stocks to 404 in 1929. It was significant of the extent to which the CME's department was constrained in capital expenditure that no more than 196 express passenger locomotives of new types were built between January 1923 and January 1935, comprising 77 'Pacifics', 76 'D49' Class 4-4-0s and 43 'Sandringhams', not to forget the experimental No 10000.

In writing this book, I have naturally made extensive references to the earlier classics of railway literature, which are listed in the bibiliography, while in more recent years my membership of the Institutions of Mechanical and Locomotive Engineers and of the Stephenson Locomotive Society has opened up a wealth of professional contacts and lasting friendships, not to mention immeasurably rich sources of technical literature.

Coming now to more personal matters, there was one association with Sir Nigel Gresley himself of which I treasure the memory, although sadly it came in the last few months of his life. When he was told that I had been commissioned to write *The Locomotives of Sir Nigel Gresley* to be serialized in *The Railway Magazine*, he wrote charmingly and sent under separate cover all his personal albums of photographs, offering to read personally each instalment as it was ready. Unhappily, he died when we had reached no more than the third. However, thanks to the sustained interest of Edward Marsden and his successors in the Chief General Manager's office of the LNER at Kings Cross, I was put in touch with the Running Superintendents in each of the Areas, and the facilities they so generously granted me for riding on the footplate were the means of establishing many more railway friendships, as well as the collecting of much valuable running data.

The author of a book such as this is deeply in debt to his illustrators in addition to those whose co-operation is acknowledged on the printed pages. I should like to honour the memory of those personal friends who are no longer with us, and whose company I have enjoyed at the lineside on many a photographic field day: Cecil Laundy, W.J. (Josh) Reynolds, Maurice W. Earley and Derek Cross.

O.S. Nock

1. Early days: the MS & L

On New Year's Day 1923, the London and North Eastern Railway, as constituted by The Railways Act of 1921, owned a total of 7,392 steam locomotives. The pre-grouping ownership was 1,359 to the Great Northern, 1,358 to the Great Central, 1,336 to the Great Eastern, 2,143 to the North Eastern, 1,074 to the North British and 122 to the Great North of Scotland. The North Eastern total had been increased in 1922 by incorporating the 137 locomotives of the Hull and Barnsley Railway, which had been absorbed prior to the major amalgamations of 1923. Faced with a total of more than 7,000 locomotives of pre-grouping origin, a high proportion of which continued in service to provide an important constituent of London and North Eastern motive power throughout the 25 years of the Railway's existence, to say nothing of the notable new locomotives added to the stock in the years following the grouping, a process of fairly rigorous selection has had to be adopted in deciding the designs that were sufficiently outstanding to be classified as 'great'. At the outset, a broad statistical analysis of the principal types existing in 1923 will, it is hoped, make the general position clear.

The constituent companies of the LNER were primarily freight carriers. Of the principal tender types thus involved, 0-6-0, 0-8-0, 2-6-0 and 2-8-0, the total was 3,165, against a total of 1,424 for the passenger types, 4-4-0, 4-4-2 and 4-6-0. Moreover, a high proportion of the 90 Great Central and 103 North Eastern locomotives included in the total of passenger types were used on fast freight services. Inevitably, the East Coast passenger service and the one-time highly competitive trains from London to the East Midlands, Yorkshire and Manchester gathered most of the limelight in the 'enthusiast'

Left *Dawn of the LNER group — one of the four remarkable 'Saltburn' Class with 7 ft coupled wheels built for the Stockton & Darlington line in 1862* (The Locomotive Publishing Company).

Below *GNR Sturrock 0-4-2 tank engine No 272 of 1866 with condensing equipment for working on the London underground lines beyond King's Cross* (British Railways).

press, but their aggregate mileage was small. It was not only the long-haul coal runs from the Durham, Yorkshire and Nottinghamshire pits that contributed so substantially to the high freight train mileage of the company; in Durham and Northumberland a very considerable output was conveyed in short runs from the collieries to the high staithes of local ports. While this trade diminished greatly during and after the First World War, it was nevertheless an important factor in the locomotive operating strategy of the North Eastern Area in steam days. It was still necessary to keep a stud of medium-powered 0-6-0 tender engines for this heavy, unspectacular though remunerative work. The units thus employed might not qualify for inclusion in the ranks of the 'great' locomotives of the LNER, though one is glad to see one of the North Eastern 'P3' Class 0-6-0s has been preserved in full working order.

Although serving contrasting territories, the Great Eastern Railway had a swarm of run-of-the-mill 0-6-0 tender engines of the 'J15' Class, first introduced in 1883 and to which the final additions were made in 1912; this was the largest class of any on the entire LNER system, a total of 273 engines at the grouping of 1923. Scrapping of the earliest members of this class, then nearly forty years old; had commenced only two years prior to grouping, at which time there were 289 of them in service. Yet, in 1923, few locomotive enthusiasts would have been

inclined to include the 'J15' Class in the category of 'great' locomotives of the LNER. Even so, their larger successors, first introduced in 1900, earned a species of reflected glory from one railway writer by possessing the same boiler as that of the 'Claud Hamilton' Class express passenger 4-4-0s, and being at that time the largest 0-6-0s in Great Britain. The locomotive history of the Great Eastern Railway is, however, distinguished enough without any artificial 'puffs' being given by chance references, and I hope adequate tribute has been paid to the work of James Holden and his brilliant assistant F.V. Russell in a later chapter of this book.

Ever since its formation, by amalgamation in 1862 of the Eastern Counties with several smaller railways in East Anglia, the Great Eastern Railway, or rather its locomotive department, seemed a trial ground for engineers using it as a stepping stone to greater things. Robert Sinclair had been Locomotive Superintendent of the Eastern Counties for five years before the amalgamation, and although he was then not more than 46 years of age he relinquished his responsibility for the locomotive department in 1866, although remaining with the company in a consultative capacity until 1869. While at Stratford, he produced one express passenger engine design which, having regard to its vintage and the use that was made of it during the rather chequered careers of some of its successors, could certainly place it among the 'nearly great' of the pioneer days. This was his 7ft 2-2-2 single of which a total of 31 was built by various contractors between 1862 and 1867. They were, however, no beauties! With outside cylinders, a double-tiered arrangement of slotted driving wheel splashers, a very tall and ungainly-looking cab, a

Great Eastern Railway Sinclair 2-4-0 express goods engine of 1859, as rebuilt with an enlarged boiler for passenger work (British Railways).

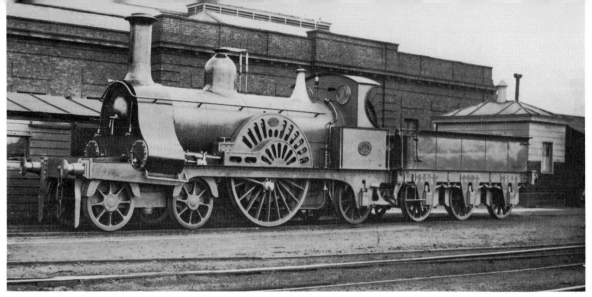

Sinclair single wheeler, rebuilt by S.W. Johnson as a 4-2-2 and painted in the Stroudley 'Brighton' yellow livery (The Locomotive Publishing Company).

stove-pipe chimney and a boiler line interrupted by a markedly raised firebox, they cut completely across the canons of what a British express locomotive then should have looked like.

After Sinclair retired in 1866, the Great Eastern had four locomotive superintendents in the next twenty years, and all except Massey Bromley went on from Stratford to fame in the engineering world. The first of these four was S.W. Johnson who came south from the North British and went on to the Midland in 1873. He left his mark on the Great Eastern with a class of very handsome 0-4-4 suburban tank engines, unmistakably the prototypes of the later well-known Midland engines of the same type. He also rebuilt with a leading bogie one of the Sinclair 7ft 2-2-2s and substitued his very shapely chimney and boiler mountings for what E.L. Ahrons once described as the 'rugged grandeur' of its former appearance. This was to no avail, however, because when Johnson went to Derby in 1873 and William Adams made the short trip eastwards from the North London works at Bow to Stratford, it was not long before stove-pipe chimneys reappeared and there-after became a standard feature until the 'Claud Hamilton' Class of 4-4-0s arrived in 1900.

Stove-pipe chimneys or not, the five-year sojourn of Adams on the Great Eastern Railway did not yield very brilliant results. He designed three large eight-wheeled main-line engines, of which the last two were left to be put into service by his successor Massey Bromley. The first lot, a class of twenty 4-4-0s introduced in 1876, were originally intended to replace the Sinclair singles, but they proved so

ineffectual that they had to be taken off and trans-ferrred to goods trains. The mixed traffic 2-6-0s, the first of the 'Mogul' type to be introduced in Great Britain, were an even greater flop. Bromley also had the job of getting the 4-2-2 singles into service, though these had a distinctly better reputation, par-ticularly in climbing the banks of the Colchester main line. Ahrons referred to them as of Bromley's design, presumably because the first batch did not come out until Adams had left for the London and South Western Railway; but, in a meaty piece describing Stratford Works, its equipment and its products in the *English Illustrated Magazine* of 1891, Alex P. Parker, then secretary to James Holden, titles an official photograph of one of them 'Adams's Express, 1879', and he should know. Railway history has little to say of Bromley's brief stay at Stratford other than that he authorised purchase from Kitsons of Leeds of another ten of the 7ft 6in 4-2-2 singles, which were put into service in 1881-2. He retired in the latter year, and two years later he was unfortunate enough to be travelling by the eastbound 'Boat Train' from Manchester when it was completely wrecked on the Bullhouse curve near Penistone. Bromley was among the 24 passengers who were killed.

Bromley's successor on the Great Eastern was T.W. Worsdell but he did not stay long enough to make any lasting impression, other than the intro-duction of the Worsdell-Von Borries system of com-pounding with two inside cylinders. All the engines that could be called 'great' of this type were, how-ever, rebuilt after he had transferred to the North Eastern Railway apart, of course, from the numerous engines using this system of compounding designed by Bowman Malcolm for service on the Belfast and Northern Counties Railway, later to become the Northern Counties Committee section of the Midland Railway of England, and subsequently of the LMS. The Worsdell-Von Borries compounds built for service in England are dealt with in the chapters that cover the locomotives of the North Eastern Railway.

Worsdell went north to the North Eastern Railway in the aftermath of one of the most dramatic episodes in nineteenth-century British railway history, in which the enginemen had virtually sacked their own boss! There have been many incidents on the majority of railways of new locomotive designs or novelties in equipment being treated with reserve, not to say thinly-veiled hostility, by the drivers and firemen who had to use them; but never before had there been a situation of such outright rebellion that the locomotive superintendent himself had to resign.

The roots of this remarkable affair lay deep in railway history before even the North Eastern Railway was formed by the amalgamation of the York, Newcastle and Berwick, the York and North Midland and the Leeds Northern in 1854. The further amalgamation in 1863 of the historic Stockton and Darlington with the North Eastern merely intensified the *status quo* as far as locomotive design was concerned. For although the veteran Edward Fletcher by successive additions to the stud through railway amalgamations remained the chief locomotive superintendent of the ever-enlarging combine, the men at the former headquarters, York, Leeds and Darlington, were left to carry on as they thought fit, with a minimum of interference from Fletcher's headquarters at Gateshead, even to the painting style of their engines. Fletcher's own superintendence gradually assumed the form of a father-figure to whom every man or boy on the strength, whether in drawing office, workshop or running shed, looked not only with complete respect but in many cases with real affection. The only trouble was that neither Fletcher himself nor the top management of the North Eastern Railway appeared to pay any regard to the succession, until an immediate appointment had to be made.

At that time in British railway history, locomotive men in search of advancement sought progressively senior posts on railways other than those on which they had been trained. The Great Eastern Railway in later Victorian days was an example of what may be termed a transitional post to which the locomotive superintendent came from a senior office on a still smaller railway then passed on after a relatively short time to greater responsibilities. Thus, ambitious men had a wide field to choose from which at that time included the whole of the British Isles. Changing railways in search of promotion, however, could be a 'dive into the lucky-bag' as much for the engineer himself as for the management making the

appointment; this was certainly so on the North Eastern when choosing the successor to Edward Fletcher. A Crewe man of the Ramsbottom and Webb era, and one, moreover, who had won his spurs on the largest and most progressive of the Irish railways, would have seemed a strong candidate for the vacant post on the North Eastern, and indeed he got the job—with disastrous results for himself and the locomotive department at Gateshead.

There has surely never been one of man's inventions more imbued with human frailties than the steam locomotive, nor, on the other hand, one in which the idiosyncracies of individual designers could reach such lengths. The appointment of Alexander McDonnell as Locomotive Superintendent of the North Eastern Railway, however, fell into neither of those complex categories. The million-dollar question inevitably arises as to how his career would have developed on a different railway. On the Great Southern and Western Railway of Ireland he had introduced the shop practice he had learned at Crewe, at that time the most advanced in Great Britain if not the whole world, and he had followed his first Irish design, which had been a close copy of the Ramsbottom 'Newton' Class 2-4-0, with a 4-4-0 development which had several notable and original features.

This was the design that he brought over from Inchicore to Gateshead, and it caused such a furore when the engines took the road that he eventually had to resign. The sad thing about this affair is that there was nothing wrong with the new engines—rather the reverse. The problem was that they did not look like Edward Fletcher's highly distinctive creations, and were damned at sight by the footplatemen! For all that, however, the McDonnell 4-4-0s lasted the best part of fifty years in a completely unrebuilt condition, and well deserve the honourable mention made of them in subsequent chapters devoted to the North Eastern Railway.

In the memorable series of articles contributed to *The Railway Magazine* on 'Locomotive and train working in the latter part of the nineteenth century' by E.L. Ahrons, which began in January 1915, I have often been intrigued by the order in which the various railways were treated. As the premier line of Great Britain it was perhaps appropriate to accord the London and North Western Railway first place, and, as their historic rivals in the 'Race to the North', the Great Northern followed next. But as the series lengthened, and later contributions came to have far more extensive treatment than the first two or three, it became fairly obvious that some editorial restraint had been imposed upon the author at first while it was gauged how the series generally would be received by the readership. Otherwise, seeing the large number of instalments lavished upon certain companies featured later in the series, the treatment meted out to the LNWR and GNR could be regarded as inadequate. Then again, the choice of the Manchester, Sheffield and Lincolnshire Railway as the third subject in the series seemed rather odd, particularly to readers south of the Thames to whom in days gone by the MS & L might well have seemed like some north country equivalent of the Somerset and Dorset!

In 1884, Professor E. Foxwell published his first book on the subject 'Express Trains', as a prelude to the more extensive work of five years later, in which he was joined as co-author by Lord Farrer and which extended the subject to 'English and foreign'. He wrote of the Manchester, Sheffield and Lincolnshire 'This is a route to breed energy', and then went on to detail the gradients. Having proceeded as far west as Sheffield, he described the line onwards to Manchester as resembling the roof of a house, beginning with 18½ miles of unbroken ascent averaging 1 in 125 to the eastern portal of the Woodhead Tunnel at 1,010 ft above sea level and followed by a descent of 22½ miles into Manchester. Breed energy or not, little of it was apparent in the speed of the passenger trains at the time Foxwell was writing, nor was it to be expected from the moderate dimensions of the locomotives concerned. This could not be blamed primarily on the locomotive engineer, Charles Sacré, whose practice was sound enough, but on parsimony from the top, in the soulless and tight-fisted Chairman, Sir Edward Watkin. It is extraordinary to recall that at the time Foxwell was writing, the MS & L was in partnership with the Great Northern in running a highly competitive express business service between London and Manchester; yet the Sheffield company did not stir itself to make any speed, even on the long descending gradients on either side of the Woodhead Tunnel.

In more recent times, the Woodhead route achieved prominence as one of the major coal train hauls, to such an extent as to be converted to electric traction. This was not the case when the ownership was the provincial MS & L. Then, the principal freight hauls were to and from Grimsby; indeed, the traffic passing thence in the first years of the present century became such as to induce the Great Central Railway to embark upon the vast port project of Immingham Dock. Until the outbreak of the First World War, traffic across what had originally been the Great Grimsby and Sheffield Railway had been a profitable two-way business involving export of coal to the Baltic states and import of timber and certain kinds of dairy produce. In Sacré's time, a high proportion of the 0-6-0 goods tender engines owned by the MS & L were stationed at Grimsby and most of

these, whether of the 4ft 9in or the 5 ft 3 in varieties, had double frames. One gathers that the Sacré 0-6-0s were very well liked by their drivers, though in common with the earlier instalments of his famous serial articles in *The Railway Magazine*, E.L. Ahrons virtually ignored the MS & L freight engines, awarding them no more than a single paragraph in a weighty three-part instalment covering the not-so-very distinguished passenger classes.

There were few of these passenger locomotives that could be called by any one of the adjectives pertaining to greatness, either in conception of design or in performance on the road. East of Retford there was no express running—none at all—and between Sheffield and Manchester the so-called fast trains ran at a seemingly even speed, uphill and downhill alike, of around 25 to 35 mph. West of Manchester, however, it was very different. There the MS & L was one-third owner with the Midland and Great Northern of the Cheshire Lines Joint Committee, and the inter-city service between Liverpool and Manchester was a highly competitive business in which the CLC was pitted against the London and North Western, over the historic route engineered by George Stephenson, and the Lancashire and Yorkshire. And, believe it or not, the partners in the CLC Joint Committee entrusted the passenger service of this prestige joint line to the Manchester, Sheffield and Lincolnshire Railway.

Foxwell's description of the result cannot be bettered: 'Since 1875', he wrote 'the whole service between Lancashire and London, and between Liverpool and Manchester, has been revolutionised by the insinuating power of this competitive wedge. An hourly service was at once started between the two great towns, doing the 34 miles in 45 minutes, with a stop at Warrington; the North Western had to follow suit (theirs is the original line made by George Stephenson 31½ miles long), and now this bit of Lancashire ground which first saw the wonder of high speed, is the focus of the smartest running in the world. At each even hour a North Western express starts from either end, and the "Cheshire Lines" at each half-past, beside which 10 other trains are thrown in that do the trip in 40 minutes without a stop. There are *sixty* (28 LNW and 32 CLC) of these express journeys every day, the average time being slightly over 44½ minutes.

'This swarm of rapid trains have cut their way through a maze of murky junctions, but they are as punctual as chronometers. The cultured Londoner must drop many a tear when he sees such a high standard of performance daily maintained in the rude provincial air.'

The route of the 'Cheshire Lines' did not involve any long or steep gradients and although the loco-

Manchester, Sheffield and Lincolnshire Railway Sacré 6 ft 0 in 2-4-0 passenger engine No 363 (The Locomotive Publishing Company).

motives mainly used were at that time small Sacré 2-4-0s with 6-ft 0-in coupled wheels and 16-in by 22-in cylinders, the non-stop trains maintained running average speeds of 60 mph over about 25 miles of the total distance. Also, the loads were relatively light, rarely as much as 100 tons.

About the time Foxwell was writing his first book, Sacré had introduced some considerably larger express engines of the 2-2-2 type. But the 12 examples of this type were not, strange to say, intended for the smartly-timed services of the Cheshire Lines but for the mountain section between Manchester and Sheffield, and though the London trains rarely touched as much as 60 mph downhill, the locomotives were provided with driving wheels as large as 7 ft 6 in diameter. About this time, however, the MS & L in partnership with the Great Northern instituted a new fast express service between London and Manchester, two trains a day in each direction covering the distance in 4½ hours. To avoid stopping at Retford to change engines, arrangements were made for the MS & L engine to continue to Grantham, non-stop from Sheffield, and so on the

Great Northern main line the Sacré 2-2-2s had a chance of using their 7-ft 6-in driving wheels to some advantage.

These competitive London expresses were very lightly loaded, in their first years usually to no more than about 70 tons, but while the standard of performance was not high, even on the 33 miles of the Great Northern main line, those 12 Sacré 'singles' had a distinguished air about them and design features which, while not elevating them to the ranks of the 'greats', certainly made them distinctive to a degree. For one thing, while Sacré coupled engines, both 2-4-0 and 0-6-0, had double frames throughout, the singles had inside frames for the driving wheels and outside cylinders encased in an elaborate framing reminiscent of Alexander Allan's Crewe style, of which the only surviving derivatives in current production in the early 1880s were on the Highland Railway. More than this, Sacrés MS & L singles had magnificently-slotted splashers to the driving wheels. These engines were considerably more powerful than the 6-ft 2-4-0s which ran the Cheshire Lines trains, with cylinders 17 ½ in by 26 in

MS & LR Sacré 7 ft 6 in 2-2-2 of 1883 built at Gorton for the Manchester-London expresses via Retford and the GN line (The Locomotive Publishing Company).

and a boiler pressure of 140 lb per sq in. However, in actual running they seem to have suffered from too short a wheelbase, resulting in a wobbling action at any speed.

Only two of the singles were needed for the London expresses working through from Manchester to Grantham, with a further three engines standing pilot, as it were—one at Gorton shed and two others at Sheffield. The remaining seven engines of the class were allocated to the Cheshire Lines. A typical run on one of the forty-minute Manchester-Liverpool trains was recorded in detail by Ahrons in 1886 behind 2-2-2 No 506 with a load of 100 tons. A speed of 60 mph was attained four miles from the start in Manchester, after which 22 miles were run at an average speed of 59 mph, with no greater variation in the milepost timings than 58 up to 63.2 mph. Then a relaying slack caused a slight delay, but milepost 30 was passed in 32 min 18 sec from the start and, despite a very slow entry into Liverpool, the journey was completed in 38¼ minutes. At one time it was proposed to remedy the bad riding qualities of these engines by fitting leading bogies, but the project was abandoned, and they were scrapped early in the 1900s.

Prior to the introduction of the fast London trains in 1883 and the 7-ft 6-in singles, the principal passenger services of the MS & L had been worked by a class of 4-4-0 engines built at Gorton by Sacré between 1877 and 1880. These had a rather curious external appearance; his partiality for outside-framed engines has already been mentioned, but on these 4-4-0s, of which there were eventually 27, the outside slotted frame of the engine was carried along to the front buffer beam, although it had no physical connection to the bogie which had inside frames only. One could not dignify with the word 'express' the trains they worked between Manchester, Sheffield and Retford in connection with the Great Northern service to London; the eastbound trains which called at Guide Bridge thereafter ran the 23.4 miles over Woodhead to Penistone at an average speed of 40 mph, and then the steeply downhill 13 miles into Sheffield at 37 mph. Afterwards, they put on a big spurt by covering the remaining 22.5 miles to Retford at an exciting start-to-stop average of 43.6 mph. However, there was some justification around 1880 for a leisurely speed downhill, as the MS & L was one of the railways then persisting in the use of the early non-automatic form of vacuum brake, the shortcomings of which twice involved the MS & L in a grievous death-roll following what would in other circumstances probably have been relatively minor accidents. At Penistone, in 1884, there were 24 killed and 60 seriously injured, and three years later, at Hexthorpe Junction outside Doncaster, the casualty

list was even heavier, with 25 killed and no fewer than 94 seriously injured.

Before the latter catastrophe, Parker had succeeded Charles Sacré as Locomotive Superintendent, and in 1887 produced at Gorton Works three of the most unusual 2-4-0s ever to run in Great Britain. They were nominally powerful engines, with 6-ft 9-in coupled wheels and 18-in by 26-in cylinders, but while they had the traditional MS & L outside frames for the coupled wheels, the leading wheels had inside frames and radial axle-boxes. It might be imagined that this latter feature was intended to cure the 'boxing' action of the Sacré singles, but the Parker 2-4-0s were reputedly even worse in this respect. This engineer, viewed from his work a hundred years later, does seem to have been something of an enigma.

In 1887, there was an exhibition in Manchester in which various large modern locomotives were to be shown. One gathers that the original intention was for the MS & L to exhibit one of the new Parker 2-4-0s, but then apparently one of those little quirks that sometimes intruded in the MS & L management occurred and the Leeds firm of Kitson & Co were instructed to exhibit a 4-4-0 of their own design on behalf of the MS & L. It is understood that the locomotive department at Gorton was fully informed of what was going on, and details of certain fittings were in accordance with current MS & L practice, but the design as a whole was in every way a Kitson job.

The resulting engine, numbered 561, was a very neat though undistinguished machine differing from all its predecessors on the MS & L by having inside frames throughout. The leading dimensions were the same as Parker's own 2-4-0s, having 6-ft 9-in coupled wheels, 18-in by 26-in cylinders and a boiler pressure of 160 lb per sq in. After the Manchester Exhibition, engine No 561 joined two of the new Parker 2-4-0s in a link of three engines working between Manchester and Grantham on the London expresses, and as such was superseding the Sacré singles. Ahrons always claimed that the Kitson 4-4-0 No 561 was far and away the best of the MS & L passenger engines, but, despite that, Parker built three more of his own outside-framed four-coupleds in 1888, although with leading bogies instead of the radial truck. These, together with the Kitson engine No 561, had the Manchester-Grantham trains to themselves until the end of 1890, when, apparently, the locomotive department at Gorton decided that the Kitson design was better than their own and built six more, Nos 562 to 567. Subsequently they became the standard express passenger class of the line; 12 more were built at Gorton (Nos 682-693) and another dozen by Kitson.

A somewhat enlarged version of the same design, introduced in 1895, proved the climax of the passenger locomotive story of the Manchester, Sheffield and Lincolnshire Railway before it blossomed forth as the twentieth-century Great Central Railway, and this final MS & L design provided another puzzle as to authorship! The distinguished journal, *The Engineer* (very ably edited by Vaughan Pendred, the first of a family of engineers who edited it in a continuous succession of father, son and grandson for more than an hundred years) published in 1894 detailed drawings of an enlarged version of the '561' Class having a larger boiler and cylinders 18½ in by 26 in. But the odd thing about this series of six engines was that they did not materialise from Gorton Works until more than a year after the drawings had been published in the technical press. By that time, Harry Pollitt, a son of the General Manager, had succeeded Parker, and while the design of the new 4-4-0s when they eventually appeared was generally credited to Pollitt, certain interested parties, including E.L. Ahrons, ascribed them to Parker under whose authority, presumably, the working drawings were made available to *The Engineer* in 1894. Other than the slightly enlarged boiler, the only design novelty was the Belpaire firebox, which the MS & L had been the first British railway to introduce on some 0-6-2 shunting tank engines in 1891. It had, however, then been new only as far as the British home railways were concerned, as the firm of Beyer, Peacock & Co had already used it extensively for export orders.

Whatever the authorship of the design of the new MS & L 4-4-0s of 1895 may have been, the six engines, numbered 694 to 699, received a remarkable publicity boost in July 1897. Six months earlier, after a year of publication as *Moore's Monthly Magazine*, the name was changed to *The Locomotive Magazine*, and, after no more than six issues in this new and ultimately very popular guise, the publishers issued what is believed to be the first-ever colour plate of a British express locomotive. It was a reproduction in coloured lithograph of one of the famous 'F. Moore' oil paintings, and the subject, believe it or not, was one of the '694' Class MS & L 4-4-0s. The production was sumptuous, and the innovation set the seal on the success of the magazine itself and the fame of the subsequent series of colour plates.

2. Patrick Stirling

For no fewer than 42 years, Patrick Stirling was at the head of the locomotive departments of major British railways, first on the Glasgow and South Western and then on the Great Northern, and when still a young man of 40 he had established the famous Stirling 'look'—the straight-backed domeless boiler and the safety valves in a shapely brass casing over the firebox—that he was to maintain without the slightest exception for the rest of his life. The first examples of this style were of the 0-4-2 type which Stirling had introduced, albeit with domed boilers, as early as 1856. These G & SWR engines were for mixed traffic and had coupled wheels of only 5 ft 0 in diameter. When the type was continued on the Great Northern, from the very first engine built at the Doncaster Plant in 1867 until the total reached 154 with the last three built in 1895, there were really little more than superficial changes in design. Doncaster's No 1 engine, which bore the running number 18 in the GNR stock, had the distinctive cab with a single circular side window that Stirling had developed when he was on the G & SWR, and which was used on GNR engines of the 0-4-2, 0-6-0 and 2-2-2 types until about 1869.

The first new locomotives that Patrick Stirling introduced on the Great Northern Railway were of a wheel arangement that he had not used in Scotland, 2-4-0, and the first batch were built by the Avonside Engine Company in 1867-68. There is room for a strong suspicion that the design itself had been completed before he left Kilmarnock because, after his young brother stepped into his shoes on the Glasgow and South Western Railway, a 2-4-0 express engine of almost identical design was built at Kilmarnock Works in 1868. The only differences between the English and Scottish versions were that the latter had

smart brass-capped chimneys and wing plates to their smokebox fronts. A writer in the Journal of the Stephenson Locomotive Society in 1950 commented that this first design of James Stirling was 'probably the neatest he ever produced. These engines were certainly more ornately finished than usual, but there was an elegance of outline about the '8' Class which he never succeeded in recapturing in his later designs'. The most likely answer was that the '8' Class was not his design at all, but that of his elder brother, the details for which had been worked out in the drawing office at Kilmarnock before Patrick left for Doncaster. The G & SWR '8' Class had the standard 17-in by 24-in cylinders and 6-ft 7-in coupled wheels used in the first GNR 2-4-0s.

Patrick Stirling immediately set out to establish standards of design and fittings that could be used throughout the entire stock of Great Northern locomotives, and in the 29 years during which he reigned supreme at Doncaster he achieved a uniformity in style that was unequalled in the British locomotive world. Leaving aside for a moment the single-driver express engines reserved for the fastest and most important services, the tender engines throughout Stirling's time were of only three types, 0-4-2 for mixed traffic, 2-4-0 for ordinary passenger and 0-6-0 for freight. Moreover, while examples of all three types continued to be built until the year that Stirling died, changes to the details of construction and the external appearance were minimal. On all three classes, the cylinder diameter was increased from 17 in to 17½ in on the batches built from 1874 onwards, but while the piston stroke was increased from 24 in to 26 in on the 2-4-0s and 0-6-0s built from this date, the 0-4-2s continued to have cylinders of 24 in stroke up to the last batches in 1895. Stirling

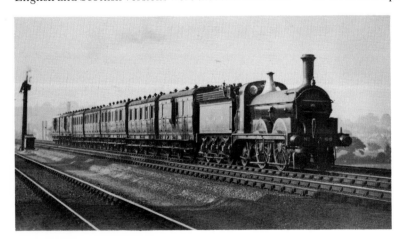

Doncaster No 1, carrying the running number 18, was an 0-4-2. An engine of this class, though with the later type of cab, No 68, is shown here hauling a down local train near New Barnet (Author's collection).

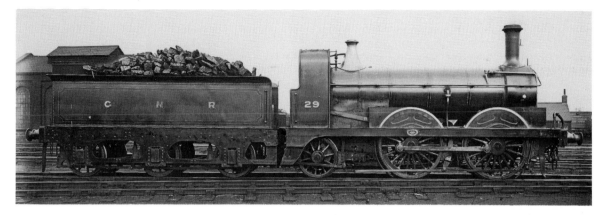

abandoned the side-windowed cab after no more than a few years at Doncaster, but, until the 1881-82 batches, the 0-4-2s and 2-4-0s continued to have slotted coupled wheel splashers as on the original lots of 1867.

While the above types were the mainstay of the main-line motive power of the Great Northern Railway, there is no doubt that it is by his single-driver express locomotives that Patrick Stirling will ever be revered by locomotive enthusiasts, and indeed by many professional locomotive engineers. In 1889, E. Foxwell wrote 'It is the straightforward dash of the Great Northern, and the high standard of excellence maintained in all its services, which have won it the distinguished place it holds in public estimation. Especially in regard to speed it was long merited the gold medal...' He continues 'Would any company except the Great Northern ever have contemplated and carried out an effective competition for traffic between London and *Manchester*, with such a roundabout route, and the extra disadvantage of having to work in harness? But in matters of speed and smartness the Great Northern has worked like an

inspiriting leaven on everything it has touched.' The situation so eulogised by Foxwell did not, however, happen overnight with the arrival of Patrick Stirling from Kilmarnock. His first real express passenger engine, of the 2-2-2 type, was of a different design from those that he had built previously for the G & SWR, and requires special mention.

At Kilmarnock, both classes of 2-2-2 that he built had outside cylinders and inside frames throughout. The first batch, with domed boilers, have been likened to Ramsbottom's 'Lady of the Lake' Class of the London and North Western. So they might have been, but Stirling's 2-2-2s on the G & SWR preceded those of Ramsbottom by about two years, having been put on the road in 1857. Stirling's second class was larger, having 6-ft 6-in driving wheels, domeless boilers and the single side-windowed cab that he took to the Great Northern, while the third series, with 7-ft wheels, could be considered a faint prototype of those that he later developed to such marked effect on the Great Northern. The later members of the eleven engines of this series, known as the '45' Class on the G & SWR, were still under construction when

Above *One of the later examples of the standard GNR 0-4-2 mixed traffic engines of which 25, including No 29, were built at Doncaster and 50 by outside contractors* (British Railways).

Right *Stirling's first express design for the GNR of 1868. Engine No 14, with his original type of cab, was the sixth of the class and only the eleventh engine built at Doncaster Plant.* (British Railways).

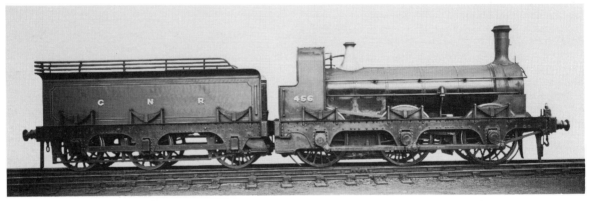

Top *Stirling and the Great Northern Railway 'house style': one of the Sturrock 0-6-0s built in 1865-6* (British Railways).

Above *A Sturrock heavy freight 0-6-0 as rebuilt by Stirling with his familiar features but still having the original large tender* (British Railways).

Left *Sturrock 2-4-0 passenger engine of the 251-260 Class of 1866, also rebuilt by Patrick Stirling* (The Locomotive Publishing Company).

Patrick Stirling left to go to Doncaster; his younger brother, James, certainly had no qualms in accepting the legacy thus bequeathed to him, for the '45' Class were excellent engines. It is all the more surprising that, once on the Great Northern, Patrick should have proceeded to design a 2-2-2 different in almost every respect, and different from the 2-2-2 that was generally acclaimed as Archibald Sturrock's masterpiece, the '229' Class of 1860.

In contrast to these latter, which had outside frames throughout, Stirling adopted the 'Jenny Lind' style, with outside frames for the leading and trailing wheels and inside frames for the 7-ft driving wheels. The first of the new engines was only the fourth to be built new at the Doncaster plant, and was allocated the running number 6. At that time, the Great Northern, like its friendly rival at Crewe, paid no attention to an ordered sequence of running numbers for individual engine classes, and the first Stirling 2-2-2s turned out from Doncaster in 1868 were numbered 6, 222, 41, 4, 21 and 14! The remaining six engines of the class, completed in 1869-70, were numbered 55, 61, 63, 215, 37 and 39. The engines built in 1868 had side-windowed cabs but the remainder had the later standard pattern, which was much more popular with their crews. These 7 ft singles had the 17-in by 24-in cylinders that Stirling adopted as a general standard in his first years at Doncaster, and until 1870 it could have been assumed that, with the 2-4-0, 0-4-2 and 0-6-0 classes already produced, the 'house style' of the next generation of the Great Northern was assured.

The slotting of the driving wheel splashers took a very artistic form, and the elegant polished brass mounting that encased the safety valves gave no clues as to whether the 'innards' were of the older, rather primitive spring balance type or the Ramsbottom type, used well nigh universally in later Victorian times. Also, studying contemporary photographs and old drawings, the fact that strikes one most forcibly is that there were no brakes on the engine itself, and only a rather primitive form of hand-brake on the tender, but despite these shortcomings, which were remedied later first with the Smith non-automatic brake and then by the automatic brake, the Stirling 7-ft singles were excellent engines. In contrast to the 2-2-2 engines on the G & SWR, which had a relatively short wheelbase and were susceptible to a species of 'boxing' action at any speed, the Great Northern 'No 4' Class had the leading wheels placed immediately beneath the smokebox at a distance of 9 ft 6 in ahead of the driving wheels, in this respect exactly the same distance as in the Sturrock '229' Class.

While in the first four designs of tender engines that Stirling produced in the years 1867 and 1868

there was a notable uniformity in the machinery, all having 17-in by 24-in cylinders, the same could not be said about the boilers, although the same principle in design, that of having a relatively low water-line with ample steam space above it, was followed consistently. The curious thing about it is that, for an engineer who was steeped in the precepts of standardization as Stirling appeared to be in other respects, the dimensional differences between one boiler and another seemed to be so relatively small. They were, however, sufficient to make interchange of boilers between the four classes impracticable. Having said that, the days when such interchanges were regular works practice were still very far ahead. In Stirling's day, general repairs took vastly longer than would have been tolerated in the 1930s, and it took a longer time to repair a boiler than the rest of the engine; consequently, a small number of spare boilers were kept in reserve, and they were interchanged freely on engines of associated classes. On the Great Northern it was usual in the 1880s for the Stirling 2-4-0s, for example, to spend four months in the shops undergoing a general repair. Boiler variations between the four 17-in by 24-in classes were as follows:

	2-4-0	0-4-2	0-6-0	2-2-2
Firebox (sq ft)	94	100	94.25	89.5
Tubes (sq ft)	991.5	975	985.5	922.5
Total (sq ft)	1,085.5	1,075	1,079.75	1,011.75

It was evident, even in his first years at Doncaster, that Stirling was thinking of bigger engines than the 17-in inside cylinder classes, and while his earlier experience with the G & SWR 2-2-2s with their unsteady riding undoubtedly influenced his choice of the 'Jenny Lind' type for his first 7-ft singles, his inclination still appeared to be towards outside cylinders after he had arrived at Doncaster. Having built the first batch of 'No 4' Class 2-2-2s, he made arrangements with the Great Eastern Railway to borrow and test in express passenger service one of the Sinclair 7-ft singles. These engines were considerably less powerful than Stirling's own singles, with only 16-in by 24-in cylinders and a working pressure of 120 psi; but the point that commended itself about their working was their steady riding. The visitor was run on the Great Northern main line not only against one of the newest Stirling 7-ft singles but also against a Sturrock 2-2-2 of the '229' Class. All the time, Stirling was contemplating a considerably larger engine, and with the use of outside cylinders a leading bogie seemed essential.

So, in April 1870, with 8-ft diameter driving wheels, the prototype bogie single express locomotive was completed at the Doncaster Plant. Its works number was No 50, but the running number, specially selected as appropriate to an era promising new standards on the GNR, was No 1. So far as nominal tractive effort was concerned, the new engine, with outside cylinders of 18 in diameter by no less than 28 in stroke, was by far the most powerful that had been built at Doncaster and had the higher boiler pressure of 140 psi as against 130. But the boiler itself seemed inadequate in that the tube heating surface was only 875.5 sq ft against 922.5 on the 7-ft 2-2-2s, and the grate area only 15.8 sq ft against 16.4 sq ft. Dimensions apart, No 1 was an exceedingly handsome and altogether impressive locomotive. The 8-ft driving wheels, with their gracefully-curved running plates and the numerous slots in the splashers, were arresting enough when the wheels were stationary, but I, for one, will never forget my first sight of No 1 in steam when she had been restored to working condition in 1938 and was making her way up to Kings Cross with the replica 'Flying Scotsman' train prior to her first reappearance as a working engine. It was a beautiful evening and my friends and I were in time to see her leaving Hitchin; the spectacle of the great connecting-rod plunging slowly back and forth on its 28-in stroke was unforgettable.

In 1870, engine No 1 was even more of a phenomenon, albeit more as a spectacle than as a motive power unit commensurate with its capable appearance. As first put to work, No 1 was far from a successful engine, and in view of the many novelties embodied in its construction it was hardly likely to be so from the outset. Stirling was experimenting with a single prototype, with the aim of working express trains of 150 tons at average speeds of 50-51 mph. It must also be remembered that the trains of 1870 had no continuous brakes, and that the running speeds had to provide a much more considerable margin for slowing down than with the automatic vacuum brake that was adopted on the Great Northern twenty years later. However, the mechanical features which Stirling was pioneering appear to have been completely successful at the outset. The bogie centre, for example, was pitched 3 ft 6 in in rear of the leading axle-centre but only 3 ft 0 in ahead of the hind axle. As a result, not only was the weight on the bogie wheels so distributed as to lead up gradually to the greater weight on the driving wheels, but also the rear wheels of the bogie had a less transverse movement than the leading pair on a curve (although the effect of this latter feature would be less marked owing to the straightness of the Great Northern main line).

The trouble with No 1 as originally built was simply that she would not steam! The comparison of heating surfaces with Stirling's 7-ft 2-2-2 singles has already been made, but the significance of those altered dimensions needs some emphasis. First of all, there was the firebox. The overall dimensions were almost exactly the same as those of the 2-2-2s, namely 5 ft 6 in long and 3 ft 11½ in wide, but the latter was ½ in *less* than that of the 2-2-2s. The grate area was 15.8 sq ft on No 1 against 16.4 sq ft on the 2-2-2s. The boiler barrel was of the same diameter on both classes, 4 ft 0½ in, but the length between the tube

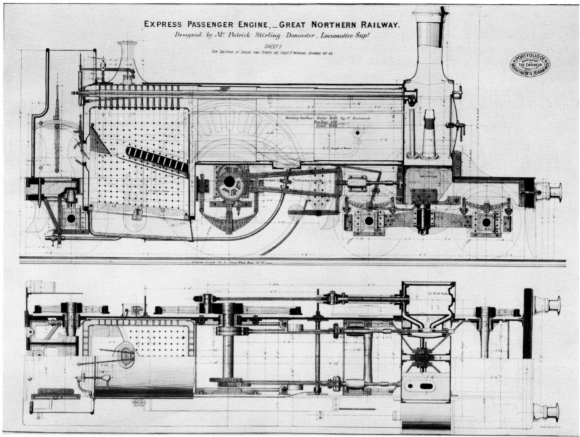

Above *Drawings of the first Stirling 8 ft single No 1 (British Railways).*

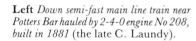

Left *Down semi-fast main line train near Potters Bar hauled by 2-4-0 engine No 208, built in 1881 (the late C. Laundy).*

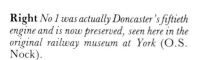

Right *No 1 was actually Doncaster's fiftieth engine and is now preserved, seen here in the original railway museum at York (O.S. Nock).*

plates was 11 ft 9 in on No 1 against 10 ft 6 in on the 2-2-2s, with 175 tubes of 1⅝ in outside diameter on No 1 against 206 tubes of 1¾ in. It would seem that a considerable amount of guesswork had been involved in determining the proportions of the first boiler used on No 1, and, having regard to the greatly increased cylinder volume of the 4-2-2 engine, some not very imaginative guesswork at that! It should not be forgotten that No 1 had a cylinder volume 30 per cent greater, so the use of tubes of a smaller diameter in a longer boiler seems inexplicable in an engineer of Stirling's calibre. Steaming troubles apart, the engine amassed a substantial mileage, running 32,000 miles in the first eight months of her life. She was then running between Doncaster and Peterborough in a link with the 7-ft 2-2-2 engines.

The inadequacy of the steaming arrangements seems to have been realised at an early date, and when construction of two further engines was begun in the late autumn of 1870 they were provided with larger fireboxes of the same cross-section but 8 in longer. A study of the general proportions of these engines makes it clear that this increase would have made it necessary to lengthen the main frames by an equal amount because of the positioning of the trailing wheel immediately in rear of the firebox. However, in addition to a longer firebox and thereby increased grate area, from 15.8 sq ft to 17.7 sq ft, these next two 8-ft singles each had a water midfeather in the firebox instead of the conventional brick-arch. This was a revival of a device Sturrock and certain other engineers had tried out when experimenting with means of burning coal instead of coke in locomotive fireboxes. The two new engines which were completed at Doncaster in December 1870 and March 1871, were numbered 8 and 33 respectively, and the latter was the subject of a

finely executed sectional drawing in *The Engineer*, which is reproduced on page 19. From this it will be seen that the suspension for the pair of trailing wheels under the cab was by a volute spring, that the safety valves were the old spring-loaded pattern and that there were no brakes on the engine.

After the completion of engine No 33 there was a further hiatus of nine months before further engines of the type were built, doubtless to allow for the effectiveness or otherwise of the midfeathers to be assessed. The result must be judged from the fact that no further Great Northern engines were built with midfeathers, and Nos 8 and 33 had them removed and brick-arches substituted after less than two year's running. The next two engines of the class, Nos 2 and 3, were completed in December 1871 and March 1872, and with them it seemed that the early experiments with boilers were ended. The tube size was settled at 1¾ in and the grate area at 17.5 sq ft, while the height of the blastpipe as originally fixed on No 1 (but subsequently lowered by no less than 5½ in) was accepted as standard for the class. The steaming troubles were cured, and the eight-footers settled down to that reliability of service that eventually made them famous. Construction proceeded in pairs from Nos 2 and 3, and, although there were some changes in detail design, the next major development came in July 1876 when engine No 221 was the first to be built with vacuum brake. In the meantime, the eight engines that followed Nos 2 and 3 were built without brakes except for the handbrakes on the tender. These engines were numbered 5, 7, 22, 48, 34, 47, 53 and 62, in that order.

The Newark brake trials took place in the summer of 1875 and as a result the Great Northern decided to equip all its passenger stock and the engines used for hauling it with Smith's simple, non-automatic

Left *One of the first Stirling tank engines of the 0-4-4 type, No 511 built in 1874, seen here on an outer suburban train to Hertford near Hadley Wood* (the late C. Laundy).

Right *One of the 1877 group of 8 ft bogie singles, No 69* (British Railways).

vacuum brake system. This was considerably cheaper than the full automatic form of the brake, but it had the fatal disadvantage that, in the event of a coupling breaking, any part of the train severed from the locomotive had no brakes at all. On the Great Northern, the equipment had not yet been fitted at the time of the grievous double collision at Abbots Ripton on January 21 1876, when the down Leeds express could not be stopped in time to avoid crashing into the derailed seven-footer which had been hauling the up Scotch express before its collision with a goods train. The Leeds engine was one of the last eight-footers to be built, No 48, and she was so badly damaged that she had to spend more than two months at Doncaster afterwards. While on the subject of rebuilding, it may be added that in the following year, 1877, the pioneer engine No 1 was fitted with a new firebox of the standard length of 6 ft 2 in, and this involved lengthening the frames by 8 in. The original frames were wrought iron, 1¼ in thick, and to cut the plates and weld a new length into position was a normal blacksmith's job at the time.

Engine No 221, and her 'twin' No 94, in addition to being the first eight-footers to have the early form of vacuum brake, included an important design change at the rear end. The original springing at the rear must have provided something of a lively ride when those big 8-ft wheels were stepping it out a bit, and, in contemplation of still faster running, Stirling decided on a change to plate springs. To enable these to be underslung it was necessary to use a larger diameter trailing wheel, 4 ft 7 in instead of 4 ft 1 in, and the outward appearance of the engines was enhanced thereby. However, the engines fitted with the earliest form of vacuum brake had a fitting that some observers regarded as an 'eyesore', the vacuum ejector mounted on the right-hand side of the smokebox wrapper plate.

There was another change on the next eight-footer to be built, No 69, in February 1877; this had the Ramsbottom type of safety valve, and to accommodate it a slightly modified profile of the beautiful brass casing had to be adopted. Hitherto these had been slightly waisted from the neck, but thereafter a fuller curve was necessary. Both were equally handsome. Engine No 69 was the sixteenth eight-footer built at Doncaster, and was the start of a spell of what was as near to 'bulk building' as the Plant reached with these locomotives. Between February 1877 and December 1879 they turned out 11 more, and, if the period is extended to April 1880, one more could be counted, engine No 95. This batch of 12 actually included six with consecutive numbering, Nos 544-549.

With the stud of eight-footers now totalling 27, it is appropriate to refer to their allocation and their work. In Stirling's own time, the eight-footers were not moved from shed to shed. Engine No 547, originally stationed at Kings Cross, was the sole 'exception that proved the rule' when, before 1885, she was transferred to Doncaster. The allocation of the first 27 engines in 1880 was Kings Cross 4, Peterborough 9, Grantham 7 and Doncaster 7. Although the class was introduced in 1870, it was not until 1875 that one of them was stationed in London.

The year 1880 was something of a milestone in the history of the eight-footers, because No 662, the first engine with the deeper front frames, was built in February 1881. This was the first of a consecutively-numbered batch of ten, built at Doncaster up to March 1883. They were not all the same, because beginning with engine No 664 in June 1881, the picturesque slotted splasher for the driving wheel was abandoned and replaced by the plain splasher

decorated only by the large oval Doncaster works-plate. When these engines were being built, the Great Northern Railway was still using the simple non-automatic form of vacuum brake, with the ejector mounted on the right-hand side of the smoke-box, but the brake-pipe was not carried forward to the front buffer beam; in Stirling's day, double-heading was absolutely forbidden on the Great Northern, and the absence of any brake connection at the front end virtually ensured this.

In 1884-85, four more eight-footers were built, Nos 771-774, generally the same as the 662-671 series, but in this period there was considerable rebuilding of the old engines of the class with new frames. In later years, after the introduction of steel frames, it was usual for the frames to last the entire life of a locomotive, and when the frames were beyond repair it was the signal for scrapping the entire machine. It was otherwise in Stirling's day, when all the eight-footers originally had wrought iron frames 1¼ in thick, and all of the older engines built between 1870 and 1880 were rebuilt with stronger frames between 1880 and 1889.

As regards speed, in those days of the non-automatic brake the up Manchester express leaving Grantham at 4.17 pm was the fastest train on the line, having a booked average speed of 53.7 mph over the 105.5 miles to Kings Cross. The usual load was not more than six six-wheeled coaches, amounting to a gross trailing load of 90 tons behind the tender, but, while this does not seem very much these days, when related to the weight of the engine and tender, the trailing load, reckoned to include the tender, was 2¾ times the weight of the engine, or not so very different from a Gresley 'A4' 'Pacific' hauling three times its own weight on 'The Talisman' in the last days of steam on the East Coast Route. The eight-footers kept very good time on the 4.17 pm up from Grantham, reaching about 75 mph down the bank from Stoke Summit, passing Peterborough in about 31

minutes from the start (29.1 miles) and then being able to take it more easily.

By December 1885, with 41 of the eight-footers on the road, Stirling seems to have had some doubts concerning his first-line express passenger motive power stud. In the first place, it is known that he was under some pressure from the top management of the GNR to reduce the costs of his department, while at the same time he seemed always to have in mind the introduction of a 'single driver' locomotive with a smaller wheel than his already celebrated eight-footers for use on the sections of line with heavier gradients, presumably north of Doncaster to Leeds. Only two months after completing the first eight-footer in 1870, he had built an isolated 7-ft 6-in 2-2-2 ostensibly to use up the driving wheels of the old Sturrock 4-2-2 No 215, which it was thought were too good to scrap. This engine, No 92, had 17½-in by 24-in cylinders and proved a remarkably free runner, though not as powerful as the eight-footers. Be that as it may, however, Stirling used this engine as a kind of prototype for the new main-line express passenger engine he was to introduce in 1885. The first two of this new class, Nos 238 and 232, had the same wheel-base as the isolated engine of 1870 but larger cylinders, 18½ in by 26 in; in fact, their nominal tractive effort was slightly greater than that of the eight-footers. As anticipated, the two new engines were both stationed at Doncaster and worked north to Leeds as part of their rosters.

Before the second of these new 2-2-2 engines was in service, however, Stirling was planning a larger version to use a boiler of the same length as that of the bogie eight-footers. The emergence of these later engines as the '234' Class in the summer of 1886 poses the inevitable question: was the outside-cylindered 4-2-2 going out of favour at Doncaster? To answer that query with an immediate negative, one can quote the chronology of express engine building at Doncaster from midsummer 1885:

Left *The 7 ft 7 in 2-2-2 express engine No 92 of 1870, with the single pair of driving wheels carried by the Sturrock 4-2-2 No 215* (the late W.J. Reynolds).

Above right *Stirling 7 ft 7 in express 2-2-2, built in 1886* (the late W.J. Reynolds).

Date	Engine No	Type
30.6.85	238	2-2-2 short frame
1.8.85	232	2-2-2 short frame
6.8.85	773	4-2-2
1.12.85	774	4-2-2
19.6.86	234	2-2-2 larger frame '234' Class
27.7.86	229	2-2-2 larger frame '234' Class
20.1.87	775	4-2-2 (steam sanding)
22.3.87	237	2-2-2 '234' Class
26.3.87	776	4-2-2 Newcastle Exhibition engine
16.4.87	230	2-2-2 '234' Class
21.9.87	777	4-2-2
24.9.87	236	2-2-2 '234' Class
23.11.87	239	2-2-2 '234' Class
26.11.87	778	4-2-2

After that, no more eight-footers were built until 1893 when the last two of the engines with 18-in cylinders wre completed at Doncaster, Nos 1001 and 1002 in August and December respectively. In the meantime, the Works had turned out the remaining 2-2-2 engines of the '234' Class, Nos 231, 233, 235 and 240, the last being completed in January 1889.

While Stirling himself originally classified the 7-ft 7-in singles as suitable for the more heavily-graded sections of the line, and arranged for the first two of them, with shorter frames, to be shedded at Doncaster, any inhibitions of that kind were apparently cast aside when the '234' Class was built, because these engines were distributed among the sheds involved with the fastest main-line running on the system, and they quickly took their place as every bit the equivalent of the eight-footers regarding performance in traffic. In view of this, it may well be wondered why Stirling went to the 4-2-2 type with outside cylinders in the first place when planning his large express passenger engine in 1870.

The answer is undoubtedly linked with the history of metallurgy. At that early date, fractures of the wrought iron axles then in use were distressingly frequent, and any proposal to use cylinders as large as 18 in diameter greatly increased the likelihood of failure with an inside cylinder engine. So, outside cylinders were essential. Fifteen years later, all was changed—cranked axles in steel instead of wrought iron made inside cylinders as large as 18½ in diameter a perfectly sound proposition, and the '234' Class was as good a traffic machine as an eight-footer for all parts of the Great Northern main line. At sheds such as Peterborough, 2-2-2s and 4-2-2s were used, I was going to add 'indiscriminately', on all the principal express workings; however, the engines were allocated to individual drivers at that time, and engine workings depended on the driver's link.

The working of the Peterborough engines on the down 'Flying Scotsman' in the first 'Race to the North' in the summer of 1888 provides a good example of the varying use of the 2-2-2 and 4-2-2 engines at that shed. At that time, the train was booked to run the 105½ miles from Kings Cross to Grantham in 119 minutes, and, while a Kings Cross eight-footer was used on the very first trip, on all the other 26 occasions Peterborough engines were used, eight-footers on 18 occasions, the remainder using 2-2-2s. The individual 4-2-2 engines were 7, 22, 48, 69, 98 and 776 and the 2-2-2s were 233, 234 and 237. It is of interest that the fastest of all these runs was made by a 2-2-2 engine, No 233, when Grantham was reached in 105 minutes at an average speed of 60.3 mph from Kings Cross. Northwards to York, the Grantham engines had the train for a week at a time, and only four, the eight-footers 3, 95, 775 and 777, were used throughout the racing period.

After the excitement of 1888, no further express locomotives were built at Doncaster until the

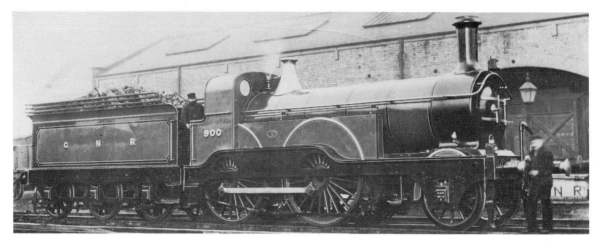

One of the last batches of Stirling 2-4-0 engines, built at Doncaster in 1894 (the late W.J. Reynolds).

beginning of 1892, when work was started on a further batch of 2-2-2s. Not even Stirling, with his love of the eight-footers, could deny that the 7-ft 7-in 2-2-2s were fully their equal in performance on the road, and the five new engines went into traffic in 1892, No 871 in January and No 875 in June. Two more eight-footers were, nevertheless, built in the following year (Nos 1001 and 1002) to be followed by 2-2-2s Nos 876-880 and 981 in 1894. By that time, Stirling himself was well over 70 years of age, and he had reluctantly agreed to the fitting of brake-pipes and coupling-hoses to the front buffer beams of this latest batch of 2-2-2s so that they could be double-headed if necessary.

He met the need for more powerful engines to deal with the heavier trains that were being worked in a manner that was less successful. For the final batch of eight-footers, Nos 1003-1008, which were turned out at Doncaster between November 1894 and April 1985, the cylinders, hitherto 18 in, were increased to the very large size of 19½ in, and the boiler pressure was increased to 170 psi. However, although the fire-box was enlarged the boiler was not, and all six

engines had to have new cylinders within a short time of their going into service. Nevertheless, after these early failures the new engines settled down to ordinary top link work, Nos 1003, 1004 and 1005 at Peterborough, No 1006 at Grantham and Nos 1007 and 1008 at Kings Cross. When Anglo-Scottish rivalry blazed up again in the second 'Race to the North' in August of that same year, 1895, none of the new engines was used. The enthusiasts, some of whom had come to worship at the shrine of Stirling as others did at that of Stroudley, were fulsome in their praise of the '1003' Class, but another of their number, who combined high professional engineering attainments with love of the eight-footers as works of art, wrote: 'Looking back over 70 years to the circumstances of their design, it is indeed difficult to justify the construction of these last six eight-footers. The writing on the wall was clear and any younger man than Stirling would have rightly and properly looked ten years or more into the future and produced a new design of express passenger engine. Stirling had done so in 1870 in his original eight-footer design, which was not out-classed for over 20 years.'

Patrick Stirling died 'in harness' on November 11 1895 at the age of 75, a much revered member of the engineering profession and a much-loved 'boss' of the locomotive department of the Great Northern Railway.

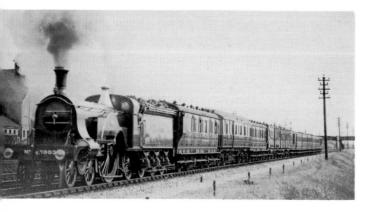

One of the beautiful '1003' Class Stirling 8 footers fitted with cylinders of 19½ in diameter; engine No 1003 is seen here on a train for the East Lincolnshire line leaving Peterborough (the late C. Laundy).

3. North Eastern: Fletcher to T. W. Worsdell

By the year 1870, the North Eastern was the most prosperous of all the home railways. The dividend paid on the ordinary shares was not less than ten per cent and the trade boom which created an ever-increasing demand for Durham and Northumberland coal was intensified during the winter of 1870-71 with the Franco-Prussian war. To deal with the increased freight traffic, particularly on the longer through hauls from Newcastle and Darlington to York and Leeds, Edward Fletcher who had been Locomotive Superintendent since 1854, put on the road in 1870 a new class of 0-6-0 main-line goods engine. This class was remarkable in that it was not only the first to be built in really large numbers for the North Eastern Railway, but also because Robert Stephenson & Co turned out the first fifty engines of the class within two years. The remaining twenty were built by Hawthorn's in 1872-73. Their numbers ran from 706 to 775, but for some reason they are often referred to as the '708' Class. They were excellent sturdy, machines, thoroughly suited to heavy work, with 17-in by 24-in cylinders, coupled wheels of 5 ft diameter, a total heating surface of 1,138 sq ft and a boiler pressure of 140 psi. They had outside frames of the 'sandwich' type, comprising a plank of wood sandwiched between wrought iron plates. Such frames were much favoured in early days as they imparted a certain degree of structural flexibility without any loss of strength at a time when permanent way was not as solid as we know it today. Fletcher retained the sandwich frames in his standard tenders, but the '708' Class were the last main line engines to be so equipped.

Such was the demand for freight engines in 1872 and afterwards, however, that before the later examples of the '708' Class were on the road, Fletcher was building an inside-framed version of the same general design. The first of these, engine No 398, was built at Gateshead in 1872, and no fewer than 160 were built by different contractors between 1872 and 1876. Construction was continued at intervals by the North Eastern Railway at Gateshead until there was a grand total of 324 engines; the last five were completed after Fletcher had retired, and had round-topped domes and Ramsbottom valves when new. Like the double-framed variant of the design, the '398' Class were excellent engines, and handled the main-line goods traffic turn and turn about with the later 0-6-0s of McDonnell and Worsdell design for many years. The boiler is of paricular interest, as it was used without major altera-

tion for the well-known 'Tennant' express engines of 1885. The barrel was 4 ft 3 in in diameter and 10 ft 7 in long; there were 206 tubes of 1¾ in outside diameter providing a heating surface of 1,028 sq ft. The firebox had a grate area of 17 sq ft and a heating surface of 110 sq ft. They had a total weight, in working order of 37.25 tons without tenders, and 66.25 tons with their tenders. As originally built, they had the elaborate colour scheme of Fletcher days, identical to that of the passenger engines, though the number was not generally carried on the tender.

In 1872 there was completed at Gateshead works the first of the locomotives for which Fletcher is best remembered, by the outside world at any event, the big 2-4-0 express engine No 901. This engine, which was turned out in October of that year, and No 902, which followed in December, were evidently in the nature of prototypes for trials, because the next order for ten locomotives of this class was given to Beyer, Peacock & Co, to be followed by an order for another ten given to Neilson's. The former batch was delivered in May to July 1873 and the Neilson lot, Nos 924-933, arrived in November and December of the same year. Gateshead added one more, No 903, in November 1873, and No 904 followed in January 1874. Thereafter, 31 more were built at Gateshead, three in 1874, nine in 1875, three in 1876, six in 1880, six in 1881 and four in 1882. Despite this, however, the main concern of the North Eastern continued to be with freight, and this point is borne out by the locomotive building activities between 1872 and 1882. During that time, 70 new passenger tender engines were added to the stock compared with 394 new 0-6-0 engines.

Nonetheless, the '901' Class express engines were Fletcher's masterpiece and the consummation of his long career, so the more fortuitous it seems that the London and North Eastern Railway decided not merely to preserve but to restore to its original condition an example of so supremely beautiful a nineteenth-century locomotive design. I remember how, in the quietude of the old Railway Museum at York, old No 910 stood in a splendour of brasswork and gorgeous colouring that made the Stirling eight-footer, *Gladstone* and *City of Truro* look plain by comparison. The adjective 'colourful' is now used more often in a figurative sense than literally, but, letting the imagination wander beyond No 910, one can picture what a kaleidoscopic array North Eastern running sheds of the 'seventies would present, when

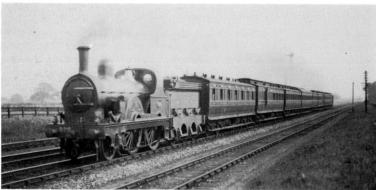

Above *An example of Fletcher's celebrated '901' Class 7 ft 2-4-0s, built first in 1872 and the mainstay of NER express service for many years* (The Locomotive Publishing Company).

Left *One of the Fletcher '901' Class, No 926 as reboiled by Worsdell, on a down express near Alne* (Author's collection).

Left *The first of four elegant 6 ft 6 in 2-4-0s built by Fletcher for the Central Division in 1882. Reboiled by Worsdell, as shown here, they lasted for thirty years* (The Locomotive Publishing Company).

all engines, passenger, goods and shunting alike, were arrayed like her and, to judge from contemporary photographs, kept in a beautifully clean condition. No 910 as now preserved in the National Railway Museum at York represents the Gateshead style of painting, and the colours, although rich and varied, are not such as to be classed as gaudy. The basic green is almost exactly the same as that of the GNR, a little darker in appearance than the pea-green of later NER days. It is beautifully set off by the myrtle-green surround on the tender and cab sides, while the broad dark bands on the boiler barrel are most effective. The under-frames are painted a claret colour and the coupling-rods, the levers to the Salter safety valves and the reversing-rod are all painted red; the last–mentioned passes through the right-hand driving wheel splasher and can be seen through the slotted openings on the splasher itself.

On the footplate, the fittings are of the simplest. The inside of the cab is lined with wood that is stained and polished, and looks most handsome. The most interesting feature is the combined lever and screw reverser; this is a development of an ingenious device brought out by Robert Stephenson & Co in 1867. By turning the wheel, the lever can be moved slowly to any desired position of cut-off, while it is also possible, by manipulating the lever direct in the usual way, to change quickly from forward to reverse, or to make any other desired quick change.

The design of the '901' Class was very sound in all respects. The basic dimensions were: coupled wheels 7 ft diameter, cylinders 17 ft by 24 in (though the diameter in the case of engines built in 1880-82 was increased to 17½ in), total heating surface 1,208.5 sq ft, grate area 16 sq ft and boiler pressure 140 psi. The slide valve dimensions, with 1¼ in lap and 4⅛ in travel in full gear, gave generous port openings and rendered the engines free-running, while the use of Fletcher's exhaust cocks, whereby the driver could soften the blast by diverting part of the exhaust from the blastpipe direct to the atmosphere underneath the cylinders, was generally considered to play a part in reducing coal consumption. In broad principle, it is something akin to the 'jumper' caps fitted to modern Great Western engines, except that they operate automatically. On the North Eastern, the exhaust cocks were a widely-appreciated feature, and, as will be seen later, an attempt to remove them met with solid opposition.

Early in 1883, Fletcher retired, and in April of that year Alexander McDonnell, until then Locomotive Superintendent of the Great Southern and Western Railway, took over at Gateshead. The events of the next two years will be debated as long as there are students of locomotive history. The new chief came over from Ireland with a brilliant record of achieve-ment behind him; a native of Dublin and an honours graduate of Dublin University, he was just 53 years of age and apparently in the prime of life. Far from having a purely academic outlook, he had acquired a most varied practical experience of railways before being appointed Locomotive, Carriage and Wagon Superintendent of the GS & WR. He was then no more than 35, and in a relatively short time he had produced order out of something bordering on chaos. Modelling his practice upon that of Crewe, in standardizing parts between one engine class and another and in effecting speed and economy in workshop practice, he laid the foundation of the noted Inchicore school of locomotive engineers which produced such distinguished men as Sir John Aspinall, H.A. Ivatt and R.E.L. Maunsell.

To McDonnell's neat and orderly mind, the locomotive department of the North Eastern Railway in 1883 must have presented a very much enlarged and more complicated version of the 'chaos' he had found at Inchicore 18 years earlier, except that the added nightmare of bad permanent way and consequent damage to locomotive springs was not present. At Inchicore he had followed a policy of letting the oldest and most decrepit engines wear themselves out, while standardizing fittings on the more serviceable ones and making such details interchangeable with those of his own new designs. But whereas in Ireland he was concerned with a few hundred engines, the North Eastern stud in 1883 must have numbered about one and a half thousand, and whether he had any real appreciation of the state of affairs up and down the line before he actually took over at Gateshead is open to doubt. He came as a stranger to a strange land, and, looking back on those eventful years, one is curious to know what steps he took to assess the situation. John Stephenson was still at York as Divisional Superintendent and George Graham was at Darlington, and although Wilson Worsdell had but recently gone to Gateshead there would have been others born and bred on the north-east coast who could have advised him.

The 'Locomotive Superintendent' of those days included the train running in his responsibilities, and the drivers and firemen came under his supervision. For many years, the locomotive department of the North Eastern Railway had been a kind of family party. Edward Fletcher was a Northumbrian himself, and, understanding his men thoroughly, he was well liked and well respected for his personality no less than his ability as an engineer. For, despite their lack of standardization, Fletcher engines ran well and economically, and the regime had, by the year 1883, gone placidly on its way for just thirty years. The majority of the men had grown up with Fletcher engines; they knew no others, and at the points where they came in contact with the outside world, at York, Leeds, Edinburgh and Carlisle, the latest of them were second to none, and superior to most. So why change? The fact that the new chief was a complete stranger naturally caused a good deal of comment, not so say apprehension; and, when that stranger began to institute certain reforms and introduced a tightening up of discipline, the tension began to rise. It rose still further when small alterations in detail were made to some of the Fletcher engines.

Discipline and reform in the various works were ill-received in themselves, but McDonnell incurred the wrath of the footplate men when he began to remove the exhaust cocks from the Fletcher engines. The men liked them and appreciated their operation, so their removal aroused a perfect fury of indignation. In the enginemen's views, for a stranger to dare to alter a Fletcher locomotive was little short of iconoclasm! The whole storm centred on those exhaust cocks, but in face of representations, indignant meetings and goodness knows what else, McDonnell stood firm; the exhaust cocks must go. So far the new chief had certainly shown the courage of his convictions, and he might eventually have ridden out this particular storm had it not been for the shortcomings of his own express locomotives which were virtually damned by the footplate men before the first of them ever turned a wheel. Their construction had not proceeded far in Gateshead before the salient features became known and were condemned outright by the men. First of all, the new engines had bogies; Mr Fletcher had never used bogies for his main-line engines, and therefore in the eyes of the men they were quite unnecessary! Then there was the shape of the chimneys. The Fletcher stove-pipes were a functional design, tapering outwards in some conformity with the shape of the cone of exhaust steam ejected from the blastpipe. The men took one look at the new chimneys and pronounced, once and for all, that the engines would not steam. The truth was, of course, that McDonnell in his reforming zeal had queered his pitch with the men before his own engines came out, and nothing he could do thereafter was right. He resigned in the autumn of 1884.

The resignation of McDonnell came at an awkward time for the North Eastern. New locomotives were needed urgently, for in the summer of 1885 the night express to Aberdeen was to be run non-stop from Newcastle to Edinburgh, a distance of 124½ miles. At the time, this was the longest non-stop run in Europe, and the McDonnell engines had been intended to handle it as well as the other heavy main-line jobs. They were, however, not powerful enough, and the situation might well have become critical had not very swift measures been taken. There could be no waiting for a new locomotive

superintendent to be appointed, to take stock of the situation and begin designing his own engines. The General Manager, Henry Tennant, summoned the divisional locomotive superintendents to a committee over which he himself presided, and that committee worked so quickly that before Hawthorn's had delivered the last of the McDonnell 4-4-0s, Darlington works had the first of the Tennant engines on the road. Wilson Worsdell, who had been assistant to McDonnell, played a leading part in the design, which could be called a model of tact, sound engineering and real aesthetic charm. No one could have been more conscious than Wilson Worsdell of the opposition to McDonnell's practice, and in the new engines every single 'bone of contention' was absent; they had no bogies, the exhaust cocks reappeared, the driving position was once again on the right-hand side of the cab and the chimney tapered outwards from the base. To the neatness of a McDonnell was restored the bright and beautiful colouring of old, while above all the pioneer 'Tennant' engine immediately showed enhanced power.

The leading dimensions of the Fletcher '901' Class, the McDonnell 4-4-0s and the 'Tennants' make an interesting comparison:

	Fletcher '901'	McDonnell 4-4-0	'Tennant' 2-4-0
Cylinders (in)	17 × 24	17 × 24	18 × 24
Coupled wheels (ft in)	7 0	6 8	7 1
Total heating surface (sq ft)	1,208.5	1,097	1,212.5
Grate area (sq ft)	16.1	16.8	18.0
Total weight of engine in working order (tons)	39.1	39.5	42.1

The 'Tennants' at first carried the same working pressure as the McDonnells, 140 psi, but, as the dimensions suggest, they were altogether more robust machines. It was significant of the gradual integration of all locomotive affairs on the North Eastern that the pioneer of the new class should have been built at Darlington, and that this engine, No 1463, was tried out in service before the remaining 19 were built. After the storm over the McDonnell 4-4-0s, it is rather amusing to see that No 1463 was sent to York and not to Gateshead, as if to introduce the new machine by degrees.

The locomotive committee responsible for the 'Tennants' need have had no fears; the engines were received by the men with enthusiasm, and

One of the 'Tennant' express 2-4-0s, No 1472, introduced in 1885 and seen here at Durham (Author's collection).

remained firm favourites throughout their existence wherever they went on the system, not excepting their last days on minor branch lines. Once the pioneer engine had been tried out, Darlington and Gateshead set to work simultaneously on the building of the class, and both works achieved a rate of output that would have done credit to Crewe. Darlington turned out Nos 1464 to 1472 in three months, while Gateshead, beginning with two per month in June and July of 1885, stepped up their output to three per month to complete the class with No 1506 in September 1885. The numbers of the Gateshead batch were 1473 to 1479 and 1504 to 1506. In addition to No 1463, York received 1465, 1466, 1467 and 1468, the three 1500s went to Edinburgh and all the rest went to Gateshead shed.

Following the success of the 'Tennant' engines, it might have been thought a logical development for Wilson Worsdell to be appointed Locomotive Superintendent, but for the second time the North Eastern board went outside the company and brought in Wilson's elder brother, Thomas W. Worsdell, then Locomotive Superintendent of the Great Eastern Railway. 'T.W.' had certainly enjoyed a distinguished career even before he joined the Great Eastern. He was the eldest son of Nathaniel Worsdell, Carriage Superintendent of Grand Junction Railway, who in still earlier days, with his father, had built the tender for the *Rocket*. It would seem only natural that 'T.W.' should spend some of his training at Crewe, but in his young days, not through any fault of his own, he

was never long in any particular job and in 1865, at the age of 27, he went to America and entered the service of the Pennsylvania Railroad. In that young country his outstanding ability found wide scope, and in a very short time he was appointed Master Mechanic at the Altoona shops, the 'Crewe of the USA' as it has often been called.

Crewe itself was to offer him still greater inducements. When F.W. Webb succeeded Ramsbottom on the LNWR, he offered Worsdell the job of Works Manager, so back to England he came and was associated with Webb when the first experiments with compounding were taking place. Worsdell's own experiments in this direction were made on the Great Eastern Railway, but they were not very successful. Then he moved to the North Eastern, and his first compound engine was completed at Gateshead works in the autumn of 1886; it was a two-cylinder machine on the Worsdell-von Borries system. On the North Eastern he applied the system first to an express goods engine, No 16, the pioneer of the celebrated 'C' Class of 0-6-0s. As originally built, the high pressure cylinder was of 18 in diameter and the low pressure 26 in diameter, the stroke of both being 24 in. The coupled wheels were 5 ft 1¼ in with new tyres. Joy valve gear was used, actuating slide valves with 1⅛-in lap, ³/₂₆-in lead and a travel of 5½ in in full gear. The boiler

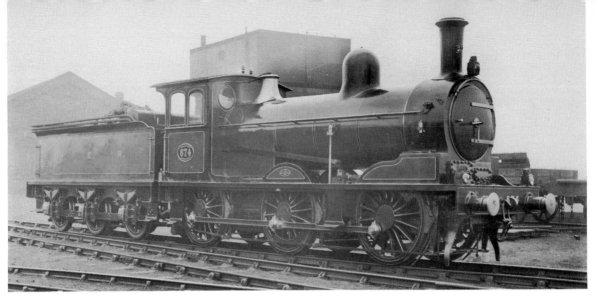

was excellent, having a tube heating surface of 1,026 sq ft, while the firebox had a grate area of 17.23 sq ft and a heating surface of 110 sq ft. The boiler pressure was 160 psi.

The spacious covered-in cab attracted much attention at the time, and it was suggested that the idea came from Worsdell's experience in America. It is ironical to reflect that when William Bouch introduced a very similar cab on his Stockton and Darlington 4-4-0s of 1860 it met with opposition from the enginemen, whereas it seems from contemporary accounts that the Worsdell cab on No 16 was well received! In general, the engine was massively built and beautifully finished, and in 1887 *The Engineer* was moved to comment 'Even if no saving in fuel is effected the North Eastern Railway Company has obtained a splendid engine which does infinite credit to the builder as well as to the designer'. While providing an excellent shelter, the cab was handsomely finished inside, with side-sheets and roof lined with painted and polished wood. The quality of the workmanship put into the North Eastern cab interiors was never brought home to me more forcibly than on a day in 1932 when I was browsing round the little shed at Penrith; two North Western 'Jumbos' were outside, several 'Cauliflowers' were also there, and there was a North Eastern 'C' Class goods, by that time, of course, converted to a two-cylinder simple. The contrast between the rough, stark ironmongery of the Crewe cabs and the comfort of the contemporary Gateshead engine could hardly have been more exaggerated.

Only one compound goods engine was built in 1886, and, while exhaustive trials were in progress, Worsdell built ten simple 0-6-0s, designated 'C1' Class, with two cylinders 18 in by 24 in but otherwise the same as the compound. In 1887, construc-

tion of the 'C' Class compounds began in earnest; 140 were built at Gateshead between 1887 and 1892, and the remaining 30 were built at Darlington. In 1894-95, Wilson Worsdell built another 20 of the non-compound series at Gateshead, and gradually the compounds were converted to 2-cylinder simples, although, as with the compound goods locomotives on the London and North Western and elsewhere, they enjoyed a much longer existence as compounds than the contemporary passenger engines; 31 were still running as compounds in 1910. Originally they were painted in the passenger colours, Gateshead style, with a dark green surround on the tender and the cab side-sheets; they carried cast brass number-plates on the cab sides, and had the initials NER on the tender. In the summer of 1951 I had a most enjoyable trip from Penrith to Darlington, and I shall always remember with something of thrill how the old engine went pedalling away up the 1 in 60 from Kirkby Stephen, over Belah Viaduct and up to Stainmore summit doing 26 mph with her load of 90 tons, and how smoothly and easily she rode at speeds of up to 55 mph on the ensuing descent to Barnard Castle.

In their early days, when they were the crack main-line goods engines of the NER, the 'C' Class, and the original non-compound 'C1' series, undertook the longer hauls, from Newcastle to York and Leeds, from Newcastle to Carlisle and from Darlington over the Stainmore route to Tebay. Also, on account of their 5-ft diameter wheels, they were suitable for semi-fast passenger and excursion working. In many ways they were a counterpart of the famous Webb 18-in goods of the LNWR, though I have never heard of them running up to 70 and 75 mph as the old 'Cauliflowers' did on occasions.

Left *One of the 170 two-cylinder compounded 0-6-0 goods engines built by T.W. Worsdell between 1886 and 1892. They were beautifully painted and lined out in the passenger livery (The Locomotive Publishing Company).*

Right *Eastbound train of coke empties near Stainmore summit, Darlington-Tebay line, hauled by 'P1' 4 ft 7 in 0-6-0 No 2068 banked in rear (R.J. Purves).*

Below *NER freight stud: a group of ex-NER Worsdell tank engines around the turntable in Tweedmouth shed (O.S. Nock).*

It was perhaps significant of the importance of freight traffic on the North Eastern Railway that T.W. Worsdell had progressed towards quantity-production of his new standard 0-6-0s before his passenger engines had passed beyond the experimental form. Towards the end of 1886, the first two-cylinder compound express locomotive, No 1324, was completed at Gateshead, and it may have been out of deference to the McDonnell storm that the engine was built originally as a 2-4-0. The coupled wheels were of 6 ft 8 in diameter, but while the cylinders and motion were the same as those of the 'C' Class goods, the boiler provided a larger tube and firebox heating surface, giving a total of 1,323 sq ft against 1,136 sq ft of the 'C' Class. No 1324 was a handsomely-proportioned and beautifully-finished engine, and, after she had spent three months on main-line traffic, she was withdrawn in order to be exhibited, along with old *Locomotion* of the Stockton and Darlington Railway, in the Newcastle-upon-Tyne 1887 Jubilee Exhibition. That three months of running experience had shown No 1324 to be a fast and free runner; indeed, *The Engineer* reported early in 1887 that Worsdell had found her too powerful for the work and was contemplating the use of smaller cylinders in further compound engines. She did, of course, represent a noticeable advance in tractive power over the 'Tennants', having 175 lb pressure against 160 with the same equivalent cylinder capacity. As a 2-4-0, however, she proved unsteady at high speed, probably as a result of the cylinders doing an unequal amount of work and thereby setting lateral forces.

T.W. Worsdell certainly seems to have used better judgement than McDonnell in planting his

innovations upon the North Eastern Railway. His 'C' Class engines were well received, his cabs were appreciated and when, following the experiments with No 1324, his new standard express engines of the 'F' Class came out in 1887 with bogies, that particular feature was accepted without apparent comment. But the overriding factor in the case of the 'F' Class engines was that they were completely master of any main-line duty that could be assigned to them, whereas in the troubled times of 1884 the McDonnell '38' Class definitely were not. Two batches of the new 4-4-0s were built in 1887, all at Gateshead works; ten were compounds with cylinders the same as in the 'C' Class, and ten had two cylinders of 18 in diameter by 24 in stroke.

Mr Worsdell, like his great contemporary at Crewe, made some show of comparing compound with simple propulsion, but, as he provided his compounds with 175 lb boiler pressure and the simples with a meagre 140, the result was a foregone conclusion! The 'F1' Class, as the simples

Worsdell-von Borries two-cylinder compound 'F' Class 4-4-0 No 779 of 1887 at the old Waverley station, Edinburgh (The Locomotive Publishing Company).

were known, had no more tractive effort than the 'Tennants'. Like No 1324, the 'F' Class proved to be very free-running engines, and considered in relation to their Great Eastern forerunners, which were so sluggish, one feature of their design appears to have been critical. To obtain a smooth action and free running it was essential for the work done in the two cylinders to be as nearly equal as possible; to do this, it was calculated that the cylinder volume of low pressure to high pressure should be about 2.3 to 1. This, however, would have resulted in a larger low pressure cylinder than could be conveniently accommodated, so Worsdell used cylinder diameters exactly the same as in his Great Eastern 4-4-0s, 18 in and 26 in, but on the North Eastern engines the Joy valve gear was arranged to give a longer cut-off in the low pressure cylinder. Typical figures were 50 per cent hp and 73 per cent lp or 70 per cent hp and 84 per cent lp. This compensated for the low pressure cylinder having to be smaller than was theoretically correct.

The Gateshead express drivers had had time to take the full measure of these engines when the race to Edinburgh took place in 1888, and it was with No 117, one of the compounds, that the great Bob Nicholson made what was then the record time

from Newcastle to Edinburgh—124.4 miles in 126 minutes with a load of 100 tons. The year 1888, however, witnessed an event that for the North Eastern Railway and, indeed, for British locomotive practice in general, was to prove of considerably greater significance than the race to Edinburgh—the introduction of W.M. Smith's piston valves on a second engine of the 'D' Class of 2-4-0 compound. Walter M. Smith, whose second name, Mackersie, was often wrongly written as MacKenzie, was an outstanding personality; he was one of the ablest locomotive engineers ever to serve the North Eastern, and in later days he became very much the 'power behind the throne'. In 1887, as Chief Draughtsman, his thoughts turned to piston valves as a means of avoiding engine failures due to broken slide valves. Smith set out to produce a piston valve that would be free in operation but would provide means of allowing trapped water to escape without damage to the pistons. It was on the second 'D' Class engine that his first design of piston valve was tried. Why this engine, No 340, was built as a 2-4-0 remains something of a mystery when the superiority of the 'F' Class 4-4-0s had been demonstrated, but built thus she was, though readily distinguishable from her sister engine No 1324 by her long, extended front to cover the tail rods on the pistons.

After some experience with engine No 340, a similar type of piston valve was fitted in 1891 to one of the 'C' Class compound goods engines, No 107, with the important difference that the valves were of the outside admission type, rather than the inside admission on No 340. From one point of view, outside admission valves are to be preferred in that they make possible a shorter and more direct exhaust. On the other hand, it is more difficult to keep the valve chest covers steamtight when they contain high pressure live steam rather than exhaust steam. In spite of this, the North Eastern standardized the use of outside admission valves. The performance of No 107 was carefully watched in comparison with the eleven other engines in her link, and, over a period of six months ending in December 1891, she showed the lowest coal consumption of any, 32.05 lb per mile. This was 3.2 lb per mile less than the average for the remaining 11 engines, and 1.6 lb per mile less than the lowest of any slide valve engine. For locomotives engaged in heavy freight work, these were in any case excellent figures, while the mileages averaged out at about 3,100 per month. Both this engine and No 340 had 2-in spring-loaded relief valves fitted at either end of each cylinder for the purpose of allowing trapped water to escape, but it was found in practice that sometimes, with less-experienced enginemen, the

relief valves did not open quickly enough and cylinder covers were broken. This led W.M. Smith to the design of an improved type of valve in which relief from excessive pressure was obtained by the use of segmental piston rings.

At that time, relations were cordial between the Locomotive Departments of the North Eastern and the Midland Railway. W.M. Smith had at one time served under S.W. Johnson on the Edinburgh and Glasgow Railway, and in the 'nineties Derby collaborated with Gateshead in the development of Smith's piston valves. So, in 1888 it may well have been the success of Johnson's new singles on the Midland that provided the inspiration for the North Eastern 'I' Class 4-2-2s. New motive power was needed for the Leeds and Scarborough expresses, and the relatively easy road and light trains doubtless underlined the view that a well-designed modern single would be ideal. Also, the invention of the steam sanding gear by Mr Holt, the Midland chief draughtsman at Derby, had cured much of the slipping problem experienced with singles. The 'I' Class engines, with driving wheels of 7 ft diameter, had what might be termed the standard North Eastern compound front end, with high pressure cylinders of 18 in diameter and low pressure of 26 in diameter, both with a stroke of 24 in; the boiler was the same as that of the 'C' Classes, and the pressure was 175 psi. The high and low pressure cylinders were on the same horizontal centre-line and the valves were located immediately above them. The wall of the low pressure cylinder extended through an aperture in the frame on the right-hand side of the engine. Ten of these engines were built at Gateshead works in 1888-90.

If the 7-ft 'I' Class engines were from the first intended for secondary main-line work, the second Worsdell 4-2-2 series, the 'J' Class, was not only a main-line job, but one intended to supersede the existing 4-4-0s in the haulage of the heaviest East Coast expresses between York and Edinburgh. The driving wheels were of 7 ft 7 in diameter and the cylinders were much larger than those of previous North Eastern compounds, being 20 in diameter (high pressure) and 28 in diameter (low pressure), both with a stroke of 24 in. The tube heating surface was no larger than that of the 'I' Class but the grate area was increased from 17.2 to 20.7 sq ft, and the grate sloped throughout. The accommodation of the huge 28-in diameter low pressure cylinders between the frames called for some ingenuity in design and was achieved by placing the cylinders at a higher level and inclined. However, this device in turn brought the cylinder so near to the underside of the boiler that there was no room for the steam chest, so both high and low pressure valve chests

Left *'I' Class 7 ft 0 in No 1531 as rebuilt as a two-cylinder simple and with outside frames for the trailing pair of wheels* (The Locomotive Publishing Company).

Right *The first engine of Class 'J', 7 ft 7 in 4-2-2 No 1517, as originally built in 1890 as a two-cylinder compound, with outside steam chests and inside frames for the trailing pair of wheels* (The Locomotive Publishing Company).

Below *'J' Class 4-2-2 No 1519 in its final form in 1919 on a York to Leeds express south of York* (R.J. Purves).

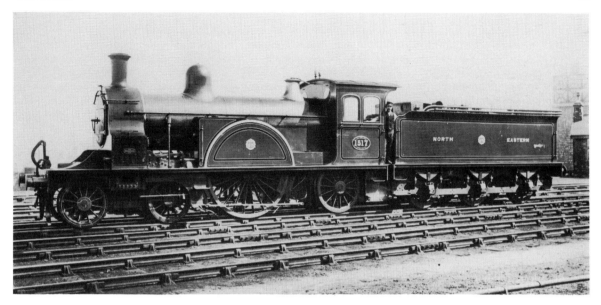

were placed outside the frames with the valves worked by rocking levers. The receiver was arranged very neatly as a curved tube within the narrow smokebox. Joy's valve gear was used, and after some experiments the following details were settled upon:

	High pressure	Low pressure
Lap	1⅛ in	1⅛ in
Travel (full gear)	4⅜ in	5¾ in
Lead	³/₁₆ in	³/₁₆ in
Exhaust clearance	⅛ in	⅛ in

These engines were designed in anticipation of the opening of the Forth Bridge in 1890, when it was thought that heavier loads would have to be worked at higher speeds. The tenders were the largest yet built for the North Eastern, and had a water capacity of 3,940 gallons.

These engines soon showed a remarkable ability to work heavy trains at high speed. No 1517, the first of the class, ran a train of 32 carriages, 270 tons behind the tender, over the 66.9 miles from Newcastle to Berwick in 78 minutes. With a load of 18 six-wheeled coaches, the same engine reached a maximum speed of 90 mph. Some of the most revealing figures were obtained on some indicator trials with No 1518, when the following results were obtained at various points between Newcastle and Berwick:

Speed (mph)	Cut-off (per cent) Hp cylinder	Lp cylinder	Indicated horsepower
5	63	78	136
17	63	78	438
23	50	68	498
30	50	68	630
50	43	62.5	662
75	47	67	1041
86	53	70	1069

The power output at 75 and 86 mph is remarkable, though from the cut-offs used it would seem that the engine was being pushed along pretty hard; it would be interesting to know for how long such an effort could have been sustained.

The difficulty with so many compound locomotives was to get the low pressure cylinders to do their fair share of the work. On the LNWR it was only with the 'Teutonic' Class that Webb achieved anything near success, but T.W. Worsdell scored a real 'bull's-eye' with the 'J' Class. Their life as compounds was, however, exceedingly short; trouble arose with the outside steam chests and broken valves, while the complicated arrangement of rocker gear from the Joy motion to the outside valve spindles was another source of weakness. So it befell that within six years of their construction the ten engines of the class had been converted to 2-cylinder simples. The brilliance of their work from 1894 onwards, however, belongs to Wilson Worsdell's regime.

4. Holden on the Great Eastern

In 1885, the Great Eastern, having had as Locomotive Superintendents S.W. Johnson, William Adams, Massey Bromley and T.W. Worsdell in fairly rapid succession, turned to the Great Western and appointed a man who, though apprenticed to his uncle, Edward Fletcher, at the works of the North Eastern Railway at Gateshead, afterwards went south to make something of a career for himself first at Shrewsbury and then at Swindon. There he rose to become chief assistant to William Dean who had become Locomotive Superintendent. At Swindon he would inevitably have been involved in the preliminary stages for the final epoch-marking liquidation of the broad gauge, in which provision for new express passenger motive power was not one of the most important of considerations. It was the same when he arrived on the Great Eastern, though the problems there were naturally not connected with any change of rail gauge.

In his celebrated series of articles contributed over many years to *The Railway Magazine*, 'Locomotive and train working in the latter part of the nineteenth century', E.L. Ahrons writes of a particular episode on the Great Eastern: 'When Mr Holden succeeded Mr Worsdell at the end of 1885 he promptly started to settle the shunting engine question. The deficiency was somewhat glaring; there were at the beginning of 1886 only 15 0-6-0 shunting and goods tank engines on a railway with a total stock of somewhat over 700 engines. The new shunting engines, with 4 ft wheels and 16½-in by 22-in cylinders, began to pour out of Stratford works for some time, and now there are about 230 of them in service. The old days of painful and laborious movements to and fro on the part of retired tender engines on half pay are now over as far as the Great Eastern is concerned'.

Ahrons was writing in 1918, and one feels that he was much more concerned with main-line matters than with the teeming network of East London, for the passage I have quoted is about all he had to say concerning those remarkable little work-horses that bore the brunt of the Great Eastern suburban service for so many years. True, a number of them were equipped only for shunting, with lever reverse and steam brakes, but many more had the Westinghouse brake and wheel reversers for passenger service. By the year 1904, a total of 210 of these engines had been built, all with 16½-in by 22-in cylinders, but with an increasing boiler power. The first fifty were certainly shunting engines and had boilers with a total heating surface of 960 sq ft, a grate area of 12.5 sq ft and a working pressure of 140 psi. They were built at Stratford from 1886 until 1888, then, in 1890, a

further 20 were built with larger fireboxes having a grate area of 15.2 sq ft. In that same year, however, construction began of the Westinghouse-fitted engines for passenger service, and these had cast steel wheels instead of cast iron. There were some slight changes in the boiler proportions, but the first eighty of the passenger 0-6-0 tanks, built from 1890 to 1896 and numbered 327 to 396 and 265 to 274, were of an unchanged design throughout. Then, from 1899, a batch of the non-passenger variety, with steam brakes and lever reverse, was built with an increased boiler pressure of 160 psi. There were twenty of this batch, and they were followed in 1900-01 by twenty more of the passenger type, Nos 189 to 198 and 160 to 169, also with 160 psi boilers. The final development so far as James Holden was concerned were the twenty passenger 0-6-0s turned out in 1904, Nos 51 to 60 and 81 to 90, which had boilers carrying 180 psi pressure, but still with 16½-in by 22-in cylinders.

With their modest proportions and undistinguished appearance, some readers might well question the validity of the claim to include these little 0-6-0 tank engines in this gallery of 'Great' locomotives, but, even carrying the Great Eastern story no further forward than the turn of the century, and remembering that F.V. Russell's celebrated 'Jazz' service was still twenty years ahead, the work that these engines were doing was colossal by any standards. In the 'crush hours', the suburban trains out of Liverpool Street were made up to 17 four-wheeled coaches, many of which, picturesquely described by Ahrons as 'dog boxes', had already been widened to seat six aside in the thirds, and one of those trains could carry as many as a thousand passengers. The fares read nowadays like some fairy-tale—from any station in the inner suburban area subsequently served by the 'Jazz' trains, the standard fare by any train arriving at Liverpool Street before 7 a.m. was *twopence*, and even those due between the more gentlemanly hours of 7 a.m. and 8 a.m. still charged no more than threepence! The fact that these packed trains ran with the punctuality of chronometers is evidence that the little engines did their jobs admirably, and that the running shed maintenance was equally first class.

In Chapter 3, I described the work that James Holden's predecessor at Stratford, T.W. Worsdell, did for the 2-cylinder compound system on the North Eastern Railway. That development had started on the Great Eastern, but Holden would have none of it. Neither would he follow Worsdell in using the Joy valve gear. In 1884, just before Holden succeeded him, some good 2-4-2 tanks were built at Stratford,

and they, like the first and only Great Eastern compounds, had Joy valve gear. They were intended for the outer suburban runs and only thirty of them were built at first, but when Holden came to multiply the class, originally to no more than ten engines in 1886 and then in a big way with another 120 in 1903-09, he used the Stephenson link motion. These 2-4-2 tanks were altogether larger engines than the

0-6-0s, with 17½-in by 24-in cylinders, coupled wheels of 5 ft 4 in diameter, a total heating surface of 1,132 sq ft and a grate area of 15.3 sq ft. The 1886 lot carried a working pressure of 140 psi, but those built from 1903 on were pressed to 160 lb. They were smart-looking engines and did excellent work on the longer-distance outer suburban trains, such as Liverpool Street to Southend and Bishops Stortford.

Above *Holden 'J69' Class 0-6-0s tank as first repainted in LNER colours. No 359 was one of more than 100 which conveyed the bulk of the GER inner suburban traffic at the time of the grouping* (National Railway Museum, York).

Below *The Stephenson link motion as used on the Great Eastern Railway.*

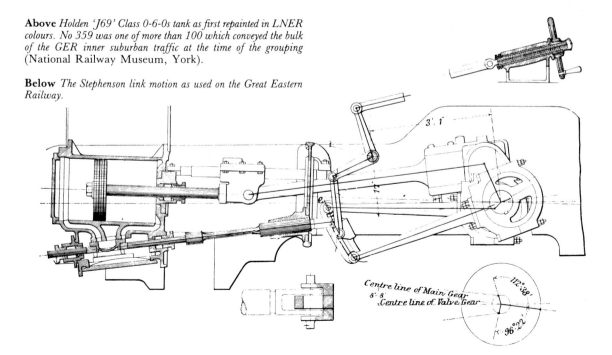

With main-line power, Holden began to make a similarly clean sweep of all the assorted classes bequeathed by his predecessors, and to replace them by a few standard classes. When he came to the top-line express passenger units, certain of the connoisseurs of locomotive practice, including E.L. Ahrons, were surprised that he had reverted to the 2-4-0 type, seeing that Adams, Bromley and Worsdell before him had built bogie engines. But Ahrons concedes 'Nevertheless, the new Great Eastern engines of 1886 to 1897, albeit without bogies, were excellent machines'. The '710' Class eventually numbered 110 engines, and they were of such general use, not only for the principal expresses, that no important shed on the line was without a considerable number of them. They had 7-ft coupled wheels, 18-in by 24-in cylinders and 1,230 sq ft of heating surface. The first hundred had a working pressure of 140 psi and the last ten had this increased to 160. They were simple, straightforward engines, ideal for the general requirements of a line like the Great Eastern. Even on the Colchester main line, the principal express trains were not timed at more than an average speed of 50 mph and the loads were usually less than 200 tons. The line to the north via Cambridge, March and Lincoln to Doncaster was a good deal busier from the passenger point of view than it became after grouping, for then the Great Eastern was in competition with the Great Northern for traffic to York and points north. More of this, however, when we come to James Holden's single-wheelers.

It would not have been surprising if his long stay on the Great Western had left Holden with some affection for the single-wheeler, even though the specimens he inherited from his predecessors at Stratford were not the best examples of the type.

However, the successful introduction of the sand blast technique on the Midland Railway and their subsequent re-introduction of single-driver express locomotives induced Holden also to 'have a go', and he took one of the '710' Class 2-4-0s stationed at Cambridge, No 721, and removed the side-rods. Running thus as a single-driver it was put to work on the GN & GE Joint Line between Cambridge and Doncaster. Although during the 127 miles there are numerous slight gradients, other than a short length of 1 in 200 between Blankney and Lincoln and a similar incline between Stow Park and Gainsborough, there is scarcely a gradient worth mentioning. It was thus an ideal route for single-wheelers, and the adapted No 721 did well. Following this, in 1889, a true single-wheeler, No 789, was built at Stratford, exactly the same as the '710' Class in all its basic dimensions but having a pair of 4-ft diameter trailing wheels beneath the cab. After preliminary trials from Stratford, this new engine was sent to Cambridge for work on the Joint Line in partnership with some of the old Adams-Bromley 7-ft 6-in 4-2-2s. Two years later, a batch of ten more 2-2-2s was built at Stratford and these new engines took over the principal express train workings on the Joint Line, with engines Nos 770 to 775 stationed at Doncaster and 776 to 779 at Cambridge. The Adams-Bromley singles were thereupon scrapped.

The introduction of the new Holden singles in everyday service on these important trains provided those who still sought to compare the merits of single and coupled engines with an unrivalled opportunity, for these new engines and the '710' Class 2-4-0s had exactly the same dimensions, even to the driving wheel diameter. On the Joint Line, as would have been expected, the new singles did well, but, when a further batch of these engines was built at Stratford in

Left *A Worsdell 2-4-2 tank of the 1884 Class, nicknamed 'Gobblers', on a Chingford train at Liverpool Street in 1936 (P. Ransome-Wallis).*

Right *One of the standard Holden mixed traffic 2-4-0s of which 100 were built between 1891 and 1902. Engine 7411 was one of those fitted by the LNER with side-windowed cabs for working on the exposed mountain section between Darlington and Penrith (O.S. Nock).*

1893 with a higher boiler pressure of 160 psi, they were distributed widely over the line, with No 1000 going to Doncaster, 1001-1003 to Cambridge, 1004-1006 to Norwich and 1007-1009 to Parkeston Quay (Harwich). In that same year, however, arrangements were made for the Great Eastern Railway to work its own trains through to York, and the first of the new singles, No 1000, together with some of the earlier batch, were transferred thence to be housed at the North Eastern shed. At the same time it was found more convenient for the 'Cathedrals Route' express trains to change engines at Ely, and so engines 1001 to 1003 were transferred thence from Cambridge to work a daily round trip from Ely to York and back. The Parkeston Quay singles also ran through to York with the North Country Continental Boat Express. This, however, involved a run of 212 miles and double-home

working shared with the '1000' Class of Norwich shed, but these locomotive workings were somewhat changed when the through London-Cromer expresses were put on in 1896, running non-stop between Liverpool Street and North Walsham, the forerunner of the 'Norfolk Coast Express'.

There were other changes, too. Before the introduction of the summer Cromer expresses in 1896, the Great Eastern Railway had adopted, in a relatively small way, the Urquhart system of burning petroleum refuse as a locomotive fuel. On the Great Eastern, the waste product was tar from the railway oil gas works. It was always realised that the supply of this form of fuel might be curtailed in due course, but while it lasted it proved very effective and economical. A small number of top-link express locomotives were fitted for this system of firing, firstly nine of the '710' Class 2-4-0s and then, in 1896, six of the singles

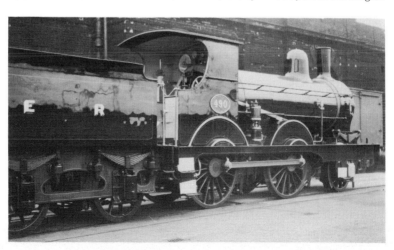

Holden mixed traffic 2-4-0 No 490, repainted in GER livery for preservation in December 1960 (R.C. Riley).

earmarked to work the Cromer expresses. For that purpose, the singles previously stationed at Parkeston Quay were transferred to Ipswich, and an arrangement of double-home working with Norwich shed was instituted. The oil-fired engines steamed very well, and, as they eliminated the labour of firing coal on these long non-stop runs, they were much appreciated. Primarily for the purpose of these runs, water troughs were installed just to the west of Ipswich Tunnel and near Tivetshall, and a small number of 2-4-0s of the '710' Class and the '1000' Class 2-2-2s were equipped with water pick-up apparatus for these particular duties. In view of the sharp gradients encountered on some sections of the main line to Norwich, not to mention those on the branch to Cromer, it might have seemed surprising that single-wheelers should have been allocated exclusively to this prestigious duty. But according to a report made by Charles Rous-Marten to the

International Railway Congress of 1898, these single-wheelers performed with complete reliability on the most severe gradients, so much so that they were able to keep the fast schedule of the Cromer express with heavy loads without needing to race on the downhill sections to make up time.

From the time the train was first introduced in July 1896 until it was withdrawn as part of the wartime restrictions in 1915, it ran to an unchanged schedule, though with ever-increasing train loads. On the down journey, Ipswich (68.7 miles) was required to be passed in 83 minutes, Trowse, in the approach to Norwich, (114 miles) in 144 minutes and the stop at North Walsham (130 miles) reached in 158 minutes, an overall average speed of 49.5 mph. On Rous-Marten's run reported to the International Railway Congress, the load was 170 tons and, in spite of several out-of-course checks, North Walsham was reached several minutes ahead of time. Encouraged

Above *One of the later batch of James Holden's 7 ft singles built in 1893 and used on the principal expresses* (The Locomotive Publishing Company).

Left *Oil-burning 7 ft single on an up Norwich express; note the ballasting of the track* (Author's collection).

Above right *One of the Holden 4-2-2 singles of 1898 built for the Cromer expresses* (National Railway Museum, York).

by the working of the '1000' Class 2-2-2s, Holden built ten more greatly enlarged singles of the 4-2-2 type in 1898, with 18-in by 26-in cylinders, 7-ft driving wheels and 160 psi boiler pressure. Ahrons wrote that he thought they had many resemblances to Johnson's famous 4-2-2s on the Midland, but I thought that they were much more nearly akin to William Dean's '3001' Class on the Great Western, particularly as the new Great Eastern engines had a decorative copper cab to their chimneys in place of the time-honoured stove-pipe of Stratford. Engines Nos 10 and 11 of the new class were stationed at Stratford, while Nos 12 to 15 and 16 to 18 went to Ipswich and Norwich respectively. The 4-2-2 engines took over the working of the summer Cromer expresses by which time the peak holiday loadings of those trains had reached nearly 300 tons. It is unfortunate that no details seem to have been preserved of the running of these very heavy trains, because the locomotive working, with Ipswich and Norwich sheds in fierce competition, was reputedly very fine.

The subsequent history of the single-driver express locomotives on the Great Eastern Railway, both of the 2-2-2 and 4-2-2 types, is rather strange. It was logical enough to transfer the '1000' Class engines that had been at Ipswich and Norwich for the Cromer expresses to the Joint Line, because on the London-Cambridge-Doncaster run there were 14 express trains a day. But the 4-2-2s had scarcely been established on the Norwich main line before Stratford built the 4-4-0 engine *Claud Hamilton*, completed in March 1900. This engine was the only one of the eventually numerous class to bear a name, and the first batch, numbered downwards from No 1899, was turned out during 1900. In due course these engines were allocated to Ipswich and Norwich sheds, where it is said that the super-top-link drivers who had the prestigious double-home workings on the summertime Cromer expresses took such a poor view of the replacement of their beautiful

oil-fired single-wheelers by the 'Claud Hamiltons' that the link workings were left unchanged until the summer service ended at the end of September. However, it was soon evident that the new 4-4-0s had come to stay. Further batches of ten locomotives each were completed at Stratford in 1901, 1902 and 1903, and, with the transference of the 4-2-2s Nos 10 to 19 to the Joint Line, the 'bell was tolled' for the earlier Holden singles. All 21 engines of this series had been broken up by the year 1906, and even the 4-2-2s followed not many years after.

Moreover, this policy of 'scrap and build' did not only affect the single-wheelers. As early as 1902, work began on an extensive programme of rebuilding the '710' Class 2-4-0s, which made it clear that coupled engines of no more than 15 years' life were not immune from alteration. To an outside observer it would have seemed that with the new century a new broom had begun to sweep very cleanly in the drawing office at Stratford as far as express passenger motive power was concerned, so much so that by February 1913 the last of '710' Class 2-4-0s that had remained unbuilt had been scrapped, of which more later. The smaller-wheeled 2-4-0s, however, remained totally immune from the general slaughter, and the honoured history of the '420' Class is described later. Apart from that, the 'new look' that came over Great Eastern passenger engines with the dawn of the new century could, I fancy, have been not unconnected with F.V. Russell's successive promotions on the staff of James Holden, eventually leading to his appointment as Chief Locomotive Draughtsman. As such he played a major part in the design of *Claud Hamilton*, while two years later there came the striking rebuild of the '710' Class, or 'T19', 2-4-0 No 769 with a much larger boiler and firebox. This, of course, was merely the prelude to the complete metamorphosis of these engines. In chronological order, however, one must first deal with the 'Claud Hamilton' Class.

The pioneer engine did no revenue-earning

Left *One of the early batches of the 'Claud Hamilton' Class 4-4-0s No 1889 on an up Yarmouth express on Ipswich troughs in 1902 (H.F. Hilton).*

Right *One of the Holden 'T19' Class 2-4-0s rebuilt with the large Belpaire boiler and leading bogie (LNER Class 'D13'). Sixty of the original 2-4-0s were rebuilt thus (National Railway Museum, York).*

service in the first year of its existence, because after its return from the Paris Exposition at Vincennes it stood pilot at Liverpool Street for some time. In the meantime, the first working batch, Nos 1890 to 1899, were winning golden opinions in traffic. They were, of course, very much larger than anything that had been produced previously at Stratford. They retained the 7-ft diameter driving wheel which had been used on all Holden's express engines so far, but the cylinders were 19 in by 26 in, and the boiler was sized proportionately, 11 ft 9 in long with a 4-ft 10-in diameter and a large firebox. The total heating surface was 1,516.5 sq ft and the working pressure 180 psi. The machinery was conventional to Stratford in the Holden regime. When he had arrived from Swindon and had immediately substituted the Stephenson link motion for the Joy radial valve, he used flat slide valves working beneath the cylinders as shown in the drawing on page 37. This particular diagram relates to an earlier Holden engine with a 24-in stroke; the valve gear of the 'Claud Hamilton' Class was similar but with larger dimensions. The characteristics of the gear were the same, with a short valve travel, less than 4 in, which necessitated the use of relatively long cut-offs with a narrow regulator opening. Despite their 7-ft coupled wheels, the 'Claud Hamiltons' were not particularly free-running engines. Their great merit was their ability to maintain an evenly high average speed on the constantly undulating gradients of the Colchester main line.

For three years after the inauguration of the class, batches of ten were turned out from Stratford, with the running numbers counting down from the original No 1900 in 1900 itself to No 1860 in 1903. During this time there was also a change in design. In 1901, the first Great Eastern engine to have a boiler with a Belpaire firebox had been an isolated 0-6-0

coal engine, but then, as will be related later, the design was used on the first of the rebuilt 'T19' 2-4-0s in 1902. Later in that same year, the first of the 'Claud Hamiltons' with the modified boiler and firebox was completed, engine No 1850, to be followed by nine more, Nos 1851-1859, in 1903-04, though the basic boiler proportions were not greatly changed. The total heating surface was increased to 1,588.9 sq ft and the firebox heating surface to 117.7 sq ft. Both varieties of boiler appeared to steam equally well. I have a particular affection for this batch of the 'Claud Hamilton' Class, for, as a very junior schoolboy, I was presented with a copy of the first edition of the Rev J.R. Howden's beautiful book *Locomotives of the World*, illustrated entirely in colour, with full-page reproductions of the famous 'F. Moore' paintings. The frontispiece was a superb opening to the book, showing the GER 4-4-0 No 1853 in its gorgeous pre-1915 livery.

By the time the Nos 1850-1859 batch of 'Claud Hamiltons' had taken the road, they were working, as might have been expected, all over the line, south, that is, of Lincoln, and there had been an interesting change in the Continental workings with the allocation of six of the new engines to Parkeston Quay. Two of these engines then worked up to London with the early-morning Hook and Antwerp boat trains, undertook intermediate work on the main line during the day and returned to Parkeston with the 8.30 pm and 8.40 pm boat trains. Raphael Tuck & Sons published a fine coloured reproduction of an 'F. Moore' painting of engine No 1872 on the inward-bound Antwerp train in Brentwood cutting. The working of the North Country Continentals was shared between Parkeston and Norwich sheds. The 6.35 am train from Harwich to York was taken by one engine as far as Ely; there, the Parkeston men coupled off and took a slow train to Norwich where

they booked off and lodged. In the meantime, a Norwich engine took a North Country train as far as Lincoln, where it coupled off, turned, and waited for the 4 pm boat train which it worked through to Parkeston Quay.

Construction of the 'Claud Hamilton' Class engines was halted temporarily during the year 1906 while Stratford Works was very busy with the rebuilding of the 'T19' Class. The first engine to be treated, No 769 in July 1902, was in the nature of a try-out. The boiler was very large for a 2-4-0, 4 ft 8 in in diameter and 10 ft long, and the Belpaire firebox had a grate area of 21.6 sq ft. The working pressure of the boiler was 180 psi, and it seemed as though the Stratford drawing office had made it as near as they could get to 'Claud Hamilton' proportions on a 2-4-0. It gave the rebuilt engine an aggressive, 'bull-dog' appearance and led to the class, eventually 21 strong, being nicknamed the 'Humpty Dumpties'. Ten of these rebuilds were turned out in 1903 and another ten in 1904. From 1898, a number of the original engines had their piston stroke increased to 25 in, though it is curious that none of them given this modest increase in tractive effort was chosen for rebuilding with the large boiler. Then a further sixty of the original 'T19's were not only fitted with the larger boiler but converted to 4-4-0s, leaving only 29 of the original design. Scrapping of these began in 1908, when eight were withdrawn; ten went in 1909, seven in 1910 and, by February 1913, the last survivors had gone.

The rebuilding of the remainder of the 'T19s' began in 1905. The boilers were of the same length as those of the 'Humpty Dumpties' but were slightly larger in diameter, and the barrel, with three rings bearing the dome on the middle one, had a pleasantly balanced appearance. It was said that the bogies were taken from older four-coupled and Bromley 4-2-2s

that had been scrapped, but it was evident that some substantial strengthening of the main frames had been necessary at the front end. The cylinders remained at 18 in by 24 in, except in the case of the few engines with the lengthened 25-in stroke. The Stephenson link motion, as illustrated on page 37, had a maximum travel in full gear of $3^{11}/16$ in and a steam lap of $\frac{7}{8}$ in. The exhaust lap was nil. With a boiler pressure of 180 psi, the nominal tractive effort, at 85 per cent of boiler pressure, was 14,163 lb for the engines with 24-in piston stroke. Ten of these engines were rebuilt as 4-4-0s in 1905 with a further 23 in 1906, 17 in 1907 and the last 10 in in 1908, and they formed a very useful increment to the express passenger power stud of the Great Eastern Railway.

Meanwhile, building of the 'Claud Hamilton' Class had recommenced, and by 1910 the total strength of the class had reached 101, with engines Nos 1800 to 1900. In 1911, preparations were in hand at Stratford for the introduction of the new 4-6-0s, and the building of the last batch of 'Claud Hamiltons', Nos 1790 to 1799, passed without more than a few paragraphs' notice in the railway press.

That last batch of 'Clauds' nevertheless included some novelties so far as Stratford was concerned, because four of the new engines were fitted with superheaters, as, apparently, a 'trial heat' before the equipment was fitted to the new 4-6-0s. Engine No 1793 was the first Great Eastern locomotive to be so fitted, and she and No 1794 had the Schmidt-type apparatus. Unlike many other early applications, there was nothing external to show for it, and the engines would have passed unnoticed in a batch of other engines of the class. Two others, Nos 1798 and 1799, were fitted with the Swindon-type super-heater, but contrary to current practice in Great Britain at that time, the superheater engines retained their original cylinder dimensions and boiler

pressures. Enthusiasts frequenting Liverpool Street Station in June 1911 might have been surprised to see No 1793 with indicator shelters fitted for her first few trips, but nothing more was vouchsafed. From 1913, a start was made on fitting the older engines of the class with superheaters, but the process was not so rapid as that applied to the 'T19' Class, 14 of which had been equipped with the Schmidt apparatus by the end of 1914.

In contrast to the fairly rapid scrapping of the remaining 2-4-0 express engines of James Holden's design, his intermediate class first introduced in 1891 and designated 'T26' survived intact, all one hundred of them, to enter London and North Eastern Railway ownership in 1923, and it was not until 1926 that the first of them was scrapped. They were extremely useful engines in a mixed traffic category, having 5-ft 8-in coupled wheels and a boiler interchangeable with the standard Holden 0-6-0s.

Half the class had cylinders of 17 in by 24 in, while the others had a 17½ in diameter. The Great Eastern had numerous special workings over other companies' lines, and because the 'T26' Class had a relatively light axle loading and were generally handy, they were much in demand for this class of work; at one time, no less than 61 of them were dual fitted to enable them to work vacuum-braked trains. After the grouping, six of them were fitted with cabs with single side windows for bad weather protection when working on the trans-Pennine line between Darlington, Penrith and Tebay. It is amusing to recall that none of the North Eastern 2-4-0s previously working over that route, the Fletcher '901' Class and the celebrated 'Tennants', ever had such consideration shown to their engine crews. By the time the ex-GER 'T26' 2-4-0s were drafted to those latitudes in 1936, however, the North Eastern 2-4-0s had been withdrawn for some years and the men had

Up express in Brentwood cutting hauled by one of the last built of the 'Claud Hamilton' Class 4-4-0s No 1792 (Author's collection).

Left *Up express on the Cambridge line approaching Broxbourne, having just detached a five-coach slip portion. The engine is a Holden 7 ft 2-4-0 rebuilt with large boiler ('T19' Class)* (Locomotive and General Railway Photographs).

Right *The famous 'Decapod' experimental 0-10-0 three-cylinder tank locomotive* (Author's collection).

become used to working passenger trains over the Pennines with the 'C' Class 0-6-0s, which had well-protected cabs.

Before concluding these references to James Holden's work on the Great Eastern, a mention must be made of the 'Decapod'. Although that isolated ten-coupled three-cylinder tank engine cannot be ranked among 'great' locomotives in that it did not do any revenue-earning passenger service, it did show what could be done with steam traction at a time when the neophytes were loud in claiming that electricity was the only power for the future. It is worthy of comment that the engineer who was the principal designer of the 'Decapod', F.V. Russell, was in later years the architect of the 'Jazz' suburban service, which proved such a monumental example of an intensively-worked steam service.

Holden was succeeded as Locomotive Superintendent by his son, S. Dewar Holden, but he seems to have featured as more of a figure-head than anything else. Certain it was that the only new design that appeared during his short tenure of office, the '1500' Class express passenger 4-6-0, was as near as possible a ten-wheeled version of the 'Claud Hamilton' as was possible to imagine. The first batches of these quite splendid engines had the Schmidt superheater, as tried out on the 4-4-0s Nos 1793 and 1794 in the previous year, but were fitted with piston valves. It was evident that some skilful design work had been put into these fine engines. First of all, the overall weight had to be kept down to 64 tons, of which only 44 tons were on the coupled wheels. The leading dimensions were cylinders of 20 in by 28 in, coupled wheels of 6 ft 6 in diameter and piston valves of 10 in diameter. The boiler itself was little larger than that of the 'Claud Hamilton' Class, having a maximum external diameter of 5 ft 1⅛ in

and a length of 12 ft 6 in, but the firebox was much larger, having a grate area of 26.5 sq ft. The heating surfaces were tubes 1,123 sq ft, superheater 286.4 sq ft and firebox 143.5 sq ft. The working pressure, as on the 'Claud Hamiltons', was 180 psi. The cab was even more commodious, and gave the engines the appearance of being larger than they actually were.

The '1500' Class were splendid-looking engines and no less excellent in their work. They steamed very freely and with their good valve gear they seemed more free-running than the 4-4-0s despite having smaller coupled wheels. The first five of the engines, completed in 1912, were stationed at Parkeston Quay for the Continental trains, and it was not until 1913 that Ipswich and Norwich received an allocation ready for the summer service which included the prestigious 'Norfolk Coast Express'. One of this second batch of engines, No 1506, met a tragic end when working the up train on July 12 1913. Passing through Colchester at speed, it collided with a light engine and was so badly damaged that it had to be scrapped; the driver and fireman were both killed. The engine itself was not replaced, and the number 1506—even in LNER days as 8506—remained blank. From their earliest days, the '1500' Class were remarkably strong engines, but their greatest years were after the end of the First World War when the outward-bound 'Hook of Holland' boat express had its pre-war timing of 82 minutes from Liverpool Street to Parkeston Quay restored, and loads that were unheard of before the war were taken nightly. While the pre-war 'Norfolk Coast Express' at peak times sometimes loaded up to 390 tons, the 'Hook Continental', with Pullmans and a heavy rake of the ordinary stock, rarely totalled less than 430 tons.

During the war, the Great Eastern changed its gay

engine livery to one of plain grey, and the former colouring was not restored afterwards. I am glad that I am old enough to have seen the 'Prussian blue' of Stratford in all its original glory. As a very small boy, I was taken to visit some relatives who had a cottage for the summer at Felixstowe. We travelled by a train that left Liverpool Street just after the 'Norfolk Coast Express', and I shall never forget the galaxy of gorgeously-polished dark blue engines in and around that great terminal station.

Above *First of the celebrated '1500' Class 4-6-0s built at Stratford in 1911* (British Railways).

Below *One of the first GER '1500' Class 4-6-0s No 61505 in BR service in 1949 on the GN of S section at Keith, fitted with a round-topped firebox* (Author's collection).

5. Great Central: the first 12 years

The first two years of the Great Central Railway, following the assumption of its new name in place of the provincial Manchester, Sheffield and Lincolnshire, could well be regarded, from the locomotive point of view, as a farewell gesture to the Victorian style of working rather than an overture to the brilliant orchestration that was to come in the ensuing twenty odd years. In charge of the former MS&L locomotive works at Gorton since Parker's retirement five years previously had been Harry Pollitt, and he had to provide for the running of the passenger and goods trains on the long extension to the south in addition to such traffic as was likely to build up from the short but important cross-connection from Woodford and Hinton, as it was known then, to Banbury on the Great Western main line to Birmingham and the north. Pollitt followed closely in the style of design set by his predecessor in building more 4-4-0s for the opening of the London extension, but with slightly larger dimensions. They had a neat though undistinguished appearance, the most characteristic feature being a plain cast iron stove-pipe chimney with a slight rim round the top.

Pollitt's London Extension 4-4-0s, of which No 268 was the first to be completed at Gorton in 1897, had cylinders 18½ in by 26 in, 7-ft diameter coupled wheels and 170 psi boiler pressure. The only appreciable change from Parker's previous 4-4-0s was the use of piston valves. Ten of these engines were built at Gorton and twenty more by Beyer, Peacock & Co in 1898. Then, in readiness for really fast running on the London Extension south of Leicester, Pollitt built a class of 4-2-2s with 7-ft 9-in wheels and generally large dimensions. The cylinders were 19½ in by 26 in, the firebox had a grate area of no less than 24.8 sq ft and the working pressure was 200 psi. The nominal tractive effort was unusually high, higher even than that of many of the much larger engines that had followed them, but with only 18.5 tons adhesion weight they would have to be handled with a very light rein on the steep inclines of the Metropolitan and Great Central Joint Line through the Chiltern Hills between Rickmansworth and Aylesbury. Actually, their capabilities were never fully tested in this direction. On the London Extension of the Great Central, no high speeds were scheduled in the first years of its operating, while the track was consolidating, and by the time it had fully settled down, Robinson's 4-4-0 engines of the '1013' Class were available. All that remains to be added is that only six of the Pollitt singles were built, Nos 967 to 972. In later days they did good work on the Cheshire Lines Committee trains between Manchester and Liverpool.

The introduction of these engines is, however, wrapped in an element of mystery. No sooner had the first of the class, No 967, been completed at Gorton, and its photograph and leading particulars published in *The Locomotive Magazine* under the authority of Mr Pollitt, than the news came that he had resigned and that J.G. Robinson, formerly of the Waterford, Limerick and Western Railway had been appointed to succeed him, taking office as early as July 1 1900. By that time, only two of the new singles had taken the road, and the second of them was reported as being painted grey. Gorton did not seem to be in any

Great Central 5.40 pm down Manchester express, passing West Hampstead in 1901 hauled by Pollitt 4-2-2 No 967 (Locomotive and General Railway Photographs).

hurry to complete the order, and in the late autumn, presumably under the influence of Robinson, some experiments were being made with a new painting style. Engine No 969 was finished in a darker green than had been used by the MS&L, and the lining consisted of black bands with a fine white line on either side; the underframes were maroon as originally. This seemed to be the final choice, and the remaining three engines were finished thus and in traffic by the end of the year. This style remained the standard Great Central livery for passenger engines for the rest of the Company's separate existence.

J.G. Robinson was one of several British engineers who were trained in English railway workshops before graduating, as it were, in Ireland and then recrossing the water to consummate their career on the home railways. However, while Aspinall and H.A. Ivatt were originally trained at Crewe, as was the unlucky Alexander McDonnell, Robinson came from Swindon where his father had a long career in the service of the locomotive department of the Great Western Railway. 'J.G.', as he became widely known on the Great Central, resigned from his work on the broad gauge at Bristol in 1884 to take up the post of assistant locomotive superintendent of the Waterford, Limerick and Western Railway; four years later, when his chief, Henry Appleby, resigned through ill-health, Robinson got the job of Chief Locomotive, Carriage and Wagon Engineer to the Company. The WL&WR was not a large railway, even in nineteenth-century Ireland, but in the twelve years that he had been in charge at Limerick the entire stock had been thoroughly modernized and, at the turn of the century, the locomotives were by common consent the best looking in Ireland. Even the goods engines were named, and the livery of all locomotives was crimson lake (although in the last years some of the goods engines were painted black, albeit smartly lined out in red).

In 1900, Robinson would in any case have been looking for another job because in that year the Waterford, Limerick and Western was to be absorbed into the Great Southern and Western. At the Inchicore works of the latter company, Robert Coey, having succeeded to the chieftainship on the departure of H.A. Ivatt for the English Great Northern in 1895, was far too well established for the absorption of a small company like the WL&W to make any difference. So, Harry Pollitt's sudden departure from the Great Central scene was fortuitous for Robinson. He was 44 years of age and certainly ripe for top engineering management. At first, his appointment was as Locomotive Engineer, but on Parker's retirement of 1902 the Carriage and Wagon Departments were also put into his charge, and his official title then became Chief Mechanical Engineer. Like most other holders of that title on the British railways in pre-grouping days, his responsibilities included locomotive running (the notable exceptions, though not yet in effect in 1902, were on the Midland and the South Eastern & Chatham Railway).

When Robinson took over in 1900, Gorton Works was already engaged on the building of forty further 0-6-0 goods engines of Pollitt's '786' Class. They were good general utility engines with 5-ft 1-in wheels, 18½-in by 26-in cylinders and the somewhat non-descript Pollitt appearance which Robinson improved by substituting his pattern of chimney and cab before the order was completed. By the late autumn of 1900, designs were well in hand for his own first engines, a main-line goods 0-6-0 with a very much larger boiler than that of the Pollitts, and a companion express passenger 4-4-0. Both classes were built by contractors, the 0-6-0s by Neilson & Co and the 4-4-0s by Sharp, Stewart and Co. They were very handsome engines, fully justifying the hopes that had already been aroused by Robinson's earlier engines in Ireland. Indeed, the 0-6-0s of the 973-1072 series, nicknamed 'Pom-poms', can be well described as the 'prettiest' 0-6-0s ever built. They had the same cylinder dimensions and wheels as the Pollitts, but had balanced slide valves, a total heating surface of 1,424 sq ft and a grate area of 19.5 sq ft. The working pressure, as in all Robinson's simple engines, was 180 psi. The 4-4-0s were equally elegant.

In introducing these first two of his Great Central designs and commenting on their handsome appearance, I am also mindful of the depredatory way in which that characteristic 'family' look was utterly destroyed, not only on these two pioneer Robinson classes but on all the Great Central engines after the grouping. It would seem that some 'social climber' at Gorton, seeking to curry favour with the new supreme command of the mechanical engineer's department at Kings Cross, began to replace the Robinson chimneys of all Great Central locomotives by shapeless alien contraptions of a pseudo-Great Northern type. The infuriating thing to all lovers of beautiful locomotives is that the depredations were confined to the types maintained at Gorton. No implanting of Great Northern chimneys or flattened dome covers occurred on the pre-grouping classes maintained at Stratford, Darlington or Cowlairs. No more striking example could be found of the way in which the profile of a chimney combined with the curves of a dome cover can impart a beauty of character to the appearance of a locomotive.

Robinson's Great Central engines, even after he had progressed to the big four-cylinder 4-6-0s, were high aristocrats in every line. As for the 4-4-0s of

1901, when attached to a six-car set of the new vestibule buffet car trains in their chocolate and cream livery, there was no doubt that the railway buffs in the southern shires of England began to waver in their former allegiances and incline towards the Great Central!

At that time, *The Railway Magazine* was still publishing the series of 'Illustrated Interviews' with prominent men in the British railway world initiated in its first issue, and in April 1902 the personality chosen was J.G. Robinson. Appropriately, the coloured frontispiece of that issue was one of the new 4-4-0s, No 1017, in the lithographed style marketed by Alfred Cooke of Leeds. Not all the pictures reproduced thus were very satisfying as to colour or register, but that of engine No 1017 was one of the better ones. In addition to including a comprehensive account of Gorton works and some of its past products, there were line drawings of three further new types of locomotive then being built. Two of

these, of which the first examples were in service in the same year, were unusual in British practice in having outside cylinders. The first, a class of mixed traffic 4-6-0s, was intended for working express fish trains from Grimsby docks to Manchester and London. They had cylinders 19 in by 26 in, 6-ft diameter coupled wheels and a large boiler and firebox with a total heating surface of 1,748 sq ft and a grate area of 23 sq ft. The valve gear was Stephenson's, with the balanced slide valves as on the 4-4-0s and 0-6-0s built in the previous year. These 'fish' engines were handsomely proportioned, and, as the earlier freighters, were finished in black lined in red and white.

Like the heavy mineral 0-8-0s also built in 1902, the 'fish' engines could be compared to Wilson Worsdell's North Eastern engines of the 'S' Class 4-6-0 and 'T' Class 0-8-0 which were designed for similar duties and also had outside cylinders. In making this comparison, one recalls the remarkable differences

Above *Manchester express beside the electrified Metropolitan line near Harrow, hauled by Robinson 4-4-0 No 1041 (the late C. Laundy).*

Right *Robinson mixed-traffic 4-6-0 No 6070 in LNER black; these were known originally as the 'fish engines' when built in 1902-04 (P. Ransome-Wallis).*

in the most elementary features of design that persisted on the British railways in pre-grouping days, particularly over such things as cabs. When Robinson came to the Great Central, his cabs were much admired for their spacious layout and improved protection from the weather, and certainly in comparison with those of some other north-going lines they were a great improvement. His design remained standard until the very last years of his time at Gorton, when he changed to the side-window type, and it received its widest application during the First World War when the Great Central 2-8-0, about which much will be said in Chapter 10, was adopted as the British standard for wartime by the Railway Operating Division of the British Army. After the war, many of these engines were absorbed into the stock of the London and North Eastern Railway, and one area where they were received with the greatest disfavour was on the former North Eastern Railway. Although the footplate arrangements of the engines built at Gateshead and Darlington were by no means so convenient, the men missed the sheltered, closed-in cabs, and called the ex-ROD 2-8-0s the 'pneumonia engines'.

The 0-8-0 heavy goods and mineral engine is not a type that lends itself to beauty of style, but in my opinion Robinson's Great Central Class, introduced in 1902, came nearest to being a really handsome 0-8-0 regardless of its cab. The shapely chimney and smoothly-rounded dome cover contributed much to the general effect, while the low continuous running-plate, although hampering accessibility to 'the works', improved the aesthetic look of the engine. The boiler and firebox were the same as that of the 'fish' 4-6-0s as were the dimensions of the cylinders and motion, but the wheels were of 4 ft 7 in diameter. These engines, of which 89 were built between 1902 and 1910, were used principally on the trans-Pennine mountain route over Woodhead hauling the heavy coal trains from Wath marshalling yard to the Manchester district. It was the application of super-

heating to this very successful type that led to the adoption of the 2-8-0 in place of the 0-8-0 to carry the extra weight at the front end, though in later years most of the ex-GCR 0-8-0s were themselves fitted with superheaters. Scrapping did not begin until 1934, but during the Second World War 25 of the survivors were converted to 0-8-0 shunting tanks, and under Edward Thompson's modernization scheme were subsequently designated an LNER standard. This procedure is referred to in the concluding chapter of this book.

Robinson's 4-4-2 passenger tanks introduced in 1903 were also very long-lived engines. The first batches, totalling forty locomotives, were drafted to short distance runs all over the system as a supplement to the 2-4-2 tanks built by Parker. The new engines were characteristically graceful in appearance until the new order at Gorton got into its stride after grouping, when there could be no more astonishing change in the 'look' of a locomotive than that presented by the 'before and after' aspect of these 4-4-2 tanks by the one detail of the chimney. Technically, they had 18-in by 26-in cylinders, 5-ft 7-in coupled wheels and 160 psi boiler pressure. Twelve further engines of the type were built at Gorton in 1907 especially for the residential trains out of Marylebone. The traffic was then increasing, and these later engines had larger coal bunkers and tank capacity. In keeping with the mixed traffic and freight engines, these 4-4-2 tanks were painted black, stylishly lined out in red and white. Although they were moved from the London district after Robinson's big 4-6-2 superheater tank engines were introduced in 1911, all 52 of the class were still in service when the LNER became part of British Railways in 1948.

By 1903, the track on the London Extension had become fully consolidated and able to sustain the highest speeds of the day; further, the Metropolitan part of the joint line had been improved to make it suitable for express running. The Great Central

Robinson Class '8A' 0-8-0 No 1077 built in 1902 (P. Ransome-Wallis).

No 267 of Robinson's beautiful 'Atlantic' express class, nicknamed the 'Jersey Lillies' (Author's collection).

management had from the very outset of their London Extension project known that they would have to fight every inch of the way for traffic, and, so far as passenger business was concerned, speed was a first essential. With the upgrading of express train timings to start-to-stop bookings of between 55 and 60 mph, at any rate south of Nottingham, first the half-dozen Pollitt 'singles' and then the new Robinson 4-4-0s coped admirably. Many of the fastest trains loaded up to no more than five of the new vestibule coaches, and even on the steep gradients of the Metropolitan Joint a single-wheeler was adequate. But the Great Central management was planning for bigger things, although some of the railway buffs of the day sought to belittle the programme of larger engine building that was initiated at Gorton from 1904 onwards, suggesting that it was merely a case of 'keeping up with the Joneses'. Be that as it may, Robinson gave the Great Central some very fine larger engines that in my own personal experience stayed the course for thirty years.

Having had the experience with the 6-ft 4-6-0 'fish'

engines, Robinson tried something larger for express passenger service, and, early in 1904, Beyer, Peacock & Co built four experimental ten-wheeled engines to his designs, two 'Atlantics' and two 4-6-0s (that were otherwise identical) with 6-ft 9-in coupled wheels. The boilers and fireboxes were somewhat larger than those used on the 'fish' engines, having a total heating surface of 1,931 sq ft and a grate area of 26.25 sq ft. There was some variation in the cylinder diameters, engines No 192 (4-4-2) and 195 (4-6-0) having 19½ in while Nos 194 and 196 had 19-in diameter, but all four engines had the usual 180 psi boiler pressure. Apparently it did not take long for the design department at Gorton to decide that the 'Atlantic' was the most suitable, because a further five, Nos 263 to 267, were built by Beyer, Peacock & Co in that same year. In 1905, a further contract was placed with the North British Locomotive Co for twelve more 'Atlantics', Nos 1083 to 1094, but with a higher boiler pressure of 200 psi. However, when further Gorton-constructed additions were made to the stud in 1906, the original boiler pressure of 180

The first Robinson 'Atlantic' No 192 with a train of the latest elliptical stock, the 12.15 pm Marylebone to Manchester, on the GW & GC line near Gerrards Cross (Author's collection).

psi was reverted to; for the record, the 1906 engines were 260-262, 358 and 360-363.

Robinson's experiments with top-line express passenger locomotives did not finish with alternative wheel arrangements, because in 1905-06 he built four additional 'Atlantics' as three-cylinder compounds. So far as the machinery was concerned, these four engines were identical to the new compounds being built at the same time by R.M. Deeley at Derby for the Midland Railway. These latter engines were of the modified type and originally numbered from 1000 upwards. Both the Great Central and Midland examples had one high pressure cylinder of 19 in by 26 in below the smokebox and two low pressure cylinders of 21 in by 26 in outside. Apart from the wheel arrangements, the only differences were that the Midland engines had 7-ft coupled wheels and a boiler pressure of 220 psi, whereas the Great Central had Robinson's standard 6-ft 9-in wheels and 200 psi, as on the 1083-1094 batch of two-cylinder simple 'Atlantics'. Outwardly there was no apparent difference between the simple and compound Great Central 'Atlantics', and, judging from their subsequent careers, little if any difference in the quality of their performance.

The compound engines in due course all received names. Hitherto the only engine to be named had been the second of the '1013' Class 4-4-0s, *Sir Alexander*, after the Chairman of the Company. Then the second of the compound 'Atlantics', No 259, was named *King Edward VII* in 1906 and subsequently the

One of the four compound 'Atlantics' No 365 Sir William Pollitt *with a Manchester express consisting of early London Extension stock near Northwood (the late C. Laundy).*

other three engines were named *The Rt Hon Viscount Cross GCB GCSI* (No 258), *Lady Henderson* (No 364) and *Sir William Pollitt* (No 365). So far as the first of these engines was concerned, the naming was carried to the extent that the noble Lord's honours were capable of misinterpretation. While it might have seemed just permissable to preface his title on the engine nameplates with 'The Rt Hon', so far as the addenda were concerned I can only re-tell the story of the senior schoolboy enthusiast who reputedly wrote to the Company management to enquire what office in the Great Central hierarchy the initials GCB and GCSI stood for! Names apart, however, the four compound 'Atlantics', like their Midland counterparts, were excellent engines, although, while they themselves remained as compounds throughout their long lives, there never seems to have been any suggestion that the simples should be converted.

Despite the enterprise of the top management, the passenger traffic on the London Extension did not develop as was hoped and the fastest expresses of the 1905-10 period were usually carrying loads of rarely more than 200 tons. It is true that the strongly competing Midland trains were no heavier, but there were many more of them, and there was a massive mineral business to provide the mainstay of the revenue. On the Great Central, the star train of pre-1914 days was the 3.15 pm Sheffield Special, running the 164.7 miles from Marylebone to Sheffield non-stop in 177 minutes. The usual load of that train was of no more than four of the big vestibuled coaches for Sheffield and a slip-coach detached at Leicester, no more than 180 tons from London, and only 145 tons over the last 61.5 miles. Even allowing for the fast point-to-point timings of this train, it was a modest task for one of the Robinson 'Atlantics', either simple or compound. Leicester, 103 miles, was scheduled to be passed in 109 minutes, but there were usually one or two minutes in hand at that station and the subsequent 23.4 miles on to Nottingham rarely took as much as the sharp 22 minutes allotted for that inter-city run, even though the speed had to be greatly reduced in the approach and passage through those stations.

Studying the records of pre-1914 running of the 'Atlantics', and it was very fully documented, I cannot resist the view that drivers and firemen of those days had a fairly easy time of it compared to what those same engines were regularly doing when I personally was travelling on the Great Central line between 1927 and 1936, when the 'Atlantics' were displaced from Leicester top-link workings by the arrival of a new batch of 'Sandringham' Class three-cylinder 4-6-0s. In those halcyon years, the 6.20 pm Bradford express from Marylebone had been restored to its pre-1914 timing of 114 minutes non-stop to Leicester, via High Wycombe. The train then carried two slip portions, one detached at Finmere, for intermediate stations to Woodford, and the second at Woodford for stations to Stratford-upon-Avon. With substantial patronage, the load was never less than 290 tons out of Marylebone, and sometimes in my experience was as much as 335 tons.

Even in stormy winter weather, on no occasion did I record a single minute lost to Leicester. While the building of such large engines as the 'Atlantics' may have been in advance of requirements in the early 1900s, it certainly paid off 25 years later.

Apart from the application of superheating, to which reference is made in Chapter 10, there was a further development of the 'Atlantics', albeit no more than experimental. In 1909, engine No 1090, one of the batch built by the North British Locomotive Co with boilers carrying a pressure of 200 psi, was rebuilt at Gorton with three high pressure cylinders of 15 ⅞ in by 26 in. The drive was divided, with the inside cylinder driving the leading coupled axle, and the outside cylinders the trailing axle. Walschaerts valve gear was used, with separate sets for each cylinder. While three-cylinder propulsion had already been used for heavy shunting engines, and, in an experimental form only, on the Great Eastern 'Decapod', the rebuilding of the Robinson 'Atlantic' was the first case that can be recalled of the use of three high pressure cylinders on a British express passenger locomotive. Of course, the practice became common enough soon afterwards on the North Eastern Railway. Fortunately, the utilization of engine No 1090 on the Great Central brought it into the light of the 'British locomotive practice and performance' feature in *The Railway Magazine*.

Despite the opening of the London Extension, the Great Central continued, with their partners the Great Northern, to run a London-Manchester service from Kings Cross, and one feature of this was its operation by Great Central locomotives as far south as Grantham. On the southbound run, the train consisted only of the four-car set from Manchester to Kings Cross, but northbound there was a tail of through carriages for destinations on the North Eastern Railway which were detached from the Manchester train at Retford. The Great Central engine thus had a load of nine or ten coaches from the start. The three-cylinder 'Atlantic' No 1090 was

Robinson 'Atlantic' No 1090, rebuilt in 1909 with three high pressure cylinders and Walschaerts valve gear (British Railways).

sometimes used on this train, and apart from the unusual acoustic effect—unusual in pre-Raven days on the North Eastern—the run from Grantham to Retford was often distinguished by some very fast running. Schedule for the 33.25 miles was 37 minutes start to stop, but with No 1090 on the job and a load of 275 tons, the actual time was usually less than 35 minutes. On the downhill start to the Trent Valley at Newark, 'even time' was achieved in 15 miles from the start at Grantham, by which time the train had been running at 77-78 mph for some distance.

Another distinguished Great Central engine which was a frequent visitor to Grantham was the 6-ft 9-in 4-6-0 No 196, and on Great Northern metals she seems to have been every bit a flyer as the three-cylinder 'Atlantic' No 1090. It is interesting that although the 'Atlantic' was favoured rather than the 4-6-0 in the first comparison of express passenger types in 1904, a further class of 4-6-0s with slightly smaller coupled wheels of 6 ft 6 in was built by Beyer, Peacock & Co in 1907. They had 19½-in by 26-in cylinders, and, while having the same sized boilers and fireboxes as the 6-ft 9-in 4-6-0s Nos 195-6, they carried a boiler pressure of 200 psi. The third engine of the new class, No 1097, was later named *Immingham* to commemorate the opening of the new East Coast docks near Grimsby by King George V and Queen Mary in 1912. A further variant of the Robinson 4-6-0 was also built in 1907, ten engines with 5-ft 3-in coupled wheels but otherwise the same as the 'Immingham' Class, as the 6-ft 6-in engines Nos 1095-1104 became known. The latter, like the 6-ft 9-in engines of 1904, were for a short time painted in the passenger colours, but were then altered to the 'goods black' to conform to the smaller-wheeled 4-6-0s.

There was an amusing sequel to this in LNER days. After grouping, it was decided that all passenger engines of whatever tractive power should be painted 'apple green', as the colour was then designated. But then, in the interests of economy, all engines except the top-line express passenger classes were to be relegated to 'lined black'. Even the GCR 'Atlantics' and 'Director' 4-4-0s were so demoted, but not so the 'Imminghams'. As if to underline their new-found status, some of them, working from the one-time Great Northern shed at Copley Hill, Leeds, were put on to certain top-link workings with the West Riding express trains. At that time, all Leeds and Bradford trains except the 'Pullmans' changed engines at Doncaster, as the 'Pacifics' were not then working over the West Riding Joint Line, and, among other London expresses, the 5.30 pm from Leeds Central to Kings Cross was worked as far south as Doncaster by the 'Imminghams', in all their 'apple green' glory. With loads that frequently topped the 350-ton mark, they took a pilot up the severe initial climb to Ardsley, but from Wakefield they gave me some thrilling runs down the West Riding Joint Line. On one trip, with engine No 1102 (LNER No 6102) and a load of 365 tons, from Wakefield over Nostell summit and downhill to signal stop at Marshgate Junction outside Doncaster, we ran 19.6 miles in 22¾ minutes, with a sustained maximum speed of 74 mph past South Elmsall.

The London Extension line was only one of many

The 6 ft 6 in express passenger 4-6-0 named Immingham *to commemorate the opening of the East Coast docks in 1912* (Beyer, Peacock & Company).

One of the special hump shunting 0-8-4 three-cylinder tank engines for Wath marshalling yard (Beyer, Peacock & Company).

enterprises embarked upon the Great Central Railway in the early years of the twentieth century. The Immingham dock has been mentioned incidentally regarding the introduction of the 6-ft 6-in 4-6-0s in 1907, and the installation of the new 'hump' marshalling yard west of Wath-on-Dearne in 1908 saw the introduction of one of the most remarkable freight locomotives yet seen in Great Britain. Wath yard was ideally located in the very heart of the South Yorkshire coalfield, whence trains could be conveniently despatched westwards across the Pennines via the Woodhead Tunnel route, southwards, or eastwards to the East Coast ports for shipment. In this new concentration yard, the shunting engines were required to push trains of 80 loaded wagons, about 1200 tons, up the maximum gradient leading to the crest of the 'hump', 1 in 146, whence the wagons would descend into the appropriate reception sidings. A single very powerful tank loco-

motive was required and for the overall duties in the yard an order for three 0-8-4 locomotives was placed with Beyer, Peacock & Co.

In order to meet demand while at the same time keep so powerful a locomotive within the limits of interchangeability which tend to promote economy in construction and working, Robinson and his staff adopted for the new engines the wheels, axles, axle-boxes, coupling-rods and outside connecting-rods and motion of the standard eight-coupled mineral 0-8-0 and the boiler as fitted to the 'Atlantic' express engines. To give the substantial extra tractive effort when propelling maximum tonnage mineral trains, three cylinders were used, the 'inside engine' maintaining the same principles of standardization by using the same inside-cylinder motion as that of the 'Pom-pom' 0-6-0 goods engines; the cranks were set at an angle of 120 degrees. The leading dimensions of these very powerful locomotives were cylinders (three) 18 in by 26 in, total heating surface 1,931 sq ft, grate area 26 sq ft and boiler pressure 200 psi; the nominal tractive effort was no less than 38,250 lb.

6. Wilson Worsdell

The retirement of T.W. Worsdell in 1890, and the appointment of his younger brother Wilson to succeed him, coincided within a year with a momentous change in the top-level administration of the North Eastern Railway; in 1891, the General Manager, Henry Tennant, retired and was succeeded by the dynamic George Stegmann Gibb. Now Gibb was a truly great railwayman, and in a very few years every department of the railway had felt the effects of his invigorating leadership, and from being a rich, leisured monopoly the North Eastern went forward with a big programme of improvements, accelerations, new works and internal reform. In the Locomotive Department, Wilson Worsdell must be counted as one of the most fortunate of Chief Mechanical Engineers. With a General Manager like Gibb behind him and two brilliant assistants, the way was cleared for striking progress, and progress there certainly was; no more than ten years after the completion of the last 'J' Class single-wheeler, Gateshead was turning out the then gigantic 'S1' express passenger 4-6-0s.

Vincent Raven had already shown himself a man of rare administrative ability and he was made Assistant Mechanical Engineer in 1895, while W.M. Smith continued as Chief Draughtsman. It should not be imagined, however, that Worsdell himself became a mere figurehead; far from it, for he was a first-rate mechanical engineer. However, by standing above the day-to-day work of his department, leaving the general administration and locomotive running to Raven and the details of design to Smith, he was able to keep the whole rapidly-changing picture in true perspective, and to guide the North Eastern through a crucial period in locomotive history with distinction and success.

Until he came to Gateshead in 1883, it might well have seemed that Wilson Worsdell was set for a career on the North Western rather than the North Eastern. He was born at Church Coppenhall, Crewe, but like his elder brother spent some of his early railway life in America. He was a pupil at the Altoona Works of the Pennsylvania Railroad during the time that his brother was Master Mechanic, and when 'T.W.' was recalled to Crewe, Wilson came also. After fulfilling various appointments, he spent nine years in charge of various running sheds on the LNWR. Vincent Raven, on the other hand, had spent his whole life since leaving school in the service of the North Eastern Railway. He became a pupil under Edward Fletcher and was appointed Assistant Mechanical Engineer in 1895. Walter Smith's early career had been the most diverse of all. He was born

at Ferry Port-on-Craig, Scotland, in 1842, and served his apprenticeship with a firm of general engineers in Glasgow. Then, after a short time with Neilson's, he joined the Edinburgh & Glasgow Railway when S.W. Johnson was Locomotive Superintendent. This early association blossomed into a lifelong friendship that came to influence profoundly the locomotive practice of both the North Eastern and the Midland Railway. When Johnson went to the Great Eastern in 1866, Smith went with him, but in 1874, at the still early age of 32, he was appointed Locomotive, Carriage and Wagon Superintendent to the Imperial Government Railways of Japan. He was one of the first British engineers to take an appointment in that country, and laid out the workshops, machinery and running sheds. In 1883, he returned to England and joined the North Eastern Railway, carrying out improvements at Gateshead Works; very soon, however, he was exerting a strong influence on locomotive design. On the retirement of T.W. Worsdell in 1890 his influence became considerably greater.

Gateshead reached the peak of its production of new engines in 1890, with 60 locomotives built in one year, and, with Darlington completing 33 in the same period, the North Eastern Railway was building almost on the scale of the London and North Western at Crewe. The years 1892-94 saw the production of the 'M', 'N', 'O' and 'P' Classes.

In December 1892, Wilson Worsdell completed at Gateshead the largest and heaviest express engine yet to be seen in Great Britain, the very celebrated No 1620. This was the first of the 'M' Class 4-4-0s, and, although it bore a strong resemblance to T.W. Worsdell's 'F' Class 4-4-0s, there were many important differences apart from the all-round enlargement of dimensions. The cylinders were increased from the old standard 18 in by 24 in to a 19 in diameter and a 26 in stroke; the total heating surface was 1,341 sq ft and the grate area 19.5 sq ft. The coupled wheels were of 7 ft 1 in diameter. At the time some considerable surprise was caused in the engineering world by Worsdell's abandonment of compounding, particularly as the previous two-cylinder locomotives on the North Eastern appeared to be so successful. Compounding was being adopted generally on the continent of Europe and in America, and there were then at least 1,000 Worsdell-von Borries compounds in service abroad. While not exactly stigmatizing Wilson Worsdell's policy as retrograde, the engineering press of the day went so far as to question why it was that the British railways could not make a success of compounding. While the appearance of

No 1620 as a simple caused general surprise, it must have been a particular disappointment to David Joy to see the link motion preferred to his radial gear. As on the 'J' Class 4-2-2s, the valve chests were placed outside the frames, and the slide valves, working on vertical faces, had a lap of 1 ¼ in and a travel and lead in full gear of 4 ¾ in and ⅛ in respectively.

Engines Nos 1621 and 1622 of this class had already been constructed when, in May 1893, a further example was built as a two-cylinder compound for comparative trials. This was the celebrated No 1619, which had one 19-in diameter high pressure cylinder and one 28-in diameter low pressure cylinder, the stroke of both being 26 in. Although the potential cylinder capacity of No 1619 was the same as other engines of the 'M' Class, she carried a boiler pressure of 200 psi against the 180 psi of the simple engines. No 1610 was followed by 16 more standard 'M' Class engines, Nos 1623 to 1638, all built at Gateshead in 1893, and it was very soon evident that they were fulfilling every expectation. With the steady increase in weight of the East Coast expresses, a considerable amount of double-heading had been necessary, especially between Newcastle and Edinburgh; but with the 'M' Class, any task of the day could be tackled without assistance.

The last engine of the class, No 1639, built at Gateshead in 1894, differed from the rest in having Smith's segmental piston valves with the valve chests outside the frames. These valves were the outcome of a period of careful study and development carried out

A celebrated 4-4-0 of Class 'M', No 1621, at Tweedmouth Junction in 1933 before preservation in the Railway Museum at York (O.S. Nock).

jointly by the North Eastern and the Midland. In referring to the earlier piston valve engines on the NER, the compound 2-4-0 No 340 and the compound goods No 107, it was mentioned that trouble occurred when water became trapped in the cylinders, but the savings in coal consumed and the increased mileage obtained from the engines so fitted encouraged further development. Johnson had obtained similar results with two Midland engines. To overcome the practical difficulties experienced, Walter Smith invented an entirely new type of valve; however, in a paper read before the Institution of Mechanical Engineers in 1902 he stated 'It was chiefly due to the assistance received at Derby in carrying out experiments there, that this form of valve took a definite shape'. This was the segmental valve, so designed to allow the segments to collapse inwards in case of excessive pressure and to allow trapped water to be relieved from the cylinders. Engine No 1639 was the first to have these valves, and the results both in mileage and coal consumption for the last six months of 1894 showed a definite superiority over the other engines. The average mileage for six months for the eight other engines in the same link was 21,024 at a coal consumption of 34.08 lb per mile; No 1639, however, achieved a mileage of 28,890 at a coal consumption of 29.55 lb per mile.

The fitting of piston valves outside the frames, though unorthodox, was in keeping with the original design of the 'M' Class engines, and the general performance details do not suggest any particular weakness from this source. Something approaching finality in the piston valve design was, however, reached in the conversion of the 'J' Class singles from compound to simple working in 1895. Eight-inch diameter piston valves were fitted, with an improved version of the segmental rings, but the valve chests were inside and above the cylinders, and a direct-drive Stephenson link motion was substituted for the complicated layout of the Joy valve gear. In 1895, these engines, despite the prowess of the 'M' Class, were in many ways the pride of the line; they were highly esteemed by the running department, and took quite a large share in the race to Aberdeen.

Gratifying though the work of the 'M' Class must have been to all concerned at Gateshead, Wilson Worsdell laid down two new 4-4-0 express passenger designs for his 1896 programme. The first of these to be completed, the remarkable 'Q1' Class with 7-ft 7-in coupled wheels, was designed purely and simply as a 'racer', to be ready for anything that might eventuate in the heat of competition for the Anglo-Scottish traffic. The 'Q' was also a high-speed engine, but intended for normal express duties. It is curious, however, that both the 'Q' and 'Q1' Classes had relatively small boilers, as will be seen from the following comparison with Class 'M':

Class	'M'	'Q1'	'Q'
Coupled wheels (ft in)	7 1	7 7	7 1
Cylinders (in)	19 × 26	20 × 26	19½ × 26
Total heating surface (sq ft)	1,341	1,216	1,212
Grate area (sq ft)	19.5	20.75	19.75
Boiler pressure (psi)	180	180	180

For beauty of appearance, the 'Q' and 'Q1' engines must stand second to none among nineteenth-century designs. The extended smokebox fitted to the 'M' class, to provide space for intermediate receivers if ever they had been converted to compounds like No 1619, was not needed, the cab was improved by the fitting of a clerestory roof, and the slide valves were placed inside and above the cylinders. Apparently Gateshead was not sure enough of the segmental piston valves to incorporate them in a large new express locomotive. The 'Q1' Class, with the largest coupled wheels in the world, were extraordinarily impressive engines although, as no race developed in the summer of 1896, only two were built; Nos 1869 and 1870 were completed in May and June respectively. Gateshead then followed with the first ten engines of the 'Q' Class, Nos 1871-1880. In the summer of 1896, the new vestibule trains for the 'Flying Scotsman' were introduced,

The early Worsdell style: 'Q' Class 4-4-0 No 1874, built in 1896 with the handsome clerestory-roofed cab (Author's collection).

although the timing was not severe. It was the night Aberdeen train that proved the toughest proposition, as the schedule was 92 minutes from York to Newcastle with a 250-ton load, and the work of the 'Q1' engines on this train was more interesting. Between Newcastle and Edinburgh, however, the 8.15 pm 'sleeper' was regularly double-headed when the load was 250 tons, the usual engines being an 'M' and a 'J'.

In November 1896, a comprehensive series of trials was conducted between Newcastle and Tweedmouth with special trains using a variety of locomotives ranging from a Fletcher '901' Class 2-4-0 to a 'Q1' 7-ft 7-in 4-4-0. Unfortunately, the tests with the 2-4-0s gave rather misleading results and are not quoted here, but the modern engines involved in addition to the 'Q1' were a 'J' 4-2-2 rebuilt as a 'simple', with piston valves, and a standard original 'M' with outside valve chests and extended smokebox. Owing to the varying conditions prevailing on the different days, one cannot place too great a reliance upon the figures obtained. We know only too well from the experience of the 1948 interchange trials on British Railways how relatively small circumstances can alter the test results obtained, but a remarkable feature of the North Eastern trials of 1896 was the excellent performance of the 'single', despite the worst weather conditions of the whole series. Complete details of the workings were given in a paper read before the Institution of Mechanical Engineers in October 1898 by W.M. Smith, and from these details I have prepared the accompanying summary. The coal consumption of the 'single', in pounds per train mile, was naturally affected by the bad weather conditions, but in his later paper, describing the development of the segmental ring piston valves, Smith said in respect of the 'J' Class in the 1896 trials 'This engine was in every respect well in advance of the others. It did not show any signs of weakness'. Seeing that the 'others' included such engines as the 'M' and 'Q1', this was praise indeed for the 'single'.

While quoting the drawbar horsepower corresponding to each of the indicator diagrams, Smith's paper does not give the average drawbar horsepower for the complete journeys. It was largely as a result of these trials that Worsdell decided to incorporate the segmental ring piston valves in the 'R' Class express passenger 4-4-0 engines, the first of which was turned out at Gateshead works in August 1899.

In the first eight years of Wilson Worsdell's superintendence, events had certainly moved fast in the locomotive department, but from 1899 the emergence of new designs continued for a time even more rapidly and testified to both an exceptional fertility of ideas and an exceptional output of work from the Gateshead drawing office under W.M. Smith's leadership. The following constitutes a bare record of developments from 1899:

Year	Class	Description
1899	'R'	4-4-0 express passenger
	'S'	4-6-0 mixed traffic
1901	'S1'	4-6-0 express passenger
	'T'	0-8-0 heavy mineral
1902	'T1'	0-8-0 heavy mineral
	'U'	0-6-2T heavy mineral
1903	'V'	4-4-2 express passenger
1904	'P2'	0-6-0 mineral
1906	'4CC'	4-4-2 compound express passenger
	'P3'	0-6-0 mineral
1907	'W'	4-6-0T heavy passenger tank
1908	'R1'	4-4-0 express passenger
1909	'X'	4-8-0T humping engine

These together with additions to existing classes

1896 Trials, Newcastle-Tweedmouth and back: 131 miles

Class		'J'	'M'	'Q1'
Load behind tender (tons)		187	187	187
Actual average speed (mph) {	Down	46.5	50.9	48.7
	Up	54.2	51.8	51.2
Net. average speed (mph) {	Down	50.9	52.7	50.5
	Up	54.2	52.4	52.4
Weather conditions		heavy NE gale and rain	calm, fine	calm, fine
Average ihp (round trip)		692	603	558
Coal used per mile (lb)		43.35	37.26	37.33
Coal per ihp hour (lb)		3.28	3.25	3.44
Coal per sq ft of grate area (lb per hour)		109.6	99.9	90.8
Evaporation, water per pound of coal (lb)		7.97	7.70	8.45

brought the combined new engine output of Gateshead and Darlington works to 474 in the eleven years 1899-1909.

The year 1898 had seen both works engaged in building freight and shunting engines. From Gateshead, however, came one further engine, strictly speaking a rebuild, that might have been a curtain-raiser to the entire twentieth-century locomotive policy of the North Eastern Railway. The two-cylinder Worsdell-von Borries compound No 1619 was completely re-designed by Smith, and came out as a three-cylinder compound with one high pressure cylinder inside and two low pressure cylinders outside. This arrangement, which was patented by Smith, was as logical as F.W. Webb's arrangement was the reverse! Instead of two small high pressure cylinders and one enormous low pressure, the three cylinders in Smith's system were all much the same size. Through its adoption on the Midland Railway, and subsequently on the grand scale by the LMS, the Smith compound system is so well known as to need no detailed description here. In its original form, however, and as first used by Johnson on the Midland, the engines were provided with a change-over valve by which the driver could, if necessary, admit a certain amount of live steam direct to the low pressure cylinders so as to develop increased power on a heavy gradient. This is sometimes termed semi-compound or reinforced compound working. A similar control was provided on all the famous de Glehn compounds in France, which also, like the original Smith compounds, had independent valve gears for the high and low pressure cylinders. This called for intelligent work on the driver's part, and on the North Eastern No 1619 certainly did well.

Apart from the arrangement of cylinders—high pressure 19 in by 26 in and low pressure 20 in by 24 in—there were certain other interesting details in the design. The high pressure cylinder had a segmental ring piston valve, but the outside cylinders had ordinary slide valves. The boiler was new, and differed from any other on the NER; a much larger fire grate was adopted, with an area of 23 sq ft, the total heating surface was 1,328 sq ft and boiler pressure 200 psi. A novel feature was the use of cross water tubes in the firebox to improve the circulation of water and to increase the heating surface; this device was invented and patented by Smith, though it is, of course, best known through its adoption by Dugald Drummond on the London and South Western Railway. No 1619 when first turned out as a three-cylinder compound bore no outward sign of these water tubes and, more importantly, no means of removing them without complete shopping of the locomotive. In August 1900, a new firebox was fitted with outside covers for providing access to the tubes.

Also, at the time of this change, a tender with increased coal space was attached to the engine carrying 5 instead of 4½ tons, and the total weight of engine and tender in working order became 94.5 tons. No 1619 proved master of any task allotted to her, and was naturally under close scrutiny from headquarters at Gateshead and handled by regular crews; nevertheless, in the first four months 21,000 miles were covered on top-grade express duty. The enginemen concerned acquired the necessary technique of manipulating the independent reversing gears and the change valve when necessary, and it might indeed have seemed that here was the prototype of the future North Eastern express locomotive.

However, Wilson Worsdell proceeded with some caution. Those controls on No 1619 were decidedly more than enginemen had been expected to understand and operate in the past. New engines were needed at once; the rapid increase in East Coast loads was making it necessary to double-head the 'M' and 'Q' Class engines north of Newcastle, and, with the results of the Tweedmouth trials of 1896 in mind, he decided upon a greatly enlarged two-cylinder simple 4-4-0. In comparison with the previous three classes, 'M', 'Q' and 'Q1', the changes in basic dimensions were significant. After increasing first to 19½ and then to 20-in cylinders, a reversion was made to 19 in for the new 'R' Class, while, on the other hand, the boiler was much enlarged to provide a total heating surface of 1,527 sq ft. The grate area was 20 sq ft and the boiler pressure 200 psi. Apart from the large boiler, the outstanding feature of the new engines was the use of Smith's patent piston valves beneath the cylinders but not on the same vertical centre line. Direct-action Stephenson link motion was used in a very simple and straightforward layout, the valves themselves being of no less than 8¾ in diameter to provide a large port area for inlet and exhaust from the cylinders. Like the previous locomotives with Smith's piston valves, the 'R' Class had outside admission which became the accepted North Eastern standard practice.

Engine No 2011 was the first of the 'R' Class to be constructed, in August 1899, and she was the subject of very special attention. Unlike North Eastern express locomotives of the day, and unlike the rest of the class, she was double-manned and ran daily from Newcastle to Edinburgh and back followed by a second round trip from Newcastle to Leeds. This daily mileage of 455 made six days a week was continued with scarcely a break for over two years, with the result that the engine had reached the exceptional, and perhaps unbelievable, mileage of 284,000 before her first visit to the shops for general overhaul. Of course, No 2011 was under very close observation, and there is little doubt that her two regular

Right *NER long-boilered 0-6-0 No 1275, built in 1874, which survived in a rebuilt form and was photographed by the author at Whitby in 1923, subsequently restored to its original condition for the Railway Centenary pageant of 1925. It is now seen on display on the original Stockton and Darlington Railway station at Darlington (J.A. Coiley).*

Below *GNR — the first of Patrick Stirling's famous 8-ft bogie single express locomotives, No 1, built at Doncaster Plant Works in 1870. It was withdrawn in 1907, but restored to working order by Sir Nigel Gresley in 1938. It is now at the National Railway Museum at York, but makes various runs in special service (J.A. Coiley).*

The first large-boilered 'Atlantic' of the GNR built at Doncaster in 1902 served 45 years in traffic, and was then restored to near original condition and livery. She subsequently made many trips on special trains in 1953-4, seen here on such a working at Basingstoke. She is now in the National Railway Museum at York (G.W. Powell).

Above *GNR — the first British 'Atlantic' tender engine No 990, Henry Oakley, built at Doncaster in 1898. On withdrawal in 1935, it was placed in the original Railway Museum at York though brought out for various functions, notably for the 'Plant Centenarian' special excursions in 1953. It is now in the National Railway Museum at York* (J.A. Coiley).

Below *NER — 'M' Class 4-4-0 No 1621, built by Wilson Worsdell at Gateshead in 1893, here seen outside the National Railway Museum at York. With its sister engine No 1620 this engine participated in making some memorable runs in the 1895 'Race to the North'* (J.A. Coiley).

Right *'R' Class 4-4-0 No 1232 crossing the King Edward Bridge, Newcastle, with the 12.20 pm 'Flyer' to York, until 1915 the fastest train in Great Britain* (R.J. Purves).

Below *'R' Class 4-4-0 No 592 as LNER Class 'D20' at Tweedmouth in 1933 when superheated* (O.S. Nock).

drivers entered into the spirit of this marathon trial and did their best to create an out-and-out record. The remaining engines of the first batch, 2012 to 2020, averaged 163,000 miles between heavy repairs which, not making such long daily rounds at No 2011, represented as much as 3½ years' service! They were all kept in beautiful condition and the regular enginemen, not having to share them with even one other crew, took great pride both in their appearance and their working efficiency. Many minor adjustments and repairs would be done by the drivers and firemen without the 'booking' of such defects at the shed, and the men naturally grew to know the individual peculiarities of their own engines and could make allowance for them when running their trains. Nonetheless, taking all this into consideration there is no doubt that the 'R' Class engines were outstanding in their general reliability.

Although the next new design to be considered, Class 'S', follows logically after Class 'R', the first

two engines to be completed, Nos 2001 and 2002, actually preceded the record-breaking No 2011 by two months. Although the 'R' was destined to prove far more useful in express traffic and to have a much longer life, it was perhaps only natural that the 'S' Class created infinitely more of a stir in 1899, not only from its size and handsome appearance but also from its pioneer position as the first passenger 4-6-0 in the British Isles.

It is most interesting to compare the dimensions of the two classes. On the first engines of the 'S' Class, Worsdell reverted to ordinary slide valves placed vertically inside the frames and actuated by direct Stephenson link motion. The valves had 1⅛ in lap and ⅛ in lead, as in the piston valves of Class 'R', but the valve travel in full gear was a fraction longer, $4\frac{21}{32}$ in against $4\frac{11}{32}$ in. The boilers of both the 'R' and 'S' engines steamed well in heavy working conditions, but an anomaly is to be seen in the use of the same blastpipe orifice on both. Unless a locomotive is to be worked with a greater back pressure than is

economical, the diameter of the blast nozzle is the limiting factor of the entire performance. It should, in some measure, be proportional to the steaming capacity of the boiler, but, as will be seen from the comparative table, although the 'S' Class engines were given a greater heating surface and a larger grate area, the blast nozzle was the same as that of the 'R' Class.

Comparative dimensions—Classes 'R' and 'S'

Description	Class 'R'	Class 'S'
Cylinders (in)	19 × 26	20 × 26
Coupled wheels (ft in)	6 10	6 1
Boiler		
Tubes (number)	255	204
Outside diameter (in)	1 ¾	2
Length between tubeplates (ft in)	11 10⅛	15 4⅛
Heating surfaces (sq ft)		
Tubes	1383	1639
Firebox	144	130
Total	1527	1769
Grate area (sq ft)	20	23
Boiler pressure (psi)	200	200
Blastpipe (inside diameter of nozzle) (in)	5	5
Adhesion weight (tons)	35¼	46¼

Technicalities apart, however, the Class 'S' locomotives when they first appeared in 1899 were impressive beyond measure. Their beautiful lines were marred a little at first by the short cab fitted to engines 2001, 2002 and 2003 to enable the engine to be accommodated on a 50 ft turntable. At the time of their construction, the North Eastern had no experience of such a long engine and trouble arose from inadequate side clearances in the coupled wheels journals and on the rods. The driving wheels had flangeless tyres so that the curves at Newcastle and York might be negotiated more readily, but for some time the class as a whole was a bit 'touchy' so far as the running gear was concerned. As motive power units, the 'S' Class engines were designed to eliminate double-heading of the heavy East Coast expresses on the Newcastle-Edinburgh section. One would imagine that the original intention was to use the 'S' engines north of Newcastle and the 'R' Class on the southern division. It did not work out quite that way, for while the 'R' Class was singularly free from trouble, the original 'S' Class was rarely out of it.

Engines Nos 2004 to 2010 were completed at various dates between December 1899 and June 1900. No 2006 was sent to the Paris Exhibition of 1900 and gained a gold medal; Nos 2009 and 2011

were used for Royal Train workings between York and Newcastle in the same year. Nevertheless, the class as a whole was not shaping as well as had been hoped, and in December 1900 the first engine of Class 'S1' appeared, No 2111. This could be described as a 6-ft 8-in version of Class 'S', although on the larger variety Smith's patent piston valves were again used, and there were certain changes in the boiler. The distance between the tube plates was 16 ft 2⅝ in, and fewer tubes were used—193 against the 204 in Class 'S'. The total heating surface remained the same at 1,769 sq ft and the grate area was also the same at 23 sq ft. Again, the diameter of the blast nozzle was 5 in. For the year 1900, the 'S1' was a huge engine and at the same time a most graceful one; in favourable conditions, the five engines of this class proved very free runners. Rous-Marten compiled a number of logs with them, and on one of these a 300-ton train was taken up to Berwick in 66 min 23 sec from Newcastle start-to-stop, or 63 minutes net, while on the moderate descending gradients of this route speeds exceeding 80 mph were reached. On the 1 in 170 gradient of Longhoughton bank, the speed was sustained at 52.5 mph. Another interesting trial was made between Darlington and York with the up afternoon 'Scotsman' when a load of 260 tons was run from the Darlington start to a signal stop at Waterworks Box just outside York in 40 min 51 sec start-to-stop. The distance is 43.9 miles, so the engine made the notable average speed of 64.4 mph. There was no exceptional maximum, but the generally high speed was well sustained throughout at 68 to 72 mph.

The remaining four engines of Class 'S1', Nos 2112-2115, were built at Gateshead in the summer of 1901, but No 2115 was scarcely completed when No 2116 the first of Class 'T', came out in August, the pioneer of the 0-8-0 heavy mineral engines. The 'big engine' spirit had certainly gripped the North Eastern locomotive department in earnest by this time, although with the enormous mineral traffic of the line there was ample justification for something larger than the 'P1' 0-6-0. By 1901, it should be recalled, the London and North Western had been building 0-8-0 mineral engines for more than eight years. One might have thought there was a case for some degree of standardization of boilers between the 'S' the 'T' Classes, but, while the boiler barrel was the same with a distance of 15 ft 4⅛ in between tube plates, the 'T' had the tube arrangements of the 'S1', namely 193 tubes of 2 in outside diameter. The firebox was smaller, with a grate area of 21.5 sq ft; this, with the reduced number of tubes, brought the total heating surface of the 'T' down to 1,675 sq ft against 1,769 in the 'S'. The cylinders were of 20 in diameter by 26 in stroke with the Smith segmental

Right *Wilson Worsdell's pioneer 4-6-0 of Class 'S', introduced in 1899 (the late W.J. Reynolds).*

Right *Class 'S1' express passenger 4-6-0 No. 2111 built in 1900 (Author's collection).*

ring piston valves of 8¾ in diameter, and the diameter of the blast nozzle was the usual 5 in. The coupled wheel diameter was 4 ft 8 in. In outward appearance, the original 'T' Class were surely the most ornate mineral locomotives ever to be built in twentieth-century England. They were bedecked in the full passenger livery—like all other NER engines of the day—with brass-capped chimneys, polished brass safety-valve covers, coats-of-arms on the sand boxes and a deep brass collar at the join of the boiler and smokebox. Possibly they may have been equalled in the splendour of their appearance by the Churchward '28XX' 2-8-0s on the Great Western, after the latter received copper-capped chimneys and the gartered coat-of-arms was put on to the tender, but they can never have been surpassed.

The 'T' Class 0-8-0s were grand engines. Some of their earliest duties lay in working coal trains from Stella Gill to Tyne Dock over the Pontop and South

Shields line. At the turn of the century, the Stella Gill district, lying about a mile north-west of the main line at Chester-le-Street, was a concentration point for coal traffic brought down the various gravity-operated inclines, and from Pelaw Colliery Junction it is a fairly level run of 11 miles to Tyne Dock. Towards the northern end, the line begins to assume a gradually descending character; after 1 in 250 for 2 miles there is an abrupt fall at 1 in 47 into the dock sidings. Over this route the 'T' Class engines handled loaded trains of 1,200 to 1,300 tons. Being almost exclusively a mineral line, apart from the intersection with the Leamside route at Washington and the level crossing with the Newcastle-Sunderland line at Pontop Crossing, the coal trains usually got a good road, and on a typical run made in 1902 a train of 1,326 tons was worked from Stella Gill to Tyne Dock in 52 minutes, an excellent average speed of 21 mph. In the reverse direction, the 'T' Class handled 60 empty coal wagons up the initial 1 in 47 out of Tyne Dock, and, if wagons were available, the empty trains were made up to 80 wagons before leaving for Stella Gill.

Ten locomotives of Class 'T' were built in 1901, their numbers being 2116-2125, and these were followed by a series with ordinary slide valves but otherwise identical, built at Gateshead between March and June 1902; these were known as Class 'T1'. A further thirty of the piston valve engines were built in 1902-04. This temporary hesitation in the use of the segmental ring piston valves for all large North Eastern locomotives is interesting, because, after the dynamometer car was built, one of the first series of tests carried out with it in July and August 1906 was to determine the relative efficiency of the 'T' and 'T1' Classes in heavy mineral working between West Auckland and Tebay. In these trails, the slide valve engine had considerably the better of it, so it was perhaps only natural that slide valves were subsequently used on future engines of this type. Twenty more 'T1' Class were built in 1907-08 and a further twenty in 1911, both batches at Darlington.

In 1901, George S. Gibb, accompanied by four senior officers of the NER, visited the USA on a tour to study American railway methods. Wilson Worsdell was one of this party and it was said that he was very much impressed with the performance of the 'Atlantic' type engines on the Reading Railroad, working the Atlantic City Flyers. When they returned, Worsdell began to work up his impressions into a design for a 'super' express passenger engine that should be the largest so far constructed in England, and he no doubt found a ready supporter in Gibb, if for no other reasons than those of prestige.

While the work of the 'S1' engines had been good, and at times spectacular, there is no denying the fact that for their size they were inferior to the 'R' 4-4-0s, and for the speeds of that day the 'Rs' were still adequate, even with the maximum loads. But it was certainly time to look ahead, and it so happened that when authority was given to proceed with the new 'super' engines, W.M. Smith, the Chief Draughtsman, was away ill and not expected back for some little time. So, concerning the design of the new engines, there has been handed down one of those stories that are inevitably connected with men of strong personality; it may be entirely apochryphal but it is certainly amusing and may have some foundation in fact. When he returned, so the story goes, the design of the new 'Atlantics' was complete and work was advanced in the shops, but Smith was strongly critical of many points and Wilson Worsdell had some very difficult days! It is somewhat significant that when Smith himself was given authority to design some further 'Atlantics', the result was very different. Whatever internal strains may have been set up within Gateshead offices and works during the building of the new engines of 1903—if indeed there were any—the outcome, so far as size and appearance went, was indeed magnificent.

The first 'V' Class 'Atlantic', No 532, was completed in November 1903, and was one of those rare locomotives in which a huge boiler is poised so as to give an appearance of elegance rather than an effect of mere massive bulk. Whatever W.M. Smith thought, N.D. Macdonald must have rubbed his hands in delight at No 532, on which the total heating surface was increased from the largest NER boiler so far, the 'S1' with 1,769 sq ft, to no less than 2,455 sq

Right *No 295 of Wilson Worsdell's huge Class 'V' 'Atlantics' of 1903 (LNER Class 'C6'), as later superheated, at North-allerton in 1933 (O.S. Nock).*

Right *The down 'Flying Scotsman' passing Lamesley hauled by 'V' Class 4-4-2 No 1680 (R.J. Purves).*

Below left *Class 'T1' heavy mineral 0-8-0 No 1709 of LNER Class 'Q5' at Darlington in 1934. This was one of 50 engines sent overseas in World War I for service with the ROD (O.S. Nock).*

ft, with a grate area of 27 sq ft. The length between the tube plates was 16 ft 2 ⅝ in as on the 'S1' Class, but within a barrel of 5 ft 6 in diameter there were 268 tubes (as against 193) and the tube heating surface alone was 2,275 sq ft. The cylinders remained at 20 in diameter but the stroke was increased to 28 in. The segmental ring piston valves were used, of 8 ¾ in diameter, and the valve setting was the same as on the 'S1' and 'T' Classes. Again, the blast nozzle was of 5 in diameter. The weight of the engine alone in working order was 72 tons.

A further result of the visit to America in 1901 was a general increase in the net loads conveyed on freight trains. The General Manager was anxious to use larger wagons; the 20-tonner became the North Eastern standard for mineral carrying, and, although the process of development had necessarily to be a gradual one, the gross freight train load increased from 276 tons in 1903 to 402 tons at the time of the grouping; these were, of course, all-line averages. To be ready for heavier loads, the 'P2' goods engine of 1904 was given an enormous boiler of 5 ft 6 in diameter, with a tube heating surface of 1,531 sq ft; the grate area was 20 sq ft and the working pressure originally 200 psi. The coupled wheels were 4 ft 7 in, as in Class 'P1', and the cylinders were 18¼ in by 26 in. With the safety valve columns arranged in a group of four and encased in a huge brass mounting, they were 'stocky' workmanlike engines. The boiler is pitched relatively low, and one hardly realizes its girth until the 'P2' is seen head-on. It is the only 5-ft 6-in boiler of which I know where the look-out from the cab is over the top! Fifty engines of Class 'P2' were built in 1904-05, thirty at Darlington and another twenty at Gateshead. Then, in 1906, came a modified version in which the cylinders were enlarged to 18½ in diameter and the pressure lowered to 180 psi. This series, beginning with a

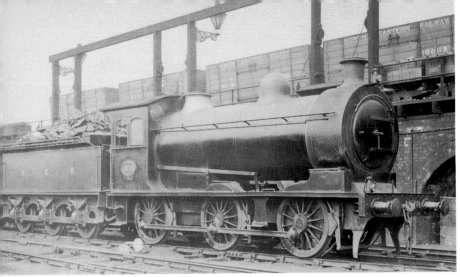

Left *Heavy mineral 0-6-0 Class 'P2' built in 1904 (LNER Class 'J26') (The Locomotive Publishing Company).*

Below *The preserved 'P3' Class super-heated 0-6-0 No 2392 on the North Yorkshire Moors Railway near Goathland in May 1977 (John Titlow).*

batch of twenty built at Darlington in 1906, was designated Class 'P3'; the last thirty five of the class were built from 1921 onwards with superheaters and piston valves.

The year 1906 was a momentous one for the North Eastern. Beginning with the resignation of Sir George Gibb, who left York to become Deputy Chairman and Managing Director of the London Underground railways, it later witnessed the death of W.M. Smith at the early age of 64. Smith died in harness, but not before he had produced his locomotive masterpiece. In addition to his pioneer engine No 1619, 'Smith compounds' were at work on the Midland and on the Great Central, but his two four-cylinder North Eastern 'Atlantics', Nos 730 and 731, must be regarded as the finest of them all. Although the boilers were no more than 5 ft in diameter, these engines were slightly heavier than the Class 'V' in total weight, and the nominal tractive effort was slightly greater too. The cylinder arrangement was the same as in Webb's 'Jubilees' and 'Alfreds' on the LNWR, with the high pressure cylinders outside (14¼ in diameter by 26 in stroke) and the low pressure cylinders inside, having the large diameter of 22 in but the same 26 in stroke. It is interesting to compare the proportions of the boiler with that of the 'V' Class:

Four-cylinder compound 'Atlantic' No 731 on the up 'Flying Scotsman' near Lamesley (R.J. Purves).

NER: Boilers of 'Atlantic' engines

Engine	'V' Class	730/731
Diameter of barrel (ft in)	5 6	5 0
Type of firebox	round-topped	Belpaire
Tubes		
Number	268	242
Outside diameter (in)	2	2
Length between		
tubeplates (ft in)	16 2⅜	14 7
Heating surface (sq ft)		
Tubes	2,275	1,782
Firebox	180	209*
Total	2,455	1,991
Grate area (sq ft)	27	29
Boiler pressure (psi)	200	225

*Including 29 sq ft from cross water tubes

Although the total heating surface was less in the case of the compounds the shorter length of tube would be an advantage in steaming and the grate area was larger. In tests made with the dynamometer car between Newcastle and York, the compounds proved markedly superior to the Class 'V' engines. Piston valves of 7½ in and 10 in diameter were used for the high and low pressure cylinders respectively and the valve gear for both cylinders was combined.

The valve spindles were driven through rocking levers, and although the cranks for each high and low pressure pair on each side of the locomotive were diametrically opposite, the valves moved in unison. This was made possible by the ingenious device of using inside admission for the high pressure cylinders and outside admission for the low pressure. This provided the usual very direct exhaust passage from the low pressure cylinders to the blastpipe, and an equally direct passage from the high pressure exhaust to low pressure admission. The blast nozzle was of 5½ in diameter. Engines Nos 730 and 731 were also alone among the NER stud in having Belpaire fireboxes. The safety valve casing was strongly reminiscent of the earliest Midland compounds, being extended to include a third valve column.

These two engines were in very truth masterpieces of locomotive design, extremely powerful, as the dynamometer car records showed, and graceful to a high degree from whatever angle they were viewed. Yet they were hardly completed before their famous designer was seized with a fatal illness and he did not live to learn of their magnificent achievements on the road. It is no disparagement to the memory of Wilson Worsdell to say that with the passing of Walter Smith an era of North Eastern locomotive history came to an end. Clear-thinking and forthright, it was once rather quaintly said of him by the Minister of Jesmond Presbyterian Church that his reports and engineering treatises were as good as a theological discourse for brilliance of reasoning. He will always be remembered for the Smith compounds, yet at the time of his death it could hardly have been foreseen that 190 more of the Midland version would be built twenty years later.

Towards the end of 1908, and for the first time

since the building of the 'Tennant' 2-4-0s, Darlington was concerned with a new main-line express engine, the 'R1' Class 4-4-0. After the experiments with 4-6-0s and 'Atlantics', the reversion to the 4-4-0 type was interesting and in many ways a confirmation of the outstanding success of the 'R' Class. It is true that the 1906 trials with the dynamometer car had shown off the remarkable capacity of the compound 'Atlantics', but they were large and expensive engines and it was perhaps only natural that Wilson Worsdell should be tempted to try a 'super R'. The cylinder and coupled wheel dimensions were the same in both the 'R' and 'R1' Classes, but the 'R1' was provided with a 5-ft 6-in diameter boiler, a grate area of 27 sq ft and a working pressure of 225 psi. This increased the nominal tractive effort from 17,025 lb to 21,900 lb although the potential capacity of the 'R1', with its much larger grate, was more than the tractive effort might suggest. The 'R1' Class had the variable blastpipe by which the orifice could be increased from a 4¾ in diameter to 7½ in at the driver's judgement. The piston valves were of no less than 10-in diameter but were fitted with the more modern spring rings, as in the 'X' Class 4-8-0s, instead of the Smith segmental type. The valves themselves were above the cylinders instead of below as in Class 'R', but the drive was still by direct Stephenson gear without the interposition of any rocking levers.

As originally built, the engines were not superheated. However, the boiler barrel was relatively short, with a distance of only 11 ft 3⅛ in between the tubeplates, and, with the tubes themselves of a 2-in outside diameter as in the much longer boilers of the 'V' 'Atlantics', the steaming would naturally be very

free. There was no lack of heating surface in spite of the short barrel; the 254 tubes contributed 1,579 sq ft, and the firebox 158 sq ft, making a total of 1,737 sq ft, nearly as large as that of the 'S1' 4-6-0s. The grate was level at the back and sloped at the front, after the Great Western fashion. That the 'R1' Class was designed for hard work with the heaviest East Coast expresses, rather than high-speed running with light trains, is suggested by the valve setting, arranged for equal cut-offs at either end of the cylinder as against equal leads. In a high-speed engine, the lead, with its effect upon 'cushioning' at each end of the stroke, is the important factor; however, one cannot have it both ways, and for getting away with heavy trains and climbing banks like Cockburnspath, a greater power output is obtained by setting for equal cut-offs. The 'R1s' had 1⅛ in lap and 4³/₃₂ in travel in full gear; in full forward gear the lead was ³/₁₆ in on the fore port and ¹/₁₆ in on the back port. A final point about these remarkable engines, emphasising still further the kind of work they were expected to do, was the adhesion weight of 42 tons. Wilson Worsdell evidently intended to have no trouble with slipping!

Technicalities aside, the 'R1s' were, above all, superb-looking engines. Although built at Darlington, the second of the class, No 1238, posed for the official photograph on the banks of the Tyne, as so many Gateshead-built engines had done previously, and when producing one of his delightful oil paintings Mr F Moore departed for once from his characteristic parkland setting and gave us instead a distant view of the Newcastle quays. Nos 1237-1239 were completed at Darlington in 1908, and the remainder of the ten in 1909.

Up 'Flying Scotsman' near Lamesley hauled by 'R1' Class 4-4-0 No 1244 (R.J. Purves).

Right *The down 'Flying Scotsman' climbing Benton bank, between Newcastle and Forest Hall, hauled by 'R1' Class 4-4-0 No 1246* (R.J. Purves).

Right *Edinburgh to London express near Belford, Northumberland, hauled by two-cylinder Class 'V1' Atlantic No 702* (R.J. Purves).

They were put to work on the heaviest East Coast trains between York and Edinburgh, taking loads of over 400 tons unassisted between Newcastle and Edinburgh, and following their introduction they as nearly monopolized the principal Scotch traffic as their numbers would permit. Schedules were not fast by later standards; the down 'Flying Scotsman' was allowed 98 minutes for the 80.1 miles from York to Newcastle and 149 minutes for the 124.4 miles on to Edinburgh, where the working time of arrival was 6.8 pm against the public time of 6.15. On one particular run, No 1239 with a gross load of 365 tons left York 2¾ minutes late yet reached Newcastle on time despite a permanent way slack at Birtley. Then, with a reduced load of 330 tons, No 1237 kept almost exact time to Edinburgh, arriving a few seconds before 6.8 pm.

Wilson Worsdell's last locomotive class, the 'V1' 'Atlantic', actually appeared after his retirement, and considered by dimensions alone it exhibits some rather curious points. Presumably with a view to reducing maintenance costs, the boiler pressure was no more than 180 psi so that the basic comparative dimensions of the three two-cylinder 'big engine' classes were as follows:

Class	'V'	'R1'	'V1'
Cylinders (in)	20 × 28	19 × 26	19½ × 28
Coupled wheels (ft in)	6 10	6 10	6 10
Boiler pressure (psi)	200	225	180
Grate area (sq ft)	27	27	27
Nominal tractive effort (lb)	23,200	21,900	19,870

Although the 'V1' was the least powerful on the above basis, it was nevertheless the heaviest, as some strengthening and deepening of the frames was made at the fore end. Both the original 'V' Class and the 'R1s' had the pressure lowered to 180 psi when they were superheated, but that change was yet to come. The 'V1' series was distinguishable from the 'V' Class not only by the deeper framing at the front end but also by the narrow splashers, following the style of the later 'S' 4-6-0s. There were ten 'V1s', numbered 696-705. Like the original 'Vs', they were capable of hard work on the road and they survived until after the Second World War. In their original non-superheated condition they ran well, but, somewhat naturally, due to their low tractive effort they could not make much of a show on heavy banks.

7. Doncaster: Ivatt and Gresley

In August 1895, when the second 'Race to the North' blazed up to its exciting climax, Patrick Stirling, veteran Locomotive Engineer of the GNR, was still very much in command at Doncaster, judging from his imperious instructions to his divisional superintendant at Peterborough. All the same, it has since become known that the General Manager, Henry Oakley, and the directors most intimately affected had already been looking round for a new Locomotive Engineer to succeed Stirling in due course, and that they had interviewed H.A. Ivatt of the Great Southern and Western Railway in Ireland, and earmarked him for the job. These negotiations had nevertheless been conducted in strict confidence, for Stirling was a well-liked officer, and, as there was then no fixed age at which senior men were expected to retire, the approach to Ivatt had been by way of an insurance policy on the part of the top management. As things turned out it was fortuitous, because Stirling died in the late autumn of that same year.

In the meantime, Ivatt himself had evidently been taking a closer look at his forthcoming new command and undoubtedly found it somewhat disquieting. While the Stirling era had pushed the Great Northern to an envied position of eminence among the railways of Great Britain, little if anything had been done to plan for the future, at any rate so far as motive power was concerned. The 8-ft bogie single express locomotives may have been the delight of the railway 'buffs', but they were hardly adequate for the traffic of the twentieth century in which sumptuous twelve-wheeled vestibuled corridor coaches loading up to trains of 300 tons or more had to be hauled at speeds of 52 to 55 mph start to stop. The plain fact was that the Stirling stud of single-wheeler express locomotives was virtually useless for heavy main-line traffic, unless the wasteful expedient of double-heading was restored to, and double-heading as a principle was anathema to all Great Northern operating men. One could understand Ivatt's words to the men of the locomotive department when he told them that although he was following in the footsteps of a very great engineer there would have to be changes; but then he assured them that they would always have plenty of steam.

The term 'scrap and build' became familiar in more modern times when, following the dictates of Sir Josiah Stamp on the LMS, W.A. Stanier was brought from the Great Western to do just that with the locomotive department. While Crewe had experienced a similar traumatic period in the early 1900s when George Whale succeeded F.W. Webb, few locomotive enthusiasts realised that a closely comparable slaughter was in progress at Doncaster at the very same time! Ivatt rebuilt eight of the 8-ft bogie singles with domed boilers, but apart from these and the six built in 1895 with 19½-in cylinders, only five of these famous engines were left at the end of 1906; fourteen of them were withdrawn in 1903 alone. A few were kept to work the level lines in Lincolnshire, working from Peterborough's New England shed, and it is noteworthy that one of the very last survivors among the 18-in cylinder engines, not cut up until 1912, was the engine that made such fine running on the Aberdeen 'racer' in 1895 between Kings Cross and Grantham, No 668. Her fastest run over the 105.5 miles was 101 minutes, or a net time of 99.5 minutes allowing for a permanent way slack near Welwyn. The 7-ft 6-in 2-2-2s, most of them rebuilt with Ivatt domed boilers, lasted longer on the main line because a use was found for them on the lightly-loaded Leeds and Bradford expresses that were run when competition with the Midland Railway was at its height. Nevertheless, all the 7-ft 6-in 2-2-2s had been scrapped by the end of 1913.

One fancies that the 7-ft 6-in and 8-ft singles would have been scrapped more rapidly if Ivatt had been ready with his new top-line express passenger designs earlier. But there was a great deal of leeway to be made up in the way of intermediate passenger and mixed traffic units. From 1897, he built a total of 95 4-4-0s with 6-ft 7½-in coupled wheels, 17½-in by 26-in cylinders and a total tube heating surface, of 1,250 sq ft, the firebox adding a further 120 sq ft. The grate area was 20.8 sq ft. Such engines could not cope with the heaviest main-line duties, but there was much they could do, and, pending the introduction of the new 'Atlantic' engines, the Stirling singles carried on, in pairs when the loads were greater than could be handled by one engine. The Ivatt 4-4-0s were quite undistinguished engines in their appearance, and the details of the successive batches differed only slightly, but they looked like what they were intended to be, a thoroughgoing utility job.

While the already famous Plant Works at Doncaster was busy turning out successive batches of these workaday 4-4-0s, the drawing office had been much involved in preparing for Ivatt's first masterpiece, the epoch-marking No 990, the first ever 'Atlantic' engine to run the rails in Great Britain, which was completed in May 1898. Naturally, the size of the new engine was the feature that first impressed the beholders, but when the technical details were published in *The Locomotive Magazine* of July 1898 there was surprise over some of the leading dimensions. When Ivatt's general utility 4-4-0s first

Above *Stirling 7 ft 7 in in 2-2-2 rebuilt with an Ivatt boiler on a train for the East Lincolnshire line near Werrington Junction* (the late C. Laundy).

Right *The 2.15 pm Leeds and Bradford 'Flyer', non-stop to Doncaster, hauled by reboilered Stirling 2-2-2 No 872 near Hadley Wood* (The Locomotive Publishing Company).

Below *The first Ivatt express locomotive for the GNR, 4-4-0 No 400, built at Doncaster in December 1896 and notable for the Stirling-type safety valve cover* (British Railways).

appeared with cylinders no larger than those of Stirling's later 2-4-0s, this was passed over as a feature of a locomotive of an intermediate power class, but with the 'Atlantic' No 990 it seemed that the new design philosophy of Doncaster was to be a complete reversal of Stirling's previous practice on the largest locomotives of having large cylinders and a relatively small boiler. The comparable dimensions of No 990 and the '1003' Class of eight-footers are startling to say the least:

Engine No	990	1003
Cylinders (in)	18¾ × 24	19½ × 28
Driving wheels (ft in)	6 7	8 0
Total heating surface sq ft	1,442	1,031
Grate area (sq ft)	26.8	20
Boiler pressure (psi)	175	170
Tractive effort (lb)	15,850	16,100

At this stage it is appropriate to mention briefly how the '990' Class engines got their famous nickname. In 1898, the world's press was centred on the news of the 'gold rush' and for a time it seemed that all ordinary ideas of business development and wealth creation were collapsing overnight. On the Great Northern Railway, such was the popular impression of an engine so far surpassing all others in power output and speed as to lead to its own 'gold rush', that they became known as the 'Klondikes'.

It appeared that Ivatt had not finished with the 4-2-2 type, for, in the same year that he startled the British railway world with the first 'Atlantic', he built a new 4-2-2, No 266, as unlike Stirling's famous eight-footers as could be imagined, though a closer relation to the 7-ft 7-in 2-2-2. Like the latter, No 266 had inside cylinders 18 in by 26 in but a much larger boiler with a tube heating surface of 1143.8 sq ft and a firebox of 125.8 sq ft. The grate area was 23.2 sq ft. The fine appearance of this engine was enhanced by the clean lines and the striding effect of the forward framing ahead of the smokebox. However, an analysis of the leading dimensions revealed that the nominal tractive effort was, at 14,000 lb, not so very much less than that of the 'Atlantic' No. 990. In private conversation, Ivatt more than once expressed a wish that a means could have been found of developing the Stirling eight-footers, seeing that they were so popular with their crews and, incidentally, with the travelling public, but the design cut so clean across his own principles that it was not practicable, and No 266 was the outcome. It was interesting to see how the weight distribution varied from that of No 990 in view of Ivatt's traumatic introduction to the Great Northern Railway with the alarming derailment of part of a train hauled by one of the final batch of Stirling eight-footers at Little Bytham early in 1896, following an incident at St Neots in the previous year. Both these accidents were caused by broken rails.

Ivatt's earliest engines on the Great Northern, including both Nos 990 and 266, were designed very much with bad track in mind. The derailment at St Neots coming on the day before Stirling died put him very much on the alert as to the effect of heavy axle loadings, and the '1003' series of eight-footers had no less than 19 tons on their driving axles. After taking over at Doncaster, he was so apprehensive about the state of the track that he walked the entire 156 miles between there and Kings Cross to see for himself, and having done so and seen the line on which some of the fastest running in England was then being made, it was said that he wished himself back in Ireland! So, far from any top-line express passenger engines with an axle-load of 19 tons, No 990 had 15 tons on the bogie, 15 tons on the first pair of coupled wheels, 16 tons on the second and 12 tons on the trailing wheels, so notably no more than 31 tons adhesion. By comparison, No 266 had 17½ tons on the bogie, 18 tons on the driving axle and 12 tons on the trailers.

Both prototype express engines of 1898 had trail-

Left *The first British 'Atlantic', Ivatt's No 990 of 1898 before being named* Henry Oakley *(the late W.J. Reynolds).*

Above right *First of the 'production batch' of Ivatt bogie 4-2-2s, No 267 built in 1900 with 19 in cylinders* (British Railways).

ing axle bearings of an unusual type, that of the 'Atlantic' proving a successful and long-lived design. It was not a trailing 'truck' in the ordinary understood form; what looked like a supplementary frameplate provided a mounting for a plate that was free to slide over the top of the axle-box and on which the springs rested. There was no side control by springs or any other means to keep the trailing wheels central when the locomotive was running on a straight track. While the Great Northern main line throughout from Kings Cross boasted a remarkably straight alignment, Ivatt felt, from his meticulous examination of the permanent way, that in a long engine like the 'Atlantic' some additional flexibility must be provided, and, by his special arrangements at the trailing end, the rigid wheelbase of No 990 was no more than 6 ft 10 in the distance apart of the coupled axles.

In 1898 it proved a successful design. At the outset, Ivatt exercised a very firm hand upon the running of his new locomotives, with instructions to the drivers to avoid all bursts of excessive speed down hill; furthermore, as a result of the accidents at St Neots and Little Bytham, much more careful attention was being paid to permanent way maintenance. By the time the two express passenger prototypes had been proved in service long enough for quantity production to be started, the scare had largely abated. In 1900, ten more 'Atlantics' were built at Doncaster with no more than detailed changes from No 990; however, at the end of that same year, when more of the 4-2-2s were also built, while the boilers were the same with only a modest increase in pressure from 170 to 175 psi, the cylinder diameter was increased from 18 in to 19 in. The nominal tractive effort at the usual 85 per cent of boiler pressure became almost equal to that of the 'Atlantics'. Another ten of the 4-2-2s were built at Doncaster, the first one at the end of 1900 and the rest in 1901.

The '266' Class, as the 4-2-2s became known, were popular with the running staff. Even after many of the *large*-boilered 'Atlantics' had been built, as late as 1910 the singles were still being regularly used on important trains such as the 5.30 pm from Kings Cross to Newcastle on the section from Grantham to York, on which the load was never less than 200 tons. On 11 runs logged by Cecil J. Allen, the average time to passing through Doncaster, 50.5 miles, was 53.25 minutes. The booked average speed over the 82.7 miles from Grantham to York was 52.8 mph, but the working was usually eased north of Doncaster as the train was getting ahead of time by then. Of the 11 runs noted, it is of interest that four of them were made by the pioneer engine, No 266, with 18-in cylinders, though whether they had been enlarged by that time I cannot say. On the descent from Peascliff Tunnel, the maximum speed down to the Trent Valley ranged up to 75 mph. The '266' Class, like all the Great Northern 'Atlantics', suffered some unsteadiness at the rear end resulting from the absence of side control on the trailing axle, but, apart from this, all of Ivatt's express passenger engines rode well.

Interspersed in Doncaster's building programme between the first of the 19-in 4-2-2s, No 267, and the rest of the class, came another twenty of the general utility 4-4-0s, and then another notable prototype, Ivatt's massive 0-8-0 heavy goods and mineral engine, No 401, also built at Doncaster in 1901. This notable engine and the standard class that followed it a year later differed from those on the North Eastern and Great Central Railways by having inside cylinders, strange though it might seem in view of Ivatt's pioneering of the outside-cylinder 'Atlantic' in 1898. Engine No 401 was a neat, gracefully-proportioned machine, carrying a boiler similar to but not the same as that of the 'Atlantics', with a rather smaller firegrate of 24.5 sq ft as against 26.75 sq ft. The cylinders were 19¾ in by 26 in, and the wheels

were of 4 ft 8 in diameter. These engines, designed for hauling heavy mineral trains and also the growing brick traffic between the various works south of Peterborough and the London district, were a further complete success for Ivatt. Although not perhaps so 'strung-out' as Robinson's outside-cylindered counterpart on the Great Central, the '401' Class on the Great Northern became nicknamed 'Long Toms'.

Reverting to the 'Atlantics', in 1902 an odd engine, No 271, was built quite apart from the regular series, with four high pressure cylinders all driving on the leading coupled axle. There had been several cases on the railways of Great Britain of four-cylinder non-compound locomotives, but most of them were so over-cylindered that the boilers could not furnish them with an adequate supply of steam. GNR No 271, however, while fitted with four cylinders each of a diameter of 15 in, thus equal to two cylinders of 21¼ in diameter, had a stroke of no more than 20 in to keep the combined cylinder volume approximately the same as that of the two-cylinder '990' Class. In this original form one cannot think the engine can have been much of a success. The famous railway journalist C. Rous-Marten always went for any new development like this with gusto, but he scarcely mentioned No 271 and in 1905 it was extensively rebuilt with Walschaerts valve gear to almost equal silence on the part of the technical press.

At the end of 1902, however, the news got around that one engine of a new batch of 'Atlantics' on the 1903 Doncaster programme was to have a very much larger boiler, and the very first number of *The Locomotive Magazine* of that year contained a note that the new engine was already running, numbered 251, with a boiler of 5 ft 6 in diameter. A fortnight later, the editor was able to publish a line diagram of this very famous engine, but as yet little technical information was divulged other than the size of the boiler. When it became known that despite the greatly enhanced steam-raising capacity no enlargement of the cylinders had been made, some commentators assumed that No 251 was just a preliminary exercise in boiler design using the chassis and engine parts of the '990' Class as a convenience. This view was reinforced when later in 1903 another batch of small-boilered 'Atlantics' was turned out at Doncaster. Their numbers ran from 250 to 260, side-stepping that used for the large-boilered pioneer. For engine No 251 *was* a pioneer, and between 1904 and 1908 no fewer than 78 engines were built at Doncaster, not merely as a logical development of No 251, but identical in all respects. Comparison with the dimensions of other large 'Atlantic' express engines then being built in Great Britain on the North Eastern, North British, Brighton, and Great Central Railways shows how inadequate the cylinder dimensions of the '251' Class appeared to be. It seemed as if Ivatt had seriously overdone the process of reversing Stirling's precepts.

A number of special runs were made for Rous-Marten's benefit when very fine hill-climbing performances were achieved, but the work noted in the ordinary course of day-to-day travelling on the Great Northern main line was indifferent so far as the large 'Atlantics' were concerned. Fortunately, the track by that time was in first-class condition, and the drivers could easily make up their deficiencies in hill climbing by fast running down hill. It is important, however, to emphasise that this was no more than a phase, albeit a significant one, in Great Northern 'Atlantic' history. It was one in which Ivatt's experiments with compounding were being undertaken, while in the year in which the last of the '251'

Left *Ivatt 0-8-0 heavy goods engine, of the class nicknamed the 'Long Toms'. The class was introduced in 1901 (No 424 built in 1908) and was one of the first Ivatt engines to be fitted with a superheater (the late W.J. Reynolds).*

Right *One of the original non-superheated large-boilered 'Atlantics' No 281, passing Holloway old station with the 2.20 pm Scotsman (F.E. Mackay).*

Class 'Atlantics' was built he had begun his first trials with superheating.

By that time, 1908, the class of 'Long Toms', by successive additions, mustered fifty strong, and it was one of the first batch, No 417, that was modified using the Schmidt apparatus. Five new 0-8-0s were built in the same year having larger cylinders, 21 in by 26 in, and a lower boiler pressure of 160 psi. On the Great Northern, as on several other British railways, the use of superheated steam was regarded as a means of securing greater economy in working rather than increased power. This was also shown in the modifications made to the first 'Atlantic' to be superheated, No 988 of the small-boilered class, in 1909. On that engine, the cylinders were enlarged to 20 in diameter and the boiler pressure reduced to 160 psi, and Schmidt's own patent piston valves were included.

In 1910, ten new 'Atlantics', Nos 1452 to 1461, were built of the large-boilered type in which the boiler pressure was lowered still further to 150 psi, so one then had this extraordinary situation as to the nominal tractive effort of the principal types of express locomotives:

Engine	251 (4-4-2)	267 (4-2-2)	988 (4-4-2)	1452 (4-4-2)
Cylinders (in)	18¾ × 24	19 × 26	20 × 24	20 × 24
Boiler pressure (psi)	175	175	160	150
Tractive effort at 85% bp (lb)	15,650	15,000	16,350	15,270

Furthermore, it was also the case that certain engines of the 1452 series of 'Atlantics' were not being so free in steaming as had been expected.

At the time when Ivatt retired in the autumn of 1911, while the locomotive department was generally in good shape, the standards of express train running had suffered a decline from the very high position they held at the end of the nineteenth century. It was not so much that the Great Northern itself had slip-

Engine No 988 at King's Cross, the first of the 'Klondikes' to be fitted with the Schmidt superheater (H. Gordon Tidey).

ped back in attainment, but that others, notably the London and North Western and the Great Western, had overtaken it. In punctuality particularly this was the case with the North Western. As the time drew near for Ivatt's retirement, it was recalled that each of his predecessors in the post of Locomotive Engineer of the Great Northern Railway had come from outside, Sturrock from the Great Western, Stirling from the Glasgow and South Western, and Ivatt himself from Ireland. In 1911 it was thought quite likely that the post might well be offered to Matthew Stirling, who had been trained under his father on the Great Northern and who had subsequently held the post of Locomotive Superintendent on the Hull and Barnsley Railway for fifteen years. He was then 55 years of age and was in the middle of a career of distinguished service, albeit in a relatively minor key compared to those of his contemporaries on the larger railways. He had developed a style of his own in the locomotives he had introduced, maintaining the family tradition of domeless boilers, although his designs also extended to a powerful 0-8-0 mineral engine, certainly equal in hauling power to Ivatt's '401' Class on the Great Northern. However, H.N. Gresley, coming to Doncaster from the Lancashire and Yorkshire Railway six years previously as Carriage and Wagon Engineer at the early age of thirty, had already made his mark with some fine new carriages, and the Board, expressing a strong preference for a younger man than Stirling, unanimously appointed him. He was then in his thirty-sixth year.

When Gresley was appointed in October 1911 it was not in express passenger motive power that the greatest need lay. A marked trend towards faster goods services all over the country was evident; the GNR was in the forefront of this movement, but strangely enough the company did not possess any engine really suitable for the traffic. In consequence, every available passenger tender engine was pressed into service, and 'Atlantics', 4-4-0s, Stirling 2-4-0s and even singles could be observed working freight trains. It was this boom in fast goods traffic that began to break down the old principle of 'one driver, one engine', for the fullest use had to be made of locomotives such as the large 'Atlantics', most of which included a fair proportion of fast goods mileage in their regular rosters. The use of these other types, however, could be regarded only as a temporary measure pending the construction of suitable engines, and such was the Great Northern's need that for the first ten years of Gresley's chieftainship at Doncaster all new engines turned out were intended for freight service.

In preparing a new design to meet contemporary needs, Gresley followed the general trend of British practice at the time for mixed traffic work, and chose the 'Mogul' wheel arrangement. Since the advent in 1899-1901 of the imported 2-6-0s on the Midland, Great Central and Great Northern, the 'Mogul' was in many quarters looked upon as an undesirable Yankee intrusion. By the year 1912, however, its popularity had been firmly assured by Churchward's '43XX' Class on the Great Western, and the new Great Northern engines appeared almost contemporaneously with 2-6-0s on the Brighton, Caledonian and Glasgow and South Western; not many years later, yet another example appeared on the SE & CR. Gresley's engine was described by *The Railway Magazine* of the day as 'a No 1 Class 0-6-0 with the addition of a pony truck', but actually the new type was a far greater departure, and, as the parents of a large and successful family of engines, the 'Moguls' of 1912 are worthy of special attention.

Ten of the type were built, and numbered 1630 to 1639. Their leading dimensions were cylinders 20 in × 26 in, coupled wheel diameter 5 ft 8 in, total heating surface 1,420 sq ft, grate area 24.5 sq ft and working pressure 170 psi. The principal feature was

Gresley's first express goods design, one of ten 0-6-0s with 5 ft 8 in wheels built in 1912 (British Railways).

Top *The first Gresley 'Mogul' of 1912, one of ten engines built for the fast night goods trains (LNER Class 'K1') (British Railways).*

Above *One of the enlarged 'Moguls' of Class 'K2', temporarily fitted for oil burning during the 1921 coal strike (British Railways).*

the front end—Walschaerts valve gear was used, working 10-in diameter piston valves. The valve setting was carefully arranged so as to give a large exhaust opening when the engine was running well linked-up. Apart from the outside Walschaerts gear and the high raised running-plate, their appearance was thoroughly Great Northern; the footplate arrangements were unaltered from the standard practice since Stirling's days, the characteristic feature of which was the pull-out type of regulator working in a horizontal plane.

The 'Moguls' of 1912 were not unduly long in showing what they could do; they worked the fast night goods to Doncaster, a 'lodging' turn, and great variety of mixed traffic jobs including express passenger trains at times of pressure. In the early days of the First World War they were often requisitioned for ambulance train workings. If there was a weakness in their design it lay in the boiler which, in proportion of the cylinder dimensions, was, by Great Northern standards, on the small side. The next batch, which came out in 1914, had boilers of a 5 ft 6 in diameter instead of 4 ft 8 in, though the cylinders remained the same. No 1640 was the pioneer of a series eventually numbering 75 engines; their later designation was Class 'K2', but on the GNR they formed Class 'E1'. As wartime train loads increased and schedules were eased, they were sometimes to be seen on regular express passenger turns, but usually there was far too much in the way of fast goods, munition and troop trains for them to be spared as deputies for the 'Atlantics'. Indeed, they never seemed quite at home on express working, but as fast freight engines they were second to none at the time of construction.

Enhanced locomotive power was needed for other

classes of freight service too. The coal traffic between Peterborough and London had already grown to large dimensions, so much so that the Ivatt '401' Class 0-8-0s, though satisfactory engines in themselves, were being worked at near their full capacity. Gresley's new design of 1913, the '456' Class of 2-8-0s, was a logical development both of the previous 0-8-0s and the '1630' Class 'Moguls', and was designed for the heaviest freight service. The pony truck, in addition to supporting a heavy and powerful front end, provided a degree of flexibility in the vehicle that was especially valuable for freight working on a route like the GNR main line, with its frequent diversions from fast to slow road and vice versa.

As motive power units, the '456' Class (LNER Class 'O1') proved as good as their ample dimensions suggest. Their cylinders were 21 in × 28 in which, in combination with the 4-ft 8-in coupled wheels and a working pressure of 170 psi, give the class a nominal tractive effort of 31,000 lb at 85 per cent of the working pressure. The boiler was the largest Doncaster had produced up to that time, the barrel being 15 ft 5 in long with a diameter of 5 ft 6 in; the heating surface of the tubes alone was 1,922 sq ft. Unlike the first 'Moguls', these 2-8-0s were fitted with Robinson superheaters; a high degree of superheat was evidently aimed at, for the heating surface provided, 427 sq ft, was large for that period. The grate area of these engines was 27 sq ft and the adhesion weight was 67.5 tons; the total weight of the engine and tender in working order was 119.25 tons. Other equipment included 10-in diameter piston valves, as in the 'Moguls', and a Weir feed-water

heater and feed pump. In outward appearance, the engines remained faithful to Great Northern traditions, and the Stirling type of regulator handle still featured among the footplate fittings.

By the beginning of 1915, immediate needs had been met and Great Northern locomotive history was entering an interesting transitional stage. All over the country, new locomotive types were being produced, and on all sides superheating was being hailed as the final and conclusive answer to the exponents of compounding, yet on the GNR nothing very much seemed to be happening, outwardly at any rate, in the realm of express passenger motive power. Elsewhere, one of the most strongly marked trends of the time was the introduction of multi-cylindered single-expansion locomotives. By 1914 the Great Western had practically standardized the four-cylinder system for crack express engines, the LNWR 'Claughtons' were out and doing good work while the Great Northern's own historic partner, the North Eastern, had already turned out a considerable variety of three-cylinder simple designs.

Throughout the Gresley regime, close study of contemporary practice, both at home and overseas, was applied to design at Doncaster works, and in the early years of his chieftainship it is not surprising in view of what was taking place elsewhere in the country that Gresley made some experiments with multi-cylindered locomotives. The first step was the complete rebuilding in 1915 of 'Atlantic' No 279 as a four-cylinder simple; this engine was one of the standard Ivatt '251' Class, having two cylinders of 18¾ in diameter, by 24 in stroke. As rebuilt, the engine was provided with four cylinders of 15 in

Left *The first Gresley two-cylinder 2-8-0 No 456 (later Class 'O1') built at Doncaster in 1913* (British Railways).

Right *Ivatt 'Atlantic' No 1447, as fitted by Gresley with a high degree superheater, on the 5.30 pm King's Cross-Newcastle express near Hadley Wood* (Author's collection).

diameter and 26 in stroke, a 40 per cent increase in cylinder volume, and the boiler was modified by the fitting of a 24-element Robinson superheater (instead of the previous 18-element version) affording 427 sq ft of heating surface. This heating surface was the same as that of the original Ivatt superheated 'Atlantics' of the 1452 series. No 279 was fitted with the Walschaerts valve gear, but only two sets were provided, the valves of the inside cylinders being actuated by rocking shafts driven off the tail rods of the outside cylinder valve spindles. This rebuilding increased the weight of No 279 from the original 65.5 tons to 73.5 tons, and the engine was, in nominal tractive effort, the most powerful on the GNR, though curiously enough she never came into the limelight to the same extent as the ordinary '251' Class.

When a start was made with the superheating of the original Ivatt 'Atlantics', bolder measures were taken, the boiler pressure being retained practically at the former figure of 175 psi. The process of transformation was gradual, for many of the engines at first retained their slide valves, while others were fitted with new 8-in diameter piston valves. The first engines to be equipped were provided with 24-element superheaters having the same amount of heating surface—427 sq ft—as Nos 1452-1461 and the four-cylinder engine No 279. In 1919, however, No 1403 was fitted with a 32-element superheater, having 568 sq ft of heating surface. This variety later became standard for the whole class, and those engines which for a time had 24-element superheaters were subsequently modified. It is important to recall that, even in their last days, by no means all

of them had been fitted with piston valves. In the late 1930s, when I was accorded the privilege of making a number of footplate trips on them, I was surprised to be given full particulars not only of the piston valve dimensions but also of the balanced slide valves with which, I was informed, a number were still fitted, then mostly on the Great Central section. The respective dimensions are shown in the following table:

GNR Large-boiled 'Atlantics': cylinders, motion etc

	Slide valve engines	Piston valve engines
Cylinders		
Diameter (in)	19	20
Stroke (in)	24	24
Motion		
Type	Stephenson	Stephenson
Valves	Balanced slide valves	8-in piston valves
Max valve travel (in)	$4\frac{3}{8}$	$4\frac{3}{8}$
Steam lap (in)	$1\frac{3}{16}$	$1\frac{1}{4}$
Exhaust clearance (in)	$\frac{1}{8}$	$\frac{5}{16}$
Lead (in full forward gear)		
Front (in)	$\frac{3}{32}$	$\frac{5}{32}$
Back (in)	$\frac{3}{32}$	$\frac{3}{64}$
Cut-off in full gear (per cent)	70	70
Tractive effort at 85% boiler pressure (lb)	15,649	17,340

8. Pre-grouping Scotland: North British and GN of S

In the British railway world of the nineteenth century, the names of several families of engineers were writ large on the pages of locomotive construction history. Several generations of Trevithicks adorned the records, not only of the London and North Western but also of the railways of Japan, India and Egypt, and the Stirling's records extended not only to the famous locomotives described in this volume, but also those of the Southern and LMS. And, equal to the Stirlings, there was the great locomotive engineering family of Drummonds.

Dugald, the elder of the two famous brothers, received his first appointment of any responsibility at no more than 25 years of age when he went to Inverness as Foreman-Erector in the Highland Railway shops under William Stroudley. Two years later he was promoted to Works Manager, but in 1870 he left the Highland to follow his old chief to Brighton, where he absorbed in five years much of the neatness in design and perfection of detail that remained with him throughout his long railway career.

In 1875, when he was 35, he was appointed Locomotive Superintendent of the North British Railway. That great system was then in no more than a half-formed stage; the great viaducts which came to form a vital part of the East Coast route to Aberdeen were not yet built, not even the first and ill-fated structure designed by Thomas Bouch across the Firth of Tay. Over the East Coast route south of Edinburgh the principal express trains were run by North Eastern locomotives, and the only truly main-line running for which the locomotive department of the North British Railway was responsible was the virtually level line between Edinburgh and Glasgow. The only obstacle there was the notorious Cowlairs Incline at the Glasgow end, up which all trains were assisted by cable haulage. For this level line Dugald Drummond built two 2-2-2s, entirely in the Stroudley style of the

Brighton Railway, and, when he followed with some 0-4-2 tank engines for more local work, it seemed as if Cowlairs Works was becoming a northern counterpart of the Brighton. Incidentally, it was only a temporary failure on behalf of one of the Drummond 0-4-2 tanks that prevented it going into the river with the wreck of the first Tay Bridge on December 28 1879—the old Wheatley 4-4-0 No 224 which hauled the doomed train was only a substitute.

Almost from his first arrival at Cowlairs, Drummond was put very much on his mettle so far as main line engine design was concerned. The construction of the far-famed Settle and Carlisle line of the Midland Railway was approaching completion, and from the summer of 1876 a new and highly competitive train service between Edinburgh and the south was programmed. The line concerned had not in any way been planned as a major express route; it was a mountainous track toiling over Falahill Summit in the Lammermuir Hills, down to Tweedside and over the Cheviots at Whitrope Summit, then down through bleak Liddesdale and so to the Border marches. It was not only the gradients, but also the curves! Not a mile out of the 98 between Edinburgh and Carlisle had been originally planned as an express route, it was a link-up of a collection of branches, built as cheaply as possible with a minimum of earthworks. There could not have been a greater contrast between this route, with its numerous sharp curves and fluctuations in gradient, and the new Midland main line between Settle and Carlisle with which it was connected to provide a new Anglo-Scottish express train service. The latter had not a single permanent speed restriction anywhere between Hellifield and the immediate approaches to Carlisle.

The North British line, which soon after its elevation to main-line status became known and there-

North British inheritance: one of the six remaining Wheatley 2-4-0s of 1873 taken into LNER stock in 1923. These engines had been rebuilt in 1900 (Author's collection).

after loved as 'The Waverley Route', must have brought to Dugald Drummond recollections of the Portsmouth line of the Brighton Railway with its numerous awkward curves and sharp gradients, but the situation was far more severe north of Carlisle. Certainly he tackled the motive power problem in a manner far otherwise from Stroudley. In 1876 he designed a bogie four-coupled express passenger engine that proved the progenitor of the leading passenger power on three successive railways for which he was the Locomotive Superintendent, and on two others, the Highland and the Glasgow and South Western, where his brother introduced a larger development of the same type. The North British '476' Class can be seen in historical perspective as one of the really great designs, not only of the nineteenth century but also, from its subsequent development, of the twentieth. Their so-called 'leading dimensions' were not exceptional for that period; the cylinders were 18 in by 26 in, the coupled

wheel diameter was 6 ft 6 in and the boiler pressure was 140 psi. The boiler was relatively large for that time, however, having a tube heating surface of 1,005.3 sq ft and a grate area of 21 sq ft.

In these engines, and still more so on the Caledonian 4-4-0s that followed, Drummond was embarking upon a scientific approach to the utilization of the steam in the cylinders far in advance of the majority of his fellow locomotive engineers. It is remarkable to find how much he departed from Stroudley's practice once he got away from Brighton, not only in his immediate adoption of a leading bogie but also in the far more important matter of cylinder design. This was a departure from the normal arrangement, having a central valve face. The steam ports were moved to the cylinder ends, and the slide valve was divided, each having its own exhaust port. It is of interest to compare the front-end arrangements with certain other well-known passenger engines of that era:

Above *Drummond 7 ft single 2-2-2, one of two built in 1876 for the level Edinburgh and Glasgow line. Engine No 474 was originally named* Glasgow *(Author's collection).*

Right *Drummond 4-4-0 '476' Class for the Waverley Route as originally built in 1876, but with the name deleted and lock-up safety valves on the dome. (Author's collection).*

Engines	LBSC Stroudley 'Gladstone' Class	Highland Jones 'Duke' Class	G & SWR J. Stirling '6' Class 4-4-0	North British Drummond '476' Class
Cylinders (in)	18¼ × 26	18 × 24	18 × 26	18 × 26
Port length (in)	15	15	16	2 × 8
Port width				
Steam (in)	1⅜	1½	1½	1⅝
Exhaust (in)	2	3	3	3¼
Exhaust port area (sq in)	30	45	48	52
Maximum valve travel (in)	3¾	3⅞	4⅜	4⁵⁄₁₆

Drummond not only changed what can be termed the 'geographical' layout of the cylinders, he also notably increased the port widths and thus the port area. More recent locomotive history has shown how similar developments greatly improved the running qualities of express locomotives, particularly where higher speeds were required, and also resulted in a marked reduction in coal consumption. While train running over the Waverley Route of the North British throughout its history has been the very opposite to any pretentions to high speed even by nineteenth-century standards, a locomotive like this with which such care had been taken in the design of the steam flow circuit would respond with a notably economical coal consumption at any speed. Perhaps more important still was the water consumption. The Waverley Route, while in no way originally planned as an express route, was virtually impossible to upgrade because of the physical conditions (indeed, the fastest running ever seen over it took place in the early 1900s before the decelerations made necessary by the First World War), but the St Pancras-Edinburgh service had not long been inaugurated before the Drummond '476' Class 4-4-0s were being called upon to run the 98 miles from Carlisle to Edinburgh *non-stop*.

From 1881 onwards, the fastest trains ran this distance in 140 minutes, an average of 42 mph, while at the zenith of Waverley Route speed certain of the trains took no more than 135 minutes. Naturally the loads were much restricted, and on the three most severe inclines regular provision was made for rear-end banking assistance (these were from Newcastleton to Whitrope going north, and for Eskbank to Falahill and from Hawick to Whitrope going south). The severity of the curves imposed a maximum speed limit of about 60 mph on all the steep descents and, while there were a few straighter lengths where one could run up to 65 mph or even more between Newcastleton and Carlisle and between Hawick and Galashiels, these brief bursts of higher speed made no difference to the overall average. Although Drummond's successor built several slightly more powerful 4-4-0s before the end of the nineteenth century which, as will be mentioned later, were used north of Edinburgh, the Drummond '476' Class had the Waverley Route to themselves for at least twenty years, a sterling tribute to their design and working efficiency.

Originally they were named after stations along the line in the Brighton style which Drummond copied from Stroudley, but Matthew Holmes deleted these names and also those on the local tank engines as soon as he took charge at Cowlairs. Before the fall of the Tay Bridge, two of these engines were originally allocated to the East Coast Route and named *Aberdeen* and *Montrose*, but after the disaster of December 1879 they were transferred to the Waverley route to join the other members of the class and to be renamed accordingly. The names borne by the twelve engines until 1883 were:

476 *Carlisle*	486 *Waverley*	490 *St Boswell's*
477 *Edinburgh*	487 *Eskbank*	491 *Dalhousie*
478 *Melrose*	488 *Galashiels*	492 *Newcastleton*
479 *Abbotsford*	489 *Hawick*	493 *Netherby*

The departure of Dugald Drummond for St Rollox, and the appointment of Matthew Holmes to succeed him, was followed by a number of those changes that were characteristic of the old highly individual days of the pre-grouping railways. The changes on the North British came to affect not only the new locomotives introduced by the incoming Engineer but also the passenger engines of his predecessor. The latter changes, such as the change in painting style and the removal of engine names, were ephemeral rather than scientific, and concerned the railway 'buffs' rather than the ordinary passengers, uniformed staff and technicians. Dugald Drummond had brought the Stroudley style of painting with him from Brighton, though one gathers the actual tone of the famous 'engine green' was a little different from the yellow immortalized on the Brighton engines. Holmes changed it to a more workmanlike bronze-green, occasionally called gamboge by some railway

Right *Early Edinburgh and Glasgow Railway 6 ft 2-4-0 No 237 as rebuilt by Drummond and with the later Holmes-type cab. Note the four-wheeled tender (The Locomotive Publishing Company).*

Below *Holmes '633' Class 6 ft 6 in 4-4-0 built for the opening of the Forth Bridge route to the north in 1890. Engines of this class were used in the 1895 'Race to the North' between Edinburgh and Aberdeen (The Locomotive Publishing Company).*

writers. This colour was the cause of many misconceptions in pre-war days because of the difficulty in obtaining a true colour-rendering on the three-colour process used in the famous series of postcards marketed by the Locomotive Publishing Company, on which the colour sometimes came out more like a sepia brown. The true colour was more accurately reproduced in early examples of the lithographed colour plates included in *The Railway Magazine*.

The changes in design made by Holmes in his new 4-4-0s were largely superficial. He discarded the Stroudleyesque cab used on the '476' Class and adopted the style that Patrick Stirling used on all his later Great Northern engines. Then, following Drummond's dictum that the fewer apertures there were in the boiler the better, he also mounted the safety valves on the dome cover, but instead of the spring-balanced type, which Drummond took to the Caledonian Railway, Holmes used two separate 'lock-up' type valves. It is interesting that when he returned to railway service after his ill-starred venture into commercial engineering practice, Dugald Drummond adopted the lock-up type of safety valve on his London and South Western locomotives.

Holmes designed five classes of 4-4-0 for the North

British Railway, the first two of which made little mark. However, for the new express services north of Edinburgh following the opening of the Forth Bridge in 1891, his '633' Class, with 18-in by 26-in cylinders, 6-ft 6-in coupled wheels, a larger boiler than the Drummond '476' Class and a higher boiler pressure of 150 psi, were excellent engines, and in due course covered themselves in glory by their spectacular running in the last stages of the 1895 'Race to the North'. It was spectacular indeed, seeing that the start-to-stop average speeds of 60 mph between Edinburgh and Dundee were not remotely equalled again in the remaining history of steam traction on the East Coast route.

A 4-4-0 for a different assignment altogether was designed at Cowlairs in 1893 ready for the opening of the far-famed West Highland line from Craigendoran Junction on the Firth of Clyde to Fort William. While the Waverley Route from Edinburgh down to Carlisle was notorious among Scottish main lines for its sinuous alignment and severe gradients, the West Highland was infinitely worse, having a ruling gradient of 1 in 60 and single track throughout. The Mallaig extension line, opened in 1901, was still worse—its ruling gradient was 1 in 50! Holmes' 'West Highland' 4-4-0s had coupled wheels of 5 ft 7

in diameter, a good boiler with 1,235 sq ft of heating surface and cylinders 18 in by 24 in. The boiler pressure was 150 psi. Ahrons has stated that these engines were designed for a load of 200 tons, but I cannot think that this specification can ever have been taken seriously, because W.P. Reid's powerful superheated 4-4-0s of the 'Glen' series, with 20-in by 26-in cylinders and 165 psi boiler pressure, were limited to 180 tons when I was doing a certain amount of footplate work on the West Highland in the 1930s. When the line was opened in 1893, the Board of Trade imposed a maximum speed limit of 25 mph throughout from Craigendoran to Fort William, and this had not been increased to more than 40 mph by the time I was doing my footplate work. I found, however, that very much higher speeds were frequently run on favourable lengths of the line, when 'higher authority' was not looking: I have, for example, logged a sustained speed of over 60 mph across Rannoch Moor.

Holmes introduced a slightly larger version of the '633' Class of the main-line 4-4-0s in 1898, with cylinders enlarged to 18¼ in and the boiler pressure increased to 175 psi. Some of these engines were drafted into service on the Waverley Route, and the fact that they were the first increase in power since the Drummond '476' Class of 1876 speaks well for the efficiency of those older engines.

Holmes' last word so far as express locomotive design for the North British Railway was concerned came in 1903, just as he was on the point of retiring. This was the very powerful '317' Class 4-4-0, with 19-in by 26-in cylinders, a larger boiler and firebox than the preceeding classes and with the working pressure stepped up to no less than 200 psi. It would seem that the neighbouring works of Cowlairs and St Rollox were then engaged in friendly rivalry as to which could produce the most powerful 4-4-0. Holmes' '729' Class of 1898 matched the 'Dunalastair II' of the Caledonian, and then St Rollox went one ahead in 1899 with the '900' Class, or third 'Dunalastair'. The Cowlairs '317' Class gave the lead to the North British by the increased boiler pressure of 200 psi against the 180 of the Caledonian, although the cylinder dimensions were the same. The most distinctive feature of the new engines, however, was the cab, which set a new style for the North British and became familiar on the range of designs introduced by Holmes' successor.

The early years of the twentieth century saw competition with the Caledonian in more serious matters than the relative dimensions of 4-4-0 locomotives, in nothing less than cut-throat competition for passenger traffic between Edinburgh and Glasgow and Aberdeen. Some beautiful new block trains had been built at the Cowlairs Works in opposition to the celebrated 'Grampian' stock of the Caledonian, and W.P. Reid, the new Locomotive Superintendent of the North British, decided upon the 'Atlantic' type rather than the 4-6-0 for haulage of the new trains. While it could be said that this was in line with East Coast practice, following the lead of the Great Northern and the North Eastern in this respect, Reid also had to provide for the augmentation of power on the Waverley Route; increased traffic from the Midland was regularly involved double-heading and banking engine assistance on the heavy gradients. It was as much the curvature of the Waverley Route as any other factor that led to the choice of the 'Atlantic', not without some considerable opposition from the civil engineers. The new engines, 14 in all, were built at the Hyde Park Works of the North British Locomotive Company in 1906, and although they had the truncated chimneys and dome covers necessary with a boiler diameter as large as 5 ft 6 in to conform to the North British loading gauge, connois-

Holmes 5 ft 7 in 4-4-0 for the West Highland line introduced in 1893 (British Railways).

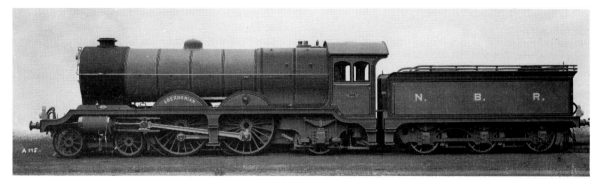

The first North British 'Atlantic' No 868 Aberdonian (North British Locomotive Company).

seurs of British locomotive practice noticed the similarity, below the top line of the boiler, to the Robinson 'Atlantics' of the Great Central, a batch of which, also with 200 psi boilers, had been built by the NBL Co in the previous year.

The North British 'Atlantics' were tremendously impressive engines. Having said this, however, it must be admitted that like a number of large engines of that vintage their performance was at first not up to the maximum expectations. In this respect they could be classed with the large-boilered 'Atlantics' of the Great Northern, and the 'V' Atlantics of the North Eastern. One supposes the same might be said of the Great Central 'Atlantics' had they had any appreciable work to do in their early years, but unlike their East Coast confrères they were always very lightly loaded. The North British 'Atlantics' had plenty of power built into them, with two cylinders 20 in by 28 in, 6-ft 9-in coupled wheels and a splendid boiler using 200 psi pressure. The cab was modelled on North Eastern lines, with two windows on each side, but, unlike other East Coast 'Atlantics', they were driven from the left-hand side of the cab in accordance with North British standard practice. Steam reversing gear was used. Despite their relatively high tractive effort, when some of these engines were allocated to work on the Waverley

Route they never seemed to take a load of more than about 250 tons without assistance on the steepest inclines. On the East Coast route, the 'Atlantics' worked through between Edinburgh and Aberdeen, and the first six of the new engines were stationed at Ferryhill, Aberdeen. All of the remainder were in Edinburgh, though I believe those allocated to the Waverley Route were originally based at St Margarets shed beside the main line about a mile east of Waverley station.

One of the most gratifying aspects about the introduction of the 'Atlantic' engines in 1906 was that naming was resumed, and in a far more imaginative and satisfying way than the old Stroudley system of using up every station on the line. At first, the names were associated with the routes the engines worked over, but in due course this was not found entirely practicable. The first fourteen engines were named and allocated thus:

Reid 'Atlantic' No 878 Hazeldean, *as originally built without a superheater in 1906* (The Locomotive Publishing Company).

Aberdeen:

868   *Aberdonian*
869   *Dundonian*
870   *Bon Accord*
871   *Thane of Fife*
872   *Auld Reekie*
873   *St Mungo*

Edinburgh, Haymarket (East Coast):

874   *Dunedin*
875   *Midlothian*
876   *Waverley*

Edinburgh, St Margarets (Waverley Route):

877   *Liddesdale*
878   *Hazeldean*
879   *Abbotsford*
880   *Tweeddale*
881   *Borderer*

The only engine that might appear territorially inappropriate is No 873 *St Mungo* were it not for the fact that the block-load Aberdeen trains included sections from Glasgow and, even though these consisted at times of no more than three coaches, they had to be 'Atlantic'-hauled for prestige purposes at the height of the competition with the Caledonian. At first, *St Mungo* was naturally reserved for this duty.

When a further six engines were added to the 'Atlantic' stud in 1911, the names chosen were equally satisfying. The first of these was No 901 *St Johnstoun*, signifying the usage of engines of this type between Edinburgh and Perth. The six new engines were:

901	*St Johnstoun*	902	*Highland Chief*
903	*Cock o' the North*	904	*Holyrood*
905	*Buccleugh*	906	*Teribus*

In the February 1912 issue of the *Locomotive Magazine* there was a beautiful colour plate reproduced from an oil painting by 'F. Moore', marred only by the basic colour of the engine, which was a rich madder brown instead of the true bronze-green. Three years earlier, the same artist made a much truer attempt at the colour in an equally fine picture of the first of W.P. Reid's 'Scott' Class 4-4-0s, *Sir Walter Scott* himself, but it was still, in recollection, too brown.

The North British 'Atlantics', from being no more than moderate performers, were absolutely transformed after superheating. They had cylinders enlarged from 20 in to 21 in diameter and the boiler pressure was lowered from 200 psi to 180. While the nominal tractive effort remained virtually unchanged, the pulling power was very much enhanced, especially on the steep gradients of the East Coast line from Edinburgh northwards. On the

Waverley Route down to Carlisle the maximum load they could take unassisted was increased from 240 to 290 tons, but to see them at their very best one had to travel behind them, or, as I was privileged to do several times, on the footplate on maximum load trains between Dundee and Aberdeen. The introduction of the eight-hour day for locomotive enginemen during the First World War resulted in some changes in the engine workings on the Aberdeen route, and on the principal trains engines were changed at Dundee instead of working through between Edinburgh and Aberdeen. Consequently, the six 'Atlantics' originally stationed at Ferryhill were transferred to Dundee Tay Bridge shed. It was of interest that five of the original allocation of six were still working north of Dundee when I was travelling on that route from 1928 onwards. By that time, however, engine No 9869 (LNER numbering) had been renamed *Bonnie Dundee*. Only *St Mungo* had been transferred away, and I travelled behind her on the Waverley Route in 1927. Two further 'Atlantics' were working north from Dundee at that time, No 9902 *Highland Chief*, one of the 1911 batch which had been built by Robert Stephenson & Co at Darlington, and No 9509 *Duke of Rothesay*, one of two built after the war. The latter was one of the finest pregrouping engines I have ever ridden upon.

Having provided for the heaviest East Coast and Waverley Route express trains, Reid turned to augmenting the stud of intermediate passenger and mixed traffic 4-4-0s. The new engines of both types had 19-in by 26-in cylinders but differed in their boiler proportions both from each other and from the preceeding Holmes '317' Class of 1903.

North British 4-4-0 Class

Date	1903	1907	1909
Class	'317'	'882'	'Scott'
Coupled wheels (ft in)	6 6	6 0	6 6
Heating surfaces (sq ft)			
Tubes	1,444	1,620	1,478.34
Firebox	133	140	139.78
Total	1,577	1,760	1,628.12
Grate area (sq ft)	22.5	21.5	21.13
Boiler pressure (psi)	200	175	190

The '882' Class 'Intermediates' were, of course, the predecessors of the well-known and popular 'Glen' Class, which did such yeoman work on the West Highland line for so many years, while the 'Scott' Class of 1909 were followed by the superheated version of the same type. The non-superheated '882' Class were not named, but the first six of the 'Scott' Class built by the North British Locomotive Co in 1909 were named as follows:

One of the two superheater 'Atlantics' built in 1921, No 509 Duke of Rothesay *in original colours (British Railways).*

895	*Rob Roy*	898	*Sir Walter Scott*
896	*Dandie Dinmont*	899	*Jeanie Deans*
897	*Redgauntlet*	900	*The Fair Maid*

These engines were originally intended to work between Edinburgh and Perth, but with the building of the second batch of ten at Cowlairs in 1912, they were spread across all the fast-running lines of the NBR. The later batch, also non-superheated, were named as follows:

243	*Meg Merrilies*	340	*Lady of Avenel*
244	*Madge Wildfire*	359	*Dirk Hatteraick*
245	*Bailie Nicol Jarvie*	360	*Guy Mannering*
338	*Helen McGregor*	361	*Vich Ian Vohr*
339	*Ivanhoe*	362	*Ravenswood*

'Scott' Class 4-4-0 No 898 Sir Walter Scott *of the non-superheated batch of 1909 (North British Locomotive Company).*

Even at this early stage in the naming of this ultimately numerous group of locomotives, it would need a specialist quiz contender to identify some of the personalities involved in some of those North British engine names! Who, for example, was 'Madge Wildfire', and who was 'Vich Ian Vohr'?

While the North British Railway had a heavy freight traffic and served many of the most industrialized districts of lowland Scotland, there had never been a need for maximum power mineral engines like those of the North Eastern, Great Northern or Great Central Railways. The runs were mostly of a short-haul nature, from collieries and steelworks in the Lowland Belt, for example, to the great shipbuilding and other engineering works in Clydesdale. Consequently the North British Railway had never found the need to develop freight engine power beyond the 0-6-0 type.

At about the same time as Reid introduced his 'Atlantic' express locomotives, he built the first twenty of his new goods engines with large boilers of 5 ft diameter having 1,605 sq ft total heating surface and a grate area of 19.8 sq ft. The cylinders were 18½ in by 26 in and the wheels were of 5 ft diameter. Con-

struction of this class continued until 1913, by which time there were 76 of them in service. A superheated version came in 1914, with the same chassis and 5-ft wheels but a still larger boiler with a total heating surface of 1,732.2 sq ft and cylinders 19½ in by 26 in; boiler pressure was, however, reduced to 165 psi. These superheated goods engines were extremely successful and eventually totalled 104. They were also fine-looking engines, and unlike their unfortunate contemporaries on the Great Central, the 'Pom-poms', they were not disfigured after the grouping by having alien chimneys and dome covers fixed to them. Such acts of iconoclasm, which were perpetrated not only on the 'Pom-poms' but throughout the Great Central stud, were entirely unnecessary in the interests of standardization or anything else, as was shown by the example of the Scottish Area of the LNER after grouping.

I grew to have a particular affection for those big North British superheated 0-6-0s, LNER Class 'J37', and I photographed them pounding up the heavy coastal gradients of the East Coast main line between Montrose and Aberdeen, and, above all, in general use on goods and passenger services alike on the Mallaig extension of the West Highland line. In my earliest explorations on Scottish railways, I approached that line by the MacBrayne mail steamer from Portree, and, staying for several days in Mallaig and exploring the surrounding country, I was at first disappointed at the complete absence of the 'Glen' Class 4-4-0s; however, after making a number of short trips I quickly appreciated the sterling worth of those 0-6-0s. They then had the 'Mallaig Road' to themselves, until the ex-Great Northern 'K2' Class 2-6-0s were introduced some years later.

The superheated goods were first built actually after the superheated versions of the two 4-4-0s of

Reid's design, the 'intermediates' of 1907 with the 6-ft driving wheels and the 'Scotts'. The first North British use of superheating was made, as in so many cases in those immediate pre-war years, with a trial of the relative merits of the Schmidt and Robinson apparatus. Two engines of the 6-ft 6-in 'Scott' Class were built first, in 1912, and then ten of the new 'Glen' Class, in 1913. The two 'Scotts' had Schmidt superheaters, while of the 'Glens' there were five of each type. The two new classes were identical except for the coupled wheel diameter, with cylinders of 20 in by 26 in, 10-in piston valves with inside admission and a boiler pressure of 165 psi. The boiler heating surfaces were, tubes 1,145.8 sq ft, superheater flues 355.2 sq ft and firebox 139.7 sq ft, making a total of 1,640.7 sq ft; the grate area was 21.13 sq ft. The first two superheated 'Scotts' were named *The Dougal Cratur* (No 400) and *Hal O' the Wynd* (No 363), two more puzzles for our quiz contestant! The first lot of 'Glens' were familiar enough, however:

149	*Glen Finnan*	307	*Glen Nevis*
221	*Glen Orchy*	405	*Glen Spean*
256	*Glen Douglas*	406	*Glen Croe*
258	*Glen Roy*	407	*Glen Beasdale*
266	*Glen Falloch*	408	*Glen Sloy*

The superheated Reid engines, both 4-4-0 and 0-6-0 alike, featured a slightly different painting style on their tenders. On the freight engines, following the inauguration of the new traffic control system on the North British Railway, the engine numbers were painted in large figures between the initials NB. On the tenders of the passenger engines the previous use of the full railway initials was shortened to NB, but with the coat of arms in between instead of the

Reid superheated 0-6-0 goods engine (LNER Class 'J37') (P. Ransome-Wallis).

The first of the superheated 'Scott' Class 4-4-0s, No 400 The Dougal Cratur, *built in 1912* (British Railways).

engine's number. In due course all North British engines carried the number on the tender or side tanks.

The superheated Reid 4-4-0s were really splendid engines. Additions were made to both classes during the war years, and, together with those added up to the time of the grouping, the class totals eventually mustered 27 superheated 'Scotts' and 32 'Glens'. The sixteen original 'Scotts' were eventually rebuilt with superheaters, though they retained their original 19-in cylinders. I treasure the memory of the many journeys I made behind these engines, whether in partnership with the 'Atlantics' in hauling the

One of the later superheater 'Scotts' in LNER black livery at Tweedmouth in 1933, No 9424 Lady Rowena (O.S. Nock).

extreme heavyweights of the East Coast service, or on the West Highland line. The introduction of third class sleeping-cars sent the load of the southbound 'Aberdonian' far above the maximum of 340 tons that was allowed for an unpiloted 'Atlantic'. One night when I was a passenger we pulled out of Aberdeen with a load of 565 tons; the 'Atlantic' *Bonnie Dundee* was leading with superheated 'Scott' *Caleb Balderstone* next to the train. I had a seat in the leading coach, and the combined roar of those two engines as they mounted the steep inclines out of Aberdeen, Stonehaven and Montrose was music to the ears of a locomotive enthusiast! So it was also when one of the two post-war 'Atlantics', *The Lord Provost,* and another 'Scott', *Lord Glenvarloch*, replaced the previous two engines for the non-stop run from Dundee to Edinburgh.

I could write pages of eulogy on the days I have spent on 'Glen' Class engines listening to them hammering their way up the fearsome inclines of the West

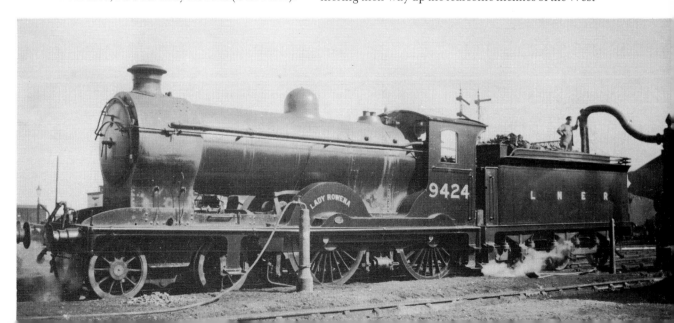

Left *'Glen' Class 4-4-0 (LNER Class 'D34') No 9100* Glen Dochart *on a Glasgow express at Fort William (O.S. Nock).*

Left *GN of SR Pickersgill 4-4-0 design of 1899, one of a batch built in 1920 and superheated. No 49* Gordon Highlander *was temporarily fitted for oil firing in 1921 (R.D. Stephen).*

Below *A scene at Macduff Harbour station in 1947 showing two Pickersgill 4-4-0s (Author's collection).*

Highland lines, but I must spare a page in the conclusion of this chapter for the locomotives of the Great North of Scotland Railway, although even the latest of them could not really have merited the description 'great'. Except for a class of 0-4-4 tank engines engaged on the Aberdeen suburban service, all the main-line locomotives of the GN of S for passenger and goods service alike were of the 4-4-0 type. The dimensions of even the largest engines never progressed beyond 18-in by 26-in cylinders, 6-ft 0-in coupled wheels and 165 psi boiler pressure, even in non-superheater engines. What became the standard main-line engine of the GN of S originated with James Manson, who was appointed Locomotive Superintendent in 1883. He introduced the basic 4-4-0 with the dimensions listed above, and it was continued, with no more than detail alterations, first by James Johnson and then by William Pickersgill, who was to be remembered more for his work on the Caledonian than on the GN of S. His one innovation in engine design, in 1899, was marked by an unfortunate occurrence for which he was in no way responsible. Ten new 4-4-0 engines ordered from Neilson & Co were provided with side-windowed cabs in the Worsdell style, but when delivery was due the railway management could not pay for them. The South Eastern and Chatham Railway bought five of them, and would have taken them all had the GN of S been able to extend credit terms to them. Eventually there were thirteen of these Pickersgill non-superheater 4-4-0s, with eight superheated versions added by Thomas Heywood in 1920-21.

Rounding off the pre-grouping story in Scotland is a list of the names of the non-superheated and superheated 'Scott' Classes. In LNER days came another series of 4-4-0 engines from south of the border which were also honoured with names of characters from the 'Waverley' novels and these make so interesting a comparison that I am including both lists.

NBR 'Scott' Classes:
Non-Superheated
895	*Rob Roy*
896	*Dandie Dinmont*
897	*Redgauntlet*
898	*Sir Walter Scott*
899	*Jeanie Deans*
901	*The Fair Maid*
243	*Meg Merrilies*
244	*Madge Wildfire*
245	*Bailie Nicol Jarvie*
338	*Helen MacGregor*
339	*Ivanhoe*
340	*Lady of Avenel*
359	*Dirk Hatteraick*
360	*Guy Mannering*
361	*Vich Ian Vohr*
362	*Ravenswood*

Superheated
363	*Hal O' The Wynd*
400	*The Dougal Cratur*
409	*The Pirate*
410	*Meg Dods*
411	*Dominie Sampson*
412	*Laird of Monkbarns*
413	*Caleb Balderstone*
414	*Dugald Dalgetty*
415	*Claverhouse*
416	*Ellangowan*
417	*Cuddie Headrigg*
418	*Dumbiedykes*
419	*Talisman*
420	*The Abbot*
421	*Jingling Geordie*
422	*Kenilworth*
423	*Quentin Durward*
424	*Lady Rowena*
425	*Kettledrummle*
426	*Norna*
427	*Lord Glenvarloch*
428	*Adam Woodcock*
497	*Peter Poundtext*
498	*Father Ambrose*
499	*Wandering Willie*
500	*Black Duncan*
501	*Simon Glover*

GCR Class 'D11' 4-4-0 (1924)
6378	*Bailie MacWheeble*
6379	*Baron of Bradwardine*
6380	*Evan Dhu*
6381	*Flora MacIvor*
6382	*Colonel Gardiner*
6383	*Jonathan Oldbuck*
6384	*Edie Ochiltree*
6385	*Luckie Mucklebackit*
6386	*Lord Glenallan*
6387	*Lucy Ashton*
6388	*Captain Craigengelt*
6389	*Haystoun of Bucklaw*
6390	*Hobbie Elliott*
6391	*Wizard of the Moor*
6392	*Malcolm Graeme*
6393	*The Fiery Cross*
6394	*Lord James of Douglas*
6395	*Ellen Douglas*
6396	*Maid of Lorn*
6397	*The Lady of the Lake*
6398	*Laird of Balmawhapple*
6399	*Allan-Bane*
6400	*Roderick Dhu*
6401	*James Fitzjames*

9. NER: three-cylinder simples and superheating

The closing years of Wilson Worsdell's time at Gateshead were marked by the production of two large tank engine designs, and the one was as bad as the other was good. The first five of the so-called 'Whitby' tanks were built at Gateshead in 1907 and they were designed to cope with the very heavy gradients of the coastal route between Middlesborough and Scarborough, where, among other exceptional inclines, there is a climb from Fyling Hall to Ravenscar of 3 miles at 1 in 39. These engines were originally built as 4-6-0s with 19-in by 26-in cylinders, 5-ft 1-in coupled wheels, a total heating surface of 1,312 sq ft and a working pressure of 170 psi. They were also equipped at first with small coal bunkers having a capacity of no more than 2¼ tons which proved inadequate and was at a later date increased to 3½ tons when the locomotives were changed to the 4-6-2 wheel arrangement. They were, appropriately, Class 'W', and their numbers ran from 686 to 695 inclusive. They had a monopoly of the passenger service over the coast line northwards from Scarborough for many years, and in 1920 and 1921 I used to see them toiling laboriously up the banks with trains of four or five flat-roofed bogie coaches. Then they were well past their heyday, and a Darlington driver who had sampled the Raven 4-4-4 tanks once remarked that the 'W' Class were 'more like dredgers than engines'!

The other Worsdell tank engine design was of more lasting significance. This was the Class 'X' three-cylinder 4-8-0 introduced in 1909 for heavy shunting duties in the hump yards alongside the river Tees between Thornaby and Middlesbrough and at Hull and elsewhere. The possibilities of a three-cylinder simple engine of high tractive effort for this class of work had been demonstrated on the Great Central Railway at Wath, where the huge Robinson 0-8-4 banking engines had been in use since 1907. Although producing an extremely powerful engine, the North Eastern did not consider it necessary to have so large a boiler, and the Class 'X' 4-8-0s had 67.5 tons of adhesion weight against 77 on the Great Central 0-8-4s. The Class 'X' engines had cylinders 18 in by 26 in, coupled wheels of 4 ft 7 in diameter and a boiler pressure of 175 psi giving the high nominal tractive effort, at 85 per cent working pressure, of 34,080 lb. The moderately-sized boiler provided a total heating surface of 1,310 sq ft and the grate area was 23.65 sq ft. Originally these engines had the variable blastpipe and ash ejector.

The Class 'W' 'Whitby' tanks had springing on the coupled wheels that was compensated throughout to suit the very difficult running conditions of the coastal route, but the coupled wheels of the 'X' Class were fitted with uncompensated plate springs to all

One of the 'Whitby' 4-6-0 tanks built in 1908. They were later altered to the 4-6-2 type to provide additional bunker capacity (British Railways).

Above *North British Railway 4-4-0 No 256* Glen Douglas *was one of the first ten of this celebrated class first built in 1913; ultimately 32 strong, they formed the mainstay of the passenger service on the West Highland line. This engine was restored to the original livery and used for special trains in connection with the Scottish Industries Fair in Glasgow in 1959. It is now preserved in the Glasgow Transport Museum (R.C. Riley).*

Below *One of the very powerful North British 'J37' 0-6-0s No 64623 in British Railways service at Inverkeithing North Junction in May 1966. These engines, first introduced in their superheated form in 1914, eventually mustered 104 strong; they also did much passenger work on the Mallaig extension of the West Highland line (Roy Hobbs).*

Restored GN of S 4-4-0 No 49 Gordon Highlander *at Stranraer on a special working in April 1963. This was one of the last engines of the type introduced in 1899. No 49 was one of seven built in 1920, and equipped with superheaters. The engine is now in the Glasgow Transport Museum (Roy Hobbs).*

Above *Ex-Great Eastern Class 'J20' 0-6-0 No 64690 at Stratford in June 1959. These engines, introduced in 1920, were the most powerful 0-6-0s in Great Britain until the advent of Bulleid's 'Q1' Class on the Southern Railway in 1942 (R.C. Riley).*

Below *'Improved Director' Class 4-4-0 No 506* Butler Henderson, *as preserved. This very successful Great Central express type was chosen by Gresley of the LNER when more 4-4-0s were required for service in Scotland in 1924 (R.C. Riley Collection).*

axles. A most interesting constructional feature of the 'X' Class shunting engines was that the three cylinders and their associated valve chests were contained in a single casting, foreshadowing the 'monobloc' construction used many years later by Sir Nigel Gresley for his 'V1' and 'V3' 2-6-2 tanks and 'V2' heavy mixed traffic 2-6-2 tender engines. In those LNER types, however, not only were the three cylinders and their valve chests cast integrally, but the smokebox saddle was included as well. Wilson Worsdell did not go far as this in his Gateshead-built 'X' Class 4-8-0s, six of which were built in 1909 and another four in 1910; their numbers were 1350 to 1359 inclusive. There is unfortunately a melancholy note about these engines in that they were the last to be built new at Gateshead works. Owing to the limited space available between the main line and the river, extensions to that historic works were not practicable, and as space for extension was available at Darlington it was decided to transfer all new construction from Gateshead.

In the spring of 1953 I was privileged to see something of the work of these historic engines, still engaged on the very duties for which they were first designed 44 years before. At that time, three of them were stationed at Stockton and eight others at Newport, and it was in the Erimus hump marshalling yards alongside the river Tees abreast of Newport shed that I saw several of them hard at work. Normally there were four in continuous humping duties, two at the outward hump and two at the inward (relating to the flow of traffic into and out of

Three-cylinder 4-8-0 humping engine for Erimus Yard (British Railways).

Middlesbrough). Each engine was in continuous service for 24 hours at a stretch, and their bunker capacity of 3 tons of coal carried them 'twice round the clock' except in exceptional circumstances during the winter months when, to help things out, it was usually the practice to top the bunker up after the fire had been made up just before leaving the shed. Even after 24 hours' working they were not in the shed for more than 6 hours; more often than not, in keeping with the very smart shed working practice of the North Eastern Region, they were out again in not more than 2 hours.

The actual work they did on the humps was remarkable in view of the fact that neither of the Erimus yards was mechanised to any extent; all point operation was by hand and the wagons were braked by shunters running alongside. Yet, on a general average, about 2,200 wagons were propelled over each hump in every 24 hours. Individual trains were mostly between 40 and 50 wagons, and the speed of humping was approximately 2 mph. At the outward yard the reception roads were on a curve, and the steady performance of the 4-8-0 tank engines in starting their loads and maintaining the requisite humping speed without any slipping was impressive to see.

When Wilson Worsdell retired at the end of May 1910, he was succeeded by Vincent L. Raven who had been Assistant Chief Mechanical Engineer for 15 years. There were no immediate changes in policy, nor indeed were there any during the remaining years of the life of the North Eastern Railway. Raven himself was one of the foremost protagonists of main-line electrification and but for the onset of war in 1914 developments in that direction would doubtless have

progressed much farther than the conversion to electric traction of the purely mineral Shildon-Newport line. So far as steam locomotives went, Raven seemed content to follow in the footsteps of Wilson Worsdell, developing his pioneer work on three-cylinder propulsion and the introduction of superheating.

The first new design to appear was the Class 'Y' three-cylinder 4-6-2 tank engine. After the success of the Class 'X' humping engines, the three-cylinder principle was now applied to a tank engine designed for the shorter coal-train hauls from the collieries to the ports. Since these were intended for work on the road rather than shunting, the boiler was considerably larger than that of Class 'X', with 1,648 sq ft of heating surface, and the cylinders were smaller, 16½ in against the 18 in of the Class 'X'. With a boiler pressure of 180 psi, the nominal tractive effort was 29,405 lb. They had all the traditional North Eastern external characteristics, including the huge polished safety valve casing, and on their side tanks they carried the large crest as used on the tenders of express passenger engines. Twenty of these fine engines were built.

The adhesion weight was 55.5 tons and with very heavy trains sanding proved an important factor. At slow speeds below 10 mph, engines of this class could sustain drawbar pulls of over 10 tons with efficient sanding, but, on some tests made near Shildon with No 1126, the engine slipped to a standstill on a bad rail when hauling a load of 864 tons up a gradient of

'Y' Class three-cylinder 4-6-2 mineral tank engine (British Railways).

1 in 185 due to a defect in the sanding gear. However, the engine started the same load from rest on a gradient of 1 in 148 and accelerated to 10 mph in just over half a mile. One of the original requirements was an ability to haul loads of 1,000 tons at 20 mph on level track, and this the Class 'Y' engines could accomplish comfortably.

In making provision for new express passenger motive power, the relative merits of the existing large engines were considered, particularly with regard to the dynamometer car trials of 1906, and on almost every count the compound 'Atlantics' stood supreme. I have good reason to believe that matters went so far as the placing of orders for ten more of these engines, but that representations made at the very last minute led to a change and eventually resulted in a three-cylinder simple being chosen instead. In those 1906 dynamometer car tests, the engines concerned were the 'R' class 4-4-0, the 'S1' 4-6-0, the 'V' 'Atlantic' and the four-cylinder compound 'Atlantic'. The table below sets out details of three journeys from Darlington to York, including the maximum and minimum speeds. The Class 'R' engine No 2028 was in average condition and was worked at 40 per cent cut-off throughout from Milepost 43½ to Milepost 7. Steam chest pressure was 150 psi going up to Eryholme, and between 130 and 140 onwards to Thirsk where a slight easing took place. The vigorous start and subsequent running were characteristic of the class with heavy trains. The 'V' Class engine, with a heavier train, made closely similar times to Northallerton but then got away to a fine burst of speed. The report contains no mention of the cut-off used, but steam chest pressure was maintained at between 160 and 170 psi throughout

NER: dynamometer car runs, Darlington-York

Engine No	2028		784		730	
Engine Class	R'		'V'		'4CC'	
Load (tons, empty/full)	343/365		373/395		435/455	
Distance (miles)	Actual time (m s)	Speed (mph)	Actual time (m s)	Speed (mph)	Actual time (m s)	Speed (mph)
0.0 DARLINGTON	0 00	—	0 00	—	0 00	—
1.2 Black Banks Box*	2 35	—	2 50	—	2 37	—
2.6 Croft Spa	4 47	51	5 02	52	4 42	55½
5.2 Eryholme	7 52	50	8 03	51	7 34	54½
10.4 Danby Wiske	13 16	63	13 22	65	12 39	66
14.1 NORTHALLERTON	16 54	60	16 55	60	16 09	60½
17.5 Otterington	20 15	62½	20 09	66	19 25	65
21.9 Thirsk	24 22	65	24 02	69	23 29	67
26.1 Sessay	28 28	60	27 46	67	27 24	63½
28.0 Pilmoor	30 21	61	29 26	69	29 11	64½
30.7 Raskelf	32 56	64	31 44	72	31 39	66½
32.9 Alne	35 01	62	33 34	71	33 38	67
34.4 Tollerton	36 28	61	34 50	71	35 00	65
38.6 Beningbrough	40 37	60	38 26	70	38 58	62
42.5 Poppleton Junction +	44 32	58½	41 51	68	42 48	58
44.1 YORK	46 56	—	44 15	—	45 33	—

*Now abolished   + Later Skelton

from Northallerton to Beningbrough. Over the 21.1 miles from Otterington to Beningbrough, where speed averaged 69.2 mph, the drawbar pull averaged 1.75 tons, within measurable distance of Churchward's famous target of 2 tons at 70 mph.

The run with the compound 'Atlantic' No 730 is of exceptional interest, not only in view of the heavy load but for details of the working. To save a good deal of description I have set out details of steam chest pressures, cut-offs etc in a separate table (below), but I can add that the steaming of the engine during the

Distance (miles)	Cut-offs (per cent)		Boiler pressure (psi)	High pressure steam chest (psi)
	hp	lp		
0.0	75	80	220	160
0.2	53	63	220	160
0.5	53	63	222	220
1.5	53	63	220	200
3.0	53	63	220	190
5.2	53	63	215	155
23.0	59	66	220	135
29.0	63	70	220	125
30.0	53	63	220	150

rapid start up to Eryholme and throughout to York was excellent, with pressure maintained at between 215 and 225 psi until the firing was eased south of Tollerton.

The mileages are the distances from Darlington at which changes were made in either the regulator opening or the cut-off or, in some cases, both. After the very fine start to Croft, speed was held steadily at 54.5 mph on the 1 in 391 to Eryholme, involving a drawbar pull of 2.9 tons and a drawbar horsepower, corrected for gradient, of 1,030. South of Northallerton, due to the lower speed, the drawbar pull was not quite so high as that of No 784 but it was sustained very evenly at 1.7 tons. For a non-superheater 'Atlantic' of 1906 vintage with a load of 455 tons this was a remarkable performance and a triumph for Walter Smith's masterpiece.

If this run was remarkable, how shall I describe the northbound journey set out in the table below? On a trip with the 'Flying Scotsman', the load was made up to no less than 456 tons tare, and No 730 handled it quite comfortably within the schedule time. For comparison there is a run with No 2114, also with the dynamometer car attached, and while this 4-6-0 did quite adequately with a normal 'Flying Scotsman' load of those days, the superiority of the compound 'Atlantic' was absolute.

In starting from York, No 2114 was linked up as follows:

Distance (miles)	Cut-off (per cent)
0.0	70
0.1	62
0.55	55
1.2	45
1.7	40

Thereafter 40 per cent was maintained throughout to Newcastle, except when the regulator was closed while coasting downhill from Relly Mill Junction through Durham. Steam chest pressure was between 140 and 155 psi from York to Eryholme, between 115 and 130 onwards to Tursdale Junction and 125 downhill through the Team Valley. The running times are very similar to those made in ordinary service, and there were no checks at all until after Bensham.

The compound, with her 475 ton load, made a

NER: dynamometer car runs, York-Newcastle

Engine No		2114		730	
Engine Class		'S1'		'4CC'	
Load (tons, empty/full)		365/385		456/475	
Distance (miles)		Actual time (m s)	Speed (mph)	Actual time (m s)	Speeds (mph)
0.0	YORK	0 00	—	0 00	—
1.0	Milepost 1	2 51	—	2 30	—
3.0	Milepost 3	5 53	—	5 11	50
5.5	Beningbrough	9 07	49	8 02	54
9.7	Tollerton	13 57	54	12 39	55¼
11.2	Alne	15 36	55	14 16	56
13.4	Raskelf	18 00	54	16 39	55
16.1	Pilmoor	21 02	53	19 38	53¼
18.0	Sessay	23 11	53	21 46	54
22.2	Thirsk	27 49	57	26 16	58
26.6	Otterington	32 29	56	31 07	52
30.0	NORTHALLERTON	36 16	52	34 54	56
33.7	Danby Wiske	40 13	60½	38 39	61
38.9	Eryholme	45 46	51½	44 00	56½
41.5	Croft Spa	48 33	59½	46 32	64
44.1	DARLINGTON	51 19	52½	49 07	57
49.5	Aycliffe	58 28	43½	55 11	51½
54.3	Bradbury	64 28	53	60 30	57½
			44		50½
57.0	Ferryhill	67 46	51	63 42	54
61.9	Croxdale	73 01	64	68 51	66½
65.1	Relly Mill Junction	76 30	46½	72 11	50
66.1	DURHAM	77 52	41½*	73 38	31*
67.5	Newton Hall Junction	79 49	48	75 44	48
70.0	Plawsworth	82 42	58½	78 31	61
71.9	Chester-le-Street	84 30	68	80 15	72/69
74.7	Birtley	86 57	69	82 39	71½
76.3	Lamesley	88 25	69½	84 00	71½
77.6	Low Fell	89 38	66	85 14	70
78.9	Bensham	91 13	—	86 39	—
		sigs		sigs	
80.1	NEWCASTLE	94 20	—	90 35	—

*Speed restriction

brilliant start out of York, reaching 50 mph in 3 miles from rest, passing Beningbrough in 8 minutes 2 seconds. The engine working details for the first 10 miles were as follows:

Distance (miles)	Cut-offs		Boiler pressure (psi)	Low pressure steam chest (psi)
	hp	lp		
0.0	75	80	220	125
0.5	63	70	217	70
1.7	53	63	210	60
4.0	53	63	190	45
10.0	41	54	200	40

The vigorous start brought the boiler pressure down a little, as well it might! However, by Alne it was back to 200 psi and it was mostly kept around that figure onwards to Ferryhill. Cut-off was advanced to 47 per cent (hp) and 58 per cent (lp) just after Thirsk, and no further changes were made except when the engine was put into full gear while coasting down from Relly Mill Junction to Durham. The drawbar pull was 1.8 tons steadily between Tollerton and Alne, and after the engine was opened out a little at Otterington it was sustained at 2.6 tons up to Northallerton while running at 55 mph. The minimum speed of 56.5 mph at Eryholme was excellent with this enormous train, but no less so was the lowest speed of 51.5 mph on the rise from Darlington to Aycliffe. For the year 1906, this was, taken all round, a magnificent piece of running.

As a result of these trials, the relative capacities of the various express engines were established as follows:

Engine class	Relative capacity	Drawbar pull at 55 mph (tons)
'R'	100	1.3
'S1'	105	1.38
'V'	128	1.66
'4CC'	145	1.88

It will be seen that although the 'V' and the '4CC' exceeded the above figures of drawbar pull considerably at times during the trials, the official figures were fixed somewhat lower to allow, no doubt, for adverse conditions in running. It is a pity, in a way, that the trials were made before the introduction of the 'R1' class 4-4-0 engines, because these, when opened out, had a fine turn of speed and high power output.

When the time came to build the new 'Atlantics' to Raven's requirements, engine-building capacity at Darlington works was fully booked for the year 1911, for, in addition to 14 Class 'Y' 4-6-2 tanks, there was an order for twenty more 'T1' 0-8-0s, and the first of the new mixed traffic 4-6-0s were to follow. So, for the first time since the McDonnell regime, orders for North Eastern express passenger engines were placed with outside contractors. During 1911, the North British Locomotive Company built the first twenty of the new 'Atlantics', ten of Class 'Z' using saturated steam and ten of Class 'Z1' with Schmidt superheaters. There were certain points of similarity in the chassis and wheelbase of the new 'Zs' and the four-cylinder compounds, but these arose no doubt from the basic arrangement of having all three cylinders driving on to the leading coupled axle. The distance from the bogie centre to this leading coupled axle was 10 ft 8 in, against 10 ft 6 in on the

Southbound Royal Train passing Low Fell hauled by non-superheated 'Z' Class 4-4-2 No 709 (R.J. Purves).

Three-cylinder 'Z' Class 4-4-2 No 2196 leaving York in LNER days with a southbound excursion train (M.W. Earley).

compounds. The three cylinders were of 15½ in diameter on the saturated engines and 16½ in on the superheated ones, the stroke in each case being 26 in. The boiler pressures were 180 psi for Class 'Z' and 160 for the superheated 'Z1s'.

The 'Z' Class had boilers similar to those of Class 'V', but the tubes were not quite so closely packed. Instead of 268 tubes, the 'Zs' had 254 as in Class 'R1', so the total heating surface was reduced as compared with Class 'V', a total of 2,340 sq ft as against 2,455. As in the Class 'X' and 'Y' three-cylinder tank engines, the three cylinders and their valve chests were carried in a single steel casting; the piston valves were of 7½ in diameter and the valve details were 1⅜ in lap, 1/16 in lead with a valve travel in full gear of 4 19/32 in for the inside cylinder and 4 15/32 in for the outside. The diameter of the exhaust nozzle was at first 4¾ in, but with a three-cylinder engine having six exhausts per revolution, the capacity for steam flow through the blastpipe is greater so that direct comparison cannot be made with the two-cylinder engines preceding the 'Zs'. In the 'Z1' engines, a high degree of superheat was aimed at, giving a steam temperature of 640'F at a

working pressure of 160 psi. A large heating surface in the superheater was needed, 530 sq ft, but despite this the ordinary tubes were so packed that the total heating surface, including superheater, was actually greater than that of the saturated engines.

The valve motion was designed for a maximum cut-off in full gear of 65 per cent, as compared with 75 per cent in Class 'V1', and the first indicator trials of No 709 showed that the engine could be worked at 15 per cent cut-off (notch 1). It will have been noticed that the steam lap is longer on the 'Zs' than on previous North Eastern engines, and the full gear valve travel of about 4½ in would be equivalent to something like 5½ in with a maximum cut-off of 75 per cent. A good port opening was obtained at 15 per cent and, after certain experiments with the valve setting, a drawbar pull of 1.3 tons at 60 mph was obtained with this setting on the reverser. Some experiments were made with a higher boiler pressure of 200 psi, and on one particular occasion the down 'Flying Scotsman' was specially made up to a tare load of 536 tons for test purposes. This, however, required a coal consumption of 85 lb per mile in working to a booked average speed of 51.2 mph from York to Newcastle. In general, the performance of the engine may be judged from the average coal consumption of about 5½ lb per drawbar horsepower hour. By present standards, this would be considered

Edinburgh-King's Cross express near Lamesley behind superheater three-cylinder 'Z1' Class 4-4-2 No 728 (R.J. Purves).

high, but the working of the 'Zs' was greatly improved by superheating. As a result of the trials of engine No 709, it was considered that the coal consumption of non-superheated 'Zs' would be, in general, slightly above that of the 'V1' Class, which averaged 53 lb per mile. It was expected, however, that the three-cylinder engines would show an overriding advantage in repair costs.

Some 13 years later, it was shown by dynamometer car trials between Newcastle and Edinburgh that the 'Zs' were considerably superior on all counts. This was a comparison of superheated engines of both the two-cylinder and three-cylinder type, 701 versus 729. Sir Nigel Gresley gave very complete details in a paper read before the Institution of Mechanical Engineers in July 1925, and supplemented this by certain details of mileages between repairs and the effects of three-cylinder propulsion on tyre wear. Although they had three sets of Stephenson link motion between the frames, the 'Zs' were popular at sheds with those responsible for

maintenance, as their mechanical simplicity and straightforwardness meant that they were very free from troubles.

NER: 'Atlantic' comparisons

Class Type	'V1' 2-cylinder	'Z'* 3-cylinder
Average coal per dhp hour on 1924 trials (lb)	6.15	4.6
Average water per dhp hour on 1924 trials (lb)	4.52	3.73
Average mileage between repairs (whole class)	58,000	73,000
Average mileage before renewal of coupled wheel tyres	252,256	333,673

*When all three-cylinder engines were superheated, the distinction 'Z1' was dropped.

Down 'Flying Scotsman' on Lucker water troughs behind non-superheater three-cylinder 'Z' Class 4-4-2 No 718 (R.J. Purves).

Left *One of the three-cylinder superheater 'Atlantics' No 729 on the King Edward bridge, Newcastle* (R.J. Purves).

Below *Up afternoon Scotsman, 2.20 pm from Edinburgh, passing King Edward Bridge Junction with 'Z1' Class 4-4-2 No 728* (R.J. Purves).

For superheated engines of 1912 vintage, the above coal consumption figures are high, that of the 'V1' exceptionally so. The original 'Z1' Class, of which No 729 was a member, had the Schmidt superheater, and the Schmidt type of piston valve ring may have been retained. The two engines in the 1924 trials had each run some 18,000 miles since their last general overhaul at the time of the tests, and the results may have been affected by steam leakage past the valve rings.

At the close of 1911, Darlington works completed the first engine of the new superheated mixed traffic Class 'S2' 4-6-0, No 782. This was an enlarged version of the non-superheated Class 'S', with a 5-ft 6-in diameter boiler and the advantage of high degree superheating. The cylinders were 20 in by 26 in and the coupled wheels 6 ft 1 in, but the boiler proportions were the subject of extended tests with engine No 797 in 1912. The boiler pressure was at first only 160 psi. Like H.A. Ivatt on the Great Northern, Vincent Raven adopted superheating as a means of obtaining an engine of equivalent power with a lower boiler pressure than previously. At the same time, he aimed at a high degree of superheat, and the 'S2' engines were originally provided with no less than 545 sq ft of heating surface in the superheater elements. As originally designed, superheat temperatures of about 575°F were obtained in tests with

Right *Newcastle-Liverpool express passing Low Fell behind two-cylinder 'S2' Class 4-6-0 No 797* (R.J. Purves).

engine No 797, but better results were obtained after a number of the small tubes had been blocked up and the steaming of the engine was, if anything, improved. The desired superheat temperature of 640° was obtained by this revised proportioning of the evaporation and superheating surfaces, and some modifications were afterwards made not only to the 'S2' boilers but also to those of the superheater 'Zs'. The grate area on the 'S2s' was 23 sq ft and the weight of the engine in working order was 70.75 tons. The 'S2' Class were intended for true mixed traffic duty, and the rosters included cases of passenger working in one direction and fast freight trains in the other. A favourite round trip from Newcastle was on the 12.30 pm Liverpool express as far as York, returning with the 3.50 pm Scotch goods.

In 1913, the first thirty engines of the new superheated 0-8-0 goods class, 'T2', were completed at Darlington. These engines had 4ft 7¼ in diameter wheels, cylinders of 20 in diameter by 26 in stroke and a boiler pressure of 160 psi. The boiler and firebox dimensions were as follows:

Small tubes	
Number	90
Outside diameter (in)	2
Superheater flues	
Number	24
Outside diameter (in)	5¼
Heating surfaces (sq ft)	
Small tubes	722.2
Superheater flues	504.0
Firebox	144.0
Superheater elements	544.8
Total	1,915.0
Grate area (sq ft)	23

In class 'T2', Raven produced an engine that could be driven 'all out' for indefinite periods at anything up to maximum mineral train speeds. Working at 72 per cent cut-off (in full forward gear) and with full regulator these engines could develop 1,000 drawbar horsepower at 19 mph, and this maximum capacity was ably demonstrated in some dynamometer car trials carried out over the heavily-worked mineral line between Newport and Shildon in 1915, the same year in which electric traction was inaugurated. The results of these trials with engine No 1250 can be summarized as follows:

Tests of 'T2' engine between Erimus and Shildon

Test ref no	A	B	C
Load (tons)	651	700	703
Distance (miles)	16.6	16.6	16.6
Total times (mins)	66.5	73	84.5
Running time (mins)	60	70.25	75
Time with steam on (mins)	55.5	66	70
Average drawbar pull (tons)	6.86	7.64	7.06
Average speed (mph)	16.6	14.2	13.3
Average drawbar horsepower	736	690	602

On certain of these tests, the engine was stopped specially on gradients to observe the restart. On a grade of 1 in 103, in Test A, the engine got away cleanly and sustained a drawbar pull of 10.5 to 11 tons for some 5 minutes while accelerating its load to 12 mph.

From the dynamometer car records, some examples of sustained performance on the rising gradients are tabulated separately:

Engine performance, 'T2' Class

Load (tons)	Speed (mph)	Gradient	Drawbar pull	Drawbar Horse-power	Cut-off (per cent)
651	27	1 in 230	6.3	1020	72
651	28½	1 in 450	5.4	920	68
700	7	1 in 103	11.7	500	72
700	14.3	1 in 147	10	860	72
700	22.3	1 in 235	7.5	1000	72
700	28.5	1 in 450	6	1060	68
703	23.7	1 in 235	6.7	950	68

A further test was made along the same stretch of line with a loaded train of 1,466 tons. The engine regulator was only opened for three very brief periods in restarting from signal stops, otherwise the train was coasting throughout. The average speed between Shildon and Erimus was no more than 10.5 mph since every care had to be taken to avoid this huge load running out of control on the descending gradients.

The runs made with engine No 1250 were to ascertain maximum power. The driver was instructed exactly how to work the engine, and for the most part the going was absolutely 'all out' — regulator full open and full forward gear. However, a test was taken with 'P3' engine No 1225 on which the handling of the engine was left entirely to the driver to work as he would have done in ordinary rather than test conditions. Although the 'P3' had a potential capacity that was some 75 per cent of that a 'T2', the performance was as follows:

Average speed	9.9 mph
Average pull	5.2 tons
Average dhp	315

The average drawbar horsepower of the 'T2', with its crew working under strictly-supervised conditions, showed an output nearly 2½ times greater than that of the 'P3', though the latter engine was apparently working well within its maximum capacity.

A further batch of forty engines of Class 'T2' was built at Darlington in 1917-19 while after the end of the war an order was placed with Armstrong-Whitworth for another fifty of these engines which were delivered between November 1919 and April 1921. Altogether, the 'T2s', or the 'Q6' Class as they became known in LNER days, were extremely successful. They carried on the North Eastern tradition of heavy freight and mineral haulage, not only in 1914-1918 and beyond, but also during a second and more desperate national emergency. As recently as 1951, I heard the 'Q6s' referred to as 'the engines that won the war'! I rode on one of them on a characteristic duty in the early spring of 1953, on a heavy train from Blackhill down the Derwent Valley line into Blaydon. We ran tender first, and from the high stance in the cab one could look out and get an excellent view of the line ahead as we eased our way down the grade.

In 1913, the stud of three-cylinder designs was increased by the new 4-4-4 superheated passenger tank engines, designed to replace the four-coupled passenger tender engines on the longer distance branch trains radiating from Darlington. The 4-4-4 wheel arrangement was chosen to provide equally good riding qualities in both directions of running, and the cab was designed to give good protection to the men when running bunker first. It was originally intended to use them on the Stainmore route, but so far as I know they never worked regularly to Kirkby Stephen or Tebay. The class lettering having reached 'Z', these new engines took the vacant letter 'D', previously used for the Worsdell compound 2-4-0s. The three cylinders were 16½ in by 26 in, the coupled wheels were 5 ft 9 in and the relatively small boiler provided a total heating surface of 1,332 sq ft; the working pressure was the usual 160 psi. The total weight in working order was 84.75 tons, of which 39.75 tons were available for adhesion. They were free-running engines, through rather prone to roll at times. They made short work of the gradients on the coastal route from Saltburn to Whitby, and also did excellent work on the residential trains from Leeds. Twenty of them were built in 1913-14 and another 25 followed in 1920-22. During LNER days they were converted to 4-6-2s (Class 'A8'), and these rebuilds were among the smoothest riding engines I have ever travelled on.

In 1919, two new types of large three-cylinder main-line locomotives were introduced at Darlington Works, the 'T3' heavy mineral 0-8-0 and the 'S3' mixed traffic 4-6-0. Five 'T3' engines were built as a first trial, whereas construction of Class 'S3' proceeded steadily after a first batch of five was com-

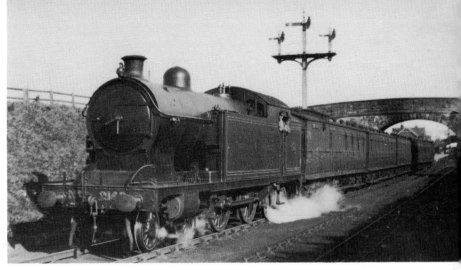

*Three-cylinder Class 'D' 4-4-4 tank engine
No 2143 leaving Whitby West Cliff with
a train for Saltburn (O.S. Nock).*

pleted in December 1919. It was not until 1924 that
further engines of Class 'T3' were built. In dealing
with design and performance, however, I will take
Class 'T3' first. The boiler was somewhat larger than
that of the 'T2' and, as originally built, the heating
surfaces in sq ft were as follows:

102 small flues of 2 in outside diameter	866
4 superheater flues of 5 ¼ in outside diameter	531.9
24 superheater elements	530.1
Firebox	166
Total	2,094
Grate area	27

With three cylinders of 18 ½ in by 26 in, 4-ft 7 ¼ -in
wheels and 180 psi boiler pressure, the nominal
tractive effort at 85 per cent of boiler pressure was
36,963 lb. With the boiler pitched higher than on the
'T2' engines, the 'T3s', with their shorter chimneys,
were much finer-looking and they very soon showed
that their higher tractive effort was no mere academic
figure. Very soon after its construction, the first
engine, No 901, was put through some dynamometer
car trials on the Carlisle road. On one of these trials
westbound the engine took a load of 1,402 tons, and
was master of it at all points on the route. The
gradients, however, were not severe in the westbound direction; the worst stretches were from
Haydon Bridge, where there were lengths of 1 in 221,
279, 243, 291 and 293, with some short easier
stretches intermediately. The train was stopped at
Haydon Bridge and an excellent restart was made on
a gradient of 1 in 298; thereafter the speed averaged
17.35 mph to a test stop at Low Row, 17.9 miles in 62
minutes stop-to-stop. The average drawbar pull
during this run was 8.2 tons, and the engine steamed
freely when working with regulator full open and a
cut-off of 74 per cent. On the return journey, loads of
up to 800 tons were handled successfully on the heavy
grade up to Naworth. For test purposes, a stop was

made on the four mile grade of 1 in 107 east of
Wetherall; with a load of 784 tons, the engine started
easily on the grade, and a drawbar pull of 12.5 tons
was registered in the process. No 901, indeed, pulled
the dynamometer car spring out to its maximum
extent, 16.25 tons, on one special occasion, when, in
addition to the train load, the car brakes were applied
to try and ascertain the maximum pull of which the
engine was capable.

In later years, the 15 engines of this class, which
became LNER 'Q7', were stationed at Tyne Dock
for working the iron ore trains up to Consett, and on
this most interesting duty I was privileged to ride on
No 63465, the old No 624 and one of the batch built
by the LNER after grouping. We had a maximum
load train of 22 hopper wagons and a brake-van,
representing an estimated load of about 690 tons
behind the tender, and, after taking banking
assistance up the sharp grade from Tyne Dock, No
63465 took this heavy train single-headed to Stella
Gill; then, of course, we were banked in rear up the
tremendous climb to Annfield Plain. We were
stopped by a signal at Pontop Crossing to allow two
passenger trains on the Sunderland-Newcastle line to
cross, after which we got away in fine style over the
gradually-rising gradients. We covered the 9 miles
from Pontop Crossing to a stop alongside Milepost
11 ½ in 47 minutes inclusive of 7 minutes stop for
water at Washington and a signal stop just prior to
this junction. Our average running speed was 14
mph, with a maximum of 23 mph on level track. The
engine was in very good trim, steaming freely and
with a good even beat. She was worked in one notch
from full gear, 65 per cent cut-off, and between
Pontop Crossing and Stella Gill the first port of the
regulator sufficed, except for a short spell on the 1 in
135-104 gradient near Harraton.

It was on restarting from Pelaw Junction with
another 'Q7' No 63471, in rear that the really
thrilling part of the journey began. From this point

up to Annfield East, the ruling gradient is 1 in 50; there are short stretches of 1 in 35 and 1 in 42, and for 35 minutes we blazed away with the main regulator practically full open and the cut-off at 65 per cent. Against this hard slogging the boiler steamed magnificently. Pressure was never below 160 psi and for the most part it was above 170 and sometimes blowing off. We maintained a full glass of water and, indeed , it seemed as though the engine could have sustained the effort indefinitely. The mileposts on this line relate to a zero at Ouston Junction on the Team Valley line, and between Mileposts 1 and 7¼ we averaged 11.7 mph on these terrific gradients. There was one especially thrilling piece on the climb; we had been pounding up the 1 in 52 above Beamish station at 9 to 10 mph when we came to a pronounced easing of the gradient for nearly half a mile at West Stanley. But there was no easing of the engines — they were allowed to charge away, 'flat out', to nearly 30 mph and the roar of the three-cylinder exhaust was indescribable. There was good reason for such tactics, for a stretch of 1 in 35 followed and we climbed it without falling below 14 mph; it was also at this precise moment that the engine blew off! But by now Annfield was in sight, the worst of the climbing would soon be at an end and the bank engine would drop off. Over the easier gradients onwards to Leadgate we averaged 18 mph and finally came to a stand at Carr House East Box just short of

Consett station in 51.5 minutes from South Pelaw Junction, 11.3 miles.

The 'S3' engines had the same boiler, cylinders and motion as the Class 'T3' but they were 4-6-0s with 5 ft 8 in coupled wheels and a nominal tractive effort of 30,032 lb. The weight of the engine alone, in working order, was 77.75 tons, against the 72.5 tons of Class 'T3'. But these new 4-6-0s constituted another thoroughly successful design, in which all the earlier North Eastern characteristics were perpetuated — Stephenson link motion, three sets of valve gear and outside admission. A high degree of superheat was obtained, and Raven used a higher boiler pressure than with his earlier superheated engines. Seventy engines of Class 'S3' were built at Darlington, as follows:

Year	1919	1920	1921	1922	1923	1924
Number built	1	21	13	5	28	2

As to their work on the road, I was fortunate enough to experience some of it in various categories of service, in express passenger work on the level lines west of Hull and working 750-ton unbraked through goods trains between York and Mexborough Yard. I found their work equally impressive on both.

Above left *Three-cylinder 0-8-0 Class 'T3' (LNER Class 'Q7')
leaving Tyne Dock with a load of iron or for Consett* (S.E. Teasdale).

*Three-cylinder Class 'S3' (LNER Class 'B16') 4-6-0 mixed traffic
engines.* **Above** *At Tweedmouth* (O.S. Nock). **Below** *No 2368
near York South* (M.W. Earley).

10. GCR: their finest years

The opening of Immingham Docks in 1912 was really no more than the high-water mark of a traffic development that the Great Central, and before it the MS & L had been fostering for a long time. Trade across the North Sea with Scandinavia, the Baltic states and, not least, Germany offered a promising reciprocal traffic to the coal of which Great Britain was then a prime exporter. The coalfields of South Yorkshire had been tapped at many of their most prolific sources by the Great Central, and the vast concentration yard with its mechanized shunting facilities at Wath-on-Dearne was well equipped to organize distribution to numerous points on the system. Before Immingham was opened, however, the Great Central locomotive department had been well aware that the building programme of the early 1900s had given them enough and to spare of first line express passenger engines for working the main-line traffic south of Sheffield. Moreover, passenger traffic was not paying its way and no new express locomotives were programmed for the years 1910 and 1911. Nevertheless, there was plenty of activity in the Drawing Office at Gorton Works. In 1909 one of the the 'Pom-pom' 0-6-0 goods engines had been rebuilt with a Schmidt superheater and Schmidt's own design of piston valves. The result was so successful that no new main-line engines were built to use saturated steam after the completion of the 1910 freight locomotive programme consisting of 18 more

0-8-0s and nine more non-superheated 'Pom-poms'.

The November 1910 issue of *The Locomotive Magazine,* published line drawings with detailed dimensional particulars of two new locomotives then under construction at Gorton, and both were fitted with Schmidt superheaters. The first was a powerful 4-6-2 tank engine designed to haul the new five-coach trains for the London outer-suburban services. These were very heavy, most palatial vehicles weighing 167 tons tare for the five, an astonishing contrast to other contemporary carriages provided for commuters! The first of the new engines came out in 1911 and was one of a batch of ten turned out between March and December of that year. They were designed for rapid acceleration in getting away from stops on the steeply-graded country lines through the Chiltern Hills. They had 20-in by 26-in cylinders, coupled wheels of 5ft 7 in but relatively small boilers, because the calls for continuous steaming were few. The boiler was actually that of the first Robinson express passenger 4-4-0, though fitted with an 18-element Schmidt superheater. The total heating surface was 1,435 sq ft and the grate area was 21 sq ft. The boiler was designed for the pressure of 180 psi as on the 4-4-0s, but, as with so many early applications of superheating in Great Britain, it was felt that a lower pressure of steam in the boiler, in keeping with larger cylinders, resulted in an increased life of the copper firebox. On these

One of the first batch of GCR superheated 4-6-2 tank engines built in 1911, as repainted in LNER passenger colours and fitted with a side-windowed cab (P. Ransome-Wallis).

first Great Central superheater engines the pressure was reduced to 165 psi. Their normal length of run was from Marylebone to Aylesbury or Princes Risborough, but at their introduction it was stated that there was an intention to run them as a far as Leicester. In any case, they were fitted with pick-up water scoops and the coal bunker had a capacity of 4 tons.

These tank engines, smartly turned out in the green livery, became immensely popular with the railway 'buffs' in the London area, and the famous model engineers, Bassett-Lowke and Company of Northampton produced a well-designed model in both 1¾-in and 2-in gauge of the first engine of the class, No 165, which earned the enthusiastic commendation of Robinson himself. The model, which was on sale for the autumn of 1912, was marketed for either clockwork or electric traction.

It has been claimed that these engines were the first-ever British 4-6-2 tank engine, but priority in this respect had already been established at Crewe by Bowen Cooke's design, the first two of which were completed in December 1910 and which had closely similar leading dimensions. Robinson's Great Central 4-6-2s, despite having coupled wheels of no larger than 5 ft 7 in diameter, were free-running engines. I shall always remember a short journey I made one Sunday evening at the end of a country walk in Metroland. I was pleased that there was a convenient Great Central train from Harrow instead of a Metropolitan electric, and 4-6-2 tank No 169, the fifth of the class to be built, gave us a spritely run into Marylebone with the usual five-coach train weighing about 180 tons with passengers. We got away smartly on the steep initial descent from Harrow and then ran at 65 mph on the level from Preston Road to Neasden. The sharp rise to Kilburn was taken in our stride and we passed Canfield Place at the entrance to the concluding tunnels in 8.75 minutes for the 7.3 miles from Harrow. We stopped in Marylebone in a few seconds under 12 minutes for the run of 9.2 miles.

The second of the new engine designs published in *The Locomotive Magazine* of 1910 was the celebrated '8K' Class 2-8-0, although the first engine built was not completed at Gorton until September 1911. This famous design was a logical development of the 0-8-0 mineral engine first introduced in 1902 and continued to the same design until 1910. The new engines had the same boiler as that of the 'Atlantics', with the same length of barrel as that of the 0-8-0s but with a 5-ft outside diameter as against 4 ft 9½ in. The 2-8-0s had exactly the same fixed wheelbase as that of the 0-8-0s with the same wheels and motion, but the cylinders were 21 in by 26 in, with inside admission 10-in diameter piston valves placed between the

frames and actuated by the ordinary link motion. The steam chests of the two cylinders were bolted together on the centre line of the locomotive, forming a very robust frame stay. Because of the use of the larger boiler, the weights on the coupled wheels of the 2-8-0 were 16.5 tons on each axle, compared to a total of 61.25 tons on the 0-8-0. On the 2-8-0, the pony truck carried a weight of 6.5 tons. The boiler proportions were firebox heating surface 153 sq ft, tube heating surface including superheater 1,538 sq ft, a total of 1,691 sq ft. The grate area was 26 sq ft, and the superheater was of the Schmidt type with 18 elements. Because of subsequent modifications and the substitution of the Robinson for the Schmidt superheater, the boiler proportions as published in the LNER records became thus:

Heating surfaces (sq ft)	
Large and small tubes	1,349
Firebox	154
Total (evaporative)	1,503
Superheater	242
Combined heating surface	1,745
Grate area (sq ft)	26.24

As in the case of the 4-6-2 tank, the boiler was designed for a pressure of 180 psi but was worked at first at 160, although in LNER days they were always worked at 180 psi.

After the building of the first of these engines, No 966, in September 1911, construction proceeded rapidly at Gorton until the autumn of the following year, by which time the GCR works had completed thirty of the class. In the meantime, such was the need for additional freight engines that orders had been given to Kitson's of Leeds for twenty more and to the North British Locomotive Company for another fifty. And as if this was not enough, no sooner were the last of the contractor-built engines delivered than Gorton works was put to work on another ten of them. Indeed, by June 1914 the combined tally of these excellent engines, both from Gorton and the contractors, was no less than 125, and the locomotive situation on the Great Central Railway generally may be summarized by the fact that, while those 125 2-8-0s were being added to the stock, only 32 other additions were made, half of which were the 4-6-2 London suburban tank engines. Furthermore, while the Great Western had been the first British railway to introduce the 2-8-0 type for heavy freight work and the London and North Western had followed by converting some of the Webb four-cylinder 0-8-0 compounds to 2-8-0 compounds, at midsummer 1914 the GW and LNW totals of the type were no more than 56 and 36 respectively, against the Great Central's 125.

Left *One of the numerous Robinson 2-8-0s seen here on GN line heavy freight duties near Hadley Wood after the grouping* (O.S. Nock).

Left *On the Woodhead route: a 2-8-0 on an up freight train mostly consisting of coal empties* (Author's collection).

Naturally, the main strength of the 2-8-0 stud was massed around the sheds in the Yorkshire coalfield area, although there were detachments as far afield as Immingham, Annersley and, of course, Gorton.

In December 1912 there was built at Gorton Works a great new 4-6-0 express passenger locomotive which was obviously intended to be the flagship of the Great Central fleet, and it was appropriately named *Sir Sam Fay* after the General Manager who had been so signally honoured with a knighthood by King George V at the ceremony of the opening of Immingham Dock in July 1912. Whether so huge an engine was necessary at that particular juncture is really not the point. It was another feature in the publicity campaign that was being waged so

vigorously over every single activity of the company. Four more of those great engines were built at Gorton in January — March 1913, and it was perhaps significant that three of them were finished in the 'goods black' livery and stationed at Immingham for working across country to Manchester and Nottingham. A sixth engine of the class was built at Gorton in December 1913. They were numbered, named and painted thus:

424 *City of Lincoln*		goods black
425 *City of Manchester*		passenger green
426 *City of Chester*		goods black
427 *City of London*		goods black
428 *City of Liverpool*		passenger green

Above *The pioneer inside-cylinder 4-6-0 express passenger engine No 423* Sir Sam Fay, *in 'works grey' with polished chimney top* (British Railways).

Right *The post-war 3.20 pm non-stop to Leicester leaves Marylebone hauled by 4-6-0 No 428* City of Liverpool (The Locomotive Publishing Company).

The precedent created over the introduction of the new 4-6-2 tank and 2-8-0 mineral engines by publishing detailed drawings well in advance of their completion at Gorton was also followed in the case of *Sir Sam Fay*, but in a more spectacular form. In the September issue of *The Locomotive Magazine*, more than three months before the engine was finished, there was published a magnificent sectional shaded drawing, the work of the Gorton Drawing Office. The original, from which the reproduction in the magazine was prepared, was a much larger affair including a schedule of all the parts of the engine to correspond with the numbers on the drawing. That there were more than 225 parts listed in the schedule was evidence of the comprehensive nature of the

drawing, and it was announced that 'copies can be procured from all booksellers, price 1/-!

Sir Sam Fay was a very handsome engine to behold. It carried the largest boiler yet built at Gorton, of 5 ft 6 in diameter and 17 ft 3 in in length, having a heating surface of 1,638.8 sq ft in the small tubes and 581 sq ft in the superheater flues. The superheater elements added another 430 sq ft and the firebox 167 sq ft, making up a combined total heating surface of 2,816.8 sq ft. It is worth noting that on this very large boiler the grate area was no more than 26 sq ft, the same size as that of the 'Atlantics'. The cylinders, 21½ in by 26 in, were the largest then fitted to a British locomotive, though they would soon be eclipsed by the 22 in used on Lawson Billinton's

'Baltic' tank engines on the Brighton railway.

Robinson's new 4-6-0 had plenty of power potential, though his next express passenger design caused further comment on the inadequacy, or otherwise, of the firebox of the *Sir Sam Fay*. The crack express trains of the Great Central at that time rarely loaded to more than 200 tons, and to maintain average speeds of around 60 mph over an undulating road did not required the sustained output of a boiler having a total heating surface of 2,816.8 sq ft, though such a boiler provided a reservoir of steam supply that was invaluable to meet intermittent demands such as those which would be needed on the heavy gradients of the northern sections of the line. It seems, therefore, that in designing a super-flagship Robinson had in mind *not* the London Extension but the old Manchester, Sheffield and Lincolnshire terrain where the loads were heavier. I have never seen a pre-war photograph of a 'Sir Sam Fay' class working anywhere south of Nottingham although the experts like F.E. Mackay were busy enough with their cameras on the line.

After the first five of the 'Sir Sam Fays', Gorton got to work on their 1913 batch of 2-8-0s, though after the first few a brief pause was made to turn out another 4-6-0 prototype in June, the giant 5-ft 7-in mixed traffic engine No 4, named *Glenalmond* after the Chairman's Scottish residence. This engine was in every way an exact 5 ft 7 in equivalent of *Sir Sam Fay*, though it was not until July 1914 that the class was multiplied. Before then, however, Bassett-Lowke stepped into the picture again with a fine scale clockwork model of *Sir Sam Fay* in gauges 1 and 2 which was ready for the Christmas trade of 1913.

The 'Sir Sam Fay' class was the first to be fitted with the Robinson superheater. When superheating was first applied to British locomotives, the Schmidt apparatus which had been well developed in Germany was generally adopted, except on the Great Western. On the Great Central, however, after his first experiences with it Robinson became aware of certain disadvantages from its use, quite apart from the financial one of paying royalties to a German firm. Furthermore, Schmidt had also developed a number of associated patents, particularly of his own design of piston valves, which were expected to be used in addition to the superheater.

While the Robinson apparatus at first glance looked very much like the Schmidt, in detail it incorporated a number of important differences, enough to establish patent rights of their own and the setting up of a manufacturing company to market the apparatus to other railways. The main feature of the Robinson superheater was that there were no flanged or other special joints for connecting the elements or superheating pipes to the header. The components were easily accessible for examination and renewal, and the superheater tubes could be readily disconnected from the header and re-expanded into it without damage. This feature prompted the Locomotive Superheater Company, which marketed the apparatus, to advertise it as 'A sound Running Shed Job' as distinct from its German rival. It was rather amusing that soon after publicity got under way advertising the Robinson superheater as a commercial proposition, *The Locomotive Magazine* contained an unsigned article clearly inspired by the rival interests entitled 'Superheater Repairs in the running shed' describing the rather complicated procedure necessary to detach the tubes from the header, from which the reader would quickly form the opinion that the Schmidt was definitely *not* a running shed job! Neither was the Robinson, in the opinion of Great Western men after the First World War when they had to take over some of the Great Central 2-8-0s which had been contractor-built for the War Office — they preferred their own Swindon type.

While *Sir Sam Fay* might have been the flagship of the GCR fleet in 1913, Robinson had other ideas as to his principal express passenger motive power, and it is sometimes thought that the spectacular success of the 'George the Fifth' class on the London and North Western Railway influenced him toward reverting to the 4-4-0 type, superheated, for the London Extension fast trains. Although a start had been made with superheating the 'Atlantics', the LNWR experience suggested that a soundly designed 4-4-0 might do the job more economically. So in the summer of 1913 came the first of the celebrated 'Director' Class 4-4-0s, on which the name of the Chairman of the Company, previously rendered in something of an attenuated form on one of the earlier Robinson 4-4-0s, was displayed in full, *Sir Alexander Henderson* (No 429). It had 20-in by 26-in cylinders and, as on the 'Atlantics' and the 'Fays', 6-ft 9-in coupled wheels, but while it also had 26 sq ft of grate area the boiler barrel was necessarily much shorter. The heating surfaces were tubes 1,502 sq ft, firebox 157 sq ft, and superheater 304 sq ft, making a total of 1,963 sq ft. Curiously enough, in not one of the published descriptions of these engines was mention made of the working pressure of the boiler. Robinson had used 160 psi on his first superheater engines while designing the boilers to take 180 if needed later. With the 'Directors' it seems that the issue had been left in doubt at the start. The engines were named as follows:

429 *Sir Alexander Henderson*
430 *Purdon Viccars*
431 *Edwin A Beazley*
432 *Sir Edward Fraser*

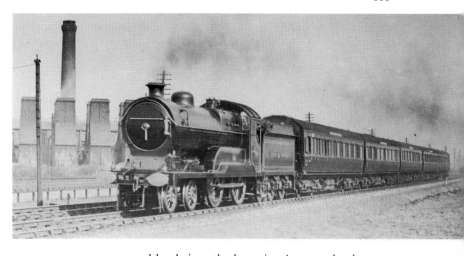

'Director' Class 4-4-0 No 431 Edwin A. Beasley *on the pre-war 3.15 pm down from Marylebone non-stop to Sheffield, passing Neasden and the Metropolitan line power station* (F.E. Mackay).

433 *Walter Burgh Gair*
434 *The Earl of Kerry*
435 *Sir Clement Royds*
436 *Sir Berkeley Sheffield*
437 *Charles Stuart-Wortley*
438 *Worsley-Taylor*

The new engines quickly made their mark in the very fastest express service between Marylebone and Sheffield; more than that, they were allocated to through workings between Marylebone and Manchester, a duty not previously worked by the 'Atlantics'. The most significant difference between the two designs lay in the length of the boiler barrel, 15 ft 0 in on the 'Atlantic' and 12 ft 3 in on the 'Director', though the shorter boiler of the 4-4-0 would tend to make it freer in steaming. When the 'Atlantics' were superheated, in sustained power output there seemed little to choose between them, but it is an important point that the 'Directors' were allocated the through Manchester turns whereas the 'Atlantics' were used on those trains that changed engines at Leicester. On a long run, trouble from the partial sooting up of the tubes would be less pronounced in the shorter boiler barrel of the 'Directors', and on these engines Robinson made his first use of his patent outside admission 10-in diameter piston valves actuated by the ordinary link motion.

The 'Directors' were very free-running engines, though not more so than the 'Atlantics', and during the war years they had more than the usual share of fast express duty meted out to British passenger locomotives. The Great Central, alone among the home railways, maintained an express train service that was the least decelerated of all by pre-war standards, so 'Director' class engines had more than the usual treatment in traffic usage, and heavier than

normal loads into the bargain. As a result, the war was hardly over when Robinson brought out an 'improved' version of the design in December 1919. The changes were a good deal more extensive than many people realized. First of all there were the boiler proportions; the superheater was retained at 24 elements but the tubes were much shorter, providing only 209 sq ft of heating surface in the superheater against 304 sq ft in the first ten engines. The boiler pressure was raised to 180 psi but the most surprising changes were those made to the motion. On the 'Improved Directors' the use of Robinson's patent form of piston valves was abandoned and 8-in piston valves used instead, though with a far longer travel in full gear. The original engines had $4\frac{1}{8}$-in travel and 1-in steam lap while the 'improved' version had $5\frac{3}{4}$-in travel and $1\frac{1}{2}$-in lap. Travelling on the GC line in LNER days, often with loads much heavier than in pre-1914 years, the performance of both varieties of the 'Director' Class engines was always very good, and sometimes outright brillant. South of Leicester, maximum speeds of up to 90 mph were occasionally attained.

Reverting to the locomotive programme in pre-war years, in July 1914 a batch of ten 5-ft 7-in mixed traffic 4-6-0s, the same as the prototype No 4 *Glenalmond*, was built at Gorton, with the same dimensions, other than the coupled wheel diameter, as the 'Sir Sam Fay' Class 4-6-0s. As one director had been omitted from those included in the 4-4-0s built in 1913, the first of these new 4-6-0s, No 439, was named *Sutton Nelthorpe*, but the rest of the class were unnamed at first. In 1915, however, to honour the memory of a great soldier of the Empire who died while visiting Imperial contingents on the Western Front in France, engine No 446 was named *Earl Roberts of Kandahar* and, at the same time, No 279 of the same class was named *Earl Kitchener of Khartoum*.

One of the smaller-wheeled inside cylinder 4-6-0s of 1913 design, No 446 Earl Roberts of Kandahar *(British Railways).*

Later in the war another 4-6-0 prototype was built, No 416, but this hardly proved a prototype at all. It was an outside cylinder engine with 21-in by 26-in cylinders, 5-ft 8-in coupled wheels and the same sized boiler as the 'Sir Sam Fay' Class. It was not until 1921 that any more of this design were built, and then no more than two.

In the New Year's Honours List of 1916, the Chairman of the Great Central Railway, Sir Alexander Henderson, was elevated to the peerage, and took the title of Lord Faringdon from the Berkshire village near to which was one of his country homes. The 'Director' Class engine which had borne his name hitherto was, for a time, unchanged in title, then, at the end of 1917, Gorton Works sprang a surprise upon the locomotive world. In the middle of a war such as Great Britain was then waging it would have been unlikely in any case that the kind of advanced publicity indulged in over the first 2-8-0, No 966, and *Sir Sam Fay* would have been repeated for the further new express passenger design contemplated in the Drawing Office at Gorton, so in 1917 what proved to be J.G. Robinson's *magnum opus* was designed, built and running its preliminary trials before the first news of it leaked out in the railway press in December. Certain journals, accustomed to the advanced warning usually given of forthcoming engineering projects on the Great Central, displayed a slight feeling of pique at being denied the opportunity of including details of the new engine in their annual review of locomotive developments in January 1918. Such was the début of the four-cylinder 4-6-0 No 1169 *Lord Faringdon*. Consequent upon the naming of this engine, the 'Director' Class

4-4-0 No 429 was renamed *Sir Douglas Haig* after the British Commander-in-Chief on the Western Front.

In utilizing the same large boiler barrel as the 'Sir Sam Fay' Class two-cylinder 4-6-0, it is interesting to see the differences that had been made as a result of four years experience of working. First of all the superheater had been increased to 28 elements, although the heating surface in the elements themselves was reduced from the 430 sq ft of the 'Fay' to 343 sq ft in the 'Faringdon'. This change prefaced the reduction in element heating surface made when the 'Improved Director' Class came out at the end of 1918, where the reduction was to 209 sq ft as compared to the 303 sq ft on the original engines. *Lord Faringdon* had a combined heating surface of 2,383 sq ft and the grate area was, as in all Robinson's largest engines, 26 sq ft. As with *Sir Sam Fay* and the inside cylinder 5 ft 7 in variants of the class, the grate area of the four-cylinder engine came in for some criticism from theorists who compared the high nominal tractive effort of 24,772 lb, at 85 per cent boiler pressure, with that of other large 4-6-0s running in Great Britain at that time, particularly their near neighbours and rivals on the London-Manchester run, the LNWR 'Claughtons'. But there was a great deal of difference between working a train of 420 tons tare at an average speed of 55 mph non-stop over the 158 miles between Euston and Crewe and the intermittent demands of the Great Central main line with rarely as much as 300 tons. In the former case there was every justification for a grate area of 30.5 sq ft, while on the GCR there would be times, with hard Yorkshire coal, when one would be firing mainly to keep the bars covered!

The design of the engine proper was very interesting because it was different from all other four-cylinder types in this country. Dugald Drummond had used a hybrid arrangement of Walschaerts gear

outside and Stephenson inside for his first LSWR 4-6-0s, while Churchward used a unique arrangement of the Walschaerts on his famous 'Star' class on the GWR; then came George Hughes on the Lancashire and Yorkshire with the Joy valve gear, and finally Bowen Cooke with his simple and readily accessible arrangement on the LNWR 'Claughton' Class. Robinson retained the use of the Stephenson link motion inside, with the outside valves actuated by rocking shafts. The inside cylinders were cast in one piece with a common central steam chest, while those outside were fed and exhausted independently. Since the adjacent cranks, outside and inside, were arranged at 180° to each other, the valves of each pair moved in unison and were driven by the two upper arms of a three armed rocking shaft, the lower of which was operated by a set of ordinary Stephenson link motion. Two sets of the latter, therefore, worked all four piston valves. The cylinders were set in one line, with the inside pair driving the leading pair of coupled wheels. In order that the outside connecting rods should not be of excessive length, the piston rods were extended and the slide bars were secured not to the cylinders but to massive cast steel brackets bolted to the frames. The cylinders were 16 in by 26 in.

Five more four-cylinder 4-6-0s were added to the stock in 1920, a little curious in their numbering and in a prominent feature of their detailed design. Two of them, Nos 1164 and 1166, were named after the great war leaders *Earl Beatty* and *Earl Haig*, and were exactly similar to the prototype, *Lord Faringdon*. Then, following the example of the London and North Western Railway a year earlier, GCR engine No 1165 was designated as a mobile war memorial; it was named *Valour* and had its name-plates extended by way of memorial plaques. This engine also differed from the three earlier members of the class in having a side-windowed cab in the style of the North

No 1166 Earl Haig *of Robinson's great four-cylinder 4-6-0 of the 'Lord Faringdon' Class, first introduced in 1917 (the late W.J. Reynolds).*

Eastern Railway. This style was adopted on the remaining two four-cylinder express passenger 4-6-0s, Nos 1167 *Lloyd George* and 1168 *Lord Stuart of Wortley*. The name of the former was afterwards removed for political reasons. The retention of the older style cab on the 4-6-0 engines 1164 and 1166 was a little strange because the side-windowed type had already been adopted on the first batch of 'Improved Directors' which had preceded the construction of the 1920 series of four-cylinder 4-6-0s. The latter engines, all stationed at Gorton, worked regularly at Marylebone on the 2.15 pm up from Manchester London Road and returned on the 3.20 pm down on the following day. In the early 1920s, when the trains were accelerated to pre-war timings, the loads were generally light, rarely more than 230 tons, and one sometimes saw one of the 'Sir Sam Fays' on the job.

I was travelling to Manchester just before Easter one year, however, and had the good fortune to catch an exceptional load, exceptional that is for the Great Central line, of all but 300 tons, and engine No 1164 *Earl Beatty* with ace-driver Chapman of Gorton shed. It was an opportunity to see what these powerful engines could really do with a reasonably big load, though I doubt if it would have been thought much of a train by North Western standards, especially when hauled by a four-cylinder 4-6-0. The big GCR engine did well up the banks, but did not run so hard as one usually expected from the 'Directors' downhill. Nevertheless, traffic was heavy on the GC line that Easter and a relief train was running in front of us. After Woodford, our driver was expecting delays

and justifiably eased up; sure enough, we were blocked in the approach to Leicester. In later years I had some far finer runs with 'Director' Class engines and loads almost as large, albeit on locomotive rosters that did not involve working further than the 103 miles between Marylebone and Leicester.

Concluding the passenger locomotive story of the last years of the Great Central Railway, I append the names given to the eleven engines of the 'Improved Director' Class, and those of the original class that were subsequently renamed:

Built 1919-20	Built 1922
506 *Butler-Henderson*	501 *Mons*
507 *Gerard Powys Dewhurst*	502 *Zeebrugge*
508 *Prince of Wales*	503 *Somme*
509 *Prince Albert*	504 *Jutland*
510 *Princess Mary*	505 *Ypres*
	511 *Marne*

In 1920, engine No 429 was renamed for the second time to become *Prince Henry*, and engine No 437 was renamed *Prince George*.

In the last years of the Great Central, two new freight locomotive classes were introduced. The first, in 1918, was a larger-boilered edition of the standard 2-8-0, using the 5-ft 6-in diameter boiler of the 'Sir Sam Fay' Class but having a 28-element superheater and a working pressure of 200 psi. The element heating surface was reduced still further from that of *Lord Faringdon*, being only 308 sq ft as against the 343 sq ft of *Faringdon* and the 430 sq ft in the same boiler barrel of *Sir Sam Fay*. Nineteen of these enlarged 2-8-0s were built between 1918 and 1921, but one can gather they were not entirely a success in that at least two of them, even before grouping, were rebuilt with the standard boilers of the very successful ordinary 2-8-0s. Mention must be made of Robinson's experiments with pulverized fuel, carried out on one or two engines of the 2-8-0 type and one of the inside-cylindered 5 ft 7 in 4-6-0s of the 'Glenalmond' Class. The experiments were long sustained and were, in-deed, continued for more than a year after grouping, but the cost of preparing the fuel as well as the difficulty of storage outweighed the savings that resulted from using a lower grade of coal.

Robinson's last locomotive design was a mixed traffic version of the 'Faringdon' express passenger 4-6-0 which had the same sized boiler, cylinders and motion and 5-ft 8-in coupled wheels. The first three were built at Gorton in May-July 1921, followed by a batch of ten produced by the Vulcan Foundry during which time two more were produced at Gorton. In 1922, the GCR works turned out eight more, while the final batch was five from the neighbouring works of Beyer, Peacock and Company, who apparently built the engines for £1500 a piece less than the Vulcan Foundry had charged for the preceding lot. These mixed traffic 4-6-0s did a lot of hard work all over the system, in heavy fast goods haulage and a modicum of passenger work as well. They gained a reputation for being somewhat heavy coal burners, but I like to remember Bulleid's words when any large locomotive was stigmatized for burning a lot of coal; he said that it merely meant that it was doing a lot of work! Such could be also said for Robinson's 5-ft 8-in four-cylinder 4-6-0s.

This account of the 22 years of Robinson's reign at Gorton cannot be ended without mention of two particular honours that were conferred upon him. When the London and North Eastern Railway was formed, and Lord Faringdon became Deputy Chairman of the new Board, he made a strong recommendation that Robinson should be Chief Mechanical Engineer of the railway. This was readily accepted by the directors who would be responsible for engineering matters, and in due course Robinson was asked to meet William Whitelaw, the new Chairman, and Lord Faringdon. Even before this, the 'grape-vine' had been operating along the corridors of power at Kings Cross and Marylebone, and 'J.G.' had a pretty clear idea of what was in the wind before he was summoned to meet the Chairman. Although

there was then no fixed age at which senior executives were supposed to retire and although he was still in good health, he felt that the job should go to a younger man. Robinson was turned 65 years of age in January 1923, so he declined the offer to live a further 20 years in a happy retirement.

The further honour that came to him, indirectly this time, was that his standard 2-8-0 goods engine was chosen by the War Office to provide a Railway Operating Division standard and multiplied to the extent that no fewer than 521 engines were built by various contractors for service overseas. They were also used after the war on various of the home railways. To meet a temporary shortfall in locomotive building, the London and North Western Railway, for example, arranged to take over from the Government no fewer than 100 of these engines while wartime arrears in the production of standard Crewe designs, 0-8-0 goods, 'Prince of Wales' 4-6-0s and 'Claughtons', were being made good. This loan of GC 2-8-0s was repaid towards the end of 1921. I have also seen photographs of these engines in service on the Caledonian Railway, lettered CR on the tender, and on the South Eastern and Chatham Railway. Of course, many of the ROD engines also went abroad via the Richborough train ferry service.

Apart from the large usage of these engines by the London and North Eastern Railway, who eventually purchased no less than 273 of the former ROD stock, the most interesting use was on the Great Western Railway. That company took fifty of the engines from the Government after the war, but unlike the North Western they did not return them, but instead absorbed them into their capital stock and maintained them to their own standards to the extent that when the Great Western Railway became a part of the nationalized British Railways network in 1948, there were still 47 of them in service, representing a cherished block of heavy freight engines. I always felt it was a pity, however, that the GWR did not acknowledge the existence of those very fine engines in any of their publicity concerning locomotives and other mechanical engineering activ . After all, they got 25 years of hard work out of them! In the first post-war engine book, issued in 1945, their existence could be inferred only from the stock totals of 226 2-8-0 tender engines; it was not until Ian Allan began to issue the 'ABCs' of Great Western locomotives that the veil was lifted and the familiar details of what were called the ROD Class were published on the same page as those of the 'Saints'. They were in good company.

11. Gresley developments on the GNR

An event which eventually proved a milestone in LNER locomotive history was the production of the first GNR three-cylinder 2-8-0 No 461. The suitability of three-cylinder propulsion for heavy freight working had already been demonstrated on the North Eastern Railway, where Wilson Worsdell's Class 'X' 4-8-0 tanks were operating successfully in the Erimus hump yard. Equally, the system would have advantages in such duties as the haulage of the Peterborough-London coal trains, in which a locomotive may have to start heavy loads from rest against a 1 in 200 gradient. A more even crank effort is obtained with a three-cylinder engine, having its cranks set at 120° to each other, than with the two-cylinder arrangement, in which the cranks are at right-angles to each other, and a smoother start is possible; it is not so much a matter of power as the way in which that power is applied to the drawbar.

No 461 carried a boiler identical to that of the 456 Class, but the two 21 in × 28 in cylinders were replaced by three cylinders of 18 in × 26 in, arranged in line and driving the second pair of coupled wheels. The connecting rods were thus much shorter than in the earlier engines, and the cylinders were steeply inclined. At the time of construction, the outstanding feature of No 461 was the valve gear. All previous three-cylinder simple locomotives built in this country — Robinson's Great Central 0-8-4 humping tanks, his one three-cylinder simple 'Atlantic' No 1090 and the various North Eastern types — used three sets of valve gear. By the use of the mechanism illustrated in principle in Figure 1, however, Gresley eliminated one set of valve motion. As applied to No 461, the details were rather different, and are shown in Figure 2. The cross-sectional view of the cylinders and valves shows why it was necessary to place the valve casing for the inside cylinder in a different transverse plane from that of the two outside cylinders; this disposition involved the use of vertical levers in the derived valve motion and made the layout of the gear rather more complicated. Eventually, the arrangement shown in Figure 1 became the standard form of the gear. Another novel feature of this engine also later become standard on all the largest LNER locomotives, the vertical screw reversing gear; the adjustment of cut-off is facilitated by the inclusion of ball-bearings in the screw mounting.

Right *Gresley's layout of valve gear on GNR 2-8-0 No 461.*

Below *Standard Gresley derived valve motion.*

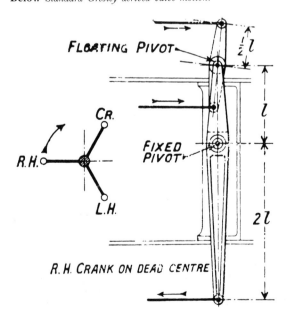

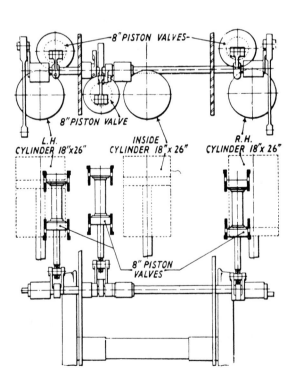

No 461 was put to work on the Peterborough-London coal trains and very soon showed a certain superiority over the '456' Class, particularly in starting. In the winter of 1918, the Technical Editor of *The Railway Gazette*, then Charles S. Lake, spent about 7½ hours on the footplate of engine No 461 while it was working a 1,300-ton 'block' coal train from Peterborough to London, and he wrote very enthusiastically of his experience. He was particularly impressed with the way the engine started from rest in difficult conditions, getting away with its very heavy train in a clean and steady fashion, and working up to speed uniformly without the jerking so noticeable, and often so impossible to avoid, with two-cylinder engines in similar conditions of loading. A cut-off of about 47 per cent and the regulator something less than half open were enough to keep the 1,300-ton trailing load running at an average of 22 mph on one of the easier sections of the line where signals were clear for about 15 miles. Of course, working a heavy mineral train on a line often busy with much faster traffic involved numerous stoppages, and the journey time from Peterborough (New England) to Hornsey (Ferne Park yard) was 6.75 hours for the 74 miles.

Details of the new engine had appeared in the technical press about midsummer, and within a remarkably short time a paper was presented at a meeting of the Northern Branch of the Institution of Locomotive Engineers at Leeds on 'Three Cylinder Locomotives'. The author was Harold Holcroft, normally on the staff of the Chief Mechanical Engineer of the South Eastern and Chatham Railway at Ashford, but at that time seconded for wartime duties to a depot of the Royal Engineers at Purfleet. His paper naturally noted earlier British examples, particularly on the Great Central and North Eastern Railways, but, coming to the most recent instance of the GNR 2-8-0 No 461, he gave a complete exposition of an alternative and much simpler way of achieving the conjugated motion by which only two sets of motion, placed outside, could be linked up to actuate the valves of the inside cylinder. In his younger days as a draughtsman in the locomotive department of the Great Western Railway at Swindon, Holcroft had in his own time designed and made a model of a conjugated valve gear which had been shown to Churchward and, on his instructions, patented in Holcroft's name. However, because of the involvement with four-cylinder express locomotives nothing further was done with it on the GWR.

Gresley was then President of the Institution as well as by then Locomotive Engineer of the GNR and from his headquarters at Doncaster he took a goodly contingent of his staff from the Drawing Office and the Works to hear the paper presented in Leeds. Apparently he was very impressed, so much so indeed that afterwards he invited Holcroft to meet him privately and discuss valve gears in general. Away from the immediate influence of Ashford by reason of his wartime duties, Holcroft saw no objection to his accepting this invitation, but it was another matter when Gresley astonished him by asking him to join his staff at Doncaster with the particular job of designing valve gears! Maunsell, of course, had to be informed, with the result that Holcroft was soon afterwards recalled from Purfleet to the SE & CR locomotive headquarters at Ashford and given the job of designing the valve gear for a three-cylinder version of the 'N' Class 2-6-0. Long before the latter engine took the road, however, Holcroft's paper and the subsequent study and analysis of it at Doncaster had borne some exceedingly rich fruit on the Great Northern Railway.

Soon after the Armistice of 1918, activity at Doncaster caused rumours that a 'super' main-line engine was under construction. Everthing pointed to a 'Prairie' at least, if not a 'Pacific'. Cecil J. Allen, then the well-established author of the regular 'British Locomotive Practice and Performance' feature in *The Railway Magazine*, was travelling every week to Teesside on his inspection for the Great Eastern Railway and was as much in the dark as anyone else outside Gresley's immediate entourage, and it was in a sense of some disappointment, one fancies, that he opened his contribution of May 1920 thus: 'So the new Great Northern main line locomotive turns out to be, not a 4-6-2 'Pacific', nor even a 2-6-2 'Prairie' type engine, but merely an enlarged version of the 'Moguls'!' To the delight of the railway 'buffs' however, this impressive and beautiful engine, No 1000 although designated for mixed traffic was painted in the passenger green livery, and *The Railway Magazine* marked the event no later than its issue of July 1920 by including a fine colour plate by 'F. Moore'.

This remarkable engine created quite a stir at the time by reason of her boiler; up until then, a diameter of 5 ft 6 in had been regarded as the maximum conveniently possible within the British loading gauge, whereas the boiler of the Gresley three-cylinder 'Mogul' was 6 ft in diameter over the smallest ring, and accommodated 217 tubes of 1¾ in outside diameter. Heating surface dimensions were tubes 1,719 sq ft, firebox 182 sq ft and 32-element superheater 407 sq ft. The grate area was 28 sq ft and the working pressure was 180 psi, a slight advance on previous Gresley practice. It was on this class of engine that a change was made from the traditional Ramsbottom type of safety valve to the Ross 'pop' type, which thereafter became a Gresley standard.

Above *The first Gresley three-cylinder 'Mogul' No 1000 painted in GNR passenger engine colours* (British Railways).

Left *Three-cylinder 'Mogul' No 1000 entering King's Cross with an express from Leeds and Bradford* (H. Gordon Tidey).

There were further features of interest at the front end, for not only was the cylinder volume far in excess of that of any eight-wheeled engine then at work on any other British railway, but there was also an alteration in the arrangement of the valve gear. The three cylinders were 18½ in diameter × 26 in stroke, and by inclining the central cylinder at a much steeper angle than the outside ones it was possible to arrange the valves so that the simple hori-

zontal rocking lever mechanism which was subsequently standardized could be used for actuating the piston valve of the inside cylinder. This was found to be a great improvement on the layout of the gear used on the 2-8-0 engine No 461.

Another detail destined to become standard practice on the LNER which made its first appearance on No 1000 was the provision of twin regulator handles, one on each side of the cab; the

Above *A contrast in boilers: the 6 ft diameter boiler of No 1000 alongside that of the Stirling 8 footer No 1* (British Railways).

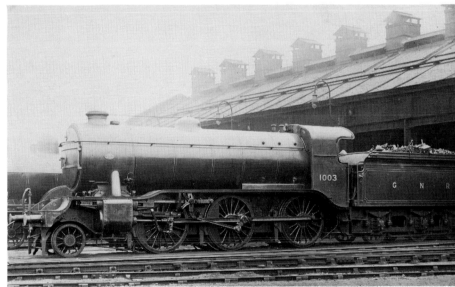

Right *GN-built three-cylinder 2-6-0 No 1003 at King's Cross shed* (the late W.J. Reynolds).

handle on the fireman's side is often of great value when a locomotive is being manoeuvred in a busy yard. The outward appearance of the cab remained faithful to Great Northern traditions, though only a tiny minority of ten in the eventually great regiment of 'K3' Moguls possessed this outward sign of true Doncaster lineage. These original engines, though intended mainly for fast goods working, came into the limelight during the coal strike of 1921, when they tackled express passenger trains loading up to 20 bogie vehicles on the fastest schedules then operating between Kings Cross and Doncaster, and showed themselves capable of 75 mph on such stretches as that from Stoke summit down to Peterborough.

After the grouping, the '1000' Class 'Moguls', only the first ten of which were built by the GNR, were adopted as an LNER standard, and towards the end of 1924 further multiplication of the class began.

A batch of fifty locomotives was turned out from Darlington works differing only in certain details, including the boiler mountings, from the original examples, and with typically North Eastern cabs. Hitherto the '1000s' or 'K3s' as they were classified, had appeared on passenger trains to only a small extent, but they were fast engines, capable of speeds of up to 75 mph, and as more became available they were frequently requisitioned for intermediate workings all over the system. After a week's strenuous work on fitted freight trains, their weekend respite often took the form of a trip with a half-day excursion train. It is a striking commentary on their tractive powers that in pre-war days with the most famous of all the fast goods trains, the 3.35 pm Scotsman, they were rostered to take a maximum of 55 wagons on the 111.75 mile non-stop run from Peterborough to York. The booked average speed was 45 mph and the gross load often rose to 650 tons behind the tender.

I had a fine trip on the footplate of No 2450 on this service in 1937, details of which are given in the accompanying table.

LNER: 6.37 pm Scotch Express Goods, Peterborough-York

Engine   Class 'K3' 2-6-0 No 2450
Load   46 wagons and brake van, 610 tons full

Distance (miles)		Schedule time (m)	Actual time (m s)	Speed (mph)	Regulator	Cut-off (per cent)	Boiler	Pressure (psi) Steam Chest
0.0	PETERBOROUGH (Westwood Yard)	0	0 00 sigs	—	Full	65	160	150
0.7	New England North Box		4 03	—	Full	40	—	—
2.4	Werrington Junction		6 40	42.5	Full	20	180	175
7.7	Tallington		13 26	51.5	Full	20		
11.5	ESSENDINE		18 10	48	Full	25	180	175
15.1	Little Bytham		23 01	43.5	Full	28	180	175
18.9	Milepost 96		28 34	41	Full	28		
20.0	Corby		30 10	44	Full	28	175	170
23.0	Stoke Box		34 30	41	½	20	175	120
28.4	GRANTHAM	40	40 33	65	⅓	15	175	120
—			easy	51	⅓	15	175	120
43.0	NEWARK	58	56 50	48	Full	20	175	170
50.3	Crow Park		65 33	56	Full	20		
54.8	Tuxford		71 52	35.5	Full	20	180	175
			sigs	15	—	25		
56.6	Markham Box		75 53	—	—	20		
			sigs (several)	—	—	—		
61.5	RETFORD	83	84 40	10	Full	22	160	155
66.8	Ranskill		93 14	52	Full	15	175	170
72.4	Milepost 149½		100 28	40.5	¾	15	175	150
76.1	Black Carr Junction		104 57	59.5	2/5	15	180	110
78.9	DONCASTER	104	108 30	46	Full	20	170	165
83.1	Shaftholme Junction		113 39	52	Full	20	177	170
88.9	Balne		120 20	54	Full	20	180	172
95.9	Brayton Junction		128 35	56	Shut	20	—	—
97.3	SELBY	127	130 30	30*	Full	32	—	—
101.4	Riccall		137 46	46	Full	22	175	170
109.1	Chaloners Whin Junction		147 14	51.5	Full	22		
111.8	YORK (Severus Junction)	149	153 25 +					

* Severe service slack   + Net time 147 min

Above *The last of the GN-built '1000' Class 2-6-0s (LNER Class 'K3') No 1009, at King's Cross in 1922 (the late* W.J. Reynolds).

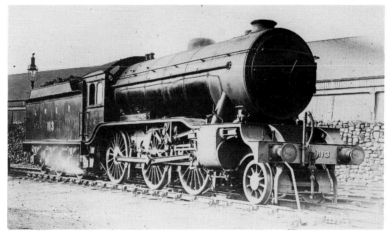

Right *Darlington-built 'K3' Class standard 2-6-0 No 113 built in 1924 (the late* W.J. Reynolds).

Below *A train of fish empties from London to Grimsby near Hadley Wood, hauled by one of the later 'K3' 2-6-0s No 231* (British Railways).

Sometimes, if the arrival from London had been exceptionally early, it was despatched at about 6.15 pm and then turned slow road from Essendine to Stoke to let the 'Silver Jubilee' go by, but on my trip we ran in the normal path. This was fortunate, as the 40 minute timing from Westwood to passing Grantham was one of the most strenuous goods train bookings to be found anywhere in the country. There must have been a strong temptation to drop a little time on this section, for it is succeeded by the much easier one of 43 minutes for the 33.1 miles from Grantham to Retford, but the driver opened out No 2450 to some purpose, made a splendid ascent and kept time.

Full regulator and early cut-off were the order of the day. The gear was linked up quickly to 20 per cent cut-off and the engine left to find her own stride. We topped the fifty mark at Tallington and it was not until we were well beyond Essendine than an advance in cut-off was made, with adjustments of 2 and 3 per cent at a time to a maximum of 28 per cent, and this by no means strenuous working took us over Stoke summit at a minimum speed of 41 mph which was no better than the booking demanded. All the way up, boiler pressure was maintained at 175-177 psi and the steam chest pressure was 170 psi. At Stoke summit the gear was linked up to 15 per cent cut-off, and down the 1 in 200 with no more than 140 psi in the steamchest we accelerated rapidly to 65 mph. North of Grantham the engine was eased and, with steamchest pressure down to 110 psi speed gradually dwindled to 48.5 mph by the time we passed Newark.

From here it was reasonably hard going right on to York. On full regulator and 20 per cent cut-off we picked up in fine style across the level of the Trent Valley, but then unfortunately just as we were getting some time in hand to offset the difficulty of the concluding point-to-point times, there came a string of signal checks culminating in a virtual stop at Retford South. 'Some bit of a passenger train in the way', remarked the driver. In getting off again, No 2450 was linked up to 15 per cent as early as Retford Canal box and we were running at 59.5 mph approaching Black Carr Junction; after easing to 46 through Doncaster we settled down to a hard spell on full regulator and 20 per cent cut-off along the faintly adverse length to Selby. The top speed here was 56 mph, but only one minute of the six lost at Retford was regained, and this was lost again on the tightly-timed last lap of 22 minutes from passing Selby to the stop at Severus Junction, a stiff booking considering that a train like the 1.20 pm Scotsman was allowed 17 minutes into York station, a run 2 to 2½ minutes easier. The slightly adverse nature of the road on this section tells heavily with such a train, and in spite of using 22 per cent cut-off instead of the usual 20 on the

level, we did not get above 50.5 mph. So we were 3½ minutes late on arrival, but our net time, at only 147 minutes, was a fine average of 45.5 mph with such a load.

This run was made with one of the later engines of the class, after left-hand drive had been standardized and the improved valve setting, described in detail in the next chapter, had been adopted. Since the grouping, a total of 183 'K3s' were built, 113 in the Company's own works, and 70 by contractors.

Returning to construction work in the last years of the Great Northern Railway, improvement was urgently needed in the motive power provided on the London suburban service. At the end of 1919, one of the Ivatt 0-6-2 tanks was superheated and what were described as exhaustive experiments were conducted between this engine, No 1598, and one of the largest-boilered two-cylinder 'Moguls', No 1646. The grapevine had it had this this was preliminary to the design of a new 2-6-2 or 2-6-4 tank engine for surburban use. Cecil J. Allen wrote feelingly in 1920: 'From intimate and painful acquaintance with the tortoise-like rate of progression current on the High Barnet branch', at the end of which he lived, 'I wish Mr Gresley all success, and shall welcome the newcomer with open arms when it materializes'. No such exotic development did take place. The superheated 0-6-2 passenger tanks, the first of which was turned out in January 1921, were just a simple and straightforward two-cylinder job, well suited to the pressing needs of the London suburban traffic. What appears to be the exceptionally high-line pitch of their boilers is rather an illusion caused by the severe restrictions of the Metropolitan loading gauge which cut the height of the engines working over the Widened Lines to 12 ft 7 in, and made it necessary to use unusually squat boiler mountings. The leading dimensions of this class were cylinders 19 in diameter by 26 in stroke, coupled wheels of 5 ft 8 in diameter, total heating surface 1,205 sq ft (of which the 17-element superheater contributed 207 sq ft) grate area 19 sq ft and working pressure 170 psi. The weight in working order, 70.25 tons, included 2,000 gallons of water and 4 tons of coal. Such preliminary experience as was necessary had already been obtained by the above mentioned superheating of one of the numerous Ivatt 0-6-2 tanks (LNER Class 'N1') No 1598, and the new locomotives, which were a logical development of Ivatt's design, were drafted to the most arduous suburban duties the moment they were broken in.

Sixty of these engines, then LNER class 'N2', were turned out very rapidly, ten by Doncaster and fifty by the North British Locomotive Co, the original numbers being 1606-1615 (Doncaster) and 1721-1770 (NBL). Further examples, without con-

densing apparatus, were built for suburban service around Glasgow and Edinburgh. They are not only powerful engines for their size but were also speedy. Before the days of the 'Pacifics' they were sometimes requisitioned to pilot main-line expresses out to Potters Bar, while their hill-climbing feats over the tremendous gradients of the High Barnet branch,

Above *One of the general service 'N2' 0-6-2 tank engines; No 2587 was built by Beyer, Peacock in 1925 (Beyer, Peacock & Company).*

Below *Gresley 'N2' superheated 0-6-2 suburban tank engine fitted with condensers for underground working (the late W.J. Reynolds).*

Above *One of the numerous and efficient 'K3' three-cylinder 2-6-0s introduced by Gresley on the GNR in 1920, and subsequently adopted as an LNER standard multiplied to an eventual total of 193 engines. No 61810, one of those built in 1924, is here seen at Norwich in May 1960* (R.C. Riley).

Left *Gresley 'N2' superheated tank engine on down Luton goods near Hatfield* (G.R. Grigs).

Below left *Class 'O2' three-cylinder 2-8-0 No 3490* (the late W.J. Reynolds).

Below *Two ex-GER engines at Norwich in May 1960: Class 'B12/3' rebuilt 4-6-0 and Class 'J15' 0-6-0 No 65452. Both engines survive in preservation on the North Norfolk Railway.* (R.C. Riley).

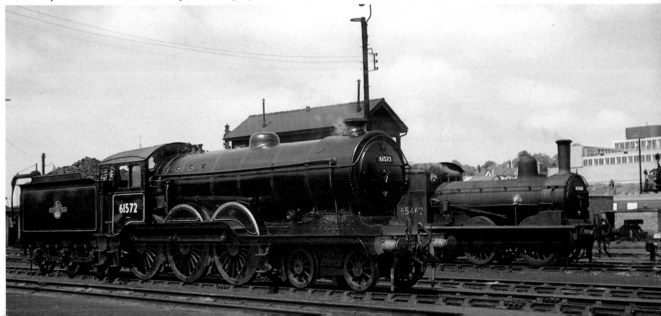

The first of the very powerful North Eastern three-cylinder 0-8-0s of Class 'T3', later LNER Class 'Q7', introduced by Sir Vincent Raven in 1919. Here seen at Consett in March 1963, this engine has now been restored by the North Eastern Locomotive Preservation Group at Grosmont (Roy Hobbs).

Above *Rebuilt 'Claud Hamilton' Class 4-4-0 ex-GER : Class 'D16/3' of the LNER, No 62529 at Cambridge in May 1957* (R.C. Riley).

Below *Two celebrated Gresley engines at King's Cross Top Shed in September 1961, Class 'V2' No 60800* Green Arrow *and the first streamliner Class 'A4' No 60014* Silver Link, *then carrying their BR numbers* (R.C. Riley).

Above *Class 'O2' three-cylinder 2-8-0 No 3485 climbing Potters Bar bank with a train of down coal empties* (James R. Clark).

though a commonplace today, were exceptional when they first came out. Up the 2½ miles at 1 in 59-63 from Finsbury Park, for example, with trains that passed a number of stations, speeds usually rose to 30 mph or so with loads of 160 tons. From the winter of 1921 I frequently travelled from Kings Cross to New Barnet on Saturday afternoons, and I can vouch for the efficiency with which those new tank engines did the job. I was sorry when the grouping came, for their smart green livery was changed to black, albeit attractively lined out.

The first of a new batch of three-cylinder 2-8-0s came out in 1921; they differed from No 461 in having the alteration to the derived valve gear that had proved so satisfactory in the '1000' Class

'Moguls'. No 477 was the first of the new series, later LNER Class '02', in which the principal dimensional changes from No 461 were an increase in boiler pressure from 170 to 180 psi and the enlargement of the cylinders from 18 to 18½ in diameter. The cylinder disposition was almost identical to that of the '1000' Class, the inside cylinder being steeply inclined so that the three steam chests could be arranged in line. This class was originally intended to be the standard heavy freight engine for the LNER, but after ten of them had been built in 1921 and another fifteen added in 1923-24, (built at Doncaster with Great Northern style cabs), the purchase of a large number of ex-ROD 2-8-0s of Great Central design obviated the need for building more of the Gresley three-cylinder engines until 1932; in that year another sixteen were built at Doncaster, with large side-windowed cabs and standard 4,200 gallon tenders.

12. The first 'Pacifics'

The locomotive history of the Great Northern Railway, as an individual concern, closed in spectacular fashion with the completion of the first two 'Pacific' engines, Nos 1470 and 1471. These behemoths fitly concluded a remarkable locomotive lineage turned out from Doncaster works between 1867 and 1922; their superiority over the '251' Class, both in mere size and tractive power, was in just about the same ratio as that of the first Ivatt 'Atlantic', No 990, over the Stirling eight-footers. Yet the trend of development had been so clearly marked in the past that the proportions of the new engines were no surpise. In view of the success of the '251s' it was hardly likely that the Wootten firebox would be abandoned, and nothing less than six coupled wheels would have been adequate to cope with the increasing East Coast loads. The girth of the boiler could be anticipated from the 6 ft boilers fitted to the '1000' Class 'Moguls'. Three-cylinder propulsion, with derived motion for the inside cylinder, was almost a certainty, and the only thing that remained in doubt was the wheel arrangement. A 2-6-2 was actually contemplated at one time; the design of the pony truck used on the 'Moguls' had already proved suitable for high-speed running, but, as the design took shape, a leading bogie was decided upon, and No 1470 *Great Northern* was the result. A story was going the rounds of engineering circles at the time that when Churchward, newly in retirement from his epoch-making career as Chief Mechanical Engineer of the Great Western Railway, heard that Gresley had built a 'Pacific' engine for the GNR he is said to have exclaimed 'Why did that young man build it, when we could have sold him ours!'.

Many problems beset the designer who puts on the road a machine that embodies such bold advances upon previous practice, if he is to produce a thoroughly sound job from the railway point of view;

the country had already witnessed the spectacle of a great engine so limited in her sphere of activity as to be more of a liability than an asset to her owners. The length of the new 'Pacific' was one of the problems in design, for although the Great Northern main line boasts one of the finest alignments in the country, matters are not so favourable to a long engine in the immediate neighbourhood of Kings Cross. By the use of heat-treated nickel-chrome steel having a tensile strength some 50 per cent greater than ordinary mild steel it was possible to make the connecting and coupling rods much lighter than usual, and thus the effect of the unbalanced forces due to the reciprocating mechanism was reduced. The fine riding qualities of the class, which had to be sampled on the footplate to be fully appreciated, were due to the springing arrangement which was arrived at only after trials of several different layouts; uncompensated plate springs are used for all three pairs of coupled wheels.

Hardly had *Great Northern* made its bow and been shown to an admiring public at Kings Cross than the counterblast came from Darlington. Sir Vincent Raven followed the precedent that had been set by J.G. Robinson on the Great Central in 1910 by issuing outline drawings, with many dimensions, of a huge 'Pacific' engine that was under construction at Stooperdale Works, the great plant north of Darlington that was the pride and joy of the North Eastern Railway, even though its large and palatial office was sometimes sarcastically called 'Buckingham Palace'! Raven had been one of the foremost protagonists of his day of main-line electrification; indeed, shortly after the war the Board of the North Eastern Railway announced their decision to electrify the main line between York and Newcastle. The Board's decision was made while the NER was still independent, and moreover one of the richest

Right *The second 'Pacific', No 1471* Sir Frederick Banbury, *in GNR colours on the 1.30 pm Leeds and Bradford express near Hadley Wood* (O.S. Nock).

Below left *The first Gresley 'Pacific', GNR No 1470 built at Doncaster in 1922* (British Railways).

and prosperous railways in the country. It was, however, another matter with the grouping in prospect, and with its forthcoming alliance with others whose finances were the very opposite. Nevertheless Raven built a prototype main-line electric locomotive and had it in service on the Shildon-Newport electrified mineral line in 1922. It was announced that he was going to retire at the end of the year, though being retained as a consultant by the LNER, but it seems he could not let Gresley have the kudos of having the only 'Pacific' on the East Coast Route, so construction was hurried forward to allow the first of the new engines to be finished in the old NER colours. The respective dimensions of the Gresley and Raven 'Pacifics' were as follows:

	GNR	NER
Cylinders (in)	20 × 26 (3)	19 × 26 (3)
Coupled wheels (ft/in)	6 8½	6 8
Bogie wheels (ft/in)	3 2	3 1¼
Trailing wheels (ft/in)	3 8	3 9¼
Steam pressure (psi)	180	200
Heating surfaces (sq ft)		
Tubes	2,715	2,211.2
Firebox	215	211
Superheater	525	695.6
Total	3,455	3,118
Grate area (sq ft)	41.25	41
Total engine weight (tons)	92.45	97
Total engine and tender weight (tons)	148.75	143.1
Tractive effort at 85 per cent boiler pressure (lb)	29,835	29,918

The unusually large fire grates of both engines caused some shaking of heads by people who thought the fireman's burden was becoming overwhelming, but in fact the Gresley 'Pacifics' were not difficult to fire; the accurate wristwork needed to shoot the coal into the back corners of the grate called for knack rather than brute force. The new engines were not long in showing what they could do. On Sunday September 3 1922, a special test run was made with No 1471, then unnamed, on which a train of 20 vehicles weighing 610 tons behind the tender was worked over the 105.5 miles from Kings Cross to Grantham in 122 minutes. The highlights of this performance were a time of 23 minutes from Hitchin to Huntingdon at an averge speed of 70 mph and a fine climb to Stoke with an average speed of 45 mph up the final 3 miles from Corby.

In ordinary service, the 'Pacifics' were not called upon to perform anything like such strenuous work as this. During the late autumn and winter of 1922 they were usually on the 4 pm and 5.40 pm trains from Kings Cross. The former, in deference to its traditionally heavy load, was then allowed no less than 101 minutes to Peterborough, but the 5.40 pm, with an average load of 500 tons and 87 minutes allowed for the Kings Cross-Peterborough run, was a stiff proposition for those days. The results obtained from Nos 1470 and 1471 were sufficiently good for a further ten 'Pacifics' to be ordered before the Great Northern became merged into the LNER group, but the first of the new series — the famous No 4472 — was not turned out of Doncaster works until January 1923.

By that time, the first of the Raven 'Pacifics' had been completed. Although the overall proportions

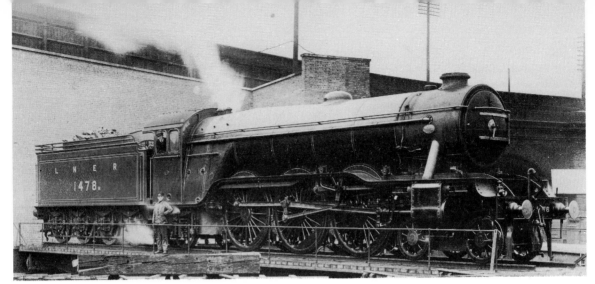

One of the first production batch of Doncaster 'Pacifics', No 1478, later named Hermit *(the late W.J. Reynolds).*

were not very different from the Gresley, the machinery was totally dissimilar. Apart from the outward 'look' of having all three cylinders driving on the leading pair of coupled wheels as on the 'Z' Class three-cylinder 'Atlantics' of the NER, there was the valve gear — three independent sets of Stephenson link motion. Also, whereas the Gresley engine had cylinders of 20 in diameter associated with piston valves of 8 in diameters, the Raven engine had 19 in cylinders and 8¾ in piston and valves working with a boiler pressure of 200 psi. In the early 1920s when I had been first admitted to the Graduates Section of the Institution of Mechanical Engineers, I recall a mild confrontation on the subject of the Stephenson link motion. My great friend, the late Roland C. Bond, was reading a paper on the Walschaerts before the Graduates Section and

at that time we youngsters were always asked if there was a particular Member of Council we would like to take the chair, if he was available and willing. On one such occasion Gresley himself was kind enough to officiate when I was reading a paper on certain features of hump marshalling yard equipment. On this earlier occasion, Bond had Sir Vincent Raven in the Chair, and after complimenting him on his paper

The first North Eastern 'Pacific', No 2400, then unnamed, with the 5.40 pm down on comparative trials between King's Cross and Doncaster in July 1923 (the late W.J. Reynolds).

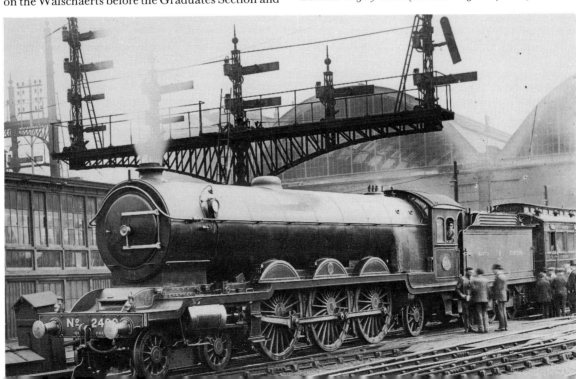

Ex-NER 'Pacific' No 2402 City of York (Real Photographs).

and congratulating Sir Henry Fowler on having such a promising young engineer on his staff at Derby, Raven rather 'tore into' the Walschaerts gear, and as good as said he would never touch it!

My first personal experience of the running of the Gresley 'Pacifics' was in June 1923 when I travelled from Kings Cross to Doncaster behind No 1473. For quite a trivial reason I decided, to my lasting regret, to go by the 4 pm train instead of by the 5.40 pm which had a faster schedule; that very day the 5.40 pm was worked by the first of the North Eastern 'Pacifics' in one of a series of trials in competition with the Gresley 'Pacifics'. Those trials were a fairly close-run thing. The North Eastern engine No 2400 was manned by a crew of the highest calibre, Driver Tom Blades and Fireman Charles Fisher of Gateshead. Blades was a great deal more than the 'senior driver' at the shed. He had fired to Bob Nicholson on the 'M' Class 4-4-0 in the concluding stages of the 'Race to the North' in 1895. Charlie Fisher became a locomotive inspector at York, and I enjoyed many trips in his company; the pair did some excellent work on the GN main line in 1923. The overall results are shown in the accompanying table, and it will be seen that by a narrow margin they favoured the Great Northern engine, none other than the historic 4472 *Flying Scotsman*. At that time, however, the engine was numbered 1472 and had not yet been named. Furthermore, her superiority over No 2400 was achieved with the original valve gear; the extent to which this was improved is described later in this chapter. Had the North Eastern engine been run against No 4472 as she was from 1928 onwards, the result would have been overwhelmingly in favour of the Gresley design. It was of course not

a straight case of Walschaerts *versus* Stephenson valve gear; it was the detail design of the gear that made all the difference.

LNER: 'Pacific' engine trials
Average results for all tests: June and July 1923

Engine No Section	1472 GN	2400 NE
Average speed (mph)	53.7	53.0
Actual 1,000 ton miles (train only)	73.11	76.5
Average drawbar horsepower	663	673
Superheat (°F)	547	574
Boiler pressure (psi)	164	197
Steam chest pressure (psi)	118	106
Cut-off (per cent)	40	40
Water:		
Gallons per mile	38.3	40.4
Lb per drawbar horsepower hour	31.0	31.7
Coal:		
Lb per mile (inclusive)	52.6	58.7
Lb per mile (exclusive of lighting up)	48.6	54.4
Lb per drawbar horsepower hour	3.94	4.29
Lb per sq ft of grate area per hour	65.2	68.9
Evaporation:		
Feed water temperature (°F)	61.0	61.6
Lb of water per lb of coal	7.47	7.7
Gallons of water used per hour	2081	2153

LNER: Grantham — Kings Cross

Engine   NER 4-6-2 No 2400
Load   483 tons tare, 520 tons full

Distance (miles)		Schedule time (m)	Actual time (m s)	Speed (mph)
0.0	GRANTHAM	0	0 00	—
5.5	Stoke Box		10 01	43½
8.4	Corby		13 05	65
13.3	Little Bytham		17 12	76½
16.9	Essendine		19 55	79
20.7	Tallington		22 56	74½
29.1	PETERBOROUGH	33	31 27	—
3.8	Yaxley		6 39	51½
7.0	Holme		9 55	62½
12.9	Abbots Ripton		16 00	47½
17.5	Huntingdon	20	20 50	73
20.4	Offord		23 16	73
24.7	St Neots		27 04	60
28.9	Tempsford		31 03	65½
32.3	Sandy		34 13	62½
35.3	Biggleswade		37 03	63
39.2	Arlesey		41 13	61
44.5	Hitchin	48	46 34	51
47.8	Stevenage		50 55	44½
51.4	Knebworth		55 04	51
58.7	Hatfield	64	62 04	71
63.7	Potters Bar		66 51	61
67.3	New Barnet		69 58	74½
71.4	Wood Green		73 35	73½
73.9	Finsbury Park		75 38	68
76.4	KINGS CROSS	84	79 24	—

So far as the individual work of the North Eastern engine was concerned, an outstanding example of its work is shown in the table above.

This relates to the hardest part of the up journey on the 10.51 am from Doncaster to Kings Cross after the train had been made up to its maximum load by attaching the through carriage from Lincoln at Grantham. It will be seen that this very heavy train was being run within the booked schedule times all the way. Moreover, this particular run, which was the last of the series made by the North Eastern engine between Doncaster and Kings Cross, was the fastest made by either of the competing engines during the test period, although, as the table of average results shows, it was made at the cost of a somewhat higher coal consumption than that of the Great Northern engine. Doubtless, under the stimulus of competition, the work of the North Eastern engine, with the crew becoming more familiar with the road, was excellent indeed and the performance tabulated appears considerably superior to the normal work of Great Northern 'Pacifics' on that same train. Nevertheless, on the overall results, particularly, regarding coal consumption, the decision was taken to put in hand a further batch of forty Gresley 'Pacifics' for general service throughout the East Coast Route.

In the summer of 1924 there was staged the celebrated British Empire Exhibition at Wembley. Railways naturally formed an important part of the exhibits, and the Great Western and London and North Eastern Railways displayed examples of their latest express passenger locomotives. To represent the latter, one of the Doncaster-based 'Pacifics', the

The first NER 'Pacific', No 2400 City of Newcastle, *leaving Berwick-on-Tweed with an express for Edinburgh* (O.S. Nock).

very one which had been engaged in the trials against the North Eastern in the previous summer, No 1472, was smartened up, given an exhibition finish, and named *Flying Scotsman*. Also, in keeping with the scheme of renumbering the entire locomotive stock of the LNER, in this case with the adding of 3000 to all the previous GNR numbers, the exhibition engine became No 4472. On the very next stand, with its tender backing on to that of No 4472 on the same set of metals, was the pride and joy of the Great Western Railway, the new four-cylinder 4-6-0 No 4073 *Caerphilly Castle*. The surrounding publicity was not backward in telling the spectators that the GWR engine was the first of a class that was the most powerful of any express passenger design yet built for the British railways. In view of the comparative size of the two locomotives displayed beside each other this might have appeared a doubtful claim, but the relative nominal tractive efforts were there in 'black and white', 29,835 lb for No 4472 against 31,625 lb for No 4073. Certain partisans who favoured Doncaster were inclined to voice the challenge 'Well, prove your superiority', and many people, when the Locomotive Interchange Trials of 1925 were announced, believed that, indeed, the challenge had come from the LNER.

Actually, at that particular time, no one in the higher ranks of the locomotive department of the LNER was anxious to try competing with the Great Western. Gresley himself was by no means satisfied with the working of his 'Pacifics', however well they had shown up against the North Eastern in 1923 so far as coal consumption was concerned. The prime mover in the Interchange Trials of 1925 was without much doubt Sir Felix Pole, the General Manager of the Great Western Railway. It was known that he was on terms of intimate personal friendship with his opposite number on the LNER the Chief General

Manager Ralph L. Wedgwood, and after the end of the British Empire Exhibition of 1924 it was generally understood, among the senior officers of the LNER, that Pole had definitely suggested the interchange of top-ranking express locomotives. Reluctantly, Gresley agreed, for he knew only too well what the challenge from the Great Western would most likely mean when he was not, as at present, prepared to meet it. The tests, after no more than a week of trial running, took place from April 27 to May 2 1925, and sure enough the Great Western staged some spectacular performances on the 'Cornish Riviera Express', twice within the week bringing in the train a quarter of an hour before time.

Feats such as these were bound to confuse the issue, and placed the competing LNER engine No 4474, whose driver had been instructed to run to schedule, at a disadvantage. The West of England main line between Reading and Plymouth is an exceptionally awkward road for a stranger, and to be practically on time at Plymouth on their very first trip with the down 'Limited' was a masterly piece of locomotive handling by the LNER crew. What is more, the coal consumption was only 50 lb per mile, which, even allowing for the higher calorific value of Welsh coal, was very little above the normal 'Pacific' figure. In the hectic excitement of what was generally regarded as a purely sporting contest, however, such considerations counted for little with the general public and the popular press.

There is no disguising the fact that the LNER was beaten on its own road. The locomotive principally concerned was No 2545, which was later named *Diamond Jubilee*, and was a hurriedly-picked second string after the first choice, No 4475, had failed with a hot box. To the chagrin of her supporters, No 2545 struck a particularly bad patch and failed to rise even to normal 'Pacific' standards. The reason is to be found in one of the hundred-and-one minor ailments that can, on any railway, jaundice locomotive performance, but that such trouble should have developed in the Company's chosen representative during so critical a week was a piece of extremely bad luck. The Great Weatern engine, No 4079 *Pendennis Castle*, certainly took the wind out of the LNER sails. On trip after trip she lifted her 475-ton trains through Finsbury Park in less than 6 minutes, and on the fastest run was through Hatfield in 23 min 25 sec. After that, short cut-offs and light steaming sufficed for speeds of average East Coast quality, and she brought her trains into Peterborough and Doncaster well before time on each journey.

The immediate results of the exchange, details of the running and certain technical items, were published by the companies concerned soon after the event. Controversy raged around the merits and demerits of the two types for many months afterwards, but much of this centred upon the differences in boiler and firebox. Each is an outstanding design peculiarly suitable for its own class of fuel and service. It is true that the Great Western engine did very well on Yorkshire coal, but a close examination of the logs of her running shows that most of the sparkle and brilliance of her work took place at the beginning of the journeys; there was never quite the same dash about the Grantham-Doncaster stage as was so noticeable between Kings Cross and Peterborough, and one wonders what might have happened had *Pendennis Castle* essayed the later

'Pacific' duty of working through from London to Newcastle or Edinburgh.

The essential difference between the two types lay in the front end — long-travel *versus* short-travel valves. It is generally recognised that long-travel valves make for more economical running and higher speeds, but few if any definite figures have been published to show exactly where the difference lies. With short-travel valves, both the admission and exhaust ports are never more than partly open when a locomotive is running well linked up, and the earlier the point of cut-off is brought, the smaller these openings become. Narrow valve openings severely throttle the steam both at admission and exhaust, and hamper an engine severely; an investigation into the cylinder and valve performance of one of the Midland compounds — generally accepted as a most efficient class — showed that when running at 68 mph 35 per cent of the total energy of the steam put through the cylinders was spent in getting through the admission and exhaust ports. By increasing the length of the valve travel, the movement of the valves can be so arranged that the full width of the exhaust ports is available even when the engine is linked up to mid gear. For many years, British locomotive engineers were inclined to look askance at the long valve travels of the GWR on account of the extra wear on valves and liners that resulted from higher valve speeds. In many ways, the term 'long-travel' valves is a misnomer; they should, strictly speaking, be called long-lap valves, for when an engine is linked

One of the first 'general service' 'Pacifics', No 2547 before being naming Doncaster, *passing Harringay on a down East Coast express* (Real Photographs).

right up and running at 70 mph the actual travel of the valves may well be *less* than that of a locomotive fitted with short-lap valves needing to be worked at comparatively long cut-offs.

At this stage in the story it is time to mention some of the younger engineers who formed Gresley's personal staff. On being appointed Chief Mechanical Engineer of the LNER in 1923, he had well-established Drawing Offices and Works at Stratford, Gorton, Darlington and Cowlairs in addition to his own at Doncaster, and the efficiency of these will have been apparent from some of the foregoing chapters of this book. He made his headquarters, however, in London, adjacent to the Chief General Manager, and formed a small personal staff at Kings Cross. O.V.S. Bulleid was his chief assistant, while B. Spencer was assistant for locomotives and N. Newsome for carriages and wagons. I came to know Bert Spencer well in later years, both as a first rate engineer and as a charming personality. From him I learned much of the inner story of the Gresley regime and particularly the period when the 'Pacifics' were still being developed. Spencer was almost always able to deal with Gresley direct without the intervention of Bulleid, and after the Interchange Trials of 1925 he was frequently pleading with Gresley to let him try some alteration to the valve gear.

Eventually, in 1926, the motion of engine No 4477 *Gay Crusader* was modified so as to give longer laps and a freer exhaust. As many as possible of the existing parts of the gear were used in carrying out this experimental rearrangement, which thoroughly justified itself; No 4477 proved decidedly more economical than the standard 'Pacifics'. This success prompted Spencer to press Gresley in authorizing a further redesign of the gear, in which the lap was increased from the original 1¼ in to 1⅝ in, and the valve travel in full gear from 4 9/16 in to 5¾ in; this was tried out early in 1927 on No 2555 *Centenary*, and trials between this engine and No 2559, with short-travel valves, showed that the altered gear reduced the coal consumption from roughly 50 to 38-39 lb per train mile. When the results were laid before Gresley, the 'great man' did not appear to be very interested and Spencer made his exit as quickly as he could. Several weeks went by, weeks very full with other pressing business, and then one day he was summoned. Gresley said immediately 'I'm very pleased with that engine ...' Spencer, with his mind full of more immediate matters, was almost on the point of interrupting him by asking 'What engine?' when he suddenly realised they were talking about the 'Pacific' No 2555 and Gresley terminated this brief interview by saying 'Have the whole lot altered'. And that was that! Apparently without telling any of his own staff he had sought out the workings of No 2555, made a couple of footplate trips and formed his own conclusions.

The more economical working of the engines was an important factor that contributed much to the feasibility of the London-Edinburgh non-stop

'Pacific' No 2555 Centenary *leaving King's Cross with the 'Queen of Scots' in 1937* (Real Photographs).

running of the 'Flying Scotsman', which was inaugurated on May 1, 1928. Engine No 4472, *Flying Scotsman*, was transferred to Kings Cross from Doncaster shed where she had been stationed ever since her construction specially for this working, and, with No 4476 *Royal Lancer*, bore the brunt of the non-stop running throughout the summer. The timing of 8.25 hours involved very easy locomotive work, and for that reason was subjected to some disparagement, but the standard of punctuality set was high and the experience gained in this, the greatest feat of locomotive endurance attempted up to that time in this country, paved the way for the more remarkable developments of later years.

The steady trend of development in locomotive engineering practice that had been so marked a feature of the Gresley regime was at a very interesting stage in the years 1927 and 1928. Long-lap valves had been tried and eventually standardized, and next there came a series of experiments leading to the adoption of higher boiler pressures. In July 1927, one of the original batch of 'A1s', No 4480 *Enterprise*, was put into traffic fitted with a new boiler having a working pressure of 220 psi. The object was to obtain comparative costs of maintenance and other data as to the life of fireboxes, stays and tubes, between boilers carrying 180 psi and 220 psi pressure. The superheater was enlarged from 32 to 43 elements, the corresponding increase in heating surface being from

525 to 706 sq ft, and the higher pressure raised the nominal tractive effort from the 29,835 lb of the standard 'Pacifics' to 36,465 lb. The heavier boiler, and a small redistribution of weight elsewhere, increased the adhesion from 60 to 66 tons.

Enterprise was, of course, fitted with long-lap valves at the time of her rebuilding, and in traffic she displayed an easy mastery over any regular task existing on the Southern Area main line at that time. In some ways she was too powerful, for even when fully linked up to 15 per cent it was not possible to use full regulator without making extravagant gains on schedule time. To investigate further the advantages to be gained from the use of higher steam pressures, another of the 'A1s', No 2544 *Lemberg*, was fitted with a boiler similar to that of No 4480 but the cylinders were lined up to an 18¼ in diameter, thus giving this high-pressure engine a nominal effort equal to that of the standard 180 psi 'Pacifics'.

A series of dynamometer car trials was then conducted, in February 1928, between *Lemberg* and No 4473 *Solario*, a standard 'A1' fitted with long-lap valves. At that time, the expresses between London and the West Riding provided the hardest daily tasks set to the 'Pacifics', and the trials were conducted on the 10.51 am from Doncaster to Kings Cross, and the regular return working, the 4 pm down. The published results of two weeks' running showed no appreciable difference between the two locomotives.

Left *The two-months-old up non-stop 'Flying Scotsman' near Potters Bar in 1928, hauled by Haymarket-based 'Pacific' No 2564* Knight of the Thistle *(Rail Archive Stephenson/F.R. Hebron).*

Right *Class 'A3' 'super-Pacific' No 2599* Book Law *on a down East Coast express at Newcastle (W.B. Greenfield).*

The average coal consumption was 3.08 lb per drawbar horsepower hour by *Solario* and 3.12 lb by *Lemberg*. The latter engine enjoyed better weather during her week, and on that account her coal consumption per train mile was less than that of her rival — 35.37 against 38.83 lb. Both, however, were excellent figures, considering that the average train loads were 431 tons from Doncaster to Kings Cross, 498 tons from Kings Cross to Peterborough and 339 tons thence to Doncaster.

In ordinary service, *Lemberg* earned the reputation of being one of the speediest of all the non-stream-lined 'Pacifics'. After the accelerations of 1932 she often worked the 8.40 am from Doncaster to Kings Cross and one could always look forward to some sparkling performance on the 63.4 mph run from Grantham to Kings Cross. One of the finest of such feats was on a day when an unusually heavy load for that train was carried, 435 tons gross. A number of delays prevented strict time-keeping, but intermediately there was some grand going, including the high maximum, for 1933, of 92.5 mph at Essendine. The net time was 97 minutes, a start-to-stop average of 65.3 mph. In the same summer she worked the 'Scarborough Flyer', loaded to no less than 570 tons gross, non-stop from Kings Cross to York, 188.2 miles in 192.5 minutes net. In view of these splendid performances it is perhaps significant that the steam port area of this engine is larger, in proportion to the total cylinder volume, than any other of the non-streamlined 'Pacifics' for when the cylinders were lined up to the 18¼ in diameter the original 8 in diameter valves were retained. This feature of her design would certainly help in giving that freedom of exhaust that is so essential for fast and efficient running.

From the data provided by the experimental rebuilding of engines 4480 and 2544, the new so-called super 'Pacific' design, Class 'A3', was prepared. No 2743 *Felstead*, the first of a batch of ten locomotives was put into service in August 1928; the boiler was identical with that of *Lemberg*, but though the cylinders were increased to 19 in diameter, the 8 in diameter piston valves, common to all previous 'Pacifics', were retained. The nominal tractive effort at 85 per cent of boiler pressure was 32,909 lb.

To conclude this chapter I have tabulated two of the finest runs I have personally experienced with the 'A1' and 'A3' 'Pacifics'. That with the 180 psi engine *Neil Gow* was made with one of the Heaton link which worked the down 'Flying Scotsman' three days a week between Kings Cross and Newcastle except in the summer season when the non-stop 'Scotsman' was running. Then the Heaton engine returned north on the 10.5 am 'Junior Scotsman'. At the time the run with *Neil Gow* was made, the schedule time to Grantham was 111 minutes, with 77 minutes to pass Peterborough, and for an 'A1' a sixteen-coach train

Above *The up 'Flying Scotsman' on Langley troughs hauled by Gateshead-based 'Pacific' No 2575* Galopin, *fitted with a Westinghouse brake* (Rail Archive Stephenson/F.R. Hebron).

Below Class 'A3' 'Pacific' No 2744 Grand Parade *on the up non-stop 'Flying Scotsman' passing York in about 1933* (Rail Archive Stephenson/T.G. Hepburn).

LNER: Kings Cross — Grantham

Train		10.5 am		1.20 pm	
Engine No		2581		2744	
Engine Name		*Neil Gow*		*Grand Parade*	
Class		'A1'		'A3'	
Load (tons, empty/full)		491/525		497/530	

Distance (miles)		Time (m s)	Speed (mph)	Time (m s)	Speed (mph)
0.0	KINGS CROSS	0 00	—	0 00	—
2.6	Finsbury Park	6 53	—	6 20	—
5.0	Wood Green	10 08	53.5	9 35	54.5
9.2	New Barnet	15 22	46	14 47	45.5
12.7	Potters Bar	20 15	42.5	19 37	43.5
17.7	HATFIELD	25 25	72	24 40	75.5
23.5	Woolmer Green	30 57	56	29 45	60
28.6	Stevenage	35 50	69/65	34 22	71/67
31.9	HITCHIN	38 36	80.5	37 00	82
35.7	Three Counties	41 15	86.5	39 40	87.5
41.1	Biggleswade	45 23	—	43 35	84
44.5	Sandy	47 42	74/79	45 50	76.5/80.5
51.7	St Neots	53 57	68.5	51 55	69.5
56.0	Offord	57 39	75	55 20	78
58.9	Huntingdon	59 56	72	57 37	74.5
62.0	Milepost 62	62 44	56	60 30	59
69.4	Holme	69 18	77.5	66 45	78
72.6	Yaxley	72 04	—	69 23	70.5
—		sigs		—	
76.4	PETERBOROUGH	77 15		73 55	
—		sig stop		—	
84.4	Tallington	90 53	61.5	84 47	57.5
88.6	Essendine	95 45	57/59	89 00	52
92.2	Little Bytham	99 24	55.5	93 20	eased
97.1	Corby	105 18	46	100 22	eased
—		sig check		—	—
105.5	GRANTHAM	117 52		111 30	

was a very tough assignment. The work both uphill and down was splendid until the signal delays from Peterborough onwards spoiled things. The companion run on the 1.20 pm 'Scotsman' was on a slightly easier schedule of 114 minutes to Grantham, but the Kings Cross driver on the 'A3' engine *Grand Parade* ran brilliantly to pass Peterborough 4 minutes early; after that, the engine was justifiably eased down. The average speeds on these two runs over the 58.9 miles from Hatfield to Yaxley, 75.8 mph by *Neil Gow* and 79.2 mph by *Grand Parade*, provide an impressive testimony to the speed of both classes of Gresley 'Pacifics' when hauling loads of more than 500 tons.

13. The grouping era: new engines great and small

Most of the individual railways that were merged to form the LNER were, it is true, fairly well equipped for the needs of the moment, though everywhere train loads showed a tendency to rise. As far as speed was concerned, train services were, with a few exceptions, stagnant. Of the Great Northern's nearest neighbours, the Great Central and Great Eastern sections were more than holding their own, though on the latter the haulage of the evening Continental boat expresses from Liverpool Street to Parkeston Quay with the 350 to 400-ton loads of that period was a task not far short of the maximum capabilities of the Holden superheated 4-6-0s, the design of which dated back to 1912. On the North Eastern, the drafting of the Gresley 'Pacifics' to the East Coast expresses released a number of 'Atlantics' for secondary duties, and it was only on the North British that anything like an immediate problem existed in the years just after the grouping. Here the greatest need was for a locomotive of intermediate power rating. In general, the Reid 'Atlantics' were well on top of their job on the heaviest turns, but these 22 engines were rather sparsely distributed between the Aberdeen, Perth and Carlisle roads, and there was a big disparity between the power developed by them and their next of kin, the superheated 'Scott' Class 4-4-0s. The use of 'Pacifics' was no doubt contemplated for the heaviest work of the future, but the immediate needs were pressing and allowed no time for the preparation of an entirely new design for immediate duty.

A locomotive designer faced with such a problem would naturally incline towards some type with which he was already familiar, and the sending to Scotland of the Great Northern superheated 4-4-0s of the '51-65' Class, designed by Ivatt, was a logical first step. These engines, then classed 'D1', had their boiler mountings cut down to conform to the North British loading gauge, and were fitted with the Westinghouse brake. They did well in Scotland, and to outsiders it seemed that this might be the beginning of a general infiltration of Doncaster types throughout the LNER system. But this seeming hint proved to be no hint at all, for the new engines built for service in Scotland were of Robinson's Great Central 'Improved Director' Class. Despite his major advancement in 1923, Gresley was known to have not only retained a strong affection for his old company and Doncaster practice, but also more than once shown evidence of his partiality towards the Great Central. After all, it was the magnanimity of

J.G. Robinson in declining to accept the job of Chief Mechanical Engineer of the LNER that opened the way for his appointment, and with W.G.P. Maclure, previously Running Superintendent of the Great Central Railway, installed at Liverpool Street in a similar post but covering the entire Southern Area of the LNER, the products of Gorton were likely to have a strong advocate at Headquarters.

The Great Central 'Director' Class had much to commend it for service in Scotland, but, before the first year of grouping had passed, other GCR engines were being tried out nearer to their home ground. One could quite imagine that Maclure, having had four-cylinder 4-6-0s of the 'Lord Faringdon' Class, with a nominal tractive effort of no less than 24,772 lb, might have wished to use them on some heavier trains than those of the Great Central main line to and from London, and the gargantuan loads frequently taken out of Kings Cross obviously gave him an opportunity to do so. Soon after midsummer in 1923 two of the 'Faringdons', engines No 1166 *Earl Haig* and No 1167 *Lloyd George* were transferred to the Great Northern line and put to work on heavy express trains between Kings Cross and Doncaster. At that time, building of the Gresley 'Pacifics' had not proceeded further than the completion of engine No 1477, as it was then numbered, and the large-boilered 'Atlantics' were still being used on some of the hardest trains like the 10.51 am up from Doncaster to Kings Cross, when one of the new engines was not available. It was on this turn, returning with the still heavier but not so sharply timed 4 pm down, that the Great Central 4-6-0 No 1166 *Earl Haig* was run. It was reported that on the latter train, which normally loaded to at least 500 tons, the severely-graded start out of Kings Cross held no terrors, and the time to passing Finsbury Park, 2.6 miles, was usually about six minutes, much the same as the 'Pacifics' with the same train. Incidentally, the companion GCR engine No 1167 had its name removed soon after this time, reputedly because an ex-Great Northern director who was a prominent Conservative MP objected to the political implications of the name!

I have no detailed logs of the working of the Great Central four-cylinder 4-6-0s with these very heavy East Coast trains, but, while there would have been plenty of power for lifting the loads up the steep bank out of Kings Cross, one could well imagine that the medium-sized fire grate would have found some difficulty in sustaining the steam supply needed for

Right *Approaching the Forth Bridge in June 1951: Crail to Glasgow stopping train at North Queensferry, with improved 'Director' Class 4-4-0 No 62687* Lord James of Douglas *in BR lined black livery* (E.D. Bruton).

Below *GC engines on the GN: the up Edinburgh Pullman, in 1927 non-stop from Harrogate, passing Wood Green hauled by GC 'Director' Class 4-4-0 No 5506* Butler Henderson *(Rail Archive Stephenson/F.R. Hebron).*

Bottom *The down Edinburgh Pullman climbing Holloway bank, hauled by 'Director' Class 4-4-0 No 5507* Gerard Powys Dewhurst *(Rail Archive Stephenson/F.R. Hebron).*

the subsequent hard running. Nevertheless, Mac-lure found another excellent opportunity for their use on the newly-instituted Pullman trains running non-stop between Kings Cross and Leeds at an average speed of 54 mph. Many fine runs were recorded, though I was disappointed that in my own journeys I always seemed to strike occasions when there was a Great Northern 'Atlantic', and not a GCR engine, on the job. In the early summer of 1924, a second Pullman train was put on, at first leaving Kings Cross ten minutes ahead of the Harrogate train. It turned off the East Coast main line at Grantham and made its way across country to Nottingham, its first stop, and thence to Sheffield. On its augural trip, duly photographed leaving Kings Cross, it was worked by a Great Northern 'Atlantic', but when I was out on the line with my camera no more than a fortnight later I was surprised and pleased to see a 'Sir Sam Fay' Class two-cylinder 4-6-0 on the job, *City of Manchester*. Both Pullman trains were GC hauled that morning; the 11.15 am had the War Memorial engine No 1165 *Valour*, still, incidentally, in Great Central colours and with the old company's name in full on her tender. The Sheffield Pullman

was not a success. After no more than a month of running, it was changed to leave Sheffield in the morning and return from Kings Cross at 6.5 pm, but it was poorly patronized.

Reverting to the North British line in Scotland, the choice of the 'Director' Class as second line express passenger engines had much to commend it. Although they did not have all that much more tractive effort than a superheated 'Scott' Class 4-4-0, the GC engines had a much larger firebox, the same size as the 4-6-0s running at that time on the Kings Cross — Leeds non-stop Pullman expresses. The new 'Directors', which had somewhat shortened boiler mountings to conform to the Scottish loading gauge, were built by contract in 1924, twelve each by Kitson & Co and Armstrong, Whitworth & Co. They were much better looking engines than many of their Great Central predecessors, which had been vandalized in the post-grouping orgy that swept Gorton, by having flower-pot chimneys and 'Pacific'-sized dome covers substituted for the previous shapely mountings. The new engines went into service mainly on the Edinburgh-Glasgow route, but also between Edinburgh and Perth. Like

Right *'Director' Class 4-4-0 No 6387*
Lucy Ashton at Edinburgh Waverley in
1927 (O.S. Nock).

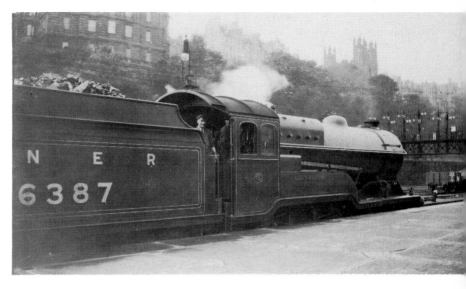

Below left *The Harrogate Pullman in*
1926, non-stop to Leeds, storms past Belle
Isle box hauled by GC four-cylinder 4-6-0
Lord Faringdon (Rail Archive
Stephenson).

the general-service Gresley 'Pacifics' of the
2543-2582 series, the Scottish engines of the
'Director' Class were unnamed when they were first
put into traffic, but by the end of 1925 the majority
had been given the names of characters in the
Waverley Novels following the 'Scott' Class engines
introduced on the North British Railway by W.P.
Reid. In such a series, one would imagine that the
more familiar characters would come first, as was
definitely the case with the 'King Arthur' Class
4-6-0s on the Southern, but with the 'Scotts',
although the non-superheated six introduced in 1909
included mostly familiar names, it was certainly not
true of the subsequent ones. When it came to the
'Directors', several of the titles, particularly of the
ladies, rang a familiar enough bell, like *Flora MacIvor,*
Lucy Ashton, and *Ellen Douglas.* The full list of both NB
and GC names is found on page 91.

Not long after these engines were put into service
I had an interesting run on the 10.7 am Highland
express from Edinburgh Waverley to Perth. It
showed the difficulties of this Scottish route, so
different from that for which the engines were first
designed. I may add that the Scottish 'Directors' had
the same motion and valve arrangement as those of
the later Great Central engines (the batch beginning
with No 506 *Butler Henderson,* introduced in 1919).
The line to Perth includes some severe banks,
notably the 11 miles graded between 1 in 74½ and 1
in 100 from the shores of the Firth of Forth at
Inverkeithing to Cowdenbeath Junction and, in the
southbound direction, the notorious Glenfarg bank
with its 8 miles of continuous 1 in 75 up from Bridge
of Earn. The run started easily with the approach to
the Forth Bridge and the restrained speed across it,

then the brief 60 mph on the sharp descent to the river
bank was cut short by the severe speed restriction
through the junctions at Inverkeithing. This, of
course, made a bad start for the heavy ascent to
Cowdenbeath. But our engine, *Lucy Ashton,* tackled
the 295-ton load in great style, not falling below 29
mph on the 1 in 83 gradient before the stop at
Dunfermline. The restart had to be made on a 1 in
74½ grade, and it was done in the same sure-footed
style, never a slip, a thunderous exhaust beat and
speed rising to 29 mph before the summit. Hard work
was finished on the northward run to Perth at this
stage. On my return, a fortnight later, however, the
load on the 8.10 pm was heavy enough for 'Director'
No 6390 *Hobbie Elliott* to need an assistant engine
throughout, a rebuilt Holmes 4-4-0; with a load of no
more than 350 tons it was easy work for the two of
them.

In 1925 a need was expressed for an 0-6-0 that
could be built as an LNER standard goods engine
and used also on intermediate passenger work of the
semi-fast type. Four constituents of the LNER had
powerful superheated classes of this wheel arrangement and of varying characteristics, the main dimensions of which are shown in the table on page 142.
I have also added a Great Central representative
which was certainly not considered in 1925 but which
came briefly into prominence in Edward Thompson's post-war standardization scheme in 1945. This
was the celebrated Robinson 'Pom-pom', rebuilt
and superheated. Apart from these, the oldest were
Gresley's 'J6' Class of the Great Northern, but by far
the most powerful of the earlier classes were the Great
Eastern 'J20s', which had the 20-in by 28-in
cylinders of the '1500' Class 4-6-0s and a 26.5 sq ft

Pre-grouping superheated 0-6-0s

LNER Class	'66'	'J11'	'J20'	'J27'	'J37'
Year Built	1911	1902/42	1913	1923	1914
Railway	GN	GC	GE	NE	NB
Number built	110	174*	25	105	104
Cylinders (in)	19 × 26	18½ × 26	20 × 28	18½ × 26	19½ × 26
Wheels (ft/in)	5 2	5 2	4 11	4 7¼	5 0
Total heating surface (sq ft)	1,230	1,386	1,810	1,326	1,732
Grate area (sq ft)	19	19.2	26.5	20	19.8
Boiler pressure (psi)	170	180	180	180	180
Nominal tractive effort (lbs)	21,875	21,959	29,044	24,642	25,211

*not superheated until 1942 and after

grate area. The North Eastern 'P3' (LNER 'J27') and the North British 'J37' were well-proved and well-liked engines, but hardly up to the needs of a universal mixed traffic unit while, particularly in respect of their grate area, these powerful classes were short-haul units designed for the specific needs of their own localities. So, Gresley, with the requirements of the entire LNER in prospect, laid down the broad specification of an 0-6-0 with a tractive effort roughly the same as the largest NE and NB classes, a large boiler and a firebox with a grate area of 26 sq ft. With this remit, the job was handed over to the Darlington Drawing Office.

With the requirements of the North British section particularly in mind, two varieties of this new standard 0-6-0 were sanctioned; the first, put into traffic in January 1926, was the 'J38' with 4-ft 8-in diameter wheels, for service in Scotland. Thirty-five engines of this class were built at Darlington between January and May of that year. Then, in September, there followed the general service variety, with 5-ft 2-in wheels, Class 'J39'. These latter engines became very much an LNER standard and construction of them continued until 1941, by which time there were no fewer than 289 of them in traffic. The enthusiastic authors who compiled the statistical booklet 'Locomotives of the LNER 1923-1937', published by the RCTS in 1941, considered that the 'J39' undoubtedly represented the finest type of 0-6-0 tender locomotive yet put into service, but I doubt if such sentiments would have been echoed at Derby! Certainly they were not shared by Gresley's successor, who chose to rebuild some of the Robinson 'Pom-poms' instead. The principal feature of the 'J39', apart, of course, from its simple and straightforward machinery, was the boiler, which was an entirely new design. The proportions were ideal for free steaming; the barrel was very short, of large diameter and with a deep, well-proportioned firebox. The design, though new in itself, bore a certain resemblance to that of the 'K3' three-cylinder

'Moguls'; the barrel length was practically the same, but of a 5 ft 6 in diameter instead of 6 ft 0 in, and the firebox had a length on the grate of 8 ft 6 in instead of 9 ft 0 in. The leading dimensions of these fine engines were as follows:

Cylinders (in)	20 × 26
Heating surfaces (sq ft)	
Tubes, large and small	1,226.28
Firebox	171.5
Superheater	271.8
Total	1,669.58
Grate area (sq ft)	26
Boiler pressure (psi)	180
Tractive effort at 85 per cent boiler pressure (lb)	25,664
Weight of engine in working order (tons)	57.85
Weight of tender with 4,200 gallons water, 7½ tons coal (tons)	52.5

Among the locomotives that took part in the historic Centenary Year procession of old and modern rolling-stock along part of the route of the Stockton and Darlington Railway in July 1925 were two which were the first of their wheel arrangements to run on any standard gauge railway in Great Britain. These were the first of two very large freight engines, two of the 2-8-2 type designed for the Peterborough to London coal traffic and the other a huge 2-8-0 + 0-8-2 of the Beyer-Garratt type for banking duties on the Worsborough Incline of the mineral train route from Wath Concentration Yard to Penistone and the Great Central main line to Manchester. These two mammoth engines were both making what was virtually their first public appearance, so much so indeed that, with the Garratt, work on the main frames of the engine had not started in Beyer, Peacock's works until June 1, yet it was steamed before the end of the month and ready to take part in the procession at Darlington on July 2. Even so, there

Above *Standard goods 0-6-0 Class 'J39'* (Beyer, Peacock & Company).

Right *Class 'J39' 0-6-0 No 2979 on an up West Highland goods train at Crianlarich* (O.S. Nock).

had been no time to apply the final coats of paint before sending it north! The official photograph published in *'The Locomotive'* no later than July 15 clearly showed this unfinished state.

Taking the two 'Mikado' engines first, they were designed to be the heavy mineral equivalent of the 'Pacifics' with the same boiler and cylinders though having valve gear providing a maximum cut-off in full gear of 75 per cent as against the 65 per cent on the 'Pacifics'. While the standard ex-Great Northern 2-8-0 mineral engines had 4-ft 8-in coupled wheels, the 'Mikados' had 5 ft 2 in, suggesting that something more than slogging along with 1600-ton coal trains may have been contemplated if and when the class should be multiplied beyond the original two. The nominal tractive effort in normal working was 38,500 lb at 85 per cent of working pressure, but, to assist in acceleration of maximum freight train loads, a booster engine was fitted to the trailing wheels beneath the cab.

In 1923, Gresley had applied a booster engine to one of the large-boilered Ivatt 'Atlantics' No 1419 to enhance the tractive effort when starting or when climbing a heavy gradient at relatively low speed. The equipment was furnished by the Franklin Supply Co of New York City, and the results from engine No 1419 were such that the same apparatus was fitted to the 'Mikado' engines Nos 2393 and 2394. The booster engine had two cylinders of 10 in diameter by 12 in stroke giving an additional tractive effort of 8,500 lb. This gave an increment of nearly 50 per cent in the case of the 'Atlantic', and boosted that of the 'Mikados' from 38,500 to 47,000 lb. Photographs of the right-hand side of these engines may have caused some mystification from the presence of a Westinghouse donkey pump half-way along the boiler side, suggesting the engines were dual fitted although the hose connections on the buffer beam did not confirm this. Actually, this pump, which was of the standard Westinghouse

type, provided compressed air for the pneumatic control mechanism of the booster engine, supplied by the American manufacturers as one of their standard products.

The 'Mikado' engines had a special six-wheeled tender designed for them. To accommodate the booster which extended rearwards underneath the footplate, the leading wheel of the tender had to be set back further than in the standard LNER tenders carrying 4200 gallons of water and 7½ tons of coal as

fitted to the 'K3' Class 2-6-0s and the 'J39' 0-6-0s. Those fitted to Nos 2393 and 2394 were 6 ft 10½ in back, against the normal 4 ft 11 in. The wheels were then spaced evenly at 6 ft 6 in, against 7 ft 3 in and 6 ft 3 in on the standard version, and the 'Mikado' tenders carried 4700 gallons of water but only 7 tons of coal.

As originally designed, of course, they were intended only for the Peterborough-London coal run and, as referred to earlier in this book, the nominal

Above *The first of the two 'P1' 'Mikado' type freight engines, No 2393 as originally fitted with the booster, on a 100-wagon coal train near Potters Bar* (F.R. Hebron).

Left *Rearward view of 2-8-2 No 2394 on an up coal train near Stevenage* (C.C.B. Herbert).

Above right *'P1' Class 2-8-2 No 2393 on a maximum-load coal train working 'flat out' on Stevenage bank* (O.S. Nock).

maximum load of these trains was 80 wagons; with the 'Mikados', it was intended to step this up to 100 wagons. Such trains were experimental from the operating point of view, and it was, indeed, a moot point whether trains of this immense length hauled by those two engines were an economical pro-position, having regard to siding, refuge loop and yard capacity. So, while the loads of 1600 tons held no terrors for those capable engines from the traction point of view, special paths had to be laid down in the working time tables for the 100-wagon coal trains which they were rostered to work from New England Yard, Peterborough to Ferme Park, Hornsey. In my various photographic expeditions to the Great Northern main line, I saw these great engines in several different circumstances, sometimes drifting down the final descent from Potters Bar but never more thrillingly than roaring up the 1 in 200 bank from Hitchin towards Stevenage, in full blast indeed. I have a treasured photograph of one of them near Wymondly box in which the great column of exhaust is seen rising quite vertically up from the funnel!

I have not been able to find any first-hand con-temporary accounts of the working of those notable engines. This to my mind is the more surprising seeing that, in Great Northern days, Charles S. Lake, the Technical Editor of *The Railway Gazette*, was accorded the most generous privileges by Gresley in order to observe the workings of his new three-cylinder 2-8-0 and 2-6-0 locomotives, and the

results were some highly interesting articles in the journals of the Tothill Press. One might have expected something of a similar kind to have resulted from the introduction of two such notable locomotives as the 2-8-2s on the Peterborough-Ferme Park coal run, particularly as it would have involved the working of the booster engine, but no such article appeared. From my subsequent association with the publishers, however, I gathered that some editorial rationalization of subject matter had taken place in *The Railway Magazine* whereby all writings on locomotive performance, and thus accounts of experiences on the footplate, would in future be dealt with under the 'British Locomotive Practice and Performance' feature. Unfortunately, the author then concerned apparently had no opportunity of making such a trip. In later years, both these great engines were fitted with high pressure boilers, one of them with a 'banjo' type dome like the last batch of 'A3' 'Pacifics'. It is of interest that in that condition the nominal tractive effort had been enhanced to no less than 46,400 lb, practically equal to the figure when the booster was in action (the booster equipment had been removed before the war). Engines 2393 and 2394 with their 220 lb boilers survived until 1945, longer indeed than the later Gresley 2-8-2 engines which were converted to 4-6-2s by Edward Thompson.

The other Gresley mammoth of 1925 had an even longer life. After the Great Central Railway had concentrated their coal operations in the great Wath

mechanized marshalling yard to avoid congestion at Barnsley, trains for destinations west of the Pennines were taken up a purely freight line through Worsborough Dale to a junction with the Sheffield to Manchester main line near Penistone. It may have avoided congestion at Barnsley, but it proved the most difficult route for heavy freight in the whole country. The great bugbear in operation was the Wentworth Incline, roughly 2½ miles long and graded at 1 in 40. In the early 1920s the maximum load for westbound trains was rostered as 63 wagons, or about 1,100 tons loaded. Such trains would come up the moderate gradients from Wath yard to Wombwell with two of the GCR Robinson 2-8-0s double-heading. A stop was then made for the assistant engine to transfer from the front to the rear of the train, and they would proceed thus on the heavier grades to Wentworth Junction, where both engines would take water. Prior to 1925, two more engines were then attached in rear for the ascent of the murderous Wentworth Incline. A load of 1,199 tons hauled by four 2-8-0s might easily take twenty minutes or more to climb the two miles of worst inclination — sometimes five engines would be needed.

For working purely on the Wentworth Incline, Gresley introduced his Garratt engine. This was the equivalent in tractive power of two standard Great Northern three-cylinder 2-8-0s and made this engine the only extra assistance needed on the worst two miles of the bank. The engine units on the Garratt were interchangeable with those of the ordinary '02' class tender engines, even having the refinement of the conjugated-type motion for the inside cylinders. It was the first time Beyer, Peacock & Co had built a three-cylinder Garratt, but from some of their staff I gathered that they hoped it would be the last! I came to know their brilliant if forthright Sales Director, W. Cyril Williams, and he always averred that LNER No 2395 was one of the least satisfying of all Garratts. I asked him why, and he said unhesi-

The LNER Garratt No 2395 (British Railways).

tatingly that it was because Gresley would not have let them have a free hand in the design. Beyer, Peacock were used to receiving a broad specification as to weights, loading gauge restrictions and tractive power, and that was that, leaving the drawing office to do the rest; they did not like being told what they must do! From one source I gathered that it was not the first time that an articulated engine had been contemplated for providing rear-end banking assistance, even in the Great Central days, but apparently the First World War led to the dropping of the project, whatever it may have been.

The boiler of No 2395 was of typical Garratt proportions, having a barrel of no less than 7 ft diameter and no shorter than 13 ft long. These ideal dimensions for free steaming were of course made possible by the characteristic Garratt design in which the boiler was mounted entirely clear of the running gear, and the wide firebox, having a grate area of no less than 56.4 sq ft and a length of 8 ft 5 in inside was conveniently arranged for servicing from the lineside. The large-diameter boiler provided space for no fewer than 275 small tubes of 2 in diameter as against 215 tubes of 2¼ in diameter on the boiler of the Gresley 'Pacifics' and 'Mikados'. The evaporative heating surfaces of the Garratt were 2,757 sq ft in the tubes and 237 sq ft in the firebox, while the superheater, which was accommodated in 45 large flues of 5¼ in diameter, provided an additional 646 sq ft. The total heating surface was thus 3,640 sq ft, as against 3,455 sq ft on the 'Mikados'. The engine was established as the largest, heaviest and most powerful that had then been built in Great Britain for service on a home railway. The total weight in working order was 178 tons, and the nominal tractive effort at 85 per cent of the working pressure of 180 psi was 72,940 lb.

As in the case of the 'Mikados', nothing in

contemporary railway literature was published about the working of the Garratt, but not long after the line was electrified and the engine itself had been transferred to banking both freight and passenger trains on the Lickey Incline, I had the privilege of riding on some of the new electric locomotives working the coal trains from Wath Yard up through Worsborough Dale to Penistone. It was not only an absorbing experience making an assessment of the new power and its capabilities, but there was also the great pleasure of riding with veteran enginemen who had worked their lives on steam and were full of reminiscences of the old days. They told me how it was far from a case of straightforward slogging and

Post-war working of the Garratt: BR No 69999 in October 1953 near Mottram on a test from Guide Bridge to Woodhead (Eric Oldham).

that perfect teamwork had been required between the locomotives at the front and rear of the train, especially on those sections where there were slight but abrupt changes in gradient due to subsidence. My hosts pointed out the spur track at the foot of the Wentworth Incline where the Garratt used to be serviced; in her heyday she usually managed about 18 trips in each 24 hours. Referring to bank engines generally, I gathered that the ex-GCR 2-6-4 freight tanks introduced by Robinson in 1916 were well liked on the Wath-Penistone run. The sheer labour of getting a 1000-ton coal train up the 1 in 40 of the Wentworth Incline takes some believing nowadays. Near the top of the bank came the two Silkstone Tunnels; neither was very long, but on a train worked by four engines and travelling at no more than 5 ½ to 6 mph, conditions could become rather grim and at one time the Garratt was equipped with respirators for the crew!

14. Intermediate power: three-cylinder engines

While Gresley was busily engaged in putting the finishing touches to his 'Pacifics' with the long-lap, long-travel valves and making the first investigations towards his monumental water-tube boiler, super-pressure compound 4-6-4, attention had also to be given to the need for replacement of many of the older intermediate units, a number of which were then more than twenty years old. From those who were closest to Gresley at that time I gathered that he was somewhat disinclined to involve himself in any detailed work on the new designs, save that they had to have three cylinders. This was a very important feature in some cases. The work of the Bridge Stress Committee, set up in 1923, still had not published its report by the end of 1928, but the findings regarding certain vital factors of locomotive design had become well known in the principal drawing offices well before then. One was that the dynamic balance of the recriprocating parts of a locomotive having three cylinders with the cranks spaced equally at 120 degrees permits a higher static load per axle than the conventional two-cylinder layout used at that time.

This attribute of the three-cylinder engine was to prove of some significance when enhanced motive power for the Great Eastern line was being considered, but, before that, the need to replace many of the intermediate classes of passenger engines, while not yet an urgent necessity, had to be borne in mind on an all-line basis. The second-line power, while little of it was in the 'first flush of youth', was generally in good shape. The 'Atlantics', whether of Great Central, Great Northern, North Eastern or North British design, were all doing first-class work, and, while the building of a further batch of GCR 'Director' class 4-4-0s specially for service on the North British section was an interim measure, the need was felt for a new intermediate express passenger class embodying all the fruits of development incorporated in the top-line 'Pacific' and mixed traffic classes.

What could be done by a modern well-designed 4-4-0 had already been shown on the LMS by the many and varied trials carried out on the superheated three-cylinder compound 4-4-0s of Midland Railway origin, which had been developed to become an LMS standard. Through his business associations with Sir Henry Fowler, Gresley would almost certainly have become aware of the remarkable results of those trials in which the compound 4-4-0 engines generally equalled, if not surpassed, much of the work of nominally higher powered 4-6-0

locomotives and on a considerably lower coal consumption. So, on the LNER the project was to produce a three cylinder 4-4-0 having a tractive power roughly equal to that of the existing 'Atlantics' but using a considerably smaller boiler and firebox. It was hoped that by utilizing the improved techniques of front end design, such as long-lap, long-travel valves, an equal output of power would be maintained from the steam-raising capacity of a smaller and cheaper boiler; in fact, the new design was based on the use of the same boiler and firebox as that of the 'J39' mixed traffic 0-6-0.

Comparative boiler proportions

Class	GN 4-4-2 (Large)	NE 'Z' 4-4-2	NB 4-4-2	Class 'J39' 0-6-0
Heating surfaces (sq ft)				
Firebox	141	185	185	171.5
Tubes	1,824	1,298	1,619	1,226.3
Total evaporative	1,965	1,483	1,804	1,397.8
Superheater	568	392	263	271.8
Total	2,533	1,875	2,067	1,669.6
Boiler pressure (psi)	170	175	180	180
Grate area (sq ft)	31	27	28.5	26

At first sight it would seem that the boiler of the 'J39' would not stand a chance when it came to sustained maximum output against such proved and prolific steam raisers as the Ivatt and Reid 'Atlantics'. Certainly neither the Great Northern nor the North Eastern 'Atlantics' had so high a tractive power as was contemplated for the new 4-4-0s, but in these latter it was hoped that the refinements of modern front end design would more than make up for any deficiencies elsewhere.

The new 4-4-0s were classed 'D49', but, as will be explained later, there were four sub-classifications. The three cylinders drove on to the leading pair of coupled wheels and the absence of a coupled axle ahead of the driving axle enabled all three cylinders to be set in line, with the three cranks at exactly 120 degrees to each other. In this respect, the 'D49' Class differed from the 'Pacifics' and the 'K3' 'Moguls'. The valve gear in the first batch of the new engines was simplified by having the rocking levers that operated the valve spindle of the inside cylinder valve *behind* the cylinders instead of in front. This arrangement eliminated the factor of expansion of the valve spindles which had to be taken into account

in the gear fitted to the previous Gresley three-cylinder locomotives. The maximum travel of the valves on those of the class fitted with the Walschaerts Gresley gear was greater than that of the 'Pacifics', 6 in as against 5¾ in, and a further important factor towards a free-running engine was the size of the piston valves; these were of 8 in diameter, large in relation to the cylinder diameter of only 17 in. The coupled wheels, as on the 'Pacifics', were 6 ft 8 in, and the weight of the engine in working order was 66 tons, of which the relatively high proportion of 42 tons was available for adhesion. The nominal tractive effort at 85 per cent of working pressure was 21,556 lb.

The 'D49' Class engines were built at Darlington Works. The first twenty were named after shires in England and Scotland:

234 *Yorkshire*	265 *Lanarkshire*
236 *Lancashire*	266 *Forfarshire*
245 *Lincolnshire*	270 *Argyllshire*
246 *Morayshire*	277 *Berwickshire*
249 *Aberdeenshire*	281 *Dumbartonshire*
250 *Perthshire*	306 *Roxburghshire*
251 *Derbyshire*	308 *Kincardineshire*
253 *Oxfordshire*	309 *Banffshire*
256 *Hertfordshire*	310 *Kinross-shire*
264 *Stirlingshire*	311 *Peebles-shire*

These had the usual Gresley arrangement of the

Walschaerts gear except tht the combination lever producing the conjugated motion for the inside valve spindle was placed behind the cylinders. Six further engines, generally considered to be part of the first batch and also named after shires, were built originally with Lentz oscillating cam poppet valves, though actuated by the Walschaerts gear. This development resulted from the fitting of the batch of GE type inside-cylinder 4-6-0s built by Beyer, Peacock & Co with the Lentz OC poppet valve gear. The members of the 'D49' Class so fitted were:

312 *Cambridgeshire*	327 *Nottinghamshire*
320 *Warwickshire*	329 *Inverness-shire*
322 *Huntingdonshire*	333 *Bedfordshire*

The final two of the 1927-28 batch of 'D49' engines were No 336 *Buckinghamshire* and No 352 *Leicestershire*. These differed from the rest of them in having poppet valve gear operated by rotating cams. They were followed later in 1929 by a further eight 'Shires' with the ordinary piston valves and Walschaerts gear:

2753	*Cheshire*	2757	*Dumfries-shire*
2754	*Rutlandshire*	2758	*Northumberland*
2755	*Berkshire*	2759	*Cumberland*
2756	*Selkirkshire*	2760	*Westmorland*

One of the piston valve 'D49' three-cylinder 4-4-0s, No 2753 Cheshire (British Railways).

My own first experience of travelling behind the new engines was in Scotland, but the Edinburgh-Perth road and the East Coast main line south of Dundee, while abounding in short steep banks, gave no impression of the capabilities of the locomotives in hard continuous steaming. There was no doubt that in both the North Eastern and Scottish Areas of the LNER the 'D49s' were intended to supersede the 'Atlantics' and, indeed, on the East Coast Route north of Edinburgh the loading limits were at first fixed equal to those of the ageing but very popular Reid 'Atlantics'. In the North Eastern Area, there were not all that many regular 'Atlantic' turns and at first the 'D49s' were rather sparsely spread around. On the Great Northern line, however, it seemed that a quite determined effort was made to establish the new engines as superior to the Ivatt 'Atlantics', albeit by the exploits of only one of them, No 245 *Lincolnshire*. Working near Kings Cross station and frequently in conversation with LNER men, I came to hear of many of the doings of that engine while she was stationed, temporarily as it turned out, at Kings Cross Top Shed in the autumn of 1928. There was no doubt that Gresley was taking a particular interest in the working of his new 4-4-0s, and having one of them at Kings Cross and under the eye of his personal assistant, B. Spencer, was advantageous.

Lincolnshire was put on to most of the prestige 'Atlantic' turns then worked from Kings Cross shed. At that time, however, the schedules were mostly at their earlier post-war level before the big accelerations began, and save for a few popular business trains they did not use 'Pacifics' for their haulage. The Pullman trains were faster, but lighter, and were then being worked by ex-Great Central engines, turn and turn about with Great Northern 'Atlantics'. The only run that reached the light of publicity in *The Railway Magazine* was rather unfortunate. Cecil J. Allen, making one of his regular business journeys to Teesside, was a passenger by the 5.30 pm from Kings Cross one

evening when *Lincolnshire* had been put on. It was normally a 'Pacific' turn, but with a load of 375 tons and a timing of 114 minutes for the 105.5 miles to Grantham, it would have been within the capacity of a Great Northern 'Atlantic' of the 32-element superheater batch. However, for some reason, explained no more than partly to the recorder, they made a complete mess of it, and arrived at Grantham 22½ minutes late. Subsequent work by this engine was vastly better, and generally up to normal 'Atlantic' standards to judge from the reports of the enthusiasts who made a platform-end study of the comings and goings of all GN line express workings. They reported that *Lincolnshire* made at least one successful return trip to Leeds, non-stop in each direction, with the 'Queen of Scots' Pullman express. Generally, however, the Southern Area running staff preferred their ever-faithful 'Atlantics' and in due course *Lincolnshire* joined the other 'D49s' further north.

With one exception, the general performance of these engines in Scotland was adequate but without any of the brilliance that came to characterize most of the Gresley three-cylinder express locomotives. The exception was one that I personally recorded, quite unexpectedly, when travelling on the 1.20 pm 'Scotsman' from Kings Cross to Edinburgh just before Easter, when traffic was very heavy. A relief train was running ahead, and, because the regular train normally detached six out of its fifteen coaches at Newcastle and was frequently taken forward by a North Eastern 'Atlantic', the 'Pacific' allocated to the job on this occasion was put on to the relief train which was to be considerably heavier north of Newcastle. It would have been, had not the station foreman suddenly decided to send three additional coaches forward to Edinburgh. So the relief engine, in this case a 'D49', was faced with the haulage of thirteen coaches, 412 tons tare and 435 tons gross. Had such a load been anticipated beforehand, a pilot engine would undoubtedly have been provided—some drivers, indeed, would have refused to start without one! But at the regulator of No 249 *Aberdeenshire* was a real character in Norman McKillop of Haymarket shed, Edinburgh, in later years well known for his writings of locomotive topics under his pen-name *Toram Beg*. That afternoon on the 1.20 pm 'Scotsman' he had not progressed beyond an extra link driver, but characteristically he took the abnormal load as a challenge and made what was undoubtedly the finest run that stands on record of the 'D49' Class.

Even with its normal load of about 320 tons tare, the 6.38 pm from Newcastle to Edinburgh included some pretty sharp timings with 'Atlantic' haulage, but north of the Border the allowance of 67 minutes for the 57.5 miles start-to-stop from Berwick to Edinburgh was supposed to include conditional stops at both Dunbar and Drem. I doubt if even a 'Pacific' could have kept time with such a load as 435 tons when both conditional stops were made as we were required to do on this evening. On the opening stage to Alnmouth, 34.8 miles, 2¼ minutes were lost on the 41 minutes booking, but a fine try was made at the next lap, 32.1 miles to Berwick in 36.5 minutes, only half a minute out with some fast level and downhill running along the Northumberland coast. It took us some time to get going up the gradients to the Border itself but once past Burnmouth the going was magnificent. From before Reston Junction, a speed of 62.5 mph had been attained, and up the six miles at 1 in 200 to Grantshouse the sustained

minimum speed was 46.5 mph, involving an output of about 1,200 drawbar horsepower. This was followed by a maximum of 80.5 mph down the Cockburnspath bank. With both conditional stops to be made it was inevitable that time would be lost, and our total time from Berwick to Edinburgh was 79 minutes; I think that without the extra stops we might just have managed the 67 minutes scheduled. It was a grand effort, but exceptional for those engines.

In the meantime, the work of the eight engines of the class fitted with poppet valve gear was being carefully observed, in particular the two engines Nos 336 and 352 with gear operated by rotating cams. The evident success of these two led to construction of further batches of engines similarly equipped, the first fifteen being completed at Darlington Works in 1932. A distinction from the piston valve 'Shire' Class had to be found for these new engines, so they were named after famous hunts, with their nameplates carrying the figure of a fleeing fox above the lettering. How this would have gone down in this age, with its growing repugnancy towards blood sports, is another matter. With the introduction of the 'Hunt' series, the original intention tht the 'D49' engine generally should supersede the various pre-grouping 'Atlantics' seems to have lapsed. The 'Hunts' were allocated to the North Eastern Area and were used mainly on what could be called cross-country routes, such as Leeds to Hull and Leeds to Scarborough. They had one important East Coast job in taking the morning Leeds-Glasgow express through to Newcastle, but the ex-NER 'V' and 'Z' 'Atlantics' remained as reserve engines for heavy main-line work. So far as the Great Northern line was concerned, the episode with *Lincolnshire* has already been told, and in Scotland experience north of Edinburgh had led to the 'Shires' being allocated one coach less than the Reid 'Atlantics' on heavy main-line duties.

One of the 'D49' three-cylinder 4-4-0 'Hunt' series with rotary cam actuated poppet valve gear, No 365 The Morpeth *(British Railways).*

As applied to the 'Hunt' series and also to the two experimental engines Nos 336 and 352 (originally named after shires but later renamed *The Quorn* and *The Meywell* respectively), the poppet valve gear provided only five positions of cut-off ranging from 15 to 75 per cent in forward gear, and it was not possible to work the engine with the gear between any two of these positions. The cut-off positions were 15, 20, 25, 35 and 45 per cent. This made the 'Hunts' somewhat inflexible in service. At about the time that these engines were built, one of the ex-NER three-cylinder 'Atlantics' of Class 'Z' (LNER 'C7') No 732 was rebuilt with an identical valve gear, and one day the inflexibility of the gear resulted in a failure to take on a special task. The engine was south-end standing pilot at York one day when the streamlined 'Pacific' on the up 'Silver Jubilee' failed and had to be taken off. The Kings Cross driver was given No 732, but quickly found that one cut-off position was not enough to do the job, and the next, if used continuously (presumably going up from 25 to 35 per cent setting), would have 'just about killed the fireman', to quote his own words. They stopped again at Doncaster and got another engine.

I did my first footplating on the 'D49' class on the 'Hunts' in the North Eastern Area and found them uniformly excellent engines, not that any of them was required to do any particularly strenuous work. They were not very comfortable to ride upon. Built at Darlington, they had the North Eastern characteristic of all earlier 4-4-0s built there and at Gateshead of huge wooden tool-boxes over each coupled wheel splasher, leaving a relatively narrow space between. There was also the North Eastern 'hooded fireplace', making it difficult for a third man

to find a corner that was comfortable to himself and out of the way! I myself usually finished up sprawling over the right-hand tool-box with my legs dangling down in the line of the fire. The engines, however, rode very smoothly and when put into mid-gear with the regulator closed they were as smooth and quiet as a passenger carriage. I have pleasant memories of a run I had from York to Scarborough on *The Albrighton*, the first of the second batch of these engines, hauling a 340-ton train, and of the technique the driver used in getting the engine smartly under way on a level track. Leaving Malton, the valves were in full gear and to guard against a slip the driver pumped the regulator handle, getting it gradually wider open until it was almost three quarters full, then he linked up to the 45 per cent position. About three-quarters of a mile out of Malton the regulator was opened to the full, and the cut-off to 35, 25 and finally to 20 per cent by which time we were doing about 45 mph. This was the running position, which took us up to a maximum of 66 mph on level track.

One of the most interesting runs I had as a passenger was on the 9 am Leeds-Glasgow express which I joined at York on a winter's morning. The load was no more than eight coaches, 271 tons tare and 285 tons full, behind engine No 370 *The Rufford*. By comparing the speeds made on level track with what I noted from the footplate of *The Albrighton* on the Scarborough line, I judged that the engine of the Glasgow train was being worked at 15 per cent cut-off on the fast level stretch between York and Darlington, and much the same after the speed restrictions around Durham. An abbreviated log of the run will be found below.

Left *'Hunt' series 'D49' No 269* The Cleveland *entering York* (O.S. Nock).

Right *Ex-GER 'B12' 4-6-0 No 8519 fitted with ACFI feed water heating apparatus for service on the GNSR line* (British Railways).

Distance (miles)		Schedule time (min)	Actual time (m s)	Speeds (average) (mph)
0.0	York	0	0 00	—
5.5	Beningbrough		8 47	37.5
11.2	Alne		14 39	58.0
22.2	Thirsk	25	25 04	64.0
30.0	Northallerton	32	32 23	63.7
44.1	Darlington	44	45 13	65.7
57.0	Ferryhill		58 19	59.0
66.1	Durham	70	67 42	57.8
78.9	Bensham		80 10	61.5
80.1	Newcastle	87	82 37	—

Turning now to East Anglia, where the 'D49' class engines were not allowed to run because of their high axle loading, no new express passenger locomotive class for the Great Eastern line had been introduced since the Holden 4-6-0s of 1912 (LNER Class 'B12'), and, while the most severe of their duties was soon to be eased by the insertion of an extra five minutes in the schedule of the outward bound 'Hook Continental' boat train between Liverpool Street and Parkeston Quay, Harwich, the heavy coal consumption of the 'B12' Class engines was a matter of concern. Because of civil engineering restrictions, their maximum axle load had been limited to 44 tons on the three axles. Attempts to reduce running costs had been made by installing the unsightly ACFI feed water heating apparatus and by having built by Beyer, Peacock & Co as late as 1928 ten new engines of the class, Nos 8571-8580, fitted with Lentz poppet valve gear instead of the normal link motion. When the project of designing a new 4-6-0 that would surpass the 'B12' was put in hand, as Spencer told me

years later, there were many obstacles put in Gresley's way. Time and again he had to start with another clean sheet on his drawing-board, and eventually he became so frustrated that he said 'Don't waste more time on it: send the whole thing up to the North British Locomotive Company'. In one of my earliest books, published forty years ago, I commented that the resulting three-cylinder 4-6-0s, the 'Sandringham' Class or 'B17', provided one of the very few instances of a new Gresley design being built other than at the railway company's own works. At the time it seemed as if Gresley himself did not want to know anything about it! The first of the new engines was completed at the end of 1928, and the initial batch of ten, numbered 2800-2809, were all put into service on the Great Eastern line. All subsequent engines, up to No 2861, were built at Darlington Works.

The basic dimensions contributing to a nominal tractive effort of 25,380 lb at 85 per cent of boiler pressure were three cylinders of $17\frac{1}{2}$ in by 26 in, a coupled wheel diameter of 6 ft 8 in and a boiler pressure of 200 psi. The boiler was of ample proportions, having an evaporative heating surface of 1,676 sq ft that included 168 sq ft in the firebox; the 344 sq ft from the 24-element Robinson superheater made a total of 2,020 sq ft. The grate area was 27.5 sq ft. The Gresley conjugated gear was used for transmitting the derived motion from the two outside cylinders to the valve spindle of the inside cylinder piston valve, and, as in the case of the 'D49' three cylinder 4-4-0s, the combination lever was located behind the cylinders instead of in front as on the 'Pacifics', 'K3' 2-6-0s and 'O2' 2-8-0s. The 'Sandringham' Class were different from the usual

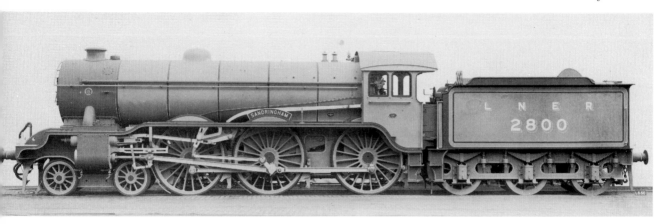

run of Gresley three-cylinder engines in having a divided drive, the inside cylinder driving the leading pair of coupled wheels. An interesting feature that in later years no doubt contributed to the very free running of these engines was that, although the cylinders had a diameter of no more than 17½ in, the piston valves had an 8 in diameter, the same as on the 'A1' 'Pacifics', which, of course, had 20 in diameter cylinders. The valves themselves had a medium long lap with a travel in full gear of 5 $^{21}/_{32}$ in. The maximum cut-off, as with the 'Pacifics', was 65 per cent. Against the very limited axle load permitted on the Great Eastern two-cylinder 4-6-0s, the 'Sandringhams' had an adhesion weight of 53.75 tons, with a total engine weight in working order of 76.65 tons.

The ten engines built by the North British Locomotive Company in 1928-29 were named after stately and historic country mansions in East Anglia:

2800	*Sandringham*	2805	*Burnham Thorpe*
2801	*Holkham*	2806	*Audley End*
2802	*Walsingham*	2807	*Blickling*
2803	*Framlingham*	2808	*Gunton*
2804	*Elveden*	2809	*Quidenham*

The overall appearance of the new engines was somewhat marred by the necessity of providing them with the very short wheelbase tender of Great Eastern design; this was caused by the small diameter of the turntables at the principal depots. The coal capacity was no more than 4 tons and the water 3,700 gallons. The carrying capacity of those tenders was brought forcibly to mind when in *The Railway Magazine* of 1929 Cecil J. Allen remarked that his first recorded performance with the new engines had been between Manchester and Sheffield on the Great Central line. It had been a time-honoured duty of Great Eastern engines of the prestigious

'Continental' link at Parkeston Quay to work also the North Country Continental boat expresses through between Harwich and Manchester, and with the infusion of the 'Sandringham' Class on the Great Eastern line this was one of the first jobs to which they were allocated. It was a lengthy journey totalling 232 miles, and took a few minutes over six hours. For much of the run the load was not particularly heavy and the booked speeds from point to point were not high, but in comparison with the 210 miles between Marylebone and Manchester worked by some engines of the class subsequently stationed on the Great Central line it could be fatiguing for one crew on a double-home duty.

On the Great Eastern main lines in East Anglia, the new engines were not set any tasks more severe than those previously worked by the Holden 4-6-0s—less so, if the deceleration of the 'Hook Continental' boat express is taken into account. Nonetheless, the coal bill would have been undoubtedly lighter, and with successive new batches of 'Sandringhams' built at Darlington Works from 1931 onwards it was found possible to release a number of the ex-GER 4-6-0s for service on the Great North of Scotland line, where more powerful engines were needed but permanent way and other engineering restrictions had hitherto precluded the use of anything larger than a 4-4-0. The Great Eastern 4-6-0s, with their light axle loading, were ideal. Although some of the later 'Sandringhams' were allocated to the Great Central line and put on some of the through workings between Marylebone and Manchester, the engines still had the small Great Eastern type tenders until the batch numbered from 2848 upwards was built at Darlington in 1936. I

gather that these tenders sometimes contributed to the rough riding attributed to the 'Sandringham' Class, but be that as it may, one of the fastest runs I ever had on the footplate over the Great Central line, including a maximum of 90 mph, was made on an engine attached to a Great Eastern type tender, and, although there was plenty of vibration, I found it no more than normal on a fast run.

It was when a batch of these engines built new at Darlington in 1936 and fitted with the standard LNER 4,200 gallon tenders was allocated to Leicester shed that they began to 'hit the headlines' in the railway press. Having more or less exhausted the list of stately homes, at least so far as eastern and north-eastern England was concerned, the next batch of 'B17' class 4-6-0s were named after popular Association Football Clubs, beginning with No 2848 *Arsenal*. Leicester shed had made a great reputation for hard running in the years since 1920 with the Robinson 'Atlantics', both simple and compound (for evidence of this, see Chapter 16) and when they received their first batch of 'B17s' (one could really no longer call them 'Sandringhams', named as they were!) the men took to them like the proverbial 'ducks to water', and were soon doing magnificent work with them. Until then, the 'B17' Class, by taking over the mantle of the Holden 4-6-0s on the Great Eastern with no heavier loads and no faster schedules, had passed largely into the nondescript stage of British locomotive performance, particularly in that the Royal Specials between Kings Cross and Wolferton, for Sandringham House, were not worked by the 'B17s' at all, but by one or other of the two 'Super-Claud' 4-4-0s stationed at Kings Lynn and maintained in a highly-burnished condition.

Above left *First of the 'B17' Class, No 2800* Sandringham, *with small-type GER tender and Westinghouse brake* (British Railways).

Left *One of the first batch of 'Sandringhams' built by the North British Locomotive Company in 1928, No 2808* Gunton *(the late W.J. Reynolds).*

Right *One of the Darlington-built 'Sandringhams', No 2822* Alnwick Castle, *as newly built in January 1931* (British Railways).

The work of the Leicester 'B17s' from 1936 changed all that. Henceforth, until still larger engines were drafted to the GC section, they continued to make front-page news.

The working of the 6.20 pm express to Bradford, non-stop from Marylebone to Leicester via High Wycombe, was always a prestige job for the 'Atlantics' (see Chapter 16), but early in 1936 the slip coaches were cut out and brief passenger stops inserted at Finmere and Woodford with little extra time added. The 'B17s' came to Leicester soon after this, and I had the very splendid run tabulated below in the early summer of that same year.

LNER: 6.20 pm Marylebone-Leicester

Engine Class 'B17' 4-6-0 No 2849 *Sheffield United*
Load 9 coaches, 310 tons tare, 325 tons full

Distance (miles)		Schedule time (min)	Actual time (m s)	Speed (mph)
0.0	Marylebone	0	0 00	—
3.0	Brondesbury		6 24	35
5.1	Neasden Junction	9	9 01	58.5/45*
8.8	South Harrow		13 49	48/56
11.6	Northolt Junction	17	17 07	42*
16.1	Denham		22 25	61.5
18.7	Gerrards Cross		25 08	56
23.0	Beaconsfield		29 36	61
27.8	High Wycombe	35	34 14	69.5/41*
32.8	Saunderton		40 46	50
36.0	Princes Risborough	45	44 08	74
41.4	Haddenham		48 11	85
45.4	Ashendon Junction		51 10	77.5
51.3	Grendon Junction		56 05	69/71
53.3	Calvert		57 50	64/69
59.0	Finmere	66	63 39	—
0.0			0 00	—
—			—	60
4.8	Brackley		7 33	53.5
8.0	Helmdon		11 29	48
12.8	Culworth Junction	15	16 11	74
14.6	Woodford	17½	18 21	—
0.0			0 00	—
2.4	Charwelton		5 12	46
9.4	Braunston		11 38	85
14.1	Rugby		15 20	68/77
17.7	Shawell		18 20	59
20.9	Lutterworth		21 29	67/58.5
29.3	Whetstone		28 32	88
34.0	Leicester	34	32 55	—

*Speed restrictions

Because of the awkward gradients and speed restrictions it was not possible to make much speed until High Wycombe was passed, but then, after climbing to the crest of the Chiltern Hills at Saunderton, the Leicester drivers, whether on 'Atlantics' or 'B17s', used to let fly, in this case reaching 85 mph at Haddenham. The short section from Finmere to Woodford was mostly adverse, inclined at 1 in 176, but the final stage included some grand racing stretches, down from Catesby Tunnel to Braunston and on the descent into Leicester. It will be seen from the log that the driver of engine No 2849 made full use of both of these, reaching 85 and 88 mph.

Towards the end of 1930 the first Gresley express tank locomotive was turned out from Doncaster works. Hitherto the company's needs in this category had been met by building more Class 'A5' 4-6-2s of the Great Central design but, although these engines together with the converted Raven 4-4-4s were holding the fort in the North Eastern Area, in Scotland there was certainly scope for something of more modern design than the Reid 4-4-2 tanks on the North British section, good engines though they were. Gresley followed Churchward's earlier example by building a tank engine version of one of his 'Mogul' mixed traffic types and using the 2-6-2 wheel arrangement. While producing an engine almost identical in tractive power to the 'K2s' Gresley adopted three-cylinder propulsion. The 'V1s', as they were classed, were compact and handsome engines with characteristically Great Northern lines. All three cylinders drove the middle pair of coupled wheels; while the outside cylinders were inclined at 1 in 30 to the horizontal, the inside one was inclined at 1 in 8, so that the connecting rod cleared the leading coupled axle. The three cylinders were combined in a single casting, a second steel casting forming the smokebox saddle and steam passages to the outside cylinders. The leading dimensions of the 'V1' engines were cylinders (3) of 16 in diameter by 26 in stroke, coupled wheels of 5 ft 8 in diameter, valve travel in full gear $6^{1}/_{16}$ in, 22-element superheater with a heating surface of 284 sq ft, total heating surface 1,609 sq ft, grate area 22 sq ft and working pressure 180 psi. The side tanks had a capacity of 2,000 gallons, and the bunker carried 4½ tons of coal. In working order the total weight of the locomotive was 84 tons, of which 57 tons was available for adhesion. The nominal tractive effort at 85 per cent was 22,464 lb.

Having dealt with the subject of the 'B17' class and their early work on the Great Eastern line, I must depart from the topic of three-cylinder locomotives for the last few paragraphs of this chapter to refer to the important rebuilding of the famous Great

Above *The great* Mallard, *restored to the LNER livery in which she captured the world record for steam traction of 126 mph in 1938. She is now preserved at the National Railway Museum at York* (J.A. Coiley).

Below *No 61656* Leeds United, *one of the later 'Sandringham' Class three-cylinder 4-6-0s introduced in 1936, climbing the Bethnal Green bank with a Norwich express in February 1959* (R.C. Riley).

Gresley 'K4' three-cylinder 2-6-0 No 3442 The Great Marquess, *built for working on the West Highland line, as privately preserved in LNER passenger livery, here seen at Worcester in 1965* (R.C. Riley).

Above *Thompson 'L1' Class 2-6-4 tank No 67703 at Ipswich in May 1957* (R.C. Riley).

Below *Peppercorn Class 'A2' 'Pacific' No 60577* Sun Chariot *at Dundee in March 1964, sister engine to the preserved* Blue Peter (Roy Hobbs).

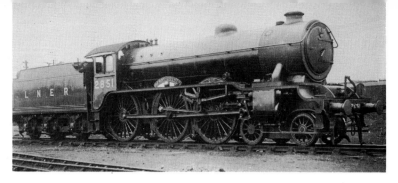

Right *One of the 'Football Club' series of the 'B17' Class with standard LNER tenders, No 2851* Derby County, *built in 1936 and stationed at Leicester GC shed* (O.S. Nock).

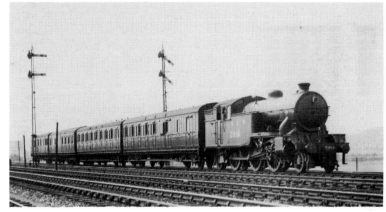

Right *One of the 'V1' Class 2-6-2 tanks, No 2916, built in 1930-31 and seen here working in Scotland on a local near Haymarket* (Author's collection).

Below *A later example of the 'V1' Class, No 465, built at Doncaster in 1936 for work in the Newcastle area* (British Railways).

Eastern locomotives of the '1500' Class 4-6-0s (Class 'B12') and the 'Claud Hamilton' Class 4-4-0s (Class 'D16'), both of which were carried out at Stratford Works. It is noteworthy that in the extensive reconstruction the greatly improved performance of both classes was obtained by the use of a more efficient boiler and the redesign of the front end, with no greater increase in total weight in the case of the 4-6-0 than from 63 to 69.25 tons. The new boiler, with a round-topped instead of Belpaire firebox, provided only a slight increase in total heating surface, from 1834 to 1874 sq ft, but the make-up of that inclusive figure yielded a higher evaporation per lb of coal fired. The small flue tubes were enlarged from 1¾ to a 2 in diameter, the grate area was increased from 26.5 to 31 sq ft and the increase in superheating surface from 202 to 315 sq ft gave a higher steam temperature with consequently greater fluidity and greater freedom in exhaust.

The new arrangement of the Stephenson link motion was arrived at after some preliminary experiments recalling the first trial of long-travel valves on the 'A1' 'Pacifics'. First, engine No 8559 was fitted with long-travel valves having a stroke, in full gear, of $6^6/_{16}$ in instead of the original $4^3/_{16}$, the increase being obtained simply by making the arms of the rocking levers unequal. Then a considerably improved setting was obtained from a thorough redesigning of the gear, first fitted to engine No 8579 in 1932, in which the principal change was the use of expansion links having longer slots than previously. One of the salient features was that, even when linked

up to 15 per cent cut-off, the new valve setting provided an opening to exhaust equal to the full width of the port. The 10 in diameter piston valves of the original engines were reduced to a 9½ in diameter in the new arrangement.

The valve arrangement fitted to No 8579 was tested carefully against that of No 8559 before a final decision was made. Coal trials made in August 1932 between Liverpool Street and Ipswich with trains of 385 tons tare showed an advantage of about 5 per cent in favour of No 8579; no dynamometer car was used, so the figures, which related to the coal actually consumed, could not be related to the drawbar horsepower developed. The trials were carried out on the 8.15 am down and the 12.23 pm up, both of which trains were then booked to make a number of intermediate stops; the 8.15 am took 110 minutes for the 68.7 miles, inclusive of 5 stops totalling 9 minutes, and the 12.23 pm took 97 minutes inclusive of 2 stops totalling 6 minutes. In such circumstances the consumption by No 8579 of only 40.6 lb per train mile on the round trip was good. In the same month, No 8579 worked a load of 288 tare on the 12.30 pm Liverpool St-Yarmouth non-stop express, returning with the 4.30 pm up non-stop from Beccles; on the round trip of 243.5 miles, involving a running average of 47.5 mph, the coal consumption worked out at the remarkable figure of 27.9 lb per train mile. Considering the numerous hindrances to fast running on the East Suffolk line, this was a striking tribute to the efficiency of the new valve gear. The valve arrangement fitted to No 8579 was used for all engines subsequently rebuilt and No 8559 was afterwards altered to correspond.

The 'B12/3s' were very fast and economical engines, but when comparison comes to be made with the original GER 4-6-0s it is no mean reputation that has to be surpassed. The nightly feats of the Parkeston drivers on the 'Hook Continental' express will live in locomotive history, but there is no denying that the coal consumption was heavy as a result of continuous working at 30 to 35 per cent cut-off. The 'B12/3s', like most Gresley engines, were worked on full regulator with 15 to 20 per cent cut-off and the first recorded attainment of 90 mph on Great Eastern metals stands to the credit of one of this class, No 8535, when a load of 305 tons was worked over the 46.3 miles from Ipswich to Norwich in a net time of 43.5 minutes.

The renewal of certain engines of the 'Claud Hamilton' Class carried out, like that of the 'B12/3s' at Stratford works, was even more complete. Originally the former had slide valves directly underneath the cylinder, whereas the new engines built on to the old chassis had new cylinders with piston valves above, similar to the 'B12/3s'. The first ten to be renewed in 1933-34, including No 8900 *Claud Hamilton* itself, had 8 in diameter piston valves with a maximum travel of $6^{1}/_{16}$ in, but a further ten were fitted with 9½ in diameter valves, in conjunction with redesigned cylinders having large steam and exhaust passages and a degree of internal streamlining. No 8861 was the first of this later batch, and was turned out in April 1936. Both batches were now classed 'D16/3', though this classification also included a number of rebuilt engines having the same enlarged boiler but retaining the original slide valves and power reversing gear. As with the 'B12/3s', the nominal tractive effort was not increased above that of the original GER engines, but the improvement in performance, particularly that of the 9½ in valve batch, was very marked.

Rebuilt 'Claud Hamilton' Class 4-4-0 No 8849 with an enlarged boiler, improved steam circuit and piston valves, on an excursion to Walton-on-the-Naze near Chadwell Heath (E.R. Wethersett).

15. The great experiment—engine 10000

By midsummer 1929, rumours had begun to circulate from Darlington Works that a very large locomotive of unusual proportions was under construction there. The secrecy with which it was apparently surrounded led to its being called the 'hush hush' project. The curiosity of those who gleaned certain scraps of information was heightened because, while the frames and machinery of a very big locomotive, and a compound at that, were being laid down, there was as yet no sign of a boiler, nor were any apparent preparations being made for building one. Then, late in October 1929, the boiler arrived at Darlington from the works of Messrs Yarrow & Co of Glasgow, and 'the murder was out'. The completion of this remarkable locomotive, which ran its trial trip on December 12 1929, was the consummation of a project that Gresley had nurtured for some time even before he had approached Mr Harold Yarrow in September 1924 and suggested that the water-tube high pressure boiler needed for marine and stationary plant might also be applied to locomotives. The technical press was favoured with illustrations and a description which were published as early as January and February 1930, but engineers in general had to wait until January 1931 for the ultimate *dénouement* when Gresley himself read his monumental paper on *High Pressure Locomotives* to the Institution of Mechanical Engineers.

A second meeting had to be held at the Institution headquarters in London to afford an opportunity for the many members who wished to discuss the paper to do so, and it was also presented and equally fully discussed at provincial meetings in Manchester, Leeds, Glasgow and Southampton. In all, the paper itself and the fully reported discussions eventually occupied 105 pages of the proceedings of the Institution. At headquarters, the President of the Institution, Loughnan Pendred, was in the chair, and at various times the following well-known railway personalities took part: Sir Henry Fowler, R.E.L. Maunsell, W.A. Stanier, A.C. Stamer, H.P.M. Beames, D.C. Urie, R.C. Bond, T.S. Finlayson and many eminent men concerned with the marine side of mechanical engineering including Sir John Thornycroft and Harold Yarrow himself.

Gresley began his paper by emphasizing that at no time during the history of the steam locomotive had such radical changes been introduced as during the past ten years. These changes had been introduced more or less simultaneously in countries supplying the locomotives of the world, and had no doubt been stimulated by the competition of electric and oil engines which offered more efficient and in some cases cheaper motive power. Twenty years before it had been thought that the steam locomotive had attained practically its maximum development, as it had nearly reached the limits imposed by the loading gauge, but the radical changes necessitated by the adoption of extra high pressures seemed to have opened up a new era, and not only did these changes render possible an increase in tractive power but should also at the same time increase the overall efficiency.

Experimental 4-6-4 high pressure compound locomotive No 10000 (British Railways).

After an early experimental run, No 10000 arrives at King's Cross in June 1930 (the late W.J. Reynolds).

After stressing the importance of economizing in maintenance costs as well as fuel consumption, Gresley then proceeded to describe briefly some notable high pressure locomotives that had been built recently in America and on the continent of Europe. Passing on to his own No 10000 which was, of course, the principal focus of interest in the paper, he said that, unlike his Continental colleagues, he had thought it advisable in designing this engine to be content with what may be regarded as only a moderate increase in boiler pressure to 450 psi. In coming to this decision he had been largely influenced by consideration of maintenance costs and the desirability of advancing by stages. Past experience of revolutionary designs had been that the spectacular advancements had not always been justified by results, and he had consequently deemed it wiser to seek progress on a less ambitious scale, recognizing that as the pressure increased the economies to be expected in fuel consumption were in a diminishing ratio.

He had decided to adopt a boiler of the water-tube type in view of the successful application of such boilers to high pressure work in ships, and large power stations. In September 1924, he had accordingly approached Mr Harold Yarrow, MIMechE of Glasgow whose firm were well known as designers and builders of water-tube boilers, and had suggested to him a design of boiler of the water-tube type which might be applied to locomotives. Such a boiler would involve a radical departure from the usual design for marine and land purposes, and upwards of three years of work on the part of Mr

Yarrow and himself had resulted in the completion towards the end of 1927 of the final design, which was patented in their joint names. Early in 1928 an order was placed with Messrs Yarrow to proceed with the construction of the boiler, which was completed and tested in October 1929.

The drums of the boiler were of sufficient diameter to allow a man to get inside for the purpose of expanding the tubes. To suit the conditions peculiar to a locomotive, it was felt that tubes of a large diameter only should be used, the tubes in the firebox end of the boiler having a 2½ in external diameter and those in the forward part 2 in. The considerations which govern the design of marine and land boilers are so entirely different from those required in a locomotive boiler that there was very little similarity between the boiler used on this engine and the ordinary type of water-tube boiler. In the ordinary water-tube boiler resting on foundations, the boiler can expand freely in any direction, and the tubes, not being subjected to vibration and racking stesses, are not liable to leak. In a locomotive, the boiler must be so secured to the frame that in addition to withstanding the shocks and vibrations consequent upon the engine running at high speed on a railway, it must be capable of withstanding the shocks which occur when the locomotive is shunting or coming into contact with buffer stops, or possibly becoming derailed.

It is necessary also to have due regard to the fact

that the boiler provides an important structural element in the construction of a locomotive and contributes to its rigidity. It will be seen from the diagram that in this boiler the large steam-drum formed the backbone of the boiler from which the tubes and the small drums depended. At the forward end, this drum was carried in a cast-steel cradle into which it was firmly secured by large strap bolts, and any fore-and-aft movement was entirely prevented by stops which were machined on the lower side of the drum. The cradle in turn was secured to the engine frame by 1 in steel plates extending downwards inside the main engine frames to which they were securely riveted. The steel drum needed to be free to expand longitudinally, however, so the back end was secured to the top of a triangular-shaped transverse plate which in turn was secured at its lower extremity to the engine frame. The drum, whilst therefore being free to expand longitudinally was constrained from side or vertical motion.

Cross-sectional drawings of No 10000.

The four smaller drums were not supported, but hung from the water-tubes. Rectangular lugs were riveted to the front and back of the lower side of each of these drums and were free to slide longitudinally in grooved castings which were secured to the engine frame; as they did not reach the bottom of the grooves, they were also free to move vertically. These lugs and grooves were provided to restrain the drums from any side movement. It was considered that this was the best way of preventing the transmission of vibration and shocks to the tubes in such a way as might cause leakage. It is interesting to note that this method of construction was completely successful, in that there was no case of the slightest leakage occurring at any of the 1,536 points at which the tubes had been expanded in the drums.

In adopting a water-tube boiler, Gresley was not unmindful of the troubles which might reasonably be expected to result from scale formation in the tubes. Unlike marine and power station boilers, in which the boiler feed is derived from the condensate and only a very small make-up of fresh water is required,

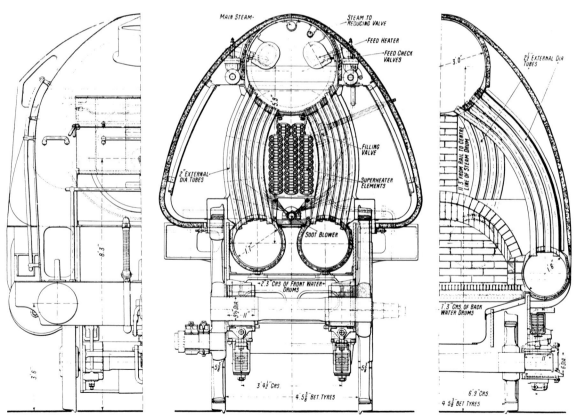

Half Front-End Elevation, Cross-sectional Elevation through Boiler and Half-Cross-Sectional Elevation through Firebox, High-Pressure Locomotive No. 10000, L.N.E.R.

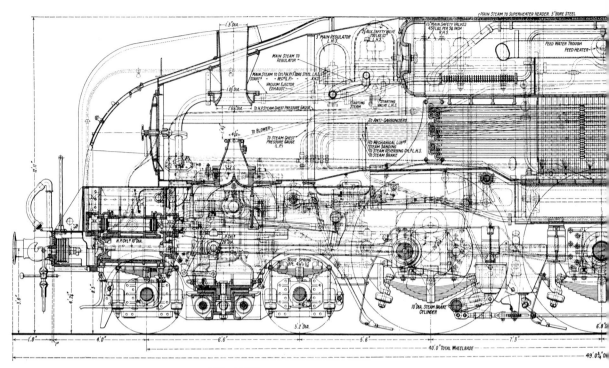

Drawing showing the internal arrangements of No 10000.

the locomotive boiler uses 100 per cent make-up water. In order to prevent as far as possible the formation of scale, Gresley decided to introduce the feed water at the highest possible temperture. It will be seen from the diagram that the feed water was introduced into a chamber at the forward end of the top drum in front of the water-tubes and separated from the evaporative portion of the boiler by a weir at a height of about half its diameter.

The water was supplied from the tender by means of two ordinary injectors, and was delivered after passing through a form of injector heater. This had two sets of cones in which the injector action was repeated by steam from the steam space in the boiler. Heat was absorbed to such an extent by the feed water that its temperature when delivered into the water chamber was over 400°F, and was therefore only about 50° less than that of the saturated steam in the boiler. Much of the scale and mud was consequently thrown down in the forward portion of the top drum.

But for this arrangement of dealing with the feed water, considerable trouble due to the formation of scale would have been expected; as it was, after running some 15,000 miles a slight deposit of hard scale was found on the inner rows of tubes in the firebox. This was at first not easy to detect, and

consequently, at the time the paper was read, about half-a-dozen tubes on each side of the firebox adjacent to the brick arch showed signs of overheating and had to be changed. The experience resulted in the development of an apparatus by which the hardest scale could be readily cut out without damage to the tubes, a process that would have been necessary when the engine had run some 10,000 to 15,000 miles, according to the class of feed water used.

On the other hand, experience had shown that this boiler could be worked for a much longer period than the ordinary type of locomotive boiler before requiring to be washed out. When stationed at Gateshead, the locomotive worked express trains from York to Edinburgh and back involving a daily run of about 420 miles. Whilst other engines of the 'Pacific' type in the same link required washing out after running 1,000 to 1,500 miles, this engine ran 5,000 miles without washing out, and when opened up it was found that the boiler was exceptionally clean and the tubes were in good condition. Moreover, it was found that the accumulation of mud and scale which usually occurs above the foundation ring in an ordinary boiler had fallen into the drums below the grate on each side of the firebox, and it remained in the form of mud and was easily removed; if it had been in the sides of an ordinary locomotive firebox,

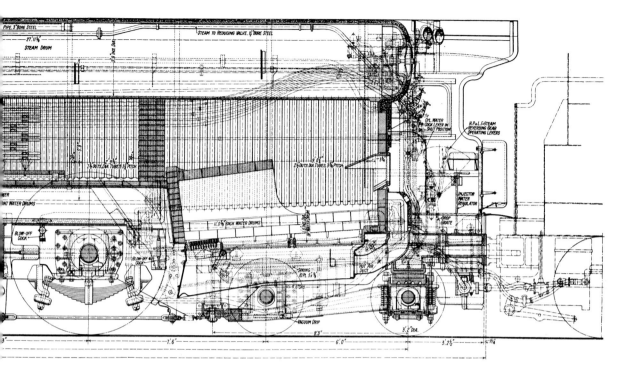

much of it would have formed into scale.

In a test which was carried out at the maker's works, an evaporation of 20,000 lb per hour at 450 psi was maintained for a period of four hours by the introduction of a steam jet up the chimney. This high rate of evaporation was possible because such a large proportion of the heating surface available was subject to direct radiant heat. In the ordinary form of locomotive boiler only the firebox is subject to radiant heat, and the evaporation per square foot of heating surface of the tubes is only about one-fifth of that of the firebox sides. Actually, the rate of evaporation maintained in the boiler of No 10000 was nothing very wonderful, even for those days. Although no measurements were then being made, in later years on tests under British Railways auspices it was demonstrated that the boilers of the ordinary Gresley 'Pacifics', both of Classes 'A1' and 'A3', could readily sustain an output of 25,000 lbs of steam per hour, and up to 30,000 lbs if pressed to the limit of the physical capacity of a single fireman.

The superheated elements in the boiler of No 10000 were located in the forward portion of the central flue and were also subject to radiant heat. In order to prevent the flames from impinging directly on the ends of the elements, a brick column was provided in the centre of the main flue immediately in front of the brick arch. Notwithstanding this

precaution, and owing to the fact that there was no data available as to the effect of radiant heat on superheater elements, the temperature to which the steam was superheated during preliminary trials was excessive, temperatures of 900°F being obtained; consequently, the lengths and area of the superheater elements were reduced so that a temperature of approximately 700°F could be obtained, and this was regarded as sufficient. The superheater elements were situated between the boiler and the regulator and were, therefore, always subject to full boiler pressure. In order to prevent overheating when the regulator was closed, the steam supplied for auxiliary services was taken from the superheater and passed through a coil of ribbed pipes laid in the feed-water chamber, thus raising further the temperature of the boiler feed and at the same time de-superheating the steam. The de-superheated steam was led to a reducing valve where its pressure was reduced to 200 psi. The steam then supplied a manifold pipe on the footplate across the front of the boiler above the firehole door and from this pipe steam at 200 psi was taken to supply all the auxiliary services, such as the injector, vacuum and steam brake, reversing gear, steam-sanding, steam-heating, whistle and turbogenerator. It had been possible to retain the standard steam fittings for all these purposes; with a pressure of even 450 psi, special designs of boiler fittings and valves would have had to be used owing to the cutting action of high pressure steam, but in this engine only the safety valves, regulators and water gauges had to be made suitable for the higher pressure.

After the hot gases had passed between the water-tubes they entered the flues located at each side of the boiler. Naturally, the walls of these flues were very hot, and in order to reduce their temperature and to make effective use of this heat which otherwise would have been wasted, the boiler was surrounded by an air space lying between the casing of the flues and the insulated outer covering. All the air required for combustion traversed this air space from the intake at the front of the engine to the ashpan, and in so doing its temperature was raised to about 250°F. It was found that even when working hard it was not necessary to supplement this supply of hot air by opening the ashpan door, and preheating the whole of the air supply was bound to augment the thermal efficiency of the boiler.

The only other feature of the boiler which called for comment was the construction of the front end and chimney. (Incidentally, the apparent absence of the chimney caused more public comment than any

Front-end view of No 10000 (British Railways).

Head-on view of No 10000 showing the arrangements for deflecting the smoke (British Railways).

other feature of the locomotive). In order to provide sufficient length for the water-tubes, it was necessary to have the top steam-drum as high as the limits imposed by the loading gauge would permit; consequently there was no room for a chimney of the conventional type. Engines having large, high-pitched boilers only had very short chimneys, and trouble had been experienced in such engines owing to smoke and steam beating down on the front windows of the cab and interfering with the driver's view of signals. Gresley enlisted the assistance of Professor W. E. Dalby and constructed a wooden model of an engine of such a type which was placed in an air flume and powdered chalk was blown up the chimney at the same time as a current of air was drawn through the flume at 50 mph. Observations through a glass window showed the course pursued by the powdered chalk and, as a result of various modifications, the design finally adopted was arrived at. In this design, the whole of the powdered chalk was lifted sufficiently to clear the cab windows, and it is satisfactory to record that in actual service the smoke and steam, whether running at slow or at high speeds, was deflected upwards to clear the cab and in no way obstructed the driver's vision.

The leading dimensions of this very noteworthy boiler were:

Grate (ft in)

Length on slope	7 6
Width	4 8
Grate area (sq ft)	34.95

Boiler (ft in)

Steam-drum:

Length	27 11⅝
Inside diameter	3 0

Forward water-drums:

Length	13 5¾
Inside diameter	1 7

Rear water-drums:

Length	11 0⅝
Inside diameter	1 6
Smokebox length	16 1
Working pressure (psi)	450

Tubes

Small:

Number	444
Outside diameter (in)	2

Combustion chamber:

Number	74
Outside diameter (in)	2½

Firebox:

Number	250
Outside diameter (in)	2½

Heating surfaces (sq ft)

Firebox	919
Combustion chamber	195
Small tubes	872
Total evaporative	1,986

Superheater

Number of elements	12
Inside diameter (in)	1.18
Heating surface (sq ft)	140
Total heating surface (sq ft)	2,126

As originally built, the engine had two high pressure cylinders of 12 in diameter and two low pressure cylinders each of 20 in diameter, all cylinders having a 26 in stroke. It was found that by reducing the diameter of the high pressure cylinders to 10 in, a more equal distribution of work between the high pressure and low pressure cylinders resulted.

The details of the motion were as follows:

Motion Gresley Walschaerts

Valves	High pressure	Low pressure
Type	piston	piston
Diameter (in)	6	8
Maximum travel (in)	8⁹/₁₆	6¹¹/₁₆
Steam lap (in)	1⅜	1⅝
Exhaust lap	nil	nil
Cut-off in full gear (per cent)	90	75

A plan view of the motion arrangement for the high and low pressure cylinders is shown in the diagram on page 166. Gresley regarded it as necessary, whilst having only two sets of valve gear, to be able to vary the cut-off of the high pressure cylinder independently of that of the low pressure cylinder. He felt that only by trial at varying cut-offs could the best results be realized. He therefore arranged that in the rocking link by which the high pressure valve is actuated provision should be made by means of a slot and die-block to vary the travel of the valve, at the same time retaining the combination lever to keep the lead constant. The reversal of the low pressure valve gear, and consequently of the whole engine, was actuated by the ordinary form of steam-reverser, and similar equipment was provided to vary the high pressure cut-off. Both these pieces of equipment were attached to the shafts they actuated, and, being so remote from the footplate, their delicate control would not have been easy but was successfully effected by the use of telemotors; another telemotor was provided for operating the cylinder cocks. The high pressure cylinders, steam ports, passages and low pressure steam receiver were formed by a single steel casting, the cylinders and steam chests having special close-grained cast-iron liners. Various minor alterations and adjustments had to be made after the engine was built, but with the exception of reducing the diameter of the high pressure cylinders and reducing the heating surface of the superheater, it was not necessary to alter any of its main features.

The discussions at the varous meetings of the Institution of Mechanical Engineers brought out many interesting points. Firstly, with regard to the boiler, Mr W. W. Marriner of Messrs Yarrow & Co said that when Mr Gresley invited Mr Yarrow to co-operate with him in the design of the boiler how pleased he and all his staff had been to do so. He added 'It was surprising how much they had learned by their association with Mr Gresley and his staff. The members had no idea of the difficulties there were in getting such a powerful machine into such a small space, and within the limits of the permissible weight. They had even learned a great deal about boiler-making itself'. Sir John Thornycroft commented on the design of the boiler, and said it appeared beautifully simple in comparison with the other more complicated continental designs which had formed a preface to Gresley's paper. At first glance it would appear to cost much less too, and he suggested that a certain amount of money could well be afforded for cleaning the firebox tubes and thereby avoiding the risks that would occur if hard water was allowed to get into them.

Some of the leading locomotive engineers of the other British railways commented on the means used

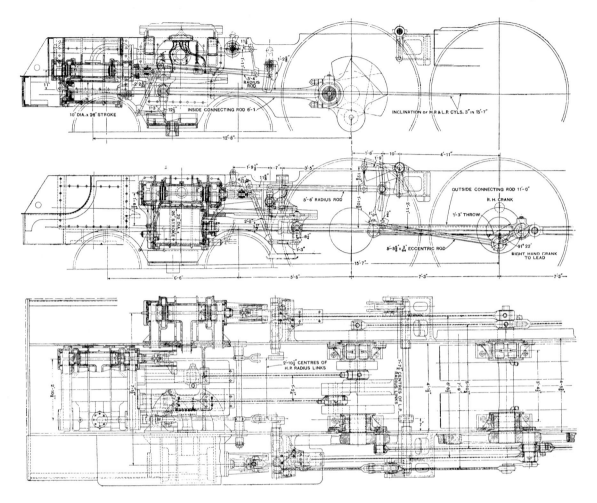

for smoke deflection. Sir Henry Fowler said 'He had been much interested in the chimney of locomotive No 10000. He was a member of a smoke prevention committee and in that capacity he had ascertained that legally a chimney was anything out of which smoke issued. There was, therefore, not the slightest doubt that the aperture in Mr Gresley's locomotive was a chimney. It appeared, however, that there was no room for the installation of a "wind-cutter". If that had been possible, the adoption of some means of causing the wind striking the locomotive to be deflected upwards would drive the steam away from the windows of the cab.'

There was also an interesting piece from R.E.L. Maunsell with regard to the arrangement for lifting the smoke. He said that 'he himself had been somewhat troubled in the same way with some engines on the Southern Railway, and they had tried numerous devices in the early part of 1930. They had

adopted the trial and error method and he wished now that they had thought of the experimental method by which Mr Gresley had got over the trouble. In his own case no device had been found to be of the slightest use except an arrangement of what were familiarly known as "blinker" plates on the sides of the engine, which induced a current of air to lift the smoke above the spectacle glasses'.

There had naturally been comment about the wheel arrangement. Once the news about No 10000 was getting around, a locomotive engineer of my acquaintance met me one day and said 'When is a 4-6-4 not a 4-6-4?'. In reply to some points in the discussion Gresley himself said 'There had been no room to put in a bogie because it would be seen that the ashpan was placed very low. The trailing axle was really a Bissel truck with Cartazzi slides for centralizing. The axle in front of it was interchangeable with that used on the ''Pacific'' engines. It was a peculiar

Left *Details of cylinder and motion of No 10000.*

Right *Footplate view of No 10000* (British Railways).

arrangement, and it had to be adopted because of the circumstance he had mentioned. The result, however, was that the engine was very easy riding'. There was always the possibility with a 4-6-4 type engine of getting a symmetrical arrangement resulting in the setting up of a swaying movement, although a dissimilar side control at the leading end from that at the trailing end tended to break the synchronization. Nevertheless, in the discussion in Manchester, Captain H.P.M. Beames raised the question of the riding and said it would seem from the diagram that the centre of gravity was pitched rather high and the engine might be unsteady. On the other hand he was given to understand that at high speed its was a particularly steady-running machine, and Gresley confirmed that in spite of outward appearances the centre of gravity of the engine was lower than that of the ordinary 'Pacifics'. Although the top drum looked very high it was comparatively

light, whereas the lower part of the boiler was fairly heavy and full of water.

At the discussion in the meeting in Glasgow on the all-important subject of coal consumption, D.C. Urie, formerly of the Highland Railway and later Chief Locomotive Running Superintendent of the LMS, took up Gresley's statement concerning the performance of engine 10000 on the non-stop 'Flying Scotsman' runs between Edinburgh and Kings Cross. Before the reading of the paper, during the summer months of 1930, the engine, stationed at Gateshead, had been frequently working on the regular double-manned turn beginning on the Leeds-Glasgow express between Newcastle and Edinburgh. The return working was on the corresponding southbound train, but continuing to York, the engine being re-manned at Newcastle. This southbound train maintained the historic 43-minute booking for the 44.1 miles from Darlington to York,

Engine No 10000 on the down non-stop 'Flying Scotsman' near Hadley Wood in August 1930 (A.L.P. Reavil).

at one time run by the lightly-loaded 1.9 pm express for Sheffield but reinstated after the First World War on the much heavier 8.49 pm up, which was then rarely taking a load of less than 300 tons. Indeed, a log was published in *The Railway Magazine* of October 1930 of engine 10000 working that train with a load of no less than 440 tons. It was in that same summer that the one and only return trip from Edinburgh to Kings Cross and back was made with the non-stop 'Flying Scotsman'. The up journey was made on July 31st and the train was then running to the original non-stop schedule of 8¼ hours for the run of 392.75 miles. I saw her arrive at Kings Cross exactly on time with a 13-coach train.

One feels that Gresley rather played down the performance of his standard 'Pacific' engines in making comparison with that one return trip of No 10000 on the non-stop 'Scotsman'. At one stage in the discussion he said 'With regard to fuel consumption the tenders of the "Pacific" engines carried 9 tons of coal, and in running a non-stop train from Kings Cross to Edinburgh burned most of that coal—about 8 tons. When engine No 10000 had finished its first trip there had been about 2 tons of coal left in the tender'. Urie, as might be expected, was critical on this point. A ton of coal saved in eight on the trip from

London to Edinburgh did not amount to much more than 10 per cent, and he saw no future for a high pressure locomotive unless its costs were not in excess of normal locomotives built for similar duties because additional capital expense would quickly absorb the coal saving under normal working conditions. Actually, the 8 tons quoted by Gresley was very much wide of the mark. On some boiler evaporation trials carried out on one of the 'Pacifics' at a steaming rate rather higher than that required by the non-stop 'Scotsman' in its 8¼-hour days, this coal consumption was less than 35 lbs per train mile against the 40-42 lb quoted by Gresley. The standard 'Pacifics', both 'A1' and 'A3' Classes, did not use more than 38 lb per mile on the hardest Doncaster-Kings Cross duties with the fastest West Riding expresses.

Reverting to the working of No 10000 on the Glasgow-Leeds express, the fast run from Darlington to York is tabulated with two roughly contemporary runs behind 'A1' 'Pacifics', the first one with the normal load of the Leeds train and a Gateshead engine on the usual 410-mile double-manned turn, and the second with a Kings Cross engine and crew working home on the up 'Junior Scotsman' with a characteristically heavy load.

LNER: Darlington to York

Engine No			2750		10000		4475	
Engine Name			*Tranquil*		—		*Flying Fox*	
Engine Class			'A1'		'W'		'A1'	
Load (tons, tare/full)			298/310		414/440		471/510	

Distance (miles)		Schedule time (min)	Actual time (m s)	Speed (mph)	Actual time (m s)	Speed (mph)	Actual time (m s)	Speed (mph)
0.0	Darlington	0	0 00		0 00		0 00	
2.6	Croft Spa		4 29	59	4 40	52	5 03	53
5.2	Eryholme Junction	7	7 07	59	7 30	56	8 01	53
10.4	Danby Wiske		11 43	75	12 30	70	13 01	69
14.1	Northallerton	16	14 43	73	15 45	67	16 20	66
17.5	Otterington		17 26	77.5	18 50	70	19 20	72
21.9	Thirsk	23	20 48	79.5	22 35	68	22 53	75
26.1	Sessay		24 14	72.5	26 20	66	26 19	73
28.0	Pilmoor		25 48	73	28 05	65	27 52	75
30.7	Raskelf		27 59	75	30 30	67	30 01	76.5
32.9	Alne	32	29 44	77	32 25	69	31 44	77.5
38.6	Beningbrough		34 44	eased	37 30	67	36 18	72
42.5	Poppleton Junction	40	38 45	—	40 50	—	39 45	—
			—		sigs		sig stop	
44.1	York	43	42 55	—	44 10	—	45 05	
	Net time (min)		43		43¾		42¾	

Tranquil, despite being nearly 300 miles out on her daily round, started the 310-ton load brilliantly by sustaining 59 mph up the 1 in 391 from the Tees viaduct at Croft Spa up to Eryholme and followed this by an average of exactly 75 mph over the 22.5 miles from Danby Wiske to Alne. By that time the train was more than 2¼ minutes early, and the driver justifiably eased up. The high pressure engine No 10000 also made a good start, accelerating up the grade to 56 mph at Eryholme and attaining 70 mph at Danby Wiske. However, after passing Northallerton and Thirsk on time, the speeds onwards to York were not up to 'Pacific' standards, and although the final approach to York was checked by signal the resulting delay did not cost more than half a minute. By contrast, *Flying Fox*'s run with no less than 510 tons was exhilarating. After a good start, the London driver went on to average 73.5 mph over the 27 miles from Northallerton to the third milepost out of York, and passed Poppleton Junction within good time to make a 43-minute run from Darlington, even though this train was allowed 46 minutes.

And what of No 10000? Following the publicity showered on it after Gresley's paper, it seems to have dropped out of the public notice. I do know that a lot of painstaking work was bestowed on it at Darlington, much of it of a fruitless and frustrating nature. At one time Bulleid was very much involved in trying to make a go of it, but it proved very troublesome to maintain and increasingly extravagant in fuel consumption. An echo of its vagaries came to me in 1933 when Gresley was planning his great 2-8-2 'P2' express engine for the Aberdeen route. Apparently there was some doubt in his mind as to the wisdom of using eight coupled wheels on express trains, so, as a practical trial, one of the two 'P1' 2-8-2 heavy mineral engines was taken off its normal return working from Hornsea to Peterborough with an empty wagon train and put on to the 7.45 semi-fast from Kings Cross, which gave the opportunity for some fast running. It was arranged that Spencer should ride on the footplate of the 'P1', and I was amused to hear from him afterwards that he had been very carefully briefed by Bulleid beforehand, including the instruction of making sure they had a pilot waiting at Hitchin in case there was any trouble. 'That', Spencer laughingly added, 'was pretty good coming from he who had recently lost half-an-hour with No 10000 on the "Flying Scotsman"'!.

16. 'Atlantic' swan-song: classic runs in the mid-1930s

Before the introduction of the Gresley 'Pacifics', the 'Atlantics' were the premier express passenger locomotive type on the East Coast Route throughout from Kings Cross to Aberdeen. Not only that, but on the Great Central line, although J.G. Robinson had introduced powerful superheated 4-4-0s and 4-6-0s from 1912, these never entirely superseded his own 'Atlantics' which, when fitted with superheaters, were able to equal the finest work done by the later engines. It was my pleasure and privilege to observe many runs made by those notable engines, quite a number from the footplate. While some of these were little more than routine timekeeping journeys, a few were outstanding and are collected in this chapter. Fortunately, my own personal records include examples from each of the four pre-grouping railways.

In the early 1930s I was travelling frequently in the North Eastern Area and was interested to see the regular use of 'Atlantics' of both 'V' and 'Z' Classes on many of the lesser East Coast trains, and, when the non-stop 'Flying Scotsman' was running in the height of the summer, a top-class train like the 1.20 pm from Kings Cross to Edinburgh was regularly taken forward from Newcastle by a 'Z'. On summer Saturdays, when there were many relief trains publicly scheduled in the timetables, the bulk of these were worked by 'Atlantics', and I made a particular study of some duties. Also, at that time the practice originally introduced on the Western Area of the Southern Railway of decelerating certain important schedules on Saturdays and busy holiday periods had not spread to the LNER, so extra and relief sections of, for example, the 'Flying Scotsman' group of trains running northward from York on summer Saturdays all had to run at the speed of the fastest. Immediately after the passage of the down 'non-stop', there was despatched the 1.34 pm for Newcastle, Berwick and

Edinburgh which originated at York and ran ahead of the 'Junior Scotsman'. This latter also had a regularly scheduled second section which did not proceed beyond Newcastle and was itself unable to dawdle because it had the sharply-timed 1.55 pm Liverpool-Newcastle express on its tail from York.

The 'Junior Scotsman' and its reliefs running fore and aft of it were all booked to cover the first 44 miles to Darlington in 48 minutes as part of a through run to Newcastle in 92 minutes. I found that with 'Atlantics' of both classes there was time to spare when the loads were not much above 350 tons. On the racing stretch north of York, speed usually rose to 67 or 68 mph on the level at Thirsk, though on the 1.34 pm with a 'V' and a load of 305 tons I have known the start out of York to be so brisk that adverse signals from the non-stop 'Scotsman' ahead were sighted; doubtless the men on that train were taking things easily prior to and during the process of remanning near Tollerton. Normally there would have been no point in trying to run as much as a minute ahead of time in so closely scheduled a procession as this, but with the Liverpool train it was different. For one thing it was booked to stop at Darlington, and moreover was allowed no more than 46 minutes for the start-to-stop run of 44.1 miles from York. At one time the North Eastern Railway had a very sharp booking of 44 minutes over this route, made with the evening dining-car express from Kings Cross; the load was generally under 200 tons, but even so an extra minute had to be added to the schedule before very long. In 1933, when I joined the 1.55 pm travelling on this occasion only to

Class 'V1' two-cylinder 'Atlantic' No 697 with the NER dynamometer-car, now preserved in the National Railway Museum at York (British Railways).

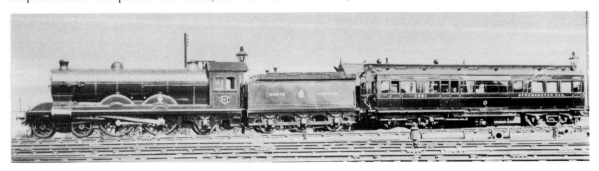

Class 'V' two-cylinder 'Atlantic' No 1776 on a Newcastle to Liverpool express near Lamesley (R.J. Purves).

Darlington, the load was 310 tons and it turned out by far and away the finest I ever experienced behind a North Eastern engine, and that for my personal records is saying a good deal!

The preliminaries proved almost as diverting as the run itself. The train was advertised as leaving from platform 14, then the most westerly and outside the wall of the main station. While I saw a 'Z' back down on to one of the centre roads to await the arrival of the second portion of the 'Junior Scotsman' which was advertised as following the first part on the main departure platform, No 9, there was no sign in the immediate vicinity of any engine to take my train. I had, however, noticed a smartly turned out 'Z' over on the furthest extent of the *up* line in a spur leading from the goods and empty carriage line near the old Waterworks signal box. When our train arrived from the LMS and its engine coupled off and ran forward to the shed, it appeared that the far-off 'Z' was indeed our engine, and a remarkable series of manoeuvres now proceeded to get it across the fullest extent of the main line and into No 14 platform to our train. I counted *six* successive shunt movements!

Direction	Move
Forward	Spur to empty carriage line
Reverse	Empty carriage line to up relief
Forward	Up relief to up main
Reverse	Up main to down main
Forward	Down main to down relief
Reverse	Down relief into No 14 platform

I wish I had thought to time those movements as the whole operation was one of the slickest I ever remember, considering that it was performed entirely with manually-operated signalling equipment.

The brilliant run of which this was the prelude is set out in the accompanying table.

LNER: 1.55 pm York-Darlington

Engine   Three-cylinder 'Z' Class 4-4-2 No 710
Load   42 axles, 292 tons tare, 310 tons full

Distance (miles)		Actual time (m s)	Speeds* (mph)
0.0	York	0 00	—
1.6	Poppleton Junction	3 54	—
5.5	Beningbrough	8 22	61
9.7	Tollerton	12 18	66
11.2	Alne	13 38	67.5
13.4	Raskelf	15 34	69.5
16.1	Pilmoor	17 58	68
18.0	Sessay	19 40	67
22.2	Thirsk	23 18	72
26.6	Otterington	27 00	69
30.0	Northallerton	30 02	66.5
33.7	Danby Wiske	33 20	73
37.2	Cowton	36 16	68.5
38.9	Eryholme Junction	37 46	67
41.5	Croft Spa	39 59	75
43.9	Darlington home signals	44 00	
		47 20	
44.1	Darlington	49 30	

*max and min at points shown

The geographic layout of the north end of York station, particularly the exit from No 14 platform with its reverse curves, is hardly conducive to making rapid starts, and there was some slipping before we got fairly under way, but once we were rounding the curve past that once grandly-named signal box, Severus, No 710 was going in first-class style. Before

saying farewell to York, at least so far as this chapter is concerned, I must voice my annoyance once again at the thought of that 'realist' (or perhaps ignoramus!) of later LNER days who expunged the classical name of the Roman Emperor who died in the city and substituted the utilitarian 'York Yard North'. 'Severus' was such a splendid name for this major signal box which housed technology that was unique on the North Eastern Railway.

However, reverting to the exploits of No 710, when the 44-minute York-Darlington timing was first introduced in the early 1900s, the engines used were often of the 4-4-0 'R' Class and they used to get away to a tremendously vigorous start, but once the mile-a-minute rate was attained there was little more acceleration. It was far otherwise with No 710. We reached 60 mph just before Beningbrough, and went ahead on the level track until we had all but topped the 70 line beyond Alne. At this point, 12.5 miles out of York, a gradual rise begins, nothing steeper than 1 in 666 and 1 in 740 but enough to stay our acceleration.

Travelling in the leading coach of the train and listening to the soft 'purr' of the engine's three-cylinder exhaust beat, I could tell that the steaming was very free. The rise in the line was cleared without speed falling below 67 mph, and on the level which was reached before Sessay we were accelerating again to reach 72 mph at Thirsk. The upward tendency of the gradients continues until the 38½ milepost out of York, just short of Eryholme Junction, and after the Thirsk 'level' there are two more sections at the modest inclination of 1 in 629 interspersed with a length of level. The speeds shown in the accompanying log reflect exactly the changes in gradient: 66.5 mph up to Northallerton, 73 mph on the level to Danby Wiske and 67 up to Eryholme.

Over the 29.2 miles from Tollerton to Eryholme, on an average rising gradient of 1 in 1320, the speed averaged all but 70 mph and the drawbar horsepower was about 800. Once over the ridge, and on a falling gradient no steeper than 1 in 391 speed leaped up to 75 mph in 2.5 miles. Having passed Croft Spa in such excellent time I was looking forward to an arrival in Darlington in 43 minutes, or a second or two under, recalling how the old 5.30 pm from Kings Cross used to run into Bank Top station in pre-grouping days. On this busy day, however, there was another train in the down main platform and after a lengthy signal check in the approach we were stopped at the entrance to the platform and held there for 3¼ minutes. I estimate that the net time for an unchecked run from York to Darlington would have been 43¼ minutes.

The East Coast main line north of Dundee, for most of the 71.4 miles to Aberdeen, is as different in its physical characteristics from the speedway south of Darlington as it is possible to imagine. Yet the North British Railway had in its own 'Atlantics' engines that were every bit as speedy as the three-cylinder greyhounds of the North Eastern. That they were rarely called upon for really fast running on the only stretch of their own line that was straight and level, between Camperdown Junction, Dundee, and Arbroath, was due mainly to the relative modesty of the schedule requirements over the 16 miles of line and to the punctuality with which the East Coast trains arrived at both starting points on this level stretch beside the northern shore of the Firth of Tay. Speed capabilities apart, the North British 'Atlantics' were tremendously strong engines, of which I had ample personal evidence throughout the East Coast route north of Edinburgh and over the Waverley route down to Carlisle even before I had

Left *Class 'Z' three-cylinder 'Atlantic' No 735 near Danby Wiske on a down relief East Coast express* (O.S. Nock).

Right *Ex-North British 'Atlantic' No 9509* Duke of Rothesay *at Ferryhill running sheds, Aberdeen, in 1935* (O.S. Nock).

the privilege of riding on their footplates. Some of the trains by which I travelled were extremely heavy, and, although the loading regulations did not spare the 'Atlantics', the introduction of third-class sleeping-cars on the night trains in addition to a goodly tally of first-class in the tourist season sent the loads of the 'Aberdonian' and the 'Night Scotsman' up towards the 500-ton mark. The latter train, northbound from Edinburgh, carried through carriages from St Pancras as well.

On the northbound road the maximum tare load for the 'Atlantics' was 380 tons, and when I was waiting for the 3.35 pm express for Aberdeen at Tay Bridge station, Dundee, I was pleased to see a solo engine, *Duke of Rothesay*, drawing down to stand on the road beside the west wall to await the arrival of the train from Edinburgh. This was to have been the second time I had ridden this 'Atlantic' engine on that day, because 'she' had been our engine on the down 'Aberdonian' that same morning. In the earlier case, however, the load had been heavy enough to need an assistant engine, a 'Scott' Class 4-4-0, *Lady of Avenel*. *Duke of Rothesay* had shown up in first-rate condition on that earlier trip and I looked forward to recording some of her unaided work on the 3.35 pm. We also had the good fortune of a load nearly up to the 'Atlantic' maximum, 359 tons tare and fully 380 tons gross behind the tender, and an equally expert and enthusiastic crew for our second run of the day, Driver Moodie and Fireman Williamson. The North British 'Atlantics' were easy and comfortable engines to ride, though lacking such luxuries as Gresley provided for his express enginemen in the form of padded seats and backrests. However, one did not look for armchair comfort on steam locomotives, and *Duke of Rothesay* and her class could be placed in the top flight among engines of

pre-1914 vintage. They had lever reversing gear and in full gear the cut-off was 74 per cent; in linking up, successive notches gave cut-offs of 67, 60, 53, 44 and 34 per cent. There was no means of intermediate adjustment.

The cold February weather with snow south of Edinburgh which had greeted our arrival earlier that day had cleared to a brisk sunny afternoon with a wind off the North Sea which was not enough to hinder our running. The immediate exit from Dundee is awkward; just before the northern end of the tunnels under the city there is a villainous S-curve, followed by a short ascent of 1 in 60 to reach the fine level stretch that extends for 15 miles along the northern shores of the Firth of Tay estuary. On clearing the tunnel and mounting the short bank to Camperdown Junction, the driver opened out to almost full regulator and notched his lever back to the 44 per cent position. Acceleration was rapid, and after two miles the lever was moved a further notch back to 34 per cent cut-off. By this time, the 'Grand Old Duke', as another of her drivers called her, was wheeling this big train along in splendid style. No more adjustments of the controls were made until slowing down for Arbroath, and the speed increased until we were doing a steady 67 mph. It was an exhilarating start, with the steaming rock steady, the engine riding as smoothly as a dining-car and the exhaust beat just a purposeful purr. Arbroath was not quite ready for us and we were stopped momentarily by signal in the approach to the station, but this was the only delay in the entire journey to Aberdeen.

The hindrances were of a physical, more geographical nature from Arbroath onwards, because the line, still not far inland, follows the rugged coastline in a steeply-graded switchback course.

Ex-NBR 'Atlantic' No 9872 Auld Reekie *on the down 'Night Scotsman' at Stonehaven* (O.S. Nock).

Fortunately, the alignment was mostly first class so that full use could be made of momentum attained on the downhill sections for climbing the next gradient. So we went pounding up the first heavy bank of 1 in 103 out of Arbroath to Letham Grange followed by a dash down to Inverkeilor at 71.5 mph and then up the 1 in 93 to the cliffs above Lunan Bay with a full-throated roar from the exhaust and speed falling to 40.5 mph at the summit. The descent thence into Montrose is, however, the one section of steeply-falling gradient on this route where one cannot make any speed. Not only is this section sharply curved but it includes the one remaining length of single-line working, between Usan signal box and Montrose itself. The viaduct over the South Esk river has not been widened and the express locomotives working north of Dundee had apparatus for mechanical token exchanging on their tenders which we used when passing Usan.

Hard climbing was resumed immediately after leaving Montrose. The gradient is 1 in 90 up the bank to join the one-time Caledonian line at the historic Kinnaber Junction, and we thundered up at 30 mph with the regulator nearly full open and 44 per cent cut-off, until slowing to 15 mph for the actual junction. At this strategic point, goal of the rival trains in the exciting 'Race to the North' in 1895, the Caledonian provided a connection for the rival North British trains with such an awkward alignment that dead slowing was required. Once over the points we were away again hard, working up speed to charge the Marykirk bank, 56 mph over the North Esk viaduct near Craigo, 44 per cent cut-off and almost full regulator. To the thrilling sound of the exhaust beat we mounted the 1 in 100 gradient, speed falling eventually to 37.5 mph, then there was a brief respite while the track dipped slightly through Laurencekirk and eased out to dead level for nearly 2 miles to Fordoun. That respite, with the lever back to the 34 per cent position, was short-lived, for when going at 66 mph the lever was set forward another notch and the regulator opened still wider for a storming ascent to the summit of the line at Drumlithie, which we topped at all but 40 mph. So, down the Fetteresso glen on easy steam to our last stop at Stonehaven.

. The last stage into Aberdeen was merely a repetition of the previous standards of running. Although there was still some stiff hill-climbing to be done, our fireman had time to talk to me about golf as we pounded up on to the cliffs north of Stonehaven, sustaining 33 mph on a 1 in 112 gradient, and in the gathering dusk the views over the sea past Muchalls and Portlethen were very fine. By this time my cup of happiness was indeed full. In the year 1935 I had seen a locomotive of much earlier vintage completely the master of a severe task, and a careful check taken at the time indicated that the coal consumption was little if anything more than 40 lb per mile. After a swift acceleration down to Muchalls, touching 64 mph round the S-curve on the cliff edge, we took the final climb in our stride and came spinning down through Cove Bay with the lever once more in full forward gear and running freely on the merest wisp of steam at 66 mph. So to the curve past Girdleness Lighthouse, past Craiginches yard and into Aberdeen to arrive a minute early. At the time I wrote most enthusiastically about the North British 'Atlantics' and their men, so much so indeed that one of my articles, published in a leading daily newspaper, caught the eye of the Divisional General Manager for Scotland, and I was glad to learn afterwards that the driver and fireman received from him a letter of warm commendation on their good work.

Altogether contrasting were the circumstances of my finest run with one of the Great Central 'Atlantics'. During the inter-war years, the 6.20 pm Bradford express was one of the most sharply-timed trains out of Marylebone, and until the summer of 1936 it was invariably worked by one of the splendid Robinson 'Atlantics', the 'Jersey Lillies' to give them their

LNER: 3.55 pm Dundee-Aberdeen

Engine NBR 4-4-2 No 9509 *Duke of Rothesay*
Load 359 tons tare, 380 tons full

Distance (miles)		Schedule time (min)	Actual time (m s)	Speed (mph)
0.0	Dundee	0	0 00	—
0.7	Camperdown Junction		2 30	—
4.0	Broughty Ferry		7 30	50
6.4	Monifieth		10 08	55.5
10.9	Carnoustie		14 34	65
12.7	East Haven		16 14	67
15.6	Elliott Junction		18 50	67
			sig stop	—
17.0	Arbroath	22	22 20	—
3.0	Letham Grange		7 00	27
6.2	Inverkeilor		10 37	71.5
8.8	Lunan Bay		13 22	46
9.7	Milepost 26¾		14 30	40.5
13.7	Montrose	21	19 43	
1.3	Milepost 32		3 07	33.5
2.3	Milepost 33		4 57	30
2.6	Kinnaber Junction		5 42	15*
4.7	Craigo		9 28	56
6.8	Marykirk		12 02	46.5
8.9	Milepost 209¼		15 05	37.5
10.0	Laurencekirk		16 46	48
13.3	Fordoun		20 17	66
17.3	Drumlithie		25 21	39.5
19.0	Carmont		27 45	49.5
21.9	Dunnottar Box		30 41	71
24.5	Stonehaven	34	33 27	
1.6	Milepost 226½		3 23	33
2.6	Milepost 227½		5 14	32.5
4.6	Muchalls		7 46	64
8.0	Portlethen		11 30	50/54.5
9.1	Milepost 234		12 45	50.5
11.4	Cove Bay		15 02	63.5
14.5	Craiginches South		17 58	66
16.2	Aberdeen	22	21 07	—

*Speed restriction

celebrated, and usually misinterpreted, nickname. Those on top link duties at Leicester shed had all been superheated and fitted with 21 in cylinders by that time. Although having a relatively short lap, the piston valves were of 10 in diameter, and the motion was suited to very fast and free running. Until the early spring of 1936, the train was booked to run non-stop from Marylebone to Leicester via High Wycombe, 107.6 miles in 114 minutes, but in February of that year the slip coaches that had hitherto been carried to Finmere, 59 miles, and to Woodford, 73.6 miles, were cut out and brief station stops made instead. No more than five minutes overall was allowed for making the two stops, slowing down for them and accelerating afterwards. Prior to the change in working I had several runs on the former non-stop train and always found the per-formance of the 'Atlantic' engines immaculate, so it was not without unusual interest that I made my way to Marylebone for a journey to Sheffield soon after the alteration. I was travelling as an ordinary passenger, so had no previous word with the driver and fireman of engine No 5363 but I knew this particular driver, Tom Newall of Leicester shed, as a thoroughgoing enthusiast, and I took my seat in the train with pleasurable anticipation.

We had a discouraging start, however. We had no sooner turned off the Aylesbury line at Neasden Junction than we were slowed for a long restriction for track repairs and by the time we passed Northolt Junction and entered the GW & GC Joint Line we were nearly three minutes late. Once over the junction, however, the driver opened up in earnest and the ensuing 47.4 miles to our first stop at

Above *One of the last two NBR 'Atlantics' of 1921, No 9510* The Lord Provost, *on an Edinburgh-Aberdeen express just after leaving Leuchars Junction* (O.S. Nock).

Left *Great Central express near Harrow, with three non-corridor bogies added to the regular train, hauled by Robinson 'Atlantic' No 1084* (the late C. Laundy).

Right *The 12.15 pm Marylebone-Manchester (via High Wycombe) express near Saunderton, hauled by 4-4-2 No 5263 in plain black with mostly modern Gresley stock* (M.W. Earley).

Finmere took no more than 47 minutes, nearly a minute ahead of time. This length included the successive climbs over the Chiltern Hills, first the section at 1 in 175-254 up to Beaconsfield and then, after the short respite to High Wycombe, the steeper pitch graded at 1 in 179-164 up to Saunderton. This was hindered by the permanent speed restriction round the curve at High Wycombe at the very foot of this incline. We ran splendidly over this length, from 61.5 mph at Denham, falling only to 55 mph up the first 1 in 175 to Gerrards Cross and recovering to 60 mph on the 1 in 254 before the first summit at Beaconsfield. Then came a quick dash up to 72.5 mph before the enforced slowing through High Wycombe. Once round the curves, I heard the exhaust open up again and on the 6-mile climb to the crest of the hills above Saunderton the speed increased to 48 mph.

This was the end of restricted speed. Down through Princes Risborough the acceleration was terrific and before Haddenham we reached 88 mph. We were then running on level track and despite the rising tendency of the line thereafter the speed had dropped little below 80 mph when the Great Western line diverged to the north-west at Ashendon Junction, and we kept up a tearing pace to the junction with the Aylesbury line at Grendon Underwood. We were now on the magnificently engineered London Extension line of the Great Central Railway and, although it runs through some hilly country in the South Midlands, the gradients are nowhere steeper than 1 in 176. Many of the inclines were considerably longer than what would be normally classed as 'momentum grades', such as could be rushed from the impetus derived from the high speed attained on a previous descent, but even so the going on this most exciting trip was such that

we were taking the rising gradients at 55 to 60 mph and the descents at 75 to 82 mph! The first stage from Marylebone finished brilliantly. On the very short fall after Calvert we were doing 70.5 mph, and then there was a length of 5 miles at 1 in 176. Finmere station was near the top of this incline, yet when we shut off steam for the stop we were still running at 60 mph.

The short section onwards to Woodford was mainly adverse though one would not realize it from the sharpness of the timing. There was a mile of 1 in 176 ascent from the start at Finmere, then 1.5 miles down followed by the Helmdon bank of 4.5 miles up at the same all-pervading incline. As the log shows, we got away in great style and touched 63 mph in the short dip before Brackley, mounting the Helmdon bank without going below 54 mph. Over the undulating gradients that followed we stormed away and reached 76.5 mph at Culworth Junction. Even so, this was not good enough to maintain such a time as 16½ minutes start-to-stop from Finmere to Woodford; in fact, the working times were adjusted two months after the elimination of the slip-coach working to provide 17½ minutes from Finmere to Woodford, and a reduced time of 66 minutes for the 59 miles from Marylebone. On my trip, the intermediate station working was as always on the Great Central line very smart, and despite our slight excess in time on the previous section we got away from Woodford practically on time, and the last stage into Leicester proved an absolute riot of high speed.

Reflecting upon this grand run, however, it is sad to remember that the route over which it was made, not only the section now under discussion but also the whole Great Central line from south of Sheffield to Aylesbury, save for the short privately-preserved length south of Loughborough, is now obliterated.

LNER: 6.20 pm Marylebone-Leicester

Engine Two-cylinder 4-4-2 No 5363
Load 242 tons tare, 260 tons full

Distance (miles)		Schedule time (min)	Actual time (m s)	Speeds (mph)
0.0	Marylebone	0	0 00	—
3.0	Brondesbury		6 38	32
5.1	Neasden Junction	9	9 20	56
—			pws	22
8.8	South Harrow		16 07	43
11.6	Northolt Junction	17	19 45	56/42*
16.1	Denham		24 58	61.5
18.7	Gerrards Cross		27 46	55
23.0	Beaconsfield		32 12	64
—	Tylers Green		34 24	72.5
27.8	High Wycombe	35	36 48	42*
32.8	Saunderton		43 31	48
36.0	Princes Risborough	45	46 56	73
41.4	Haddenham		51 03	88
45.4	Ashendon Junction		54 06	78
51.3	Grendon Junction		59 08	67.5/69
53.3	Calvert		60 57	65/70.5
59.0	Finmere	67½	66 50	—
4.8	Brackley		7 18	63/57
8.0	Helmdon		10 48	54
12.8	Culworth Junction	14	15 15	76.5
14.6	Woodford	16½	17 11	—
2.4	Charwelton		4 52	46
9.4	Braunston		11 09	82.5
14.1	Rugby		15 07	63.5/73
17.7	Shawell		18 15	56.5
19.9	Lutterworth		21 31	66.5/61
24.8	Ashby		25 08	74
29.3	Whetstone		28 27	87
33.0	Leicester South Goods		31 06	80.5
34.0	Leicester Junction	34	32 23	—

*Speed restriction

There is a poignancy about a passage in a topographical book on Northamptonshire written more than seventy years ago to which I had recently to make reference. The author wrote 'Woodford Halse, so called from the name of the manor to which it belongs, was once as rural as any village in the country round, but the advent of the Great Central Railway changed all this, and now it is a thriving railway settlement, with all the air of a miniature Swindon or Crewe'. As the junction of the important link line to the Great Western at Banbury, Woodford had running shed accommodation double that of both Leicester and Nottingham! Enough of reflections, however, for now engine No 5363 was roaring her way up to the short level where the Charwelton water troughs were situated. Thereabouts the line topped the limestone ridge that extends north-eastwards across England from the main bulk of the Cotswold massif to Grantham, and through which the line of the GCR plunged in the two-mile Catesby Tunnel. We had attained 46 mph when we entered the tunnel and with the gradient changing at once to

Bradford-Marylebone express on Charwelton troughs hauled by 'Atlantic' No 5360 just after the grouping (Author's collection).

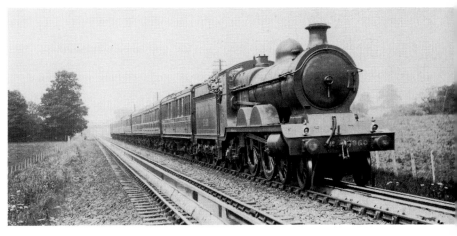

1 in 176 down we were soon flying.

We emerged at 70 mph and continued down the bank to reach 82 mph at Braunston, and thereafter a tearing pace was kept up to the near approaches to Leicester. From Braunston the road is adverse in its general tendency for the next 14 miles, with 8 miles of it rising at the standard 1 in 176, but the inclines were 'charged'—63.5 mph over the Rugby 'hump', 56 up the longer bank before Lutterworth and 61 at the final summit between the latter station and Ashby. It was thrilling to experience the immediate changes in speed as each of the intermediate summit points was passed, particularly at Rugby where the Central station was passed at a minimum speed of 63.5 mph, and the subsequent acceleration was so rapid that the long lattice girder viaduct over the LMS line was crossed at 73 mph. Having passed the last summit point at 92 miles from London, the driver indulged in a glorious last dash for home, and the speed rose to a maximum of 87 mph. So well was this sustained that after 3 further miles of only nominally falling gradients from Whetstone, the speed was still 80 mph a mile from Leicester Central station. I just had time to congratulate Driver Newall and his fireman Lees on a grand run before they coupled off in that very smart engine change for which Leicester was famous; only four minutes were allowed for the operation.

When the Pullman trains were first put on the East Coast main line, W.P.G. Maclure from the Great Central was Locomotive Running Superintendent of the Southern Area of the LNER and, with Gresley's whole-hearted approbation, a few of the latest Robinson express locomotives were transferred from the Great Central section to work turn and turn about with the Ivatt 'Atlantics'. The Kings Cross-Leeds workings of the newly-introduced 'Harrogate Pullman' in 1923 provided the longest non-stop runs yet operated by the four-cylinder 4-6-0s of the 'Lord Faringdon' Class, and by and large they did very well

on the job. When the Pullman service was extended to Edinburgh, and non-stop running was introduced for a time between Kings Cross and Harrogate via Church Fenton and Wetherby, a few of the 'Director' Class 4-4-0s were put on to the job, and they remained shedded at Copley Hill, Leeds, for a few years after the 'Queen of Scots' Pullman had resumed its original routeing via Leeds.

When the opportunities came for me to make some journeys, I found that the Ivatt 'Atlantics' were in sole possession of the job. In referring to the original designer, however, one must not forget the extent to which the design had been developed in Gresley's time. It was not only the superheating itself, with larger cylinders and piston valves, but also the substitution of 32-element for the original 24-element apparatus that worked such a transformation. In fact, many engines of the class retained their slide valves until their last years, yet all eventually had 32-element superheaters. So far as I know, however, all engines of the Pullman link were of the piston valve variety.

In the years 1930-36, I made a total of eight non-stop runs on the Pullman trains between Leeds and Kings Cross, and the only occasions on which I did not observe strict end-to-end time to be kept were on two winter Sunday evenings when the number of signal and permanent way checks proved more than could be recovered. Surpassing all my other records was the sweltering hot summer day in 1935 when I had the privilege of a footplate pass; furthermore, the incidence of track repairs on the up main line at Werrington Junction rendered the water troughs there out of action, and we had to make a special stop at Peterborough to top up the tender tank. This took nearly five minutes of precious time, but so resolutely was the engine handled and so splendidly was the mechanical condition of the machinery revealed that Kings Cross was reached just over five minutes early!

This was all the more notable in that the engine concerned was not one of the regular Kings Cross Pullman link. Going down the previous day, the driver had to report a defect on arrival at Leeds that could not be put right in time for the return working on the following day. Copley Hill shed had no spare 'Atlantic' so they had borrowed one from Doncaster, fortunately in very good condition.

When I boarded engine No 4456 at the sheds for the short run down to the Central Station at Leeds, I was then halfway through my day's footplate riding on Pullman engines, for I had already come non-stop from Kings Cross on the down 'Queen of Scots'. The shade temperature at midday was about 85 degrees, so it can well be imagined what it had been like in the confined cab of a Great Northern 'Atlantic'. The Copley Hill men on engine No 4423 gave me a magnificent run, arriving in Leeds 2½ minutes early despite delays totalling eight minutes en route. Their work included my first personal record of a maximum of 90 mph, but, in the heat of the day which was sustained throughout the journey, I was glad of the 1½ hours respite between the outward and return trips. The log of the return journey is included, and, though it was recorded now more

than fifty years ago, it still remains one of the absolute classics in my personal records of steam locomotive running.

From the very moment we got away from Leeds, it was evident that No 4456 was a very strong engine. Up the 1 in 100 to Ardsley the driver worked her with full regulator and 50 per cent cut-off and she responded with by far the highest minimum speed I had ever noted up that bank, 39 mph against the usual 31 to 32 mph for the Pullman trains. We were through Wakefield in record time and then the fun began. At any appreciable speed No 4456 became one of the wildest things I have ever ridden. I have certainly timed faster runs on the Pullman trains down the West Riding line when travelling passenger, which was perhaps just as well; on the footplate she pitched, she corkscrewed and the 'tail-wag' at the rear end was transmitted to the tender. No coal pusher was needed on this engine, and by the time we began to slow down for the junctions in the approach to Doncaster the footplate was ankle-deep in coal. When passing through Wakefield, the cut-off had been shortened to 35 per cent, and thus it remained all the way to Peterborough. We had left Leeds on time, but, in anticipation of the time that

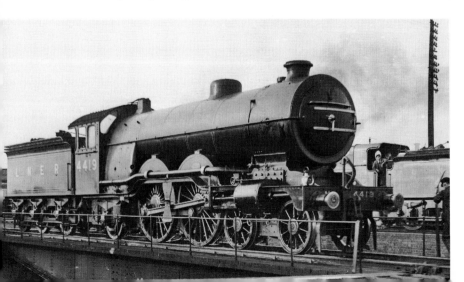

Above *Early days of the East Coast Pullman series: the up Harrogate Pullman leaving Wood Green tunnel in 1924 hauled by engine No 1427N (so numbered at the time)* (Rail Archive Stephenson/F.R. Hebron).

Left *Booster-fitted 'Atlantic' No 4419, at one time regularly used on the King's Cross-Leeds Pullman trains* (Rail Archive Stephenson/T.G. Hepburn).

LNER: 'Queen of Scots' Leeds-Kings Cross

Engine 4-4-2 No 4456
Load 7 Pullmans, 277 tons tare, 290 tons full

Distance (miles)		Schedule time (min)	Actual time (m s)	Speed (mph)
0.0	Leeds Central	0	0 00	—
2.5	Beeston		6 12	43
5.6	Ardsley		10 52	39
9.9	Wakefield	18	15 52	slack
11.6	Sandal		17 53	59
15.4	Nostell		22 10	50
23.3	Hampole		29 22	76.5
——			sig check	—
29.8	Doncaster	39	36 05	—
32.6	Black Carr Junction		39 48	59
36.3	Milepost 149½		43 48	52.5
47.2	Retford	56	54 00	73
52.1	Markham Box		58 33	60
59.4	Carlton		64 20	82
65.7	Newark	73	69 30	64
70.4	Claypole		73 52	68
76.1	Barkston		79 10	58
80.3	Grantham	88	83 24	64
85.7	Stoke Box		88 55	55
88.7	Corby		91 38	77.5
93.6	Little Bytham		95 10	90
97.2	Essendine		97 32	93/90
101.0	Tallington		100 03	92
103.9	Helpston Box		102 01	88
——			pw check	35
106.3	Werrington Junction		104 19	—
109.4	Peterborough (pass)	117	arr 109 40	—
			dep 114 25	
113.2	Yaxley		121 00	54
116.4	Holme		124 07	68.5
122.3	Abbots Ripton		129 44	57
126.9	Huntingdon	135	133 58	79
134.1	St Neots		139 40	71
141.7	Sandy		145 58	76.5
147.2	Langford Bridge Box		150 47	65
150.1	Three Counties		153 24	69
153.9	Hitchin	160	156 56	62.5
157.2	Stevenage		160 29	53.5
160.8	Knebworth		164 08	64/60
168.1	Hatfield	174	170 23	82
173.1	Potters Bar		174 40	69
176.6	New Barnet		177 40	74
180.8	Wood Green		181 09	70
183.2	Finsbury Park		183 25	—
			two sig checks	
185.8	Kings Cross	193	189 35	

The short-lived Sheffield Pullman, then the 6.5 pm from King's Cross via Nottingham, near Hadley Wood with 'Atlantic' No 4461 (Rail Archive Stephenson/F.R. Hebron).

would be spent taking water, the driver was trying to get something in hand. As the log shows, he had gained two minutes as early in the journey as Doncaster.

The good work continued until after Retford. In earlier days, it was regular practice on the Great Northern Railway to slow down to about 40 mph when picking up water. Although that restriction had been much relaxed by the time I was travelling regularly on the East Coast main line south of York, the one-time Great Northern express drivers never seemed to share the carefree habits of their rivals on the West Coast route who used to lower their scoops at anything up to 85 mph! On my footplate trip on engine No 4456, the driver eased down from the 82 mph at which we had passed Carlton to 64 mph over Muskham troughs, but it was then, after we passed Newark, that the running became really exceptional. The regulator was now half over on the quadrant plate, though in the absence of a steam chest pressure gauge one could not estimate how far from full boiler pressure steam was being admitted to the cylinders. Certainly the overall effect was tremendous. On the rising gradients from the Trent Valley, speed, gradual at first, rose to 68 mph at Claypole. The steepening gradients brought us down to 58 mph at Peascliffe Tunnel, but on the level and slight rise beyond we rallied quickly to 64 mph through Grantham, where we were 4½ minutes early.

On the final five miles continuously at 1 in 200 to Stoke summit box, exactly 100 miles from Kings Cross, we settled down to an absolutely steady 55 mph. This worked out at an equivalent drawbar

horsepower of a little over 1000, an astonishing effort for a locomotive of such relatively limited tractive power. On passing Stoke box, I was surprised, not to say a little thrilled, to see no change whatever made in the driver's working of the engine, and we continued down towards Peterborough with the regulator still halfway open and with 35 per cent cut-off. The result was an average speed of exactly *ninety miles per hour* over the 10.3 miles from Little Bytham to Helpston signal box. Strangely enough, at this tremendous speed the engine itself was riding quite steadily, a tribute to the superb track maintenance on that part of the line. So, despite the slowing down needed over Werrington troughs, we stopped at Peterborough for our water stop seven minutes *before* we should have been due to pass through on an ordinary run. Magnificent running was resumed when we got under way once more, so much so that we passed Finsbury Park, 73.8 miles from the restart, in 69 minutes, having averaged 67 mph from Yaxley. Although signals delayed us in the approach to the terminus, we still arrived in Kings Cross 3½ minutes early. Allowing for the incidental delays on this run as well, of course, for the special stop for water, the net time for the run of 185.8 miles from Leeds was no more than 176 minutes, an overall average of 63.3 mph, and a gain of no less than *seventeen minutes* on this crack schedule.

17. The streamline era

Gresley abhorred double-heading. The introduction of third-class sleeping-cars on the principal night trains on the East Coast Route to some extent nullified the advantage gained by the extension of 'Pacific' duties north of Edinburgh, because the loading of the up 'Aberdonian' with restaurant as well as sleeping-cars between Aberdeen and Edinburgh usually exceeded the maximum tonnage for a 'Pacific' southbound which was 440 tons. Experience with the 'K3' three-cylinder 2-6-0s on fast passenger trains on the Great Northern line had shown that there was no objection to the use of pony trucks on locomotives intended for fast express duties, and so the large new 2-8-2, with 6 ft 2 in coupled wheels, was designed at Doncaster, and the first two examples appeared in 1934. With three cylinders of 21 in diameter by 26 in stroke and the then usual 220 psi boiler pressure, these huge engines had a nominal tractive effort of 43,462 lb. The boiler was of commensurate proportions, and the grate area was 50 sq ft. The first two engines differed from each other in respect of their valve gear, for while the second of the two, No 2002 *Earl Marischal*, had the standard Gresley arrangement of the Walschaerts gear with conjugated motion for driving the inside valve spindle, the first engine, No 2001 *Cock o' the North*, had rotary cam type poppet valves, to some extent a sequel to the successful application of such valves to the 'D49' class express passenger 4-4-0s.

Cock o' the North was the subject of special and sustained investigations throughout the summer and autumn of 1934, mainly between Kings Cross and Doncaster, and some of them were 'full-dress' with the Darlington dynamometer car and indicating apparatus housed in shelters round the front end. These latter tests were usually made on the 10.51 am up from Doncaster returning on the very heavy 4 pm Yorkshire express from Kings Cross. I managed to get a trip as far north as Peterborough on one of these tests, travelling as an ordinary fare-paying passenger; with no recourse to the data recorded in the dynamometer car, observation revealed no performance superior to that which one could have noted with one of the standard Gresley 'Pacifics' on that train. It would have been very different on another occasion when I witnessed a departure from Kings Cross. Gresley had a visit from his friend Monsieur Lancrenon, Chief Mechanical Engineer of the Northern Railway of France, and it was arranged to put *Cock o' the North* on to the 1.20 pm Scotsman which had a much faster timing than the 4 pm Yorkshire train, passing Peterborough in 80 minutes as against 87 minutes. With the addition of the dynamometer car, the load of the Scottish express would have been at least 550 tons behind the tender. I photographed the engine, but unfortunately other duties prevented my travelling in the train on that occasion.

The outward appearance of *Cock o' the North* was not exactly prepossessing. The shields adjacent to the smokebox were in the style of the high pressure compound 4-6-4 engine No 10000, and it was hoped that they would lift the exhaust steam clear of the cab. With the sharp blast from the poppet valves of No 2001 this was successful, but it was not so on the piston valve engine No 2002. The soft blast when this

The widespread use of 2-6-0 'Moguls' proved the acceptability of pony trucks for fast passenger running (E.R. Wethersett).

Left *Dynamometer-car trials with* Cock o' the North *at Peterborough on the 4 pm down Yorkshire express* (O.S. Nock).

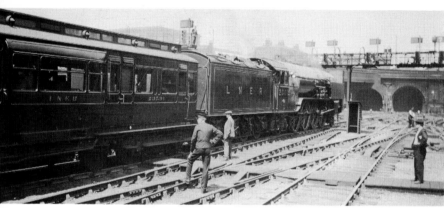

Left *Special dynamometer-car test for Monsieur Lancrenon of the Northern Railway of France on the 1.20 pm* Scotsman *waiting to leave King's Cross* (O.S. Nock).

Above right *Top-level view of* Cock o' the North *showing the twin chimney arrangement* (British Railways).

Below right Cock o' the North *on an early trial run in 1934 entering King's Cross on up Leeds and Bradford express* (Author's collection).

latter engine was running with a short cut-off, even though the regulator might be wide or even full open, resulted in the exhaust flopping down on to the unbroken line of the boiler barrel and obscuring the driver's view ahead. The remedy was to fit extra shields on each side of the smokebox as the Southern Railway had done on certain of their larger express locomotives. This expedient, which in my own subsequent experience on the footplate was entirely successful, did not however improve the looks of a somewhat unattractive locomotive.

Before *Earl Marischal* had taken the road in the late autumn of 1934 and had been used at first between Doncaster and Kings Cross, *Cock o' the North* had made its sojourn on the route for which it was designed, being stationed at Haymarket shed. During that summer and early autumn, certain Edinburgh-based 'Pacifics' were working through between Waverley and Aberdeen, north-bound on the 9.55 am and 2 pm expresses and returning on the 3.45 pm and the up 'Aberdonian'. This sometimes caused difficulties; the load of the last-mentioned

train was often above the maximum of 440 tons for a 'Pacific' on a southbound journey, and double-heading was not permitted with those engines north of Edinburgh. I saw *Cock o' the North* several times on the 9.55 am from Waverley during that summer, but what the manning arrangements were I do not know. I was otherwise engaged in my footplate work in Scotland at that time, and from a close friend who clocked an interesting run on the up 'Aberdonian' with a 550-ton load, no further information was forthcoming other than the excellent running times made. After a time, however, it was found that the cams actuating the poppet valves were sustaining damage on their operating surfaces, ostensibly from the high loads experienced when lifting them against full pressure, and, despite being generally favourable otherwise, Gresley was not satisfied with the engine.

On several occasions previously he had deplored the lack of a modern locomotive testing station in Great Britain, the Great Western plant at Swindon then being regarded as inadequate and out of date. So, considering the importance of getting *Cock o' the*

North thoroughly vetted he persuaded the top management of the LNER to allow him to incur the very considerable expense of shipping the engine across to France to enable trials to be made at the French station at Vitry-sur-Seine. Bulleid went with it, and, speaking French like a native, was immediately able to establish close and cordial relations with all concerned with the experimental work. It was a baffling time for Bulleid, and all his French colleagues for that matter, for the engine developed heating troubles which were apparently unrelated to the power or speed attained. On road tests between Tours and Orleans, very high horsepowers were registered in the dynamometer car, and the output would have been still higher according to the French driver had the English shovel been larger. The fireman had been hard pressed by the large number of shovelfuls he was having to fire, whereas with the usual French shovel, it was pointed out to Bulleid, they could fire double the amount of coal at each shovelful. Returning to the Vitry testing station after the road trials, the engine began to heat again. There were more examinations and it was eventually found that it was not the axle-box and axle that were heating but the tearing of a piece of white metal from the face of a bearing due to the rupture of the oil film. In view of this, Bulleid stopped all tests and arranged for the engine to be sent home.

After this, silence descended on the working of both of the 'P2' engines during the early months of 1935. It was at that time that the experiments with smoke deflection on No 2002 were taking place, and on the way back from some footplate work in

Left Cock o' the North *on the 2 pm Edinburgh-Aberdeen express near Inverkeithing* (E.R. Wethersett).

Below *The second 'P2' 2-8-2* Earl Marischal *at Aberdeen on the 10.25 am up to Edinburgh* (O.S. Nock).

Scotland I had as fellow travellers from Doncaster southwards some of those who had been concerned with the problems imposed by No 2002. Fortunately, these problems were only those affecting smoke deflection, though the practical solution did not please Gresley. Later that year he found a much more pleasing answer. Other than its front-end appearance, *Earl Marischal* was a superb locomotive. On the other hand, *Cock o' the North* underwent certain modifications at Doncaster on its return from France. Originally, the valve gear fitted was capable of giving fine adjustments in cut-off, and the tests on

the Great Northern main line in the summer of 1934 included reports of the usage of cut-offs of 10, 12, 15, 20, 22, 25 and 30 per cent. But when the engine was put into regular service on the Aberdeen route in the summer of 1935, the cams had been altered to give only three steps, 18, 25, and 35 per cent. Any intermediate adjustments had to be made by the regulator opening. In that summer, No 2001, stationed at Haymarket, was working only between Edinburgh and Dundee, making two return trips daily, outward on the 9.55 am and 6.10 pm from Waverley and returning on the 12.45 from Aberdeen and, as from

Dundee, the up 'Aberdonian'. Engine No 2002 was stationed at Dundee and regularly worked the same trains as I had noted 'Atlantic' *Duke of Rothesay* pulling, as described in the last chapter, but as my footplate journeys were made in the height of the summer tourist season the loads were much heavier. On the up 'Aberdonian', with 'P2' haulage throughout from Aberdeen to Edinburgh, we had a gross trailing load of 535 tons.

Both engines handled this huge load with relative ease; indeed, the firemen did not appear to me to be unduly hard pressed, although the engines were hauling such greatly enhanced loads.

LNER: maximum loads Aberdeen to Edinburgh

Type	4-4-2	4-6-2	2-8-2
Class	'C11'	'A3'	'P2'
Nominal tractive effort (lb)	23,312	32,909	43,462
Max tare load (tons)	340	440	550

It will be seen from the table that while the maximum tare loads allocated to the North British 'Atlantics' and the 'Pacifics' were roughly in accordance with their nominal tractive efforts, to achieve the same proportion the 'P2' engines would be expected to handle a tare load of 600 tons. With trains of such magnitude, however, there would have been operational difficulties such as station lengths and so on in addition to tractive power, and time would be lost in drawing up twice at stations like Montrose and Stonehaven. As it was, the extra tractive effort of the 'P2' engines was a bonus for the motive power department.

Before even the 'P2' engines had taken up their regular work on the Aberdeen route, another great Gresley project was in hand at Doncaster. The story has been told several times before of how he became interested in the performance of the German high-speed diesel railcar train, the 'Flying Hamburger', to the extent of going over to Germany and having a ride in the train. But the surprise came when the manufacturers of the German train, for all its spectacular performance on its own lines, could not promise a better time than 4¼ hours from Kings Cross to Newcastle, taking account of all the regular speed restrictions that were then in operation. While Gresley was still considering this disappointing response to his invitation, Sir Ralph Wedgwood, Chief General Manager of the LNER, with whom Gresley was on terms of the closest personal friendship, suggested that they could do much better than the Germans with a standard 'Pacific' engine

hauling a train of ordinary corridor coaches which would provide far more comfortable accommodation than the 'Flying Hamburger'. The result of his suggestion was the celebrated trial run to Newcastle and back on Tuesday March 5 1935. Sir Ralph's claim was fully borne out, in that with a six-coach train of 214 tons tare the journey of 268.3 miles was covered in 237 minutes northbound and 231¾ minutes on the return, despite incidental delays en route amounting to seven minutes on the down journey and 12½ minutes on the up.

The performance of the standard 'A3' 'Pacific' No 2750 *Papyrus* on that memorable day was such that Gresley and his staff might well have felt confident that the working of the projected four-hour service from Kings Cross to Newcastle, with an intermediate stop at Darlington, could be safely entrusted to them. But the year 1935 was the Silver Jubilee of the reign of King George V, and there were many national celebrations. No less important, however, was another great impending event in the autumn, the centenary of the birth of the Great Western Railway; their rivals could well expect some spectacular happenings from that quarter. So, with the enthusiastic instigation of Bulleid, Gresley and his staff embarked upon the design not only of a super-'A3' 'Pacific' but also a new, fully streamlined Silver Jubilee train. In retrospect, it seems that the aim of the LNER was not only to celebrate the great national event most fittingly but to 'wipe the eye' of the Germans and, in advance, anything that the Great Western was cooking up.

The LNER attempts at locomotive streamlining had so far not been particularly successful. The front end cowling on *Cock o' the North* had been effective mainly due to the sharp blast from the poppet valve gear exhaust but had been a failure on *Earl Marischal*. While in France, Bulleid had seen the Bugatti high-speed railcars running between Paris and Deauville and he commended their form of aerodynamic styling to Gresley, who knew Bugatti and took up the suggestion of making a few trips himself. He became very impressed with the way that the wedge-shaped front of this car passed through the atmosphere with a minimum of disturbance, and from this experience the external form of the new high-speed locomotives began to take shape.

On the other hand, the performance of the 'P2' engines had shown the effectiveness of the *internal* streamlining embodied in their design. In riding on the 'A1' and 'A3' 'Pacific' engines, I had always noted that when the regulator was fully opened the steam chest pressure, as registered by the separate gauge, was about 10 psi less than the boiler pressure. That difference represented the 'wire-drawing' effect of passing through the various passages between

entry to the regulator valve and arrival in the steam chest. On *Earl Marischal*, however, there was practically no drop, and steam was entering the cylinders at the full boiler pressure of 220 psi. This feature was manifested in still more striking fashion on the streamlined version of the 'Pacifics' to be introduced in the early autumn of 1935.

That the new engines were to be fully streamlined externally was in no doubt from the outset, but how? The Bugatti rail-car no doubt gave the original inspiration, but there was no deposit of exhaust steam in their case. Gresley resorted to the wind tunnel in the aeronautics department of the City and Guilds Engineering College at South Kensington to determine the form of the chimney and, more important still, the shape of the aerofoil casing at the top of the boiler immediately behind it. The end result was a triumph both in the dispersal of the exhaust steam clear of the driver's view and in the publicity effect the novel appearance had on the travelling publiic and everyone who was interested in railways. Some of the older enthusiasts, however, were not exactly impressed. They felt that the LNER was pandering to a craze of the moment, and streamlining in itself did not make any difference to the working of the engine. There were others, much more scientifically minded, who criticized the actual shape of the streamlining, pointing out that the wedge-shaped front derived from Bugatti was not true streamlining at all, and that Gresley and his staff were a lot of amateurs who did not know what they were doing!

Nonetheless, apart from providing a clear look-out for the driver and some immensely important publicity for the LNER, the streamlining did prove to be a means of saving a not inconsiderable amount of power. Further tests at the National Physical Laboratory measured the horsepower required to overcome head-on air resistance with models of the standard 'A3' 'Pacific' and the proposed new streamliner, and it was shown among many other results that with a train speed of 90 mph running against a head wind of 10 mph, the saving in horsepower between the two designs would be not less than 190.

Turning to the 'power to pull' of the new engines, one of the most important changes from the predecessors of the 'A3' Class was the advance to a boiler pressure of 250 psi. Only the Great Western 'King' Class 4-6-0s and the Stanier 4-6-2s of the LMS had so far advanced to this figure, and on the new Gresley 'Pacifics', Class 'A4', it was also accompanied by a slight reduction in the cylinder diameter from 19 in to 18½ in. Another important change in the steam circuit, which no doubt made no small contribution to their free running, was the increase of the piston valve diameter from 8 in to 9 in. There were also some significant changes in the boiler proportions, but although the effectiveness of the twin-orifice blastpipe with the associated petticoats of the full Kylchap arrangement had been demonstrated on the 'P2' engines, and particularly on No 2002 this feature was not incorporated in the 'A4' engines at first. The way the boiler design differed from that of the 'A3's is shown in the following table:

LNER: 'Pacific' boilers

Class	'A1'	'A3'	'A4'
Boiler pressure (lb)	180	220	250
Tubes			
Number	168	125	121
Outside diameter (in)	2¼	2¼	2¼
Superheater flues			
Number	32	43	43
Outside diameter (in)	5¼	5¼	5¼
Heating surfaces (sq ft)			
Small tubes	1,880	1,398.8	1,281.4
Flues	835	1,122.8	1,063.7
Firebox	215	215	231.2
Superheater elements	525	706	748.9
Total	3,455	3,442.6	3,325.2
Grate area (sq ft)	41.25	41.25	41.25
Length between tube plates (ft in)	18 11¾	18 11¾	17 11¾

Perhaps the most interesting change is that embodied in the last line of the above tabulation; while the distance between the tube plates was one foot shorter than in the 'A1' and 'A3' classes, the firebox was one foot longer. The firebox design, however, did not follow the 'P2' in having a 50 sq ft grate area; instead, the standard grate of 41.25 sq ft was used, with a combustion chamber one foot longer than in the earlier 'Pacifics'. Although the superheater flues were that much shorter, the elements themselves had an increased heating surface by being 9 in longer towards the firebox tube plate, as was done on the 'P2' boilers. Nonetheless, it is interesting to see that the 50 sq ft grate was not followed in the 'A4s', since the new 'Pacifics' were intended for high-speed continuous steaming rather than the 'stop-go' demands for maximum power on the Edinburgh to Aberdeen route.

The 'A4s' introduced primarily for the 'Silver Jubilee' service in September 1935 were an immediate and well-nigh sensational success. While it had taken a certain amount of pounding to push the 'A3' engine *Papyrus* up to the maximum of 108 mph in the descent of the Stoke bank in the trials of March 1935, the very first demonstration of the 'Silver Jubilee' train, hauled by the streamlined engine No 2509 *Silver Link*, attained 112 mph with ease in the normal course of steaming. The driver on that occasion was not one of the most noteworthy 'speed merchants' of Kings Cross shed; I had many runs behind him, once riding on the footplate, but while I would not rank him as anything but an absolutely first-class engineman he never seemed the one to break records. That is why his running with *Silver Link* on September 27 1935 appeared so significant to me, because one could be very sure that the engine would not have been pressed to make such speeds. Although only three weeks out of the Doncaster Plant, she twice on that day attained 112.5 mph, and sustained an average of 100 mph for 43 miles on end. A noteworthy feature of this demonstration run was the average of 108.7 mph over the 10.6 miles from Biggleswade to St Neots, a stretch that includes as much adverse as favourable grading.

Three days later, the 'Silver Jubilee' train went into regular service between Kings Cross and Newcastle, and it achieved a marvellous record for

Above left *The 'Silver Jubilee' climbing at 70 mph near Hadley Wood, hauled by engine No 2510* Quicksilver *(Rail Archive Stephenson/F. R. Hebron).*

Right *The 5.45 pm down Newcastle express near Hadley Wood hauled by 'A4' Class 4-6-2 No 4498* Sir Nigel Gresley, *with the author on the footplate (E.R. Wethersett).*

punctual running on these fast schedules. Three of the original 'A4' class engines were stationed at Kings Cross shed, while the fourth was at Gateshead. When the train was first put on, its manning was confined to four specially selected crews from the top link Kings Cross men whose regular duties included the London-Newcastle double-home turns like the 'Flying Scotsman' on its winter working. The 'Silver Jubilee' did not run on Saturdays, and accordingly the Kings Cross engine and its men who had worked the trains on Friday evening returned south with the up 'Flying Scotsman' on the Saturday. We had numerous reports of the running of the 'Jubilee' in the first few months of its service, though naturally nothing so exciting as the demonstration run on September 27. In fact, a very close scrutiny was maintained over all its working, but the use of the 'A4' engines on the ordinary East Coast trains, particularly on the up 'Flying Scotsman' on Saturdays, provided an added interest. I was at York on business in mid-December 1936, and purposely delayed my return home until the Saturday afternoon; the second of the streamliners, No 2510

Quicksilver, was on the job, and with the usual fifteen-coach train the running had many points of interest. Indeed, it proved so interesting after careful examination of the notes I took while travelling as an ordinary passenger that I determined to take the earliest opportunity of going again, and making the whole journey from Newcastle with the added privilege of spending some time on the footplate.

This run provided some performance data of deep significance, especially in the comparisons I was able to make with the working of the standard non-streamlined 'Pacific' engines. The section of line between Darlington and York proved ideal for making such comparisons because a large amount of data had been accumulated over the years, not only for 'Pacifics' but for North Eastern engines ranging back to the days when the 43-minute timing was first put on and the engines were the 'R' Class 4-4-0s, later LNER Class 'D20'. At that time, the train was the 12.20 pm from Newcastle to Sheffield, usually carrying a very light load. Why that particular train should have been deemed worthy of such preferential treatment so far as speed was concerned I do not

LNER: Darlington-York

Run No	1	2	3	4	5	6
Engine No	1207	2172	2570	4494	4475	2510
Engine Name			*Tranquil*	*Woodcock*	*Flying Fox*	*Quicksilver*
Class	'R'	'Z'	'A1'	'A4'	'A1'	'A4'
Load (full, tons)	135	215	310	335	515	515
Distance (miles)	m s	m s	m s	m s	m s	m s
0.0 Darlington	0 00	0 00	0 00	0 00	0 00	0 00
2.6 Croft Spa	4 30	4 40	4 29	4 40	5 03	4 36
5.2 Eryholme	7 10	7 03	7 07	7 16	8 01	7 19
10.4 Danby Wiske	11 35	11 33	11 43	11 31	13 01	12 06
14.1 Northallerton	14 45	14 45	14 43	14 23	16 20	15 19
17.5 Otterington	17 40	17 40	17 26	16 56	19 20	18 09
21.9 Thirsk	21 05	21 05	20 48	19 55	22 53	21 34
26.1 Sessay	24 35	24 35	24 14	22 49	26 19	24 59
28.0 Pilmoor	26 10	26 05	25 48	24 10	27 52	26 25
30.7 Raskelf	28 25	28 10	27 59	26 03	30 01	28 34
32.9 Alne	30 05	29 45	29 44	27 31	31 44	30 20
34.4 Tollerton	31 15	30 55	30 55	28 30	32 54	31 28
—	—	—	—	—	—	pws
38.6 Beningbrough	34 30	34 12	34 34	31 24	36 18	35 44
	pws	—	—	sigs	sigs	sigs
44.1 York	42 50	41 25	42 55	39 35	45 05	43 12
Net time (minutes)	41	41.5	43	38.5	43.5	41
Average speed, Otterington-Beningbrough	75.0	76.2	73.5	87.2	74.3	76.2
Max speed	80.5	79.5	79.5	89	77.5	80

know, because its basic make-up was a set of four NER non-corridor bogies and one or two Midland coaches destined for south of Sheffield. When the timing was restored in the autumn of 1922, it was applied to the evening Glasgow-Leeds dining-car express, an altogether heavier train which needed an 'Atlantic' for its haulage. I have tabulated the details of two fine runs from this earlier period both including lengthy spells at sustained rates at around 80 mph. At that time, such speeds with loads of more than 200 tons, as displayed by the three-cylinder 'Z' class 'Atlantics', were judged to be the capability of Great Western 4-6-0s and very few other British locomotive classes.

With the establishment of the Gresley 'Pacifics' on the East Coast Route, more particularly after the improvement of the valve gear of the 'A1' Class, the load of the Glasgow-Leeds 'diner' was frequently made up to over 300 tons and the 43-minute timing more than maintained. The third column in the accompanying table shows a characteristic run by one of the Gateshead based 'A1' engines on a bitterly cold February night in 1935, when *Tranquil* was working the normal double-manned roster of Newcastle-Edinburgh, Edinburgh-Leeds and back to Newcastle. It will be seen from the table that although the engine had already covered nearly 300 miles on her daily round she ran as fast as the 'Z' 'Atlantic' with 100 tons less load. The run in the fourth column of the table is actually a post-nationalization experience that I had on the footplate on the 'Tees-Tyne Pullman', when that train was unexpectedly stopped by signals in the middle of York station and thus provided a start-to-stop comparison with the other runs. The streamlined engine *Woodcock* was linked up to 17 per cent cut-off when no more than 1.25 miles out of Darlington, and this was further reduced to 15 per cent on passing Eryholme. The regulator was partially closed approaching Danby Wiske and from there until the 6½ milepost from York we were running with a steam chest pressure of around 200 psi instead of nearly 250 had the regulator been fully opened. Yet while *Tranquil* had averaged 74 mph over the 21.1 miles from Otterington to Beningbrough, *Woodcock* averaged 87 mph! This was, of course, a striking demonstration of the freedom with which the 'A4s' could run, but it came as no surprise to me from my experiences with these engines in their earlier days.

Of this I had no more interesting example than that of *Quicksilver* working the up 'Flying Scotsman' on a snowy January in 1937, having run the 'Silver Jubilee' down to Newcastle on the previous evening. Again for comparison I have included the log of a run of the same train just over four years earlier made by one of the crack Kings Cross drivers who were

entrusted with the running of the 'Silver Jubilee' in 1935. The superiority of the work of the streamlined engine with the same load was shown from the outset, with the acceleration to 57.5 mph up the incline from Croft Spa to Eryholme as against 52.5 mph by the 'A1' *Flying Fox*. Then, over the fast section from Otterington to Tollerton, 17 miles, the respective averages were 75 mph by *Flying Fox* and 78 mph by *Quicksilver*. However, there was a wealth of difference in the running conditions on the two occasions, for while *Flying Fox* had a calm sunny day in early autumn, *Quicksilver* had to contend with blizzard conditions, the strong east wind and snow making things rough and very unpleasant. I had gone through the corridor tender just after passing Northallerton by which time the engine was working at 15 per cent cut-off with the regulator wide, though not fully open. The steam chest pressure was then hovering around 200 psi. In these conditions, we reached a full 80 mph at Thirsk, but the high easterly wind hampered us from attaining a still higher speed on what was usually the fastest stretch of all, near Alne, where *Flying Fox* from her 75 mph at Thirsk made a maximum of 77.5 mph. In these rough weather conditions, however, I was interested and pleased to see how effectively the front-end streamlining deflected the exhaust steam completely clear of the look-out from the cab.

By the time I had made the run with *Quicksilver* on the 'Flying Scotsman', plans were well advanced for the introduction of further streamlined trains for the celebration of the Coronation year of 1937. Dynamometer test runs with the 'Silver Jubilee' train in the summer of 1936 had shown that the addition of the extra vehicle did not impose any undue extra burden on the locomotives, and arrangements went ahead for a heavier train for the 'Silver Jubilee' for the new 'Coronation'. When the train took the road in June 1937, connoisseurs of train working were surprised to see that the standard rake included nine vehicles, a beaver-tailed observation-car being attached in rear of the ordinary passenger accommodation. The tare weight of this very beautiful train was, however, no less than 312 tons, as against the 220 tons of the 'Silver Jubilee', and, as the train would be required to run at the same speed, there were some who wondered whether too severe a tax would be imposed upon locomotive capacity despite the proved abilities of the 'A4' engines. When the working details for the 'Coronation' train were announced, that one 'A4' engine was going to work through over the 392.7 miles between Kings Cross and Edinburgh, speculation as to the schedule's practicability as a year-round proposition grew. It was one thing to run the summer 'Flying Scotsman' between London and

Edinburgh non-stop at an average speed of 56.1 mph, but quite another to average 65.5 mph over the same distance including one stop.

Despite some forebodings, the new 'Coronation' service was introduced with brilliant success. From the very outset, Gateshead shed had to take the lion's share of the working. At first, the only stop in the down direction was at York, made in 157 minutes from Kings Cross at an average of 71.9 mph, and there the enginemen were changed. On the up journey, the only stop was at Newcastle, and thence the 268.3 mile run to Kings Cross was made in 237 minutes at an average speed of 68 mph. I had several runs in that first summer, all of superb quality, including one in which a maximum speed of between 104 and 106 mph was sustained between Little Bytham and Helpston Box, an average of 105 mph for 10.3 continuous miles. In the winter months it

'A4s' on the non-stop 'Flying Scotsman' in 1937: the southbound train near Barkston, hauled by engine No 4492 Dominion of New Zealand (Rail Archive Stephenson/T.G. Hepburn).

was often a different story. The East Coast Route is particularly susceptible to adverse cross winds, and I have been on the footplate not of the streamlined trains but of ordinary corridor stock when a load of 370 tons was pulling like 500 to judge by the way a standard 'A1' 'Pacific' was having to be thrashed to keep time even on a moderately fast, let alone streamlined, express. Instances have been quoted when the up 'Coronation' had to stop at Hitchin for assistance over the last 32 miles because the coal supply was

The 'Coronation' at full speed near Hatfield behind 'A4' Class 4-6-2 No 4492 Dominion of New Zealand (E.R. Wethersett).

becoming exhausted. I could never understand, when the stop on the down journey was inserted at Newcastle, why the logical step was not taken of changing engines, thereby eliminating the hazards of coal shortage on these very severe runs.

When the building of further engines of the 'A4' Class began at the end of 1936 in readiness not only for the 'Coronation' but also for the general introduction of the class on to the more important East Coast services, the first new engines, named after the fleetest birds of the air, were painted in the standard LNER passenger livery of green, and very fine they looked hauling the trains of varnished teak stock. But when it came to the Coronation train itself, which was to be finished in a two-tone colour scheme of Garter-blue bodies and Cambridge-blue upper panels, the five 'A4' 'Pacifics' specially allocated to its haulage and named after the principal units of the British Empire were themselves painted Garter-blue. So, by the autumn of 1937 the LNER had four of its 'A4' fleet painted silver-grey for the 'Jubilee', five in Garter-blue and the rest in the standard apple green. When the third streamlined service was put on in October, 'The West Riding Limited' between Kings Cross, Leeds and Bradford, two more blue 'A4s' were added to the stock, No 4495 *Golden Fleece* and 4496 *Golden Shuttle*, but by then the inconvenience from the operating point of view of having certain engines of the class restricted as to the trains they could work by their *colour* was already becoming apparent. So, the decision was taken that all future 'A4s' should be painted blue, and those in silver and green repainted as the opportunity presented itself. Actually, the Garter-blue blended very well with both the silver of the 'Jubilee' and the varnished teak of the standard East Coast stock. The first of the 'A4s', No 2509 *Silver Link*, was repainted in blue in December 1937.

This account of the streamlined engines and their activities has stepped one year ahead of an event in the life of their distinguished designer, for in July 1936 Gresley was summoned to Buckingham Palace to receive the accolade of a knighthood from King Edward VIII. The continued building of the 'A4' engines in the winter of 1937-1938 was marked by the completion at Doncaster of the one hundredth 'Pacific' to be built there, and this event was commemorated most fittingly by a pleasing ceremony at Marylebone station on November 26 1937, when the name-plates of engine No 4498 were unveiled by William Whitelaw, Chairman of the LNER—*Sir Nigel Gresley*. All his senior staff were there, and also in the group photograph posed in front of the locomotive was F. Wintour, then retired, who was Works Manager at Doncaster when the first Gresley 'Pacific' was built for the Great Northern Railway in 1922. Bulleid was also included, although he had been installed as Chief Mechanical Engineer of the Southern Railway barely two months earlier.

On the LNER itself, Spencer's colleague on Gresley's personal staff at Kings Cross, N. Newsome, assistant for Carriages and Wagons, had been for some little time engaged on tests to improve the braking of the streamlined trains. Gresley, through the advocacy of my one-time chief, Capt. Bernard Peter, Managing Director of the Westinghouse Brake and Signal Company, had shown strong preference for the Quick Service Application valve (QSA), designed by one of my brake colleagues, over the Direct Application valve (DA), which Stanier from his Great Western associations was then introducing on to the LMS. From time to time, tests were being carried out on Sundays with one of the two 'Coronation' set trains in conjunction with Westinghouse using the special apparatus that the firm had developed for this and other similar projects. At intervals during the spring and early summer of 1938 a team of Westinghouse engineers would be called out for a Sunday run, usually from Kings Cross to Peterborough and back, during the course of which four stops at predetermined locations and speed were made. The timing was usually approximate, nothing more accurate than the reading of the locomotive speedometer by an observer on the footplate and a second man clocking what mileposts he could spot while hanging out of a window in the train. The test stops had to be made between times, when the ordinary Sunday traffic was not flowing, and, as some very rapid accelerations had to be made, top link drivers and 'A4' engines were essential.

When the Westinghouse team were called for a test run on Sunday July 3 1938, no unusual arrangements were foreshadowed until they arrived at Kings Cross, then it was noticed that one two-car unit of the usual 'Coronation' train set had been removed and the LNER dynamometer car marshalled next to the engine. Moreover, to those who noticed such things, the engine itself, No 4468 *Mallard*, was one that had not been used before and the driver, instead of speaking in the familiar Cockney accents of Kings Cross Top Shed, was a broad Yorkshireman. However, the test crew piled in and set up their instruments and it was not until they were actually under way that their LNER confrères 'came clean' and told the Westinghouse senior engineer what the true purpose of this particular outing was to be. The outcome has been told in every railway history book, of how *Mallard* achieved the as yet unbeaten world record speed with steam traction of 126 mph. Of the 'cloak and dagger' business that preceded it, however, a story must be told. Gresley had been

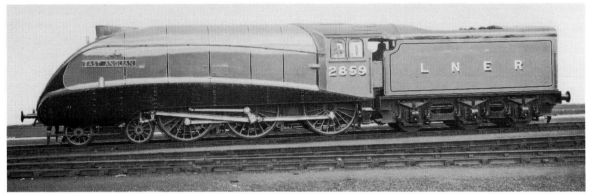

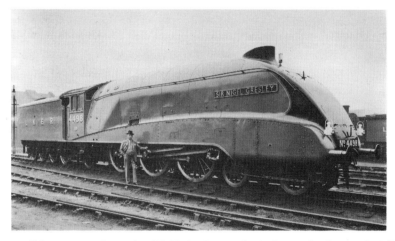

terribly upset when the LMS had snatched the British speed record with the controversial 114 mph entering Crewe with the 'Coronation Scot' on June 29 1937, and, by some mismanagement on behalf of the locomotive inspector concerned, the maximum speed attained down the Stoke bank on the 'invitation run' of the 'Coronation' on the following afternoon did not exceed 109 mph. The brake trials in the following year gave him the opportunity he needed.

Secrecy beforehand was essential, not only from their railway rivals but from other operating departments of the LNER. While the civil engineer had turned a blind eye to certain bursts of high speed down the Stoke bank there was no certainty that permission to run up to 120 mph or more would be given. After all, the official limit was still 90 mph! So, I believe, the civil engineer was not told. The triumph of *Mallard*, like so many historic occasions, was 'a close run thing', with the engine having to come off the train at New England shed with the inside valve gear in some disarray. But the great record was secure, though when the train eventually arrived back in Kings Cross to receive the acclaim of the Press it took some explaining as to why it was hauled by an Ivatt 'Atlantic'!

18. Mallard and the aftermath: the three-cylinder saga continues

In all the glory of breaking the world record for the maximum speed for a steam locomotive, a record that is still unsurpassed today nearly fifty years later, the unfortunate fact that in doing so the engine had been driven to the point of collapse of the inside valve motion was passed over, naturally so as far as the media publicity was concerned. To locomotive engineers, and indeed the many outsiders who took a sustained interest in East Coast express running, such failures were almost commonplace with the Gresley 'Pacifics' of all classes. Four occurred on the 1.20 pm Scotsman alone when the rostered 'A3' 'Pacific' had to be taken off the train at Grantham (in one case at Newark) with a hot middle big end. The relieving engines were in all cases Ivatt large-boilered 'Atlantics', and such was the brilliance of the subsequent running and the publicity it earned in the technical press that the ignominy of the 'Pacific' failures was largely forgotten! It would seem that it was much the same with Gresley himself when the 'A4s' failed on the streamlined trains, and some brilliant feats of time recovery by the 'A3' Class engines were reported to him. However, some events of 1938 other than the *Mallard* run must be set on record.

One of the photographs in my personal collection shows the 'Coronation' running about three-quarters of an hour late hauled by a Gresley 'A1' 'Pacific' No 2575 *Galopin* nearing Low Fell on the southern approaches to Newcastle. What the circumstances were prior to putting that engine on

the streamliner I do not know, but another instance of an 'A4' failure on the down 'Coronation' that same summer was fully documented when my friend and former publisher Ronald Nelson was a passenger. This time the failure of the booked engine took place before Hitchin, where a stop was made to substitute a Great Northern 'Atlantic'. At that time, no bigger engines were available at Peterborough and with this inadequate power the London driver had to carry on as best he could to Grantham, where they had an 'A3' waiting for him. With more than an hour's notice the shed there had got No 2744 *Grand Parade* fully coaled up and ready to run through to Edinburgh, but by then the streamliner was well out of its normal path and with signal checks they could do no more than keeping the running times until Newcastle, where the engine was remanned. Then, with a Haymarket crew in charge, there came some startling work. Even then, with several 'niggling' hindrances due to permanent way restrictions, the Scottish driver could not really open out until Alnmouth Junction had been passed, but then the recovery in time began in real earnest.

Up the 1 in 170 gradient of the Longhoughton bank, speed was worked up to 61 mph and on the subsequent falling and level stretches to the Northumberland coast truly record times were made with speed reaching a maximum of 99 mph at Beal. On the steep gradients north of the Border, speed was sustained at no less than 68 mph on the 1 in 200 bank that extends for five miles between Reston Junction and Grantshouse, and down the Cockburnspath bank a maximum of 95 mph was attained. Over the Lothian coastal plain numerous slight checks were made to observe local speed restrictions, but in

'A3' 'Pacifics' were often called upon to relieve 'A4' failures. This is No 2751 Humorist *fitted with smoke deflectors in 1933* (British Railways).

between these the driver managed to achieve a further maximum of 90 mph at Inveresk. In passing Dunbar in 87¼ minutes, nearly six minutes had been regained on the working times of the stream-liner in the 95.1 miles from Newcastle, but because of the final restrictions the total time for the 124.4 miles was 115¾ minutes against the level two hours scheduled. Furthermore, this run was made in high summer when the beaver-tailed observation-car was carried and the total load behind the tender was 325 tons. It was in any case a magnificent performance by a hurriedly-prepared non-streamlined engine on such an exacting duty.

Whether the 'A4' engines working the 'Corona-tion' were in any similar trouble during the following winter I cannot say, but the up service certainly struck it with a vengeance in the week ending March 25 1939. First of all, when the driver from Edinburgh climbed down at Newcastle to give the usual 'once over' before handing over to the Kings Cross man who was to take the train non-stop to London, evidence of heating was found, and the booked engine was exchanged on the spot for an 'A3' No 2595 *Trigo* which was in the station. Although leaving Newcastle eight minutes late, the train was on time by Retford, having covered the 129.7 miles in 120½ minutes. Onwards to London only a single minute was lost on the fastest part of the schedule, in spite of about five minutes loss in running time caused by temporary permanent way restrictions. The net time from Newcastle was about 225 minutes, a gain of 13 minutes on schedule and an average speed of 71.75 mph.

This thrilling performance had an amusing sequel the next day. At that time, Gresley was engaged on what were expected to be the final arrangements for the equipping of the streamlined trains with the Westinghouse 'QSA' valve, which the prolonged

tests in the previous year had shown to yield greatly reduced stopping distances from high speed. The imminence of war in 1939, however, postponed the decision. On the morning following the run of *Trigo* on the 'Coronation', the General Manager's office at Kings Cross, delighted with the news, sent a note of it to Gresley, who at that time was in conference with Capt. Bernard H. Peter, the Managing Director of the Westinghouse Brake and Signal Company. Gresley excused himself while he read the note, and as he did so a broad smile spread over his face. Then he handed the note to his visitor saying 'There you are Peter, any of my "blue pencil" engines can do the job, whether they have a tin case on or not!'. There is no report of how he reacted two days later, however, when another of the 'A4s' failed on the same train, getting no further south than Berwick and being replaced by the Tweedmouth Junction standing pilot, a North Eastern 'Atlantic', to get the train as far as Newcastle. The same Kings Cross driver and fireman as two days earlier were awaiting to take over, this time with engine No 2507 *Singapore*, and they made an equally praiseworthy effort to make up lost time, although because of the delay further north they were 34 minutes late away from Newcastle and with further checks they were not able to regain more than 8½ minutes.

To revert to new engine building, and to the year 1936, at about the same time as the later 'P2' 2-8-2s were being built with the same form of front-end streamlining as that so successfully introduced on the 'A4' 'Pacifics', the first five of the very celebrated 'V2' Class 2-6-2s were being turned out from Doncaster Plant. Gresley, from his experience with the 'K3' 'Moguls', and more recently with the huge 'P2' engines both in France and on the Edinburgh-Aberdeen route, had come to place complete confidence in his pony truck design for fast express

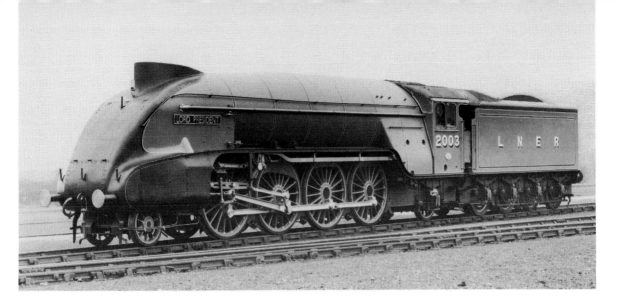

Above *'P2' Class 2-8-2 No 2003* Lord President, *one of the series built in 1936 with the 'A4'-style front end* (British Railways).

Above left *First of the last batch of 'A3' 'Pacifics', No 2500* Windsor Lad, *built in 1934* (British Railways).

Right *Class 'V2' 2-6-2 No 4830 on the 6.20 pm Marylebone-Bradford express near Saunderton, GW & LNE joint line* (H.K. Harman).

working. Thus, for this new project for a high-powered mixed traffic engine that could if necessary deputize for a 'Pacific' on the fastest and heaviest East Coast duties (short, of course, of the streamlined trains), he had no hesitation in using the 2-6-2 wheel arrangement. Boiler-wise, the 'V2' was simply a shorter-barrelled 'A3' with the same firebox and grate area and a 43-element superheater. However, while the elements of the traditional Gresley front end were all there, the design was entirely new, with the cylinders, steam chests, smokebox saddle and outside steam-pipes incorporated in a single steel casting. It was a beautiful piece of designing and, with the usual Gresley valve timing, resulted in a very free-running engine. The riding was also very smooth, even at speeds of more than 80 mph. The comparative dimensions of Classes 'V2' and 'A3' are shown in the following table:

Class	'V2'	'A3'
Cylinders (3) (in)	18½ × 26	19 × 26
Coupled wheel diameter (ft in)	6 2	6 8
Length of boiler (ft in)	17 0⅛	19 0
Total evaporative heating surface (sq ft)	2,431	2,736.6
Grate area (sq ft)	41.25	41.25
Boiler pressure (psi)	220	220
Adhesion weight (tons)	65.6	66.15
Total weight in working order (tons)	144.1	154.15
Nominal tractive effort at 85 per cent working pressure (lb)	33,730	32,909

As in the 'P2s' and in the last batch of 'A3' 'Pacifics', the boiler was fitted with a steam collector instead of a dome. All steam that entered the regulator had to pass through this collector, sometimes colloquially called the 'banjo dome', and it cannot be said that this device improved the appearance of the engines. Indeed, Gresley's successor, that iconoclast of much that had gone before, discarded it on the 511-524 series of 6 ft 2 in 'Pacifics' introduced in 1947, but it proved very effective in countering any tendency to prime and, to minimize any 'wire-drawing' effects at the point of entry to the collector, the cross-sectional area of the slotted holes cut in the top of the boiler barrel-plate was double that of the full regulator opening.

Despite the use of coupled wheels of a diameter six inches less than that of the standard 'Pacifics', the 'V2s' proved every bit as speedy as the 'A1' and 'A3' Classes. In addition to the steam collector, the appearance of the 2-6-2 engines suffered from the height of the running-plate which left the coupled wheels completely exposed, though this might be considered a desirable feature from the accessibility point of view. The wedge-shaped front of the cab was a touch of distinction on a mixed traffic locomotive; it was designed to induce air currents for deflecting any exhaust steam that tended to beat down and obscure the look-out. This was another feature that Thompson discarded on his 'A2' 'Pacifics'.

The first five of the 'V2' engines were stationed at widely separated depots, foreshadowing their eventual use as express passenger and mixed traffic engines over the entire length of the East Coast Route. In 1936, No 4771 was stationed at Kings Cross, Nos 4772 and 4773 at York, No 4774 at Peterborough and No 4775 at Dundee. The pioneer engine, named *Green Arrow* after the express goods service which was a feature of the commercial enterprise of the LNER at that time, was regularly used on the crack 3.35 pm 'Scotch Goods' between Kings Cross Goods and Peterborough, but apart from the climb to Potters Bar with this heavy train of 550 tons it was relatively easy work compared to the express passenger duties allocated to later engines of the class when they were in general use. A further batch of twenty of these engines, Nos 4776 to 4795, was built at Darlington Works between July and December 1937. They proved very popular with the running staff for all duties below the heaviest East Coast and streamlined trains.

At that time, Gresley was faced with the job of providing replacements for the many express passenger engines of medium power, mainly 'Atlantics', that were becoming life-expired, and at a conference with the running superintendents covering all the Areas, English and Scottish alike, he proposed the building

of more 'Sandringhams' to the financial limit of his allocation for new express passenger engines. The unanimous reaction of the running men to this proposal surprised him; they recommended that he spend this financial allocation on a lesser number of 'V2s' because the 2-6-2s were not only more powerful but their utilization potential was so much greater. Gresley was not slow to act on this reaction and in the next three years, despite the onset of war, no fewer than 95 more 'V2s' were built.

In regular express passenger service before the war, their work was practically indistinguishable from that of the 'Pacifics'. At first they were chiefly to be seen on relief portions of regular trains, but their running in these circumstances was such that, as more became available, they were regularly drafted to top link duties; the 'Yorkshire Pullman', with its 60 mph timing between Doncaster and Kings Cross, was a case in point. With loads of about 400 tons, their speeds down the Stoke bank were just as fast as those of the 'Pacifics' on the Leeds Breakfast Flyer. Details were published in *The Railway Magazine* of a run by No 4817 during which a maximum of 93 mph was attained near Essendine, and the 17.6 miles from Corby to Werrington Junction were run at an average speed of 86.2 mph. The load behind the tender on this occasion was 380 tons gross. Speeds of 90 mph were also not uncommon with 'V2s' on the Great Central section. With the exception of the special test runs with engines Nos 4472 and 2750 before the introduction of the 'Silver Jubilee' service, speeds of 90-92 mph had seemed to be about the maximum regularly attained by the 'A1' and 'A3' 'Pacifics', and thus it would appear that air resistance rather than piston speed was the limiting factor, where other considerations such as front-end design were equally favourable. A piston speed equivalent to that of No 4817 at Essendine would be equal to 101 mph on a 'Pacific'.

It is one of my regrets that in pre-war years an opportunity never arose for riding one of them on a really fast train like the 'Yorkshire Pullman' or the 6.20 pm from Marylebone to Leicester, as from some accounts the smoothness of their riding, no less than the speed they developed, was remarkable. All my footplate journeys were made on turns more appropriate to a mixed traffic engine. One of them, however, on the wartime 6.45 am from Colchester to Edinburgh, or more particularly that part of it when we were worked by engine No 4838 from March to Doncaster, contained some highly significant performance. Speed was then limited to a maximum of 60 mph over the whole of the LNER system, and in consequence the booked point-to-point times were somewhat slower than those worked by the pre-war 'North Country Continental' boat express which

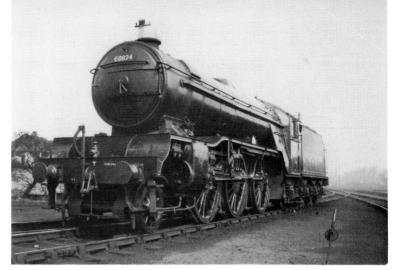

Right *'V2' Class 2-6-2 at Ferryhill shed, Aberdeen, in British Railways livery, showing the unusually high running-plate* (O.S. Nock).

Right *The pioneer 'V2' 2-6-2 No 4771 Green Arrow being prepared for the 'Scotch Goods' at King's Cross Top Shed alongside the 'Coronation' engine No 4490 Empire of India* (O.S. Nock).

Below *Later in the run No 4771 waits with the 'Scotch Goods' for the 'Coronation' to pass at Hitchin South* (O.S. Nock).

used to run in the same timetable path northwards from Ipswich. We had a very heavy and crowded train totalling 440 tons behind the tender, and even on a slower than pre-war schedule the run yielded some highly interesting locomotive work. The shabby, unkempt look of the locomotive itself gave not the slightest clue to her potentiality as a motive power unit, though I gathered from the crew that No 4838 was not the regular engine for the job. They were used to having a 'Sandringham' Class 4-6-0 and were strange to the 'V2' Class, but they quickly became acclimatized and made a remarkably fine run.

The only previous footplate experience I had on a 'V2' had been on the pioneer engine, *Green Arrow* itself, when she was relatively new, stationed at Kings Cross Top Shed and turned out as if she was ready to work the Royal Train. The driver had worked her as I had been accustomed to seeing 'A1' and 'A3' 'Pacifics' worked, on a minimum cut-off of about 18 per cent and using a partially opened regulator if any easier steaming was required. But on the 'V2' No 4838, once the driver had taken the measure of her, he continued to use absolutely full regulator and as soon as the speed was getting to about 50 mph he 'wheeled her up' well inside the 15 per cent mark to a reading marked 7 per cent on the scale. In other circumstances I could have believed that the reading on the scale may not have been the true cut-off, but the long stretches of level track on the GN & GE Joint Line, extending for at least fifty miles northwards from March, and the exactitude whereby the driver observed the 60 mph limit on each start-to-stop run from March to Spalding, on to Sleaford and then on to within nine miles of Lincoln, enabled me to make a fairly accurate estimate of the drawbar horsepower with the engine working at 7 per cent cut-off with the regulator fully open. Using the Johansen formula for train resistance which applied to pre-war standards of rolling stock, the drawbar horsepower required to keep a train of 440 tons running on level track was about 810. Comparing this with the results obtained when another engine of the class was subjected to exhaustive tests on the Swindon stationary testing plant in British Railways days, as referred to in Chapter 20, it does seem as though the actual cut-off was longer than the 7 per cent indicated.

Quite apart from cut-offs and estimates of drawbar horsepower, however, I was impressed and delighted by the smooth running of this engine. It was not only the steadiness on the track (and not many of my footplate journeys were so dignified in 1944-45!) but the sweetness of the action from the front end. Of vibration from the motion there was none, and after the purgatorial 'B1' 4-6-0 I had ridden from Ipswich

in the early stages of the same journey it was like heaven. We made no speed records on that trip, but, as an example of sound locomotive operation, it was admirable, particularly in view of the anti-Gresley campaign that was being waged from one quarter of the top management of the LNER at that time. It was a campaign that was doubly distressing to me personally because it was taken up by one or two self-appointed publicity agents of the new regime, who by the apparent cogency of their arguments cut considerable ice in the non-technical enthusiast press. Even though the basic Gresley three-cylinder design, with its derived gear for driving the motion of the inside cylinder, had been damned from the very moment the new CME was appointed, construction of the 'V2' class continued until 1944, by which time there were no fewer than 184 of them in service. Their numbers eventually ran from 4771 to 4799, 4800 to 4899 and 3641 to 3695. Then, at the very end of the line, came four engines in the same numerical series, Nos 3696-3699, having the same boiler but carrying the ungainly 'Pacific' wheel arrangement that had disfigured the rebuilt 'P2' 2-8-2s, to be mentioned in the following chapter. Like these latter engines, of the 'Pacifics' Nos 3696-3699 the less said the better!

Reverting to Sir Nigel Gresley's work in pre-war days, at the end of 1937 an interesting high-powered streamlined engine was built on the chassis of the high pressure compound 4-6-4 No 10000, and was thought by some to be prototype of a still further advanced high-speed express passenger class. Taking advantage of the longer chassis of the original 10000, a boiler and firebox approximating to the 'P2' Class, with a 50 sq ft grate but with a higher boiler pressure of 250 psi, was used. The three cylinders were 20 in diameter by 26 in stroke and the motion was the Gresley standard for maximum power express passenger engines. The nominal tractive effort at 85 per cent of boiler pressure was no less than 41,437 lb, the highest of any in Great Britain at that time. Despite the success of the 'A4' 'Pacifics' and of the 'P2' engines in Scotland, there is no doubt that by the end of 1937 Gresley was thinking of still more powerful engines, both for the streamlined trains and the ordinary East Coast expresses, and the building of a new 10000 could well be regarded as a tentative step in this direction.

While the new 10000 had a very high tractive effort, some surprise was caused by the piston valves being of no more than 8 in diameter in contrast to the 9 in valves used on the 'A4s'. It was felt that the size of the valves might prove a bottleneck in the steam flow circuit which would prevent the development of a power output commensurate with the nominal tractive effort and the size of the boiler and firebox.

The new 10000, a streamlined three-cylinder simple, in 1937 (the late W.J. Reynolds).

In actual performance on the road, after some early work on the heavy East Coat trains between Kings Cross and Newcastle, the engine was stationed at Doncaster and worked on the heaviest of the West Riding trains to and from Kings Cross until the war years. Certainly No 10000 gave every evidence of her high tractive effort, particularly in starting some immense wartime loads out of Kings Cross, but before the emergency timetables no instance of exceptional speed, as one had come to expect from the 'A4s', came to my personal notice. Being a 'rebuild', at least from an accountant's viewpoint, it had to be done as cheaply as possible, and there is little doubt that the patterns of the 20 in cylinders of the 'A1' 'Pacifics' with their incorporated 8 in piston valves were used as an expedient.

Judging from the history of locomotive development on the LNER as revealed by a fascinating paper presented to the Institution of Locomotive Engineers in March 1947 by B. Spencer, Gresley's personal assistant for locomotives, one might infer that the new 10000, whatever its makeshift character, was in some ways a try-out for two new express passenger classes that Gresley had in mind, and which, according to Spencer, would both have been built in the autumn of 1939 but for the onset of war. Operation of the 'Coronation' service with the maximum loading had shown that there were times when the 'A4s' were being extended practically to their limit, and there was a proposal for a super-'A4' carrying a boiler pressure of 275 psi. Whether this project provided for any increased coal-carrying capacity on the tender was not stated. The second project, which Spencer illustrated with a fine drawing, was of a huge 4-8-2, with the usual three cylinders, 21 in by 26 in in this case, the 'P2' boiler and firebox and a working pressure of 250 psi. This engine, with 6 ft 8 in coupled wheels and a tractive effort of 45,700 lb, was not to be streamlined, but from the drawing it would seem that the front end was to be modelled in the same style as that of the 'V2s', with a single steel casting embracing three cylinders, valve chests, smokebox saddle and outside steam-pipes. According to the drawing, however, this great engine would have had a single and not a Kylchap blastpipe. There was no mention of a mechanical stoker in Spencer's paper, though I fancy that to realize the full capability of 45,700 lb of tractive effort the limits of hand-firing would surely have been reached.

The introduction of another interesting three-cylinder design took place in 1937 on the West Highland line in Scotland. Because of civil engineering restrictions, the largest locomotives that could be used until then had been the ex-Great Northern 'K2' 'Moguls'; they were strong, reliable engines in themselves, but having a tractive effort of no more than 22,070 lb the maximum tare load that they could take on the long 1 in 60 gradients of that line was 220 tons. With the heavy holiday loads worked in the summer tourist season, and the frequency with which heavily-freighted fish-vans were added on to the rear of southbound trains from Mallaig, double-heading was rife. To save 'K2s' for other duties, it was often the practice to use a pair of 'Glen' Class 4-4-0s on the heaviest trains. To provide for enhanced locomotive power for this exacting line, Gresley and his design staff were in some difficulty. They would have liked to have used a smaller-wheeled version of the very successful 'K3', which with its 6 ft diameter boiler, 28 sq ft grate and large superheater had been widely used over the major routes of the LNER. In 1937, no fewer than 193 of them were in service. Unfortunately, the boiler was too large and the adhesion weight of 60¾ tons more than could be accepted for service on the West Highland line. Darlington Works therefore designed a special boiler for the job. It looked the same as that used on the 'J39' 0-6·0, but the firebox was actually larger, having a grate area of 27.5 sq ft against 26 sq ft. The machinery of the new Class 'K4' 2-6-0 was the same as Class 'K3'.

When first put into service in the early summer of 1937, the pioneer engine, No 3441 *Loch Long*, was working at a pressure of 180 psi, and this was quoted in the publicity issued by the LNER at the time, but the boiler had actually been designed for 200 psi, and when I was privileged to make a footplate trip on the engine in September of that same year the pressure had already been raised to 200. I found *Loch Long* to be an excellent engine. On the early morning 5.45 am from Glasgow to Fort William we took a load not far off the maximum of 300 tons rostered for this class, 286 tons tare and 305 tons full, and in observing the relative ease with which the engine climbed the steep gradients and the consistently good steaming it was also borne home to me the effect of the incessantly sharp curvature of some of the most heavily graded sections. In Glen Falloch, between Ardlui and Crianlarich, the cut-off was 32 per cent with full regulator to make speeds of between 25 and 27 mph, whereas on the much straighter incline from Bridge of Orchy, no less steep, a cut-off of not more than 27 per cent was needed to maintain a minimum of 28-29 mph. Both these cut-offs were in striking contrast to the percentages of 45, 50 and even 60 per cent needed for the 'K2s' working the maximum loads of 220 tons which they were permitted to take unpiloted. Because of their adhesion weight of 58.4 tons, the 'K4s' were not allowed to be piloted.

Following the successful introduction of *Loch Long* in 1937, five more engines of the class were built at Darlington Works in 1938-39. Unlike the pioneer

engine, which was painted black, the later 'K4s', which received the names of Scottish leaders famous in West Highland history, were painted in passenger green. The numbers and names were:

3442	*The Great Marquess*
3443	*Cameron of Lochiel*
3444	*MacCailin Mor*
3445	*Lord of the Isles*
3446	*Macleod of Macleod*

It was not until the end of the second World War that I had an opportunity to ride on these engines, and the first trip, again on the early morning service from Glasgow, was dismal. At that time, lodging turns had been abolished and we had an Eastfield crew working through to the crossing point with the first south-bound train, in this case at Tulloch. This made a long round trip from Glasgow to Tulloch and back without any respite at the halfway point. Our engine on this occasion was No 3443 *Cameron of Lochiel*, with a good train of 276 tons tare. The crew, however, were not the experts I had noted on the West Highland line in pre-war days. Even before we got to Craigendoran and the really hard work began, the fireman seemed to be making rather heavy weather of it, and, with little help from the driver who I learned later had earned the unenviable nickname of 'Sticky Joe', we made a thorough mess of it!

On arrival at Fort William, I continued on the footplate of an exhilarating but very rough-riding 'K2' to Mallaig which restored the esteem I had previously had of West Highland locomotive work. Returning from Mallaig later on another 'K2', with the intention of continuing as far as Crianlarich, I was disappointed to see that the fresh engine was to be once again *Cameron of Lochiel*. Had I not been staying in Fort William that night, and had there not been a prospect of a better run back from Crianlarich on another engine, I would seriously have thought of

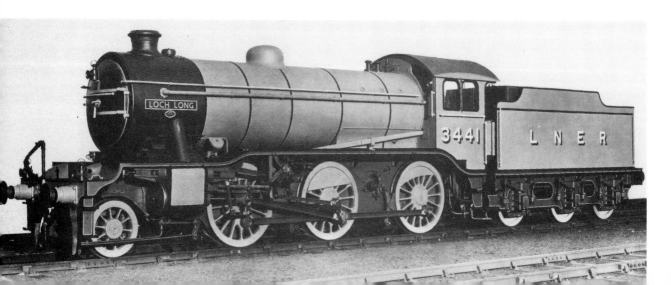

ending my footplate work for that day there and then. After all, it was mid-afternoon and I had been 'in the saddle', as it were, from soon after 5 am. However, I climbed up on to No 3443 and, in the hands of a competent and very enthusiastic Fort William crew, she seemed a different engine altogether. With the various additions to the train that we had brought from Mallaig, we now had 253 tons tare behind the tender, 275 tons full, and I was thrilled to see that the driver showed the engine no mercy in the way he flogged her in the first miles out of Fort William. For over an hour there is absolutely no respite on the southbound run. In the 28 miles up to Corrour, the line climbs to an altitude of 1,347 ft above ordnance datum, and I need not add that the start is made no more than a few feet above tide water. That gruelling 28 miles was covered in 64 minutes, including a total

of all but 7 minutes at the three intermediate station stops at Spean Bridge, Roy Bridge and Tulloch. In competent hands, *Cameron of Lochiel* was a superb locomotive and equally so was the companion engine of the class, *Lord of the Isles*, on which I accompanied the same enthusiastic pair of enginemen back to Fort William the same evening.

In 1946, the Locomotive Running Superintendent in Scotland was an ex-Great Northern man, and, as a staunch Gresley supporter, he was anxious that I should sample the work of one of the two 'V4' 2-6-2 engines, both of which were then allocated to the Scottish Area and reputedly doing excellent work despite the strong disfavour of Gresley's successor as CME. The completion of what proved to be Gresley's last design was considerably delayed by the outbreak of war. Although by 1939 a sufficient

Left *The 'K4' 'Mogul' No 3441* Loch Long *in 'photographic grey' at time of construction at Darlington Works in 1931* (British Railways).

Above *'K4' Class 2-6-0 No 3446* Macleod of Macleod (British Railways).

Right *'K4' Class 2-6-0 No 3443* Cameron of Lochiel *on a southbound goods train at Crianlarich* (O.S. Nock).

Above *'K4' 2-6-0* Cameron of Locheil, *with its new number 61995 but still in LNER apple-green livery, on a Fort William to Mallaig express near Banavie in the shadow of Ben Nevis* (E.D. Bruton).

Left *'V4' Class 2-6-2 No 3401* Bantam Cock *with a Glasgow express ready to leave Fort William* (O.S. Nock).

Below *The second 'V4' 2-6-2 No 3402; note the wartime ARP screens over the footplate* (British Railways).

number of powerful modern locomotives had been built to cover practically all main-line requirements of the LNER, a need was expressed for a general utility design with a fairly high nominal tractive effort yet at the same time a sufficiently light axle-loading to permit working over sections where the existing heavy main-line engines were not allowed to run. In adopting a maximum axle-load of 17 tons in the new 'V4' Class, Gresley produced a locomotive that could be used over a total of 5,000 route miles, nearly five-sixths of the entire LNER system.

The use of the 2-6-2 wheel arrangement has led to the 'V4' engines being referred to sometimes as smaller versions of the 'Green Arrows', but the general characteristics of the two designs differ considerably. Although the factor of adhesion was roughly the same in both cases, the boiler and firebox of the 'V2' were much larger in relation to the nominal tractive effort than in the 'V4', which was designed to put forth a high drawbar pull for short periods rather than to sustain a big effort continuously. The leading dimensions of the pioneer 'V4', No 3401 *Bantam Cock*, were cylinders (three) 15 in diameter by 26 in stroke, coupled wheels diameter 5 ft 8 in, total heating surface 1,799.9 sq ft, grate area 28.7 sq ft and boiler pressure 250 psi; nominal tractive effort at 85 per cent of working pressure was 27,420 lb and total weight in working order (engine only) was 70.5 tons. A second locomotive of the 'V4' class was completed shortly after No 3401, and it seemed that these two were to be forerunners of yet another numerous Gresley class. As in the case of the first two 2-8-2 express engines of the 'P2' Class, there were certain differences in the design of 3401 and 3402, the relative merits of which were to be investigated. No 3401 had a copper firebox, a miniature version of the standard LNER wide type as used on the 'Pacifics', 2-6-2s and 2-8-2s, while No 3402 had a box of similar proportions but built in steel and

of completely welded construction. In view of their widespread use abroad, the trial of steel fireboxes on the LNER was in itself a most interesting development, and the firebox of No 3402 was in addition fitted with a thermic syphon.

As with the first introduction of the 'V2' Class in 1936, the two 'V4' engines were allocated to widely dissimilar areas, No 3401 to the Great Eastern line and No 3402 to Scotland. The former engine, with a nominal tractive effort of 27,420 lb, represented a useful increase on that of the 25,380 lb of the 'Sandringhams', while the smoothness of the riding made the new engine very popular wherever she went; good engines though the 4-6-0s were, they were not always the most comfortable to ride, and the Great Eastern men looked forward to having many more 'V4s'. After Gresley's death, however, and the introduction of the rough-riding Thompson 'B1' Class 4-6-0s, to the disappointment of the Southern Area running inspectors No 3401 was transferred to Scotland and it was on the West Highland line, in 1946, that I had a footplate pass to ride her from Fort William to Glasgow. With their lesser tractive effort it was not possible for these two 'V4' engines to take the same loads as the 'K4s'; they were rostered for 250 tons as against 300. On the day of my journey we had 235 tons tare, but on the morning train from Fort William, which had to cross the 5.50 am from Glasgow at Tulloch and exchange enginemen, I was unfortunate to strike the same indifferent Eastfield crew who had made such a dismal showing with the 'K4' *Cameron of Lochiel*, and their performance with No 3401 was disastrous. I need only quote the start-to-stop times made on four journeys over the ten very severe miles between Tulloch and Corrour to show the difference.

I was sorry I could not record a more representative performance with a 'V4', as they were excellent engines on their day.

LNER: West Highland Line, Tulloch-Corrour

Engine No	9035	4698	3401	3443
Engine Name	*Glen Gloy*	*Loch Rannoch*	*Bantam Cock*	*Cameron of Lochiel*
Class	'D34'	'K2'	'V4'	'K4'
Type	4-4-0	2-6-0	2-6-2	2-6-0
Load (tons, E/F)	180/190	216/225	234/250	253/275
10 miles Tulloch to Corrour (min/sec)	22 41	23 41	30 21	23 38
Average speed (mph)	26.4	25.3	19.7	25.4

19. A period of recession

The death of Sir Nigel Gresley in April 1941 came to pose many problems for the top management of the London and North Eastern Railway. After Bulleid left for the Southern Railway in the autumn of 1937, Gresley had taken no immediate steps to replace him, at any rate with anyone of comparable status and personality. D.R. Edge, the new assistant, had been a carriage and wagon man, and the situation left Spencer as even more Gresley's right-hand man so far as locomotive design was concerned. The latter's death was relatively sudden, and unfortunately neither he nor the top management had made any arrangements for a successor. Certainly the circumstances, in the midst of the most desperately critical war this country has ever faced, were hardly propitious, and Sir Ronald Matthews, the Chairman, turned to the most senior of the divisional officers, Edward Thompson, Mechanical Engineer of the Southern Area, who had his headquarters at the famous Plant Works of the old Great Northern Railway at Doncaster. In appointing him Chief Mechanical Engineer, however, a considerable part of Gresley's former responsibilities were detached. Hitherto, the CME of the LNER had been in charge also of electrical engineering, but under the new arrangements the Electrical Engineer, H.W.H. Richards, was granted 'chief officer' status and independence from the CME.

The reorganisation of the former Chief Mechanical Engineer's department was extensive and significant. Gresley's two personal assistants, Spencer and Newsome, went into the wilderness and were posted to wartime duties as far as possible from LNER territory. The five divisional centres with their respective works were placed under A.H. Peppercorn (Doncaster), F.W. Carr (Stratford), R.A. Smeddle (Darlington), J.F. Harrison (Gorton) and T.E. Heywood (Scotland), but Peppercorn, who had previously been divisional engineer North Eastern Area at Darlington, was given the additional and heavy responsibility of Assistant Chief Mechanical Engineer, and was to deputize for Thompson in his absence. Peppercorn had had a varied career, much of it on the carriage and wagon side, and for a time he had also been Locomotive Running Superintendent, Southern Area, after I.S.W. Groom retired in 1937. Thompson himself, who had been domiciled at Doncaster before his new appointment, decided to make the CME headquarters there instead of at Kings Cross, and thus he and Peppercorn were quartered in the same building.

It was generally known that Thompson had never got on well with Gresley. He was a son-in-law of Sir Vincent Raven, and the thinly-veiled rivalries of the locomotive chiefs of the former Great Northern and North Eastern Railways, particularly over valve gears, had seemingly rubbed off on Thompson. At the time of the Railway Centenary celebrations, some rather patronizing remarks made by Gresley about the Stephenson link motion had not gone down too well in the North Eastern area. It was also known that in more recent times Thompson had received a 'rap over the knuckles' from Gresley for his interference with the driver on the occasion on the southbound dynamometer-car trial with the 'Silver Jubilee' train on August 27 1936, when *Silver Fox* suffered the same kind of failure that affected *Mallard* two years later. Thompson's work had hitherto been concerned almost exclusively with maintenance of locomotives and there is no doubt that he had developed a 'thing' about the Gresley conjugated valve gear for the three-cylinder engines; as soon as he was appointed Chief Mechanical Engineer, he sought the earliest means of securing authority to dispense with it. I have told elsewhere of the tactics he used to obtain that authority, and the outcome was the production of some 'Pacific' engines that could not, even in the most extenuating circumstances, be called 'great'. However, before the depredations began with the rebuilding of one of the 'P2' 2-8-2s as a 'Pacific' in 1943, a more logical new design of mixed traffic 4-6-0 had been introduced in the previous year.

In the last chapter, the design and purpose of the elegant 'V4' 2-6-2 mixed traffic locomotive was described. The first engine, *Bantam Cock*, was very well received by the running staff in the Southern Area, but in Thompson's view it had the proscribed conjugated valve gear and was therefore not to be considered. The 'V4' was in any case something of a 'Rolls-Royce' of an engine, and while some locomotive men on the LNER might have looked forward to its multiplication as a new standard class in more propitious times, that was not the case in 1942. In that year, Darlington works was continuing to build 'V2' 2-6-2s up to engine No 3685, turned out in the summer of 1943, but at the end of 1942 the Works also turned out the first of Thompson's 'B1' Class 4-6-0s. Although only five were included in that first batch, and five more were built in 1944, they were intended to be a new standard class, and several hundreds were, in fact, added to the stock in post-war years. They were the first, and undoubtedly the only, Thompson locomotive class that could be described as 'great', and even then one must make

Right *Down express fish empties leaving Hadley North tunnel hauled by Class 'B1' 4-6-0 No 61142 (E.D. Bruton).*

Below *A St Margarets-based 'B1' No 61398 climbing the last stage of the Cockburnspath bank with an Edinburgh-Berwick stopping train in 1954 (E.D. Bruton).*

some very significant reservations.

The 'B1' was a cheaply-produced, workmanlike wartime austerity counterpart of two famous 6 ft 4-6-0 designs, the 'Hall' Class of the Great Western and the 'Black Five' of the LMS. Thompson produced it by assembling a synthesis of standard components, which was economical in wartime because it involved the very minimum of new tools and no new patterns. The boiler was that of the 'Sandringham' 'B17' Class 4-6-0, strengthened to take a pressure of 225 psi instead of 200. The 6 ft 2 in coupled wheels were the same as those of the 'Green Arrow' 'V2' Class 2-6-2s, and the cylinders were

those of the 'K2' ex-Great Northern 'Moguls', 20 in diameter by 26 in stroke. The valves and valve gear were the one feature where an advance upon previous LNER practice was shown, for the piston valves were of 10 in diameter, having a $6\frac{3}{8}$ in travel in full gear and a lap of $1\frac{5}{8}$ in. The nominal tractive effort at 85 per cent of boiler pressure was 26,878 lb. The new engines, painted wartime black and devoid of any lining, had a handsome outline fully in keeping with well-established LNER traditions; the tenders were simply lettered 'NE'.

In July 1945, I was favoured with a footplate pass for the wartime equivalent of the 'North Country

Left *Up 'Queen of Scots' Pullman leaving Newcastle behind 'B1' Class 4-6-0 No 1259* (H. Gordon Tidey).

Right *Thompson 'A2' 'Pacific' No 60519* Honeyway *on the Cocksburnspath bank with the 'Heart of Midlothian' express in 1954* (E.D. Bruton).

Continental', then originating at Colchester instead of Harwich to provide facilities for the many service-men stationed in the vicinity of the former town. The train was worked by one of the new 4-6-0s between Ipswich and March, and it was an interesting and revealing experience. Recalling how the use of the three-cylinder system of propulsion had been used in the 'Sandringham' Class to reduce the dynamic axle-loading and make the design acceptable for the restricted track loading of the Great Eastern main lines, it was interesting to observe, or try to observe, the effect that the substantial reduction in weight of reciprocating balance would have on the behaviour of the locomotive as a vehicle. Not long after the first of the 'B1' 4-6-0s was built, some comprehensive tests were made on certain bridges on the Great Eastern line at speeds of up to 85 mph (specially authorized in view of the wartime limitation of speeds throughout the LNER to a maximum of 60 mph) and in these tests the 'B1' engine produced total stresses slightly less than those produced by the three-cylinder 'Sandringham' Class. With this result, the 'B1s' were given a clean bill of health, by the civil engineer at any rate. Their total weight was also slightly less than that of the 'Sandringhams'; in this respect there had been a certain amount of skimping in the extraneous fitments which was later repaid in rough riding and vibration.

My footplate journeys on these engines, not only the very first in 1945 but all subsequent ones on many members of the class and on routes extending as far afield as Newcastle to Carlisle and from Glasgow to Oban, were all made with permission from the respective running superintendents. They were made in order to collect data on the performance of the locomotives in relation to the gradients and running characteristics of the various routes. As the reports I made were destined for publication in the technical press, as well as in some more popular journals, my scripts had to be submitted for approval, and I had necessarily to 'play down' the incidental happenings. In any case, my job then was to report on the technical aspects of the locomotive performance, not to enlarge upon the etceteras which would have made good, if sometimes rather sensational, 'copy'. Any adventures in this latter respect would immediately have earned me the 'order of the blue pencil', and probably prejudiced my applications for further facilities for footplate riding. Now, however, looking back thirty years or more on the collective experience I gained on the 'B1' Class engines, I feel inclined to echo Sir Nigel Gresley's comments on the riding of a 'King Arthur' 4-6-0 which he tested during the Ministry of Transport enquiry after the Sevenoaks derailment of one of the 'River' Class 2-6-4 tank engines. Gresley 'slammed' the 'King Arthur', to use a present day journalistic expression, as giving a ride that was 'very rough and uncomfortable'! So also could all my runs on 'B1s' be collectively described.

On the footplate I did not have any examples of running that could in any way be called exceptional, and I remember more the rough and tumble conditions and incessant vibration that one sustained at any kind of speed. By far the most interesting run I had with one of them was when travelling as a passenger during the Locomotive Interchange Trials of 1948 when a 'B1' was one of the mixed traffic designs tested between Bristol and Plymouth. On the up journey, combining the Torquay and Cornwall portions at Exeter made the loads up to about 450 tons tare and 475 tons full including the

dynamometer car. The schedules were not unduly severe even with those heavy loads, 38 minutes was allowed for the 30.8 miles from Exeter to Taunton and 53 minutes for the remaining 44.8 miles on to Bristol. I was a passenger on the second trip made by the 'B1' engine, when on account of permanent way work farther west we were five minutes late from Taunton, and the visiting Eastern Region driver made a splendid final effort in his brief stay in the West of England by bringing his train into Bristol one minute early. On the long level stretches of line between Cogload Junction and Yatton, this heavy train, which I judged to scale at least 485 tons behind the tender, was run at speeds varying between 66 and 69 mph. We passed Nailsea, 36.7 miles, in 36¼ minutes, and after a very slow run into Bristol stopped in Temple Meads in 47½ minutes at a start-to-stop average of 56.6 mph from Taunton.

Over Thompson's rebuilding of the Gresley 'P2' Class 2-8-2s, and still more the pioneer Pacific No 4470 *Great Northern*, I prefer to drop the veil of obscurity rather than repeat again the arguments that were advanced at the time by certain self-appointed publicity agents of the new regime. It is sufficient commentary on the efficacy of Thompson's version that even before he retired his drawing office at Doncaster were, unbeknown to him, working on a modified version! To do them justice, however, Thompson's own 6 ft 2 in 'Pacifics' of the 60511 to 60524 series could do good work in favourable conditions, as on the East Coast main line south of Darlington. But the maintenance difficulties weighed against them, as also did the charges incidental to the firegrate which, at 50 sq ft, was certainly not needed for the work they were called upon to do. I was riding down from Kings Cross to

Newcastle one afternoon on the 'Heart of Midlothian' express which at that time stopped at Peterborough instead of Grantham and changed engines there; we got a new Thompson 'A2/2', No 60520 *Owen Tudor*, to haul our thirteen-coach train of 475 tons gross. The 'A2/2s' had the same boiler barrel as those of the Gresley 'A3' Class, but with the higher pressure of 250 psi and the 50 sq ft grate they had a considerably higher tractive effort of 40,340 lb.

Following Thompson's precepts, the three cylinders, with separate sets of Walschaerts gear to each, were spaced so that each one had the same length of connecting rod, necessitating the ungainly wheel spacing and bad riding on track that was not up to the highest British standards. In the immediate aftermath of the Second World War, there were many stretches of line that could be stigmatized thus. The Thompson 'Pacifics' also differed from the Gresleys in having 10 in diameter piston valves instead of 9 in as on the 'A4s', and a considerably longer travel in full gear of 6¾ in; this was partly because the cut-off in full gear was 75 per cent, as against 65 per cent on all the Gresley 'Pacifics'. Theoretically, the 'A2/2' Class should have been very powerful and swift-running engines but their inherent physical faults sadly inhibited them. I was glad, then, that I had this one opportunity of seeing one of them at their very best, in ideal running conditions on the East Coast main line north of Peterborough. Relieving the London engine there, and starting five minutes late, speed was worked up to 61.5 mph in no more than 3.25 miles from the start, and in the next 20.6 miles up to Stoke signal box where the line rises at an average of 1 in 345 the average speed was 65.3 mph. The maximum intermediate speed was 72 mph, and the minimum after 3 miles at 1 in 178 to the summit was 58.5 mph. The cut-offs indicated on the scale were shown as between 12 and 15 per cent. This spell of fast running was all that was necessary to restore punctual working on the easy schedule in force at that time.

On the good track on this stretch, however, there was slight though unmistakable evidence of the yawing propensities of which I had found other Thompson 'Pacifics' so badly susceptible in less favourable conditions. On this engine, too, I was to experience later another facet of their shortcomings. From Peterborough we had a pair of first-class enginemen; the driver was working the engine to restore punctual running as quickly as possible and his fireman was stoking with precision. At York, however, these men were relieved by a less expert crew, and the fireman in particular seemed to find trouble in managing that huge 50 sq ft grate, even though the demands for steam on those leisurely train schedules were not excessive. No further out from York than Alne, 11.2 miles, boiler pressure was down to no more than 180 psi and had there not been a locomotive inspector riding on the footplate to give some tuition to the fireman we could soon have been in real trouble for steam. Why Thompson perpetuated the 50 sq ft grate of the 'P2' 2-8-2s on his own 'Pacifics', when the 41.25 sq ft grates of all the Gresley engines had been shown to be ample even in the most strenuous pre-war running, is a mystery.

Looking to further post-war developments in the medium power engine range, Thompson considered that the Darlington-inspired 'J39' Class 0-6-0 was unsuitable for further building because of its inside cylinders and rather inflexible frame structure, or so it was averred in 1945. Consequently, he took one of Gresley's 'K4' 2-6-0s built for the West Highland line and rebuilt it with two cylinders and a front end identical to the 'B1'. The new boiler was a shortened version of that of the 'B1', and with 5 ft 2 in coupled wheels and a working pressure of 225 psi the nominal tractive effort was reduced from the 36,598 lb of the 'K4' to 32,081 lb. The particular 'K4' chosen for rebuilding was No 3445, *MacCailin Mor*. It retained that name after alteration and went back to work on the West Highland line, but I am afraid it was then an even more unpopular engine than ever at Fort William. The Clan Campbell had never been welcome in that gathering ground of Camerons, MacDonalds and others once fiercely loyal to the Stuart cause, and, when the engine named after the Chief of Clan Campbell returned in its new guise with a reduced tractive effort and all the harsh going of a 'B1', the West Highland men were not amused! I had one run on the footplate southbound from Fort William, but with less tractive power than a 'K4' we had a 'K2' 'Mogul' to assist, and the run was of no

value for assessing the locomotive's performance. It was as well we had some assistance because on the long climb from Tulloch to Corrour summit, although we started with a full 225 psi, pressure had dropped to 140 approaching the summit. What with the rough riding in the cab, I had had enough of it by Crianlarich and rode the rest of the way to Cowlairs in the train.

Thompson retired on June 30 1946, leaving a situation in which standards of shop repair and shed maintenance had dropped to abysmal depths and morale generally was at an all-time low throughout the CME's department. Peppercorn was appointed to succeed him, but few if any of the top management of the LNER realized what they had let him in for. Peppercorn himself was well enough aware of the situation so far as Doncaster Works was concerned, but, facing the whole of the LNER, his closest associates sensed that he was rather over-awed by the magnitude of the job and already wished he was out of it! However, there was all the difference in the world in his appointment; everyone liked him and wished him well. His first step was to recall Spencer from his banishment 'out in the sticks' to assist Windle on new design work, but, as Peppercorn himself was the first to realize, new engine building was about the least of his problems in the autumn of 1946. This, however, is a book about locomotive design and development, not about the problems of workshop administration, and before he quit the scene Thompson had laid down certain parameters which he expected his successor to follow. First and foremost was his design for the big engines, of which none of his senior staff, least of all the running inspectors, approved.

The first of the new A2 'Pacifics', No 500, was completed at Doncaster not long before Thompson retired. It was the 2000th locomotive to be built at the famous Plant, and although he was not present at the official inspection of the engine by the press on May 22 1946, as reported in *The Railway Gazette*, as a gesture to him from the top management at a little private ceremony at Marylebone station on May 31 the Chairman, Sir Ronald Matthews, named the engine *Edward Thompson*. It is to be feared, however, that few of his staff, and still fewer of the many hundreds of connoisseurs of LNER locomotive practice, appreciated the gesture. Naming engines after locomotive superintendents as on the London and North Western Railway in pre-grouping days or on the Southern in more recent times was reserved for eminent engineers who had passed on and who were historical figures. The one exception was that of Sir Nigel Gresley, very worthily honoured while he was still in office.

Thompson had secured the authorization for a

Thompson 'A2' 4-6-2 No 518 Tehran in LNER livery at Edinburgh Waverley in April 1948 (C.C.B. Herbert).

batch of 28 of his new 'A2s', but, immediately after he retired, the design of the modified version, started surreptitiously at Doncaster before even he had gone, was pushed ahead. The last of the Thompson batch, No 524, was completed in September 1947, and the first of the Peppercorns, No 525, in December of that year.

When he had set up his headquarters at Doncaster, Thompson had abolished the small design office at Kings Cross set up by Gresley, and new design work had been done in the main drawing office at

Doncaster under Windle's supervision. So far as the 'A2' 'Pacifics' were concerned, the immediate thing was to get the front end design changed to avoid the awkward spacing of the wheels, and the cylinder layout closer to the Gresley model. Naturally, the conjugated valve gear for the middle cylinder was not restored, and the improved valve events and 10 in diameter introduced by Thompson were retained. While the 250 psi pressure and 50 sq ft grate were also retained, the twin orifice blastpipe of the Kylchap type was abandoned, at any rate for the time being.

Down 'Queen of Scots' Pullman entering Newcastle Central behind Thompson 'Pacific' No 60512 Steady Aim (H. Gordon Tidey).

On the other hand, the 'banjo' type steam collector which had been used in all Gresley's largest engines from the 'P2' of 1934 onwards, and which Thompson had abandoned on the fifteen 'A2' 'Pacifics' Nos 500 and 511 to 524, was restored on the 'Peppercorns'. In saying this, and attributing the design to the new CME, it should be pointed out that Peppercorn was not in any way an engine designer. He was primarily a running man. He brought Harrison down from Scotland as his assistant, particularly to cope with the all-important job of the immense backlog of engine repairs, but as far as new design went, that of the new express passenger 'Pacifics', which Thompson had intended should follow the rebuilt *Great Northern*, was extensively changed under the triple influence of Windle, Spencer and Harrison.

The LMS had recently introduced the self-cleaning smokebox as a means of reducing shed duties. When the idea was first mooted, certain engineers of other railways thought that a considerably sharper blast would have been necessary to overcome the resistance to the flow of gases when they had to pass under the diaphragm, and that the diaphragm itself would be an obstruction to tube cleaning. Experimental installation proved that this was not so, on the LMS 'Black Five' at any rate and the self-cleaning smokebox became standard on all the engines of the class built after the war. The Doncaster triumvirate under Peppercorn decided to equip the new 'Pacifics' similarly and, as there was no room in the smokebox as designed, they abandoned the Kylchap twin-orifice blastpipe which had been very successfully used on the 'P2' 2-8-2s, the last few Gresley 'A4s' and all of the Thompson 'Pacifics'. The result was that rarest of locomotive phenomena, an LNER 'Pacific' that would not steam! Of course, I know

there have been occasions when I myself have been on the footplate when individual engines have 'gone off the boil', as it were, but there were extenuating conditions to account for these lapses. The Peppercorn 'A2s', however, were brand new engines! Certain of the Gresley 'V2' 2-6-2s had also been fitted and they too suffered from the same trouble. Most of the new 'A2s' were based in Scotland and the situation there became so serious that a complaint was submitted to Doncaster. As it was realized that the self-cleaning smokebox arrangements were the root cause of the trouble, and the 'V2' 2-6-2 was equally involved, one of the latter class was sent for examination on the Swindon stationary testing plant.

To clear the way for the new express passenger 'Pacifics', which were expected to be 'the cat's whiskers' as far as LNER maximum power units were concerned, the remaining Gresley 'Pacifics' which had not been converted to 'A3' were reclassified 'A10'. The new 'Peppercorns' became class 'A1'. Except for the restoration of the Kylchap exhaust arrangements and consequently a somewhat longer smokebox, the new 6 ft 8 in express passenger 'Pacifics' were the same as the 'A2s' except in the matter of coupled wheel diameter, and, so far as CME headquarters was concerned, were destined to supercede the 'A4s' as the principal express locomotives of the East Coast Route. Although the London-Edinburgh non-stop run had been reintroduced in the summer service of 1948, the need for engines fitted with corridor tenders was very limited and thus far none of the new 'A1s' had been

The first of the Peppercorn Class 'A2' 'Pacifics' No 525 built in 1947 and named after the CME (British Railways).

The down 'Flying Scotsman' passing York in the autumn of 1949 when the train was running non-stop from Grantham to Newcastle; the engine is 'A1' 'Pacific' No 60148 before it was named, and the author is on the footplate (the late Bishop E. Treacy).

so provided. Another factor precluded the anticipated usage of these engines. The 'yawing' action noticed on the Thompson engines had generally been considered to have been derived from the wide spacing of the bogie ahead of the leading pair of driving wheels, but there was consternation when it was found that the 'Peppercorns' had a yawing motion far worse. It had not been so bad with the 'A2s', which were mostly in the North and not required to run at fast speeds, but it was another matter when some of the new 'A1s' were allocated to Kings Cross and put on to schedules on which the engines had really got to run.

When I made my own first journeys on those engines, the 'Flying Scotsman' was running non-stop between Grantham and Newcastle with Gateshead-based engines. The timings were very easy, and I was impressed by the economy of the working. The North Eastern men with whom I travelled took evident pride in their enginemanship, both drivers and firemen, and, although the schedules were not very demanding, care was being taken to keep to them on the minimum of coal and water. Unlike the 'A2s', the larger-wheeled engines with their Kylchap blastpipes were very free steaming, and anything in the way of 'slapdash' firing could result in much blowing off from the safety valves and waste of steam. On one trip on the

up 'Flying Scotsman' from Edinburgh to Newcastle with Gateshead men, I was very impressed by the way the boiler pressure was held between 230 and 240 psi. The summary of this particular performance was thus:

Engine number	60142
Engine name	*Edward Fletcher*
Load (gross tons behind tender)	440
Length of trip (miles)	124.4
Total booked time (mins)	150
Net time (mins)	142
Net average speed (mph)	52.6
Maximum speed (mph)	69
Net average speed over 112.9 miles, Inveresk to Forest Hill (mph)	55.2
Approximate average dhp over 2 hour duration	640

The above tabulation clearly indicates the light nature of the work, and, except during the ascent of the Cockburnspath bank, the cut-offs were entirely between 12 and 18 per cent with the regulator no more than partly open. This crew, however, were exceptional in the artistry with which they handled the engine; I did not note such precision and economy in any other runs I made on the Peppercorn

Down Newcastle express leaving Hadley North tunnel hauled by 'A1' Class 4-6-2 No 60149 Amadis *(E.D. Bruton).*

'A1' 'Pacifics'. Nor did I experience such smooth and comfortable riding.

I gathered that the Peppercorn 'A1s' were not very popular in Scotland. Around 1950, when the practice was established at Edinburgh's Haymarket shed of allocating the top link drivers to regular engines and no other, that *corps d'élite*, as indeed it was, consisted entirely of Gresley 'A4s'. When the locomotive running superintendent of the Scottish Region, who, after nationalization, was an ex-LNER man, had to help the LMS side out of a temporary shortage of top link motive power, he transferred three of the 'A1s' from Haymarket to Polmadie shed, Glasgow, and these engines were put on to the double-home turns ordinarily worked by the 'Converted Scot' 4-6-0s between Glasgow and Crewe. I had a footplate pass

to Carlisle and back one October day in 1951, and, after an uneventful run southwards on the 'Royal Scot', I returned by the Birmingham train which, I was interested to see, was brought into Carlisle by an 'A1', No 60156 *Bonnie Dundee*. My thoughts went back immediately to the ride I had enjoyed sixteen years earlier on the North British 'Atlantic' of the same name from Aberdeen to Dundee, but pleasurable thoughts vanished soon after we started away, for that 'A1' gave me the roughest ride I had ever experienced on a steam locomotive; indeed, there were times when we were lurching so much on the curves by Kirtlebridge at 70 mph that I was really scared. I was very relieved when the driver eased down for the reverse curves between Castlemilk sidings and Lockerbie. It was not just a case of vibration, but of violent hunting. I was not surprised to learn that the Kings Cross top link men had complained so bitterly about their 'A1s' that the engines were removed from the fastest trains until something was done about their riding.

20. Gresley 'Pacifics': Indian summer

At the end of 1949 Peppercorn retired, as did his fellow CMEs of the old independent railways such as Hawksworth of the Great Western, while Bulleid had already gone over to Ireland in October of that same year. The road was then apparently clear for the boffins at 222 Marylebone Road to spread their influence nationwide. In the meantime, however, the results of the somewhat hastily-organized Locomotive Interchange Trials of 1948 had been published with many details that cannot have been to the liking of the ex-LMS men who constituted the backbone of the Railway Executive. In the group of trials involving the top link express passenger trains, the Gresley 'A4' 'Pacific' seems to have been a rather hurried second choice, as the preliminary notices, which were published very soon after the national railway organization was established, gave the Eastern Region participant as 'Pacific latest type'. At that time, the latest was the Peppercorn 'A2', and immediately before that the Thompson types. The latter had quickly fallen into disfavour and were not to be considered by the Eastern Region men, while the first of the Peppercorns had been introduced no

Nationalization: Class 'A3' 'Pacific' No 60039 Sandwich in 1948, sporting LNER apple-green livery but BR number and lettering at King's Cross (Author's collection).

more than a few months before the trials were due to start. So somewhat reluctantly on the part of the organizers at 222 Marylebone Road, the Eastern Region had to fall back on the Gresley 'A4'.

This was a misfortune from the forward planning point of view. The Gresley three-cylinder engine layout, with the conjugated gear for driving the piston valves of the inside cylinder, had been discredited in the higher echelons of the LNER motive power department, though not among the majority of running inspectors. But for the seemingly precipitate haste in which the Interchange Trials were organized, there was no doubt one of the Peppercorn engines would have participated. However, when the results were published, the Gresley 'A4' 'Pacifics' came out with the lowest coal consumption of any of the express passenger engines tested. Of course, they earned black marks from three total failures on the road requiring the removal of the engines from their trains and consequent delays. They were the only engines that suffered thus in the whole series of trials, and naturally the blame was laid on the conjugated valve gear which was doubly damned in certain people's eyes. But one of the principal villains of the piece, though not by any means the predominating one, was the low standard of maintenance that had been allowed to develop in

the later stages of the war and thereafter. There were many Gresley 'Pacifics' in first-class fettle in 1948-49, as the runs I was privileged to make on the footplate at that time showed, but it was unfortunate that the chosen ones let the side down.

When the venturesome step was taken in the summer service of 1948 to restore non-stop running between Kings Cross and Edinburgh, although there were then many Peppercorn 'A1' 'Pacifics' in service, and apparently winning many honours in working the train services which at that time were not very fast, none of them had been fitted with a corridor tender, so dependence for the haulage of the 'non-stop' had to remain with the Gresley 'A4s', and right royally they responded to the challenge. The restored

service ran from May 21 until the afternoon of August 12 when rainstorms culminating in a cloudburst of unprecedented violence caused complete breaching of the main line between Berwick and Dunbar in no fewer than *ten* places. All through traffic was diverted from Tweedmouth Junction via Kelso and Galashiels. At first, there was no thought of continuing to run the 'Flying Scotsman' non-stop. Rear-end banking assistance was necessary on the southbound run from Hardengreen Junction up to Falahill, where the gradient was 1 in 70 and on which the maximum load for an unassisted 'Pacific' was 400 tons. Also, in view of the length of the run to the first set of water troughs at Belford, 90 miles out of Edinburgh by the diversion route, it was thought

Above *The 1948 Interchange Trials:* Mallard *hauls the down 'Atlantic Coast Express' near Basingstoke, with the Great Western dynamometer-car, on June 8* (M.W. Earley).

Left *The up 'Flying Scotsman' passing King Edward Bridge Junction, Newcastle, with an unkempt 'A4' No 60002* Sir Murrough Wilson *(S.E. Teasdale).*

Right *The 'Capitals Limited' with a garter-blue 'A4' No 60012* Commonwealth of Australia *ready to leave King's Cross on its non-stop run to Edinburgh (the late W.J. Reynolds).*

advisable to take water at Galashiels. Although the route was no more than 15.9 miles longer than by the direct line via Dunbar, the heavy gradients between Portobello and St Boswells and the lengths of restricted speed between the latter junction and Tweedmouth Junction caused the overall time between Edinburgh and Kings Cross to be increased by about 70 minutes.

After no more than twelve days of this emergency working, the pride of the Scottish enginemen in the running of the 'non-stop' inspired the Haymarket crew on the up train to try to get through without any stop at all, even though they had a load of 435 tons instead of the stipulated maximum of 400; with engine No 60029 *Woodcock* they succeeded, making a new world record non-stop run of 408.6 miles. That was on August 24 1948, and thereafter, before the summer service ended, this remarkable feat was repeated on sixteen occasions, eight in each direction. *Woodcock* was very much the favourite engine on the job because it featured in no fewer than nine of the sixteen runs made non-stop via Galashiels, five in the up direction and four going down. Others that participated were *Commonwealth of Australia* (3), *Merlin, Sea Eagle, Golden Plover* and the historic *Mallard.* (Engine No 60028 *Sea Eagle* was afterwards renamed *Walter K Whigham.*) I had no opportunity of travelling by the train on the summer service but Scottish Region later gave me a footplate pass to ride the southbound 'Flying Scotsman' from Edinburgh to Tweedmouth. With the heavy winter load of 480 tons tare it was necessary to stop for a bank engine at Hardengreen Junction and also for water at Galashiels. The engine was *Merlin*, and they made a good job of it.

In the following summer, the three Regions covering the East Coast Route combined to put on a new non-stop Scotsman at a considerably accelerated timing, the 'Capitals Limited', running half an hour ahead of the 'Flying Scotsman' and taking 7 hr 20 min for the journey of 392.7 miles. Two years later, when I had a footplate pass to ride the down train, we had the same 'A4' that had done so well in the 1948 emergency, No 60029 *Woodcock*. However, at no time during the long run could it be said that the engine was steaming freely, but to the lasting credit of the two crews concerned, they not only surmounted difficulties on the footplate but recovered all but 4¼ minutes of *twenty-nine* minutes that had been lost by exceptional circumstances by the time Grantham was passed. The ensuing 287.25 miles to Edinburgh Waverley were covered in exactly 5 hours at an average speed of 57.5 mph, including two more moderate checks. It was a great run.

When Ivatt succeeded Fairburn as CME of the LMS, he initiated certain measures designed to improve the availability of locomotives, particularly those of the general utility type such as the Stanier 'Black Five' 4-6-0. One of these measures was the fitting of the so-called self-cleaning screens in the smokebox. Unburnt particles of fuel carried forward through the tubes were arrested by these screens and caused to fall down to the bottom of the smokebox. This accumulation could then be more easily removed; in fact, it was claimed that the LMS engines so fitted could run for a week without their smokeboxes being opened. After nationalization, at

the regular meetings of the Regional locomotive engineers the attributes of the LMS-inspired self-cleaning smokebox were no doubt discussed freely, and the Eastern Region decided to fit similar screens to some of the Gresley 'V2' 2-6-2s in view of their general utility nature. These engines had emerged from the war years with a far better reputation than most of the Gresley three-cylinder classes, and with the departure of Edward Thompson from the Doncaster scene they were largely restored to their original fame. When a few of them were fitted with self-cleaning screens in the smokebox, however, their steaming, to use a colloquialism, was 'knocked for six'. While the standard 'V2s' were able to sustain a steaming rate of 25,000 lb easily, those with the screens inserted were not able to reach half that figure.

In the meantime, the Locomotive Testing Committee of the Railway Executive had fully settled into its stride. In this particular activity it was fortunate that the inter-railway rivalry, which had dogged the early proceedings of the Executive, had quickly ended with the senior engineers at 'No 222' realizing that the Swindon Stationary Testing Plant, as modernized by the Great Western Railway in the 1930s, was a magnificent tool of management. It was fully equal, in its technical potentialities, to the recently commissioned plant at Rugby, and was also backed by a wealth of experience in the testing staff which the new plant did not then possess. At the time of nationalization, Swindon was busily engaged on tests with 'Castle' Class 4-6-0s with varying degrees of superheat. These were conducted under the former GWR drawing office organization in which the testing staff reported to the Chief Draughtsman. When these tests were finished, further work came under the authority of the Railway Executive, and a series of tests on mixed traffic locomotives began simultaneously at Swindon and Rugby. It was quickly realized that the Swindon procedure, which was accepted by the Railway Executive and also adopted at Rugby, provided an admirable means of analysing faults and of trying out alternatives and this was done with certain LMS-designed mixed traffic engines at Swindon.

In the summer of 1951, H.G. Ivatt, the last of the CMEs of the old privately-owned railways, was due for retirement. His going would give Riddles the opportunity he desired of doing a major exercise in cross-breeding of Regional Mechanical Engineers. Harrison, who had succeeded Peppercorn at Doncaster, was to go to Derby, K.J. Cook, from Swindon, was to take charge of the Eastern and North Eastern Regions and Alfred Smeddle, originally from the North Eastern, who, after Bulleid's departure, had been Deputy CME of the Southern, was to go to Swindon. It did not work out quite that way, at any rate so far as Doncaster, Darlington and Swindon were concerned. Cook, at first, was not at all keen on the transfer. He had been at Swindon all his life, and although his position was much diluted from that previously held by Hawksworth and his predecessors by the detachment of the Carriage and Wagon department and the Locomotive Running, he was still sitting in the chair of Churchward, and that meant a good deal to a Great Western man. Although constrained by the circumstances of the times, he felt that there was much he could do to get the Locomotive Department back to its pre-war levels of efficiency, particularly as Keith Grand, the Chief Regional Officer, was constantly pressing for acceleration of train services.

At his new headquarters at Doncaster, Cook found the design staff in the throes of the 'V2' problem. Spencer, who had been reinstated after the departure of Thompson, had been appointed Chairman of the small sub-committee of the main Locomotive Testing Committee of the Railway Executive charged with responsibility for the detail work in testing the individual locomotives selected for examination. In his main sphere of responsibility, locomotive design at Doncaster, Spencer was much concerned with the troubles encountered on the fitting of the self-cleaning screens to the 'V2s'. He had been intimately concerned with the original design of those engines under Gresley's direction, and was well enough aware that, in spite of the wartime vicissitudes, there had not been any basic troubles with steaming up until then. He discussed the problem with Cook, his new Chief, who, Spencer confided to me some months afterwards, 'was the nicest chap we've had at Doncaster since Gresley'. As a result of their efforts, arrangements were made to include one of the modified 'V2s' in the programme of locomotives to be examined on the Swindon plant. I have no information as to why Swindon was chosen instead of Rugby, except to suggest that if Cook himself had any part in making the decision one can be sure that he would have plumped heavily for his former headquarters on the dual grounds of its past record of achievement and the expertise of its current staff.

Under the masterly direction of Sam Ell, one of the most erudite of experimental engineers, the problem was soon laid bare. Having done some preliminary steaming trials on the Stationary Plant with the engine as received, confirming its dismal performance, the screens were then removed, and further trials restored normal 'V2' steaming. Then the blast arrangements were studied, and various alternatives tested, the upshot of which was that an entirely new draughting arrangement was designed. As finalized,

Class 'V2' 2-6-2 No 60845 on a 610 ton dynamometer-car test run (20 coaches) from Reading to Stoke Gifford sidings, here seen approaching Hullavington. The author is seen with Sam Ell in the dynamometer-car (Kenneth H. Leech).

not only was the steaming rate even with the self-cleaning screens re-inserted fully restored, but, by expert firing, as was undoubtedly made on certain pre-war record runs with these engines, enhanced. I was privileged to witness some of the concluding tests on the Plant and also to ride in the famous Churchward dynamometer-car on confirmatory road tests, and very impressive they were. I travelled on a day when the test load was 20 coaches, 610 tons and saw this huge load hauled at a steady speed of 60 mph on level track.

Details were given in the Test Bulletin issued by the Railway Executive later of a performance with a still heavier load of 25 coaches totalling 761.7 tons, on which the steam rate to the cylinders was constantly maintained for the whole trial time of 69 minutes during which the average speed was exactly 60 mph. The test began when speed from the start at Stoke Gifford sidings had reached 30 mph on the rising 1 in 300 gradient. Thenceforward, the variations in speed were 43 mph attained and sustained on the continuing 1 in 300 to Badminton, 75 mph at Little Somerford, 54 mph minimum at Wootton Bassett and 70 mph sustained on the easy descending gradients, maximum 1 in 754, between Swindon and Didcot. The regulator was full open throughout the test, and, apart from the period of acceleration from the initial 30 mph to full running speed, the cut-offs varied from 30 per cent on the rising 1 in 300 gradient down to 22 per cent for the fast running between Swindon and Didcot. The steam rate to the cylinders was 23,950 lb per hour, showing a handsome margin in reserve from the maximum of 31,000 lb per hour attained on the Swindon Stationary Testing Plant. Cook was so pleased with the results that when the engine No 60845 got back to Doncaster he decided to earmark it by fitting a copper-capped chimney as evidence of its stay at Swindon. Unfortunately someone very high up at '222' objected, and he was ordered to take it off!

The year 1953, the Coronation Year of Her Majesty Queen Elizabeth II, was celebrated on British Railways in a variety of ways, notably by the renaming of the East Coast non-stop London-Edinburgh express the 'Elizabethan'. Before coming to that splendid train, which enabled the Gresley 'A4' 'Pacifics' to see steam out on the East Coast Route in a blaze of glory, the saga of the 'V2' was continued in a further and unexpected way. In the late spring of that year, certain defects on the 'Merchant Navy' engines of the Southern led to the temporary withdrawal of the whole class. Fortunately this trouble was detected and rectified before the full summer service began, but even so for a time there would have been a serious shortage of engines. With the building of large numbers of the new Peppercorn 'Pacifics', the Eastern Region had plenty of engines at that time of year and was able to lend the Southern a number of 'V2s'. These put in good work on a variety of services. I saw them at various times working the 'Bournemouth Belle' and also sections of the West of England trains both east and west of Salisbury. Unfortunately, I had no opportunity of travelling in a train hauled by one of them.

It was not necessary for an experienced locomotive

Class 'V2' No 60893 on loan to the Southern Region in may 1953, leaving Bournemouth Central with the up 'Bournemouth Belle' Pullman express (R.C. Riley).

engineer to study technical papers for dimensional details to appreciate that the Gresley three-cylinder designs, 4-6-2, 2-6-2, 4-6-0, 2-6-0 and 2-6-2 tank alike, had been built with greater clearances in the working parts than were then customary in British practice. An acute observer at the lineside could tell from the musical 'ring' of the motion parts when steam was shut off, quite apart from the 'clanking' of the connecting and coupling rods, that there was something typically 'Gresley' about the way of their going. That there was no inherent weakness in this was shown by the splendid record of reliability of the Gresley stud as a whole during the twenty years, 1921-1941, that they had been in service under his personal surveillance. The often-publicized failures of 'Pacific' engines with overheated middle big-ends arose mainly in cases of very high power output at maximum speed. To K.J. Cook, however, with a lifetime's service on the Great Western and the exacting experience of serving as Locomotive Works Manager at Swindon under that perfectionist of Chief Mechanical Engineers, C.B. Collett, any rattles in the motion of a steam locomotive, however musically they might ring, were anathema, and he sought to eliminate them, at any rate so far as the Gresley 'Pacifics' were concerned.

At Doncaster, manufacturing facilities in the erecting shop where the largest and most powerful engines were built were then such that the frame alignment was not so exact as that standard at Swindon, or even that at Crewe, and consequently greater clearances had to be allowed in the working parts. When he first went there, Cook was said to have remarked concerning clearances in motion parts that Swindon scrapped at the point Doncaster fitted as new! He was an expert in such matters, for in the early 1930s, when he was still Assistant to Hannington, Collett had installed the Zeiss optical system for the lining up of frames, cylinder centre lines and main bearings. It was applied to a new batch of 'Castles' then about to be laid down, and its success was manifested in the improved performance of the engines, not necessarily in the power output but in reduced maintenance costs. Cook naturally thought of this system for improving the performance of the Gresley 'Pacifics', but the apparatus installed at Swindon was of German make and was no longer available after the war. Fortunately, a British manufacturer was found who could work to the stringent specification that Cook laid down, and, from the time of the installation of the new equipment, all 'A3' and 'A4' 'Pacifics' submitted for major overhaul at Doncaster were subjected to optical lining up of frames, cylinders and main axle bearings.

The results were astonishing, not only acoustically but in the general working of the engines. The first one that I had personal experience of was an 'A3', in particularly enlightening circumstances. I was riding from Leeds to Edinburgh by the Midland route on the long-defunct 'Thames-Forth Express', and on arrival from the south I was disappointed to find that Whitehall Junction shed had nothing better than a scruffy old 'Black Five' to take us forward to Carlisle, and, with a load of more than 300 tons, we had to be piloted. A superannuated Midland 7 ft Class '2' 4-4-0 was coupled ahead of us, and in stormy autumnal weather we had a tempestuous ride through the mountains. There was no difficulty in keeping time with two engines, but on arrival in Carlisle we found an 'A3' in absolutely spanking condition waiting to take us on to Edinburgh. Purely for the sake of creature comfort I was glad enough to exchange the somewhat spartan conditions of a run-down 'Black Five' cab for the padded bucket seat comfort of a Gresley 'Pacific', but when we started I could not believe my own senses. Gone completely were the clankings and vibration from the motion. We rode the sharply curving length from the junction with the Caledonian line past the former North British engine sheds in almost complete silence, and so smoothly! When we got on to the open road and could make some reasonable express speed our going was immaculate—there was no other word for it. The Waverley Route, however, with its many restrictions and booked running times requiring no higher speeds than about 65 mph, was not the place to try the running qualities of these rebuilt engines, and I looked forward to riding them between Kings Cross and Newcastle.

The first opportunity that arose was soon after 'Elizabethan' had been put on. I was given a footplate pass for the southbound run, but although the work was absolutely top class throughout, it was one of those occasions when one could not judge the power that was being developed. A strong westerly wind was blowing throughout the length of England, and on the open stretches of line—and that meant most of the way between Berwick-on-Tweed and Hitchin—I estimated from the engine working that our 415-ton train was pulling something like 500 tons on a calm day. The two pairs of enginemen did remarkably well to bring the train into Kings Cross 2½ minutes early on the newly accelerated schedule of 6 hrs 45 min after checks that cost 10½ minutes. The net time of 392 minutes was thus equal to an

average of 60 mph overall, but the most interesting impression of this long run on *Silver Fox* was the complete absence of the usual 'clatter' from the running gear, especially when coasting, and the evenness of the beat. Because of the strength of the wind, we did not exceed 78 mph between Alne and Beningbrough though working on 20 per cent cut-off and full regulator, nor more than 88 mph down the bank from Stoke Tunnel towards Peterborough.

A year later, the schedule of the 'non-stop' was still further quickened to 6½ hours and it became one of

The inaugural 'Elizabethan' non-stop express to Edinburgh on June 29 1953 climbing the Holloway Bank with Class 'A4' 4-6-2 No 60028 Walter K. Whigham *(Brian Morrison).*

The down 'Elizabethan' in June 1954 passing Monktonhall Junction behind No 60030 Golden Fleece. *Although nearing the end of the long non-stop run there appears to be plenty of coal left on the tender* (E.D. Bruton).

the hardest and most spectacular tasks ever set to a British steam locomotive. This qualification must not be misunderstood. There were other duties that involved greater outputs of power for shorter distances, but in running the 'Elizabethan' it was the length of run to be made non-stop that overrode every other consideration. There were times when the most careful management of the fire was needed on that long run to keep a good head of steam. On my first run with the accelerated train in 1954, only the second day it ran, all went very smoothly, and I was able to see from the footplate how easily speeds approaching 100 mph were attained by these engines in the ordinary course of running. Because of certain track improvement works then under construction at Potters Bar and south thereof, the schedule inwards from Hatfield had necessarily to include some substantial recovery time, and the allowance for the 375 miles from Edinburgh to Hatfield was no more than 362 minutes. On the run south we experienced five out-of-course slowings, and still passed Hatfield 2¼ minutes early. The engine was No 60030 *Golden Fleece*, and the standard 11-coach train totalled a load of 425 tons gross behind the tender.

It is of interest to analyse the sections totalling 298.6 miles over which fast running was sustained in between the various temporary and permanent speed restrictions, and from the following table it will be seen that this length was covered at an average speed of 67.4 mph:

Stretch	Distance (miles)	Actual time (m s)	Average speed (mph)
Monktonhall Jc—East Linton	17.4	16 49	62.3
Dunbar—Marshall Meadows	27.2	26 36	61.3
Tweedmouth—Pegswood	47.2	40 45	69.5
Stannington—Heaton	12.2	11 56	61.4
Relly Mill Junction—Skelton	64.5	51 38	73.8
Templehirst—Crow Park	42.4	39 29	64.4
Newark—Tallington	35.3	31 10	68.0
Fletton Junction—Connington South	7.6	7 11	63.5
Abbots Ripton—Hatfield	45.8	40 24	68.3
Totals	298.6	256 58	67.4

The complete run of 392.7 miles from Waverley to Kings Cross occupied 385 min 10 sec, and the net time was 369 minutes, an average of 63.9 mph.

The fastest speeds were over the 42.5 miles from Darlington to Skelton Box, averaging 78.5 mph with a maximum of 84 mph, from Corby Glen to Tallington, 12.3 miles averaging 89 mph with a maximum of 96 mph. The footplate conditions in which the latter maximum was attained are worth recalling. At Grantham the train was running just over three minutes early, and speed was allowed to fall to 53 mph at Stoke summit. Then the driver let the engine make its own pace, continuing to work at 15 per cent cut-off. We topped the 90 mph mark just before Little Bytham, and ran between 90 and 96 mph for about nine miles until speed had to be reduced for a permanent way restriction south of Tallington. I was on the footplate during this fast spell and found the smoothness and quietness of the engine most impressive. The fastest overall time I have been able to trace with the 'Elizabethan' was made in 1960 when my friend Baron Gerard Vuillet of Paris made a round trip on the footplate of engine No 60027 *Merlin*, and on the southbound run he logged an actual overall time of 380 minutes, thus arriving at Kings Cross *ten minutes early*! The net time, allowing for incidental delays, was no more than 362 minutes. *Merlin* was a favourite engine in Scotland; she carried a plaque presented by the Naval Establishment in Fife, 'HMS Merlin', past which the engine worked in one of the regular assignments of the top link 'Pacifics' at Haymarket shed.

It was in that same year, 1954, that I logged the first run to include a maximum of over 100 mph that I had witnessed from the footplate. It was on the up 'Tees-Tyne Pullman' and we had been stopped by signal at York so there was time to be made up. The engine, No 60029 *Woodcock*, was in first-class trim and the driver was going rather harder than usual from Newark onwards, using 20 per cent cut-off up to Stoke summit. Grantham was passed at 75 mph and the speed fell to 65.5 mph at the top of the 1 in 200 gradient. At a point about a mile over the crest, when the speed had reached 75 mph again, the cut-off was shortened to 15 per cent still with an almost full regulator, and the milepost timings from 97 southwards were as follows:

Milepost	Time from passing post 100 min sec	Average speed (mph)
97	2 18	—
96	2 58½	88.9
95	3 37½	92.3
94	4 15½	94.8
93	4 52½	97.5
92	5 28½	100.0
91	6 07½	102.7
90	6 40	98.7
89	7 17½	96.0

The regulator was eased at milepost 91 to give a much reduced steam chest pressure of 140 psi, instead of the 200 used on the earlier part of the descent. Otherwise, I think we would have attained a much higher maximum than the actual 103.5 mph, but it was, in any case, an exhilarating experience.

By the year 1958, the 'A3s' that had been fitted with the Kylchap exhaust arrangement in addition to having had their frames and cylinders optically linked up were being used turn and turn about with the 'A4s' on the principal East Coast expresses, excepting only the non-stop Scotsman in the summer months. By that time the English Electric Type 4 diesels were coming into use and it really did seem that the end of the road was approaching for steam. In early December of that year, when I was travelling from Edinburgh to Kings Cross by the 'Flying Scotsman', we were hauled by steam throughout, and moreover by 'A3s'. At that time, the famous train was running non-stop from Newcastle and carrying no more than a moderate load of eleven coaches. The schedule was fast, however, and I had a footplate pass for the section south of Newcastle; on engine No 60061 *Pretty Polly* I recorded some absolutely first-class work. Signal delays from Hatfield inwards precluded a punctual arrival in London, but we were five minutes early when passing Sandy, 224.2 miles in 228¾ minutes, despite two severe restrictions for track relaying at Alne and before Newark. The overall time for the 268.3 miles from Newcastle to Kings Cross was 289¾ minutes, but although we were thus nearly four minutes late in arriving, the net time was no more than 267 minutes, an average of just over 60 mph throughout.

The engine working was immaculate. The general position of the reverser was at 15 to 20 per cent cut-off, often with the regulator only partly open. On the racing stretch of the North Eastern line we averaged 75 mph over the 32.9 miles from Darlington to Alne, and reached a maximum of 84 mph on level track with cut-off at 17 per cent, while on the flying descent from Stoke tunnel during which a top speed of 90 mph was attained the cut off was 16 per cent. The regulator was not fully open and the steam chest pressure gauge registered around 180 psi against a boiler pressure near to the full 220 without blowing off. As with all Gresley 'Pacifics' which had been given the 'Cook' treatment at Doncaster, *Pretty Polly*'s riding and mechanical action were faultless. It was the last time I rode on one of these engines on a high-speed East Coast main-line express, and I could not have wished for a better finale.

The 'A4s' were being withdrawn from service from 1963 onwards, not from any inability to run but to make way for the exceedingly *puissant* 'Deltics'. The historic *Mallard* was earmarked for preservation, but in the last year of her active service as an ordinary traffic department engine she made a run that in many ways surpassed her high-speed achievement of

July 1938. This was no well-organized publicity venture—nothing more, in fact, than a determined effort by a keen crew to make a punctual run in the face of severe delays. On the day in question, *Mallard* was on the 2 pm express from Kings Cross non-stop to Grantham on a schedule equal to the fastest ordinary East Coast expresses of pre-war days, 111 minutes for the 105½ miles. Before leaving Kings Cross, it was known on the footplate that two severe engineering slacks would be experienced, both in locations where speed would be high, but what was not expected was a signal stop for 2½ minutes at Langley Junction costing at least 4½ minutes in running time between Hatfield and Hitchin. Despite this and the effect of the slack to 18 mph before Huntingdon, the train was only three minutes late passing Peterborough. By that time, there was only 28 minutes left to make a punctual arrival in Grantham 29.1 miles away, much of it 'against the collar' and with the second of the two severe permanent way checks still to come.

What happened may be studied in detail from the accompanying tabulated log. Suffice it to say that the uphill running from the 20 mph slow was the most astonishing piece of power output I have ever seen from a Gresley 'Pacific'. I was not travelling in the train myself, but the timing was done by one of the correspondents who wrote regularly to me during my authorship of the 'Locomotive Practice and Performance' feature in *The Railway Magazine* which I contributed monthly from 1959 until December 1980. Between Peterborough and Stoke summit my friend made a continuous record at every milepost, and, as the log shows, the 11.5 uphill miles from Essendine were covered in 8 min 35 sec at an averge of 80.6 mph, while the sustained minimum speed on the 1 in 200 up to milepost 96 was 80 mph. This tremendous effort, which involved an output of 2,450 equivalent drawbar horsepower, may well be set as a record for all time, and it brought the train into Grantham on time.

One of the last regular 'A4' duties in Scotland, the down 'Granite City', Glasgow-Aberdeen express near Bridge of Allan in March 1963 behind No 60012 Commonwealth of Australia *(the late Derek Cross).*

BR: 2 pm Kings Cross—Grantham

Engine 'A4' 4-6-2 No 60022 *Mallard*
Load: 11 coaches, 390 tons tare, 415 tons full

Distance (miles)		Schedule time (min)	Actual time (m s)	Speed (mph)
0.0	KINGS CROSS	0	0 00	—
2.5	Finsbury Park		7 19	—
5.0	Wood Green		10 24	55
12.7	Potters Bar	18	18 38	58
17.7	HATFIELD	23	23 04	73
26.7	Langley Junction		32 20	signal
			34 45	stop
31.9	HITCHIN	37	41 34	75
37.0	Arlesey		45 19	86/83
41.1	Biggleswade		48 12	87
44.1	Sandy	46	50 18	84/87
51.7	St Neots		55 42	82
			pws	18
58.9	HUNTINGDON	60	66 29	59
62.0	Milepost 62		69 24	66
67.4	Connington South		73 34	84
			sigs	
76.4	PETERBOROUGH	80	83 00	20
			pws	20
84.8	Tallington		94 11	69
88.6	Essendine	94	97 16	78
92.2	Little Bytham		99 58	82
96.0	Milepost 96		102 45	80
97.1	Corby Glen		103 34	82
100.1	Stoke Box	105	105 51	78
102.0	Great Ponton		107 18	83
105.5	GRANTHAM	111	110 39	—

Appendix: Preserved locomotives of the LNER and its constituents

Great Central
4-4-0 No 506 *Butler Henderson* ('Director' Class); Great Central Railway, Loughborough (on loan from NRM)
2-8-0 (Class 'O4') No 102; Dinting Railway Centre (on loan from NRM)

Great Eastern
0-6-0 No 564 (LNER Class 'J15'); North Norfolk Railway
0-6-0 No 1217 (LNER Class 'J17'); Bressingham Steam Museum (on loan from NRM)
0-6-0T No 87 (Class 'P57'); National Railway Museum, York
0-6-2T No 999 (LNER Class 'N7'); Chappel Steam Centre
2-4-0 No 490 (Class 'T26'); National Railway Museum, York
4-6-0 No 61572 (Class 'B12'); North Norfolk Railway

Great Northern
4-2-2 No 1 (Stirling 8 ft); National Railway Museum, York
4-4-2 No 990 *Henry Oakley*; National Railway Museum, York

4-4-2 No 251 (first large-boilered); National Railway Museum, York
0-6-0T No 1247 (LNER Class 'J52'); North Yorkshire Moors Railway (property of Captain W.G. Smith)
0-6-2T No 4744 (LNER Class 'N2'); Great Central Railway, Loughborough (property of the Gresley Society)

Great North of Scotland
4-4-0 No 49 *Gordon Highlander*; Glasgow Museum of Transport

North British
4-4-0 No 256 *Glen Douglas*; Glasgow Museum of Transport
0-6-0 No 673 Maude (1891); Scottish Railway Preservation Society, Falkirk

North Eastern
2-2-4T No 66 *Aerolite*; National Railway Museum, York
2-4-0 No 910 (Fletcher design); National Railway Museum, York
0-6-0 No 1275 (Long-boilered goods); North Road Museum, Darlington

2-4-0 No 1463 (Tennant type); North Road Museum, Darlington

0-6-0 No 876 (Class 'C' goods); Beamish Open Air Museum

4-4-0 No 1621 (Class 'M'); National Railway Museum, York

0-6-0 No 2392 (Class 'P3' goods); North Yorkshire Moors Railway

0-8-0 No 2238 (Class 'T2'); North Yorkshire Moors Railway (property of the North Eastern Locomotive Preservation group)

0-8-0 No 63460 (Class 'T3'); North Yorkshire Moors Railway (on loan from NRM)

London and North Eastern

4-6-2 No 532 *Blue Peter* (Class 'A2/3'); Dinting Railway Centre

4-6-2 No 4472 *Flying Scotsman* (Class 'A3'); Carnforth

4-6-2 No 11 *Bittern* (Class 'A4'); Dinting Railway Centre

4-6-2 No 4468 *Mallard* (Class 'A4'); National Railway Museum, York

Above *'The Plant Centenarian' commemorating 100 years of Doncaster works on September 20 1953; the down special near Stoke summit is hauled by Great Northern 'Atlantics' Nos 990* Henry Oakley *and 251, now both at York* (W.A. Camwell).

Left *Stockton and Darlington Railway No 1275, built by Dubs & Co in 1874, as restored to its original condition and painting* (National Railway Museum, York).

Right *No 4472* Flying Scotsman *on the 'Cumbrian Coast Express' at Ravenglass in August 1978* (the late Derek Cross).

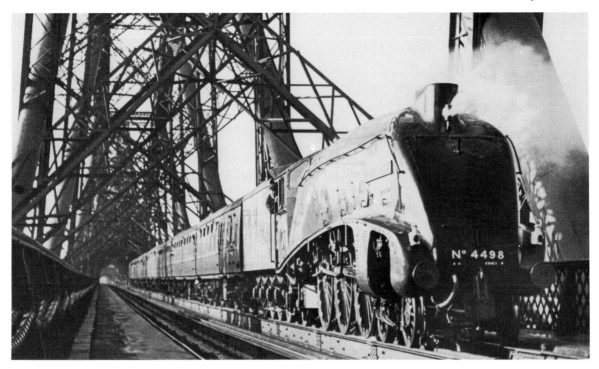

Preserved 'A4' No 4498 Sir Nigel Gresley *on a special train crossing the Forth Bridge* (The A4 Locomotive Society).

4-6-2 No 4498 *Sir Nigel Gresley* (Class 'A4'); Carnforth (property of the A4 Locomotive Society)

4-6-2 No 60009 *Union of South Africa* (Class 'A4'); The Lochty Railway

4-6-2 No 60008 *Dwight D. Eisenhower* (Class 'A4'); USA National Railway Museum, Green Bank, Wisconsin

4-6-2 No 60010 *Dominion of Canada* (Class 'A4'); Canadian Railway Historical Association Museum, Delson, near Montreal

4-6-0 No 1306 (Class 'B1'); Great Central Railway, Loughborough

4-6-0 No 61264 (Class 'B1'); Great Central Railway, Loughborough

4-4-0 No 246 *Morayshire* (Class 'D49'); Scottish Railway Preservation Society, Falkirk

2-6-0 No 2005 (Class 'K1'); North Yorkshire Moors Railway (property of the North Eastern Locomotive Preservation Group)

2-6-0 No 3442 *The Great Marquess* (Class 'K4'); National Railway Museum, York

2-6-2 No 4771 *Green Arrow* (Class 'V2'); National Railway Museum, York

Bibliography

Technical Papers

Institution of Mechanical Engineers
1902 Application of Cylindrical Steam Distributing Valves to Locomotives, Walter M. Smith
1907 Road Trials of Three Express Passenger Locomotives on the GNR in 1906, Henry A. Ivatt
1925 Three-Cylinder Locomotives, H.N. Gresley
1931 High Pressure Locomotives, H.N. Gresley
1936 Presidential Address, H.N. Gresley
Institution of Locomotive Engineers
1947 The Development of LNER Locomotive Design 1923-41, B. Spencer

Journals

Engineering, The Engineer, The Locomotive, The Railway Engineer, The Railway Gazette, The Railway Magazine

Books

British Steam Railway Locomotive
Vol 1 1825-1925, E.L. Ahrons, Ian Allan, 1960
Vol 2 1925-1965, O.S. Nock, Ian Allan, 1966

British Locomotives of the 20th Century
Vol 1 1900-1930, O.S. Nock, Patrick Stephens, 1983
Vol 2 1930-1960, O.S. Nock, Patrick Stephens, 1984
Vol 3 1960-the present day, O.S. Nock, Patrick Stephens, 1985
Classic Locomotives: Great Northern 'Atlantics', O.S. Nock, Patrick Stephens, 1984
Gresley Pacifics, Parts 1 and 2, O.S. Nock, David & Charles, 1973, 1975
Locomotives of the Great Northern Railway, G.F. Bird, Locomotive Publishing Co Ltd, 1903
Locomotives of the North Eastern Railway, John S. MacLean, Locomotive Publishing Co Ltd, 1924
Locomotives of the North Eastern Railway, O.S. Nock, Ian Allan, 1954
Locomotives of Sir Nigel Gresley, O.S. Nock, The Railway Publishing Co Ltd, Longmans Green & Co, 1945
Locomotive and Train Working in the latter part of the Nineteenth Century, Heffer, Cambridge, 1952
Vol 1 (GNR, MS & LR, NER, GER), E.L. Ahrons
Vol 3 (NBR, GN of SR), E.L. Ahrons

Index

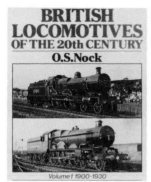
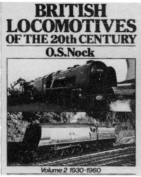
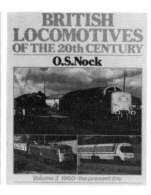
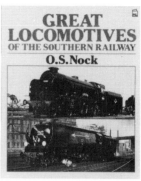

British Locomotives of the 20th Century

In this three-volume major work of reference **O. S. Nock**, Britain's leading railway author, tells the story of British locomotive development from 1900 to the present day.

The first volume covers the pre-grouping era up to 1930 and the technicalities of locomotive design, construction and performance. Each chapter contains a tabular summary of the dimensions of the locomotives introduced in the periods concerned.

The second volume covers British locomotive development from 1930 to 1960 and recalls with relish the exciting advances in train speed. This volume traces the history of the British locomotive through the last years of steam and is packed with tables, line drawings and photographs.

The third and final volume covers the period from 1960 to the present day. Details include the launch of the great modernisation plan, the introduction of diesel services, the extension of main line electrification, the Inter-City 125 High Speed Trains and the IC 225 Advanced Passenger Train.

Great Locomotives of the Southern Railway

'Jubilees', 'Schools', 'King Arthurs' and many other familiar names will be found among the *Great Locomotives of the Southern Railway*, all described in **O. S. Nock**'s customary authoritative and entertaining style. Here are not only the histories and technical details of every major class of locomotive to run on the rails of the Southern Railway, but also the stories of the designers and their philosophies. A wealth of the author's personal recollections of the era and a fascinating collection of photographs make this book a must for the shelves of every railway enthusiast.

Booster-fitted 'Atlantic' No 4419, at one time regularly used on the King's Cross-Leeds Pullman trains (Rail Archive Stephenson/ T.G. Hepburn).